Microsoft Access 2000

Illustrated Second Course

Lisa Friedrichsen

**COURSE
TECHNOLOGY**

THOMSON LEARNING™

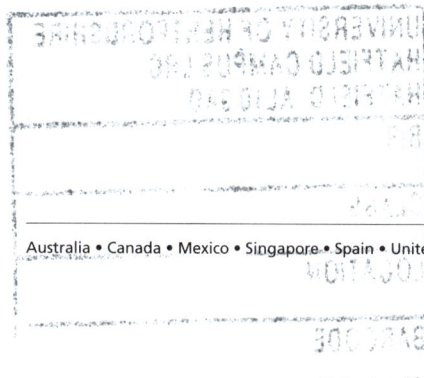

Australia • Canada • Mexico • Singapore • Spain • United Kingdom • United States

The Illustrated Series Vision

Teaching and writing about computer applications can be extremely rewarding and challenging. How do we engage students and keep their interest? How do we teach them skills that they can easily apply on the job? As we set out to write this book, our goals were to develop a textbook that:

- ▶ works for a beginning student
- ▶ provides varied, flexible and meaningful exercises and projects to reinforce the skills
- ▶ serves as a reference tool
- ▶ makes your job as an educator easier, by providing resources above and beyond the textbook to help you teach your course

Our popular, streamlined format is based on advice from instructional designers and customers. This flexible design presents each lesson on a two-page spread, with step-by-step instructions on the left, and screen illustrations on the right. This signature style, coupled with high-caliber content, provides a comprehensive yet manageable introduction to Microsoft Access 2002—it is a teaching package for the instructor and a learning experience for the student.

ACKNOWLEDGMENTS

This Access book is dedicated to my students, and all who are using this book to teach and learn about Access. Thank you. Also, thank you to all of the professionals who helped me create this book.

Thanks to the reviewers who provided feedback and ideas to us, especially Stephanie Hazen and Dr. Dominic Ligori.

Lisa Friedrichsen
and the Illustrated Team

COURSE TECHNOLOGY

THOMSON LEARNING ™

Microsoft Access 2002 - Illustrated Second Course

Lisa Friedrichsen

Managing Editor:
Nicole Jones Pinard

Product Manager:
Emily Heberlein

Associate Product Manager:
Emeline Elliott

Production Editor:
Catherine DiMassa

Developmental Editor:
Lisa Ruffolo

Editorial Assistant:
Christina Kling Garrett

QA Manuscript Reviewers:
John Freitas, Ashlee Welz, Alex White, Harris Bierhoff, Serge Palladino, Holly Schabowski, Jeff Schwartz, Marianne Broughey

Text Designer:
Joseph Lee, Black Fish Design

Composition House:
GEX Publishing Services

Preface

Welcome to *Microsoft Access 2002 – Illustrated Second Course.* Each lesson in the book contains elements pictured to the right in the sample two-page spread.

▶ How is the book organized?

The book is organized into eight units on Access, covering sharing information with other Office programs, creating data access pages, creating advanced queries, forms and reports, managing database objects, and creating macros and modules.

▶ What kinds of assignments are included in the book? At what level of difficulty?

The lesson assignments use MediaLoft, a fictional chain of bookstore cafés, as the case study. The assignments on the blue pages at the end of each unit increase in difficulty. Project files and case studies, with many international examples, provide a great variety of interesting and relevant business applications for skills. Assignments include:

- **Concepts Reviews** include multiple choice, matching, and screen identification questions.

- **Skills Reviews** provide additional hands-on, step-by-step reinforcement.

- **Independent Challenges** are case projects requiring critical thinking and application of the skills learned in the unit. The Independent Challenges increase in difficulty, with the first Independent Challenge in each unit being the easiest (most step-by-step with detailed instructions). Independent Challenges 2 and 3 become increasingly open-ended, requiring more independent thinking and problem solving.

- **E-Quest Independent Challenges** are case projects with a Web focus. E-Quests require the use of the World Wide Web to conduct research to complete the project.

- **Visual Workshops** show a completed file and require that the file be created without any step-by-step guidance, involving problem solving and an independent application of the unit skills.

Each 2-page spread focuses on a single skill.

Concise text that introduces the basic principles in the lesson and integrates the brief case study (indicated by the paintbrush icon).

Access 2002 Unit K

Creating a Delete Query

A delete query deletes a group of records from one or more tables as defined by a query. Delete queries always delete entire records, and not just selected fields within records, so they should be used very carefully. If you wanted to delete a field from a table, you would open Table Design View, click the field name, then click the Delete Rows button. Because the delete query deletes all selected records without letting you undo the action, it is wise to always have a current backup of the database before running any action query, especially the delete query. ▸ Now that Fred has the first four months of attendance records archived in the Jan-April 2003 Log table, he wants to delete them from the Attendance table. He uses a delete query to accomplish this task.

Steps

1. Click **Queries** on the Objects bar, double-click **Create query in Design view**, double-click **Attendance** in the Show Table dialog box, then click **Close**

2. Double-click the *** (asterisk)** at the top of the Attendance table's field list, then double-click the **Attended** field
   All the fields from the Attendance table are added to the first column of the query design grid by using the asterisk. The Attended field is added to the second column of the query design grid so you can enter limiting criteria for this field.

3. Click the **Attended field Criteria cell**, type **<=4/30/03**, then press **[Enter]**
   Before you initiate the delete action, check the datasheet to make sure that you have selected the same 131 records that were added to the Jan-April 2003 Log table.

4. Click the **Datasheet View button** on the Query Design toolbar to confirm that the datasheet has 131 records, click the **Design View button** on the Query Datasheet toolbar, click the **Query Type button list arrow**, then click **Delete Query**
   Your screen should look like Figure K-15. The Query Type button displays the Delete Query icon, and the Delete row was added to the query design grid. The delete action is ready to be initiated by clicking the Run button.

QuickTip
The default sort order for the records in a datasheet is ascending order based on the values in the primary key field.

5. Click the ! on the Query Design toolbar, click **Yes** to confirm that you want to delete 131 rows, then close the query without saving the changes

6. Click **Tables** on the Objects bar, double-click **Attendance**, click **any entry in the LogNo field** (if it's not already selected), then click the **Sort Ascending button** on the Table Datasheet toolbar

TABLE K-2: Action queries

type of action query	query icon	description	example
Delete		Deletes a group of records from one or more tables	Remove products that are discontinued or for which there are no orders
Update		Makes global changes to a group of records in one or more tables	Raise prices by 10 percent for all products
Append		Adds a group of records from one or more tables to the end of a table	Append the employee address table from one division to the address table from another
Make-Table		Creates a new table from data in one or more tables	Export records to another Access database or make a back-up copy of a table

▶ ACCESS K-14 **CREATING ADVANCED QUERIES**

Hints as well as troubleshooting advice, right where you need it — next to the step itself.

Quickly accessible summaries of key terms, toolbar buttons, or keyboard alternatives connected with the lesson material. Students can refer easily to this information when working on their own projects at a later time.

Every lesson features large, full-color representations of what the screen should look like as students complete the numbered steps.

FIGURE K-15: Creating a delete query

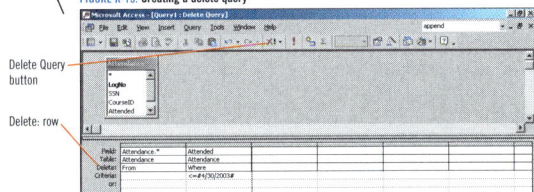

Delete Query button

Delete: row

FIGURE K-16: Attendance table without January–April records

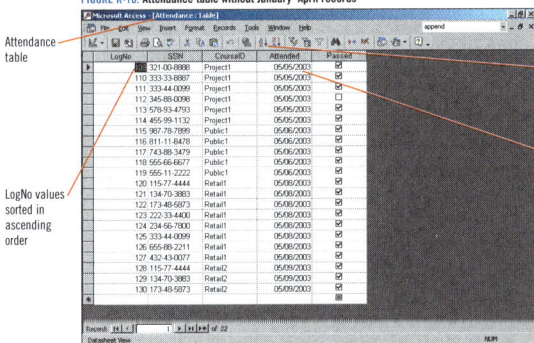

Attendance table

Sort Ascending button

May dates are the earliest dates

LogNo values sorted in ascending order

CLUES TO USE

Reviewing referential integrity

Referential integrity between two tables is established when tables are joined in the Relationships window. Referential integrity ensures that no orphaned records currently exist or are added to the database. Related tables have an orphan record when information in the foreign key field of the "many" table doesn't have a matching entry in the primary key field of the "one" table. An orphan record is sometimes called an unmatched record. The term "orphan" corresponds to general database terminology which often refers to the "one" table as containing parent records, and the "many" table as containing child records. Using this analogy, referential integrity means that a child record cannot be created without a corresponding parent record.

CREATING ADVANCED QUERIES   ACCESS K-15 ◄

Clues to Use boxes provide concise information that either expands on the major lesson skill or describes an independent task that in some way relates to the major lesson skill.

The pages are numbered according to unit. K indicates the unit, 15 indicates the page.

Access 2002

► **What distance learning options are available to accompany this book?**

Visit www.course.com for more information on our Distance Learning materials to accompany Illustrated titles. Options include:

MyCourse.com

Need a quick, simple tool to help you manage your course? Try MyCourse.com, the easiest to use, most flexible syllabus and content management tool available. MyCourse.com offers you brand new content, including Topic Reviews, Extra Case Projects, and Quizzes, to accompany this book.

WebCT

Course Technology and WebCT have partnered to provide you with the highest quality online resources and Web-based tools for your class. Course Technology offers content for this book to help you create your WebCT class, such as a suggested Syllabus, Lecture Notes, Practice Test questions, and more.

Blackboard

Course Technology and Blackboard have also partnered to provide you with the highest quality online resources and Web-based tools for your class. Course Technology offers content for this book to help you create your Blackboard class, such as a suggested Syllabus, Lecture Notes, Practice Test questions, and more.

► **Is this book MOUS Certified?**

When used in conjunction with *Microsoft Access 2002 – Illustrated Introductory,* this book is approved courseware for the Core and Expert Exams for Access and has received certification approval as courseware for the MOUS program. See the inside front cover for more information on MOUS certification.

The first page of each unit includes MOUS symbols to indicate which skills covered in the unit are MOUS skills. A grid in the back of the book lists all the exam objectives and cross-references them with the lessons and exercises.

Instructor Resources

The Instructor's Resource Kit (IRK) CD is Course Technology's way of putting the resources and information needed to teach and learn effectively into your hands. All the components are available on the IRK (pictured below), and many of the resources can be downloaded from www.course.com.

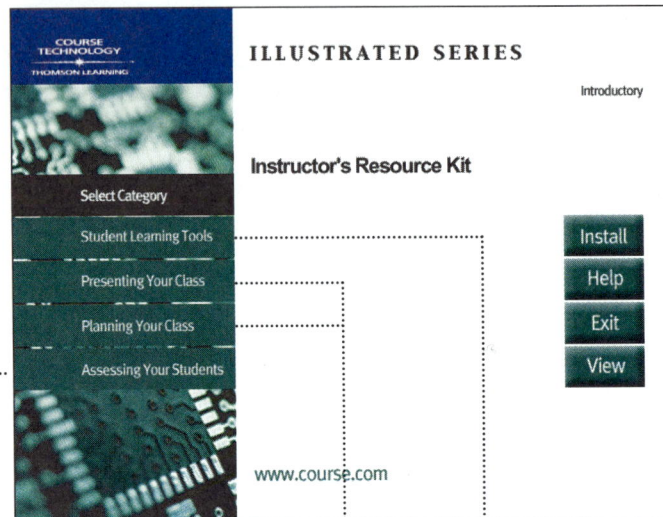

ILLUSTRATED SERIES

Introductory

COURSE TECHNOLOGY
THOMSON LEARNING

Instructor's Resource Kit

Select Category

Student Learning Tools

Presenting Your Class

Planning Your Class

Assessing Your Students

Install
Help
Exit
View

www.course.com

ASSESSING YOUR STUDENTS

Solution Files
Solution Files are Project Files completed with comprehensive sample answers. Use these files to evaluate your students' work. Or, distribute electronically or in hard copy so students can verify their own work.

ExamView
ExamView is a powerful testing software package that allows you to create and administer printed, computer (LAN-based), and Internet exams. ExamView includes hundreds of questions that correspond to the topics covered in this text, enabling students to generate detailed study guides that include page references for further review. The computer-based and Internet testing components allow students to take exams at their computers, and also save you time by grading each exam automatically.

PRESENTING YOUR CLASS

Figure Files
Figure Files contain all the figures from the book in .jpg format. Use the figure files to create transparency masters or in a PowerPoint presentation.

STUDENT TOOLS

Project Files and Project Files List
To complete most of the units in this book, your students will need **Project Files**. Put them on a file server for students to copy. The Project Files are available on the Instructor's Resource Kit CD-ROM, the Review Pack, and can also be downloaded from www.course.com.

Instruct students to use the **Project Files List** at the end of the book. This list gives instructions on copying and organizing files.

PLANNING YOUR CLASS

Instructor's Manual
Available as an electronic file, the Instructor's Manual is quality-assurance tested and includes unit overviews, detailed lecture topics for each unit with teaching tips, comprehensive sample solutions to all lessons and end-of-unit material, and extra Independent Challenges. The Instructor's Manual is available on the Instructor's Resource Kit CD-ROM, or you can download it from www.course.com.

Sample Syllabus
Prepare and customize your course easily using this sample course outline (available on the Instructor's Resource Kit CD-ROM).

INTRODUCING SAM XP

Your skills-based Office assessment solution.
SAM (Skills Assessment Manager) is a powerful testing and reporting tool that measures your students' proficiency in Microsoft Office XP applications through real-world, performance-based questions. (Available separately from the IRK CD.)

Brief Contents

Contents

Access 2002

Sharing Access Information with Other Office Programs

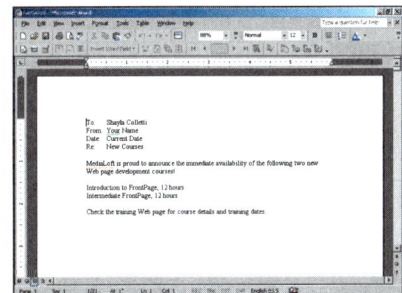

Contents

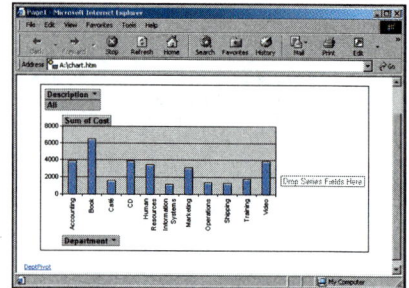

Creating Advanced Queries

Contents

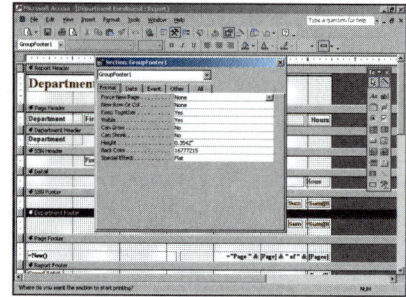

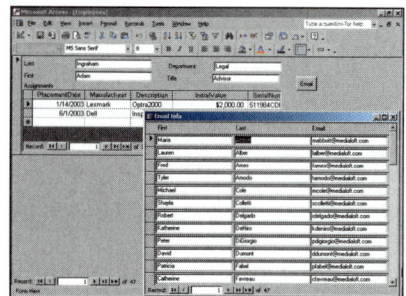

Creating Macros   ACCESS N-1

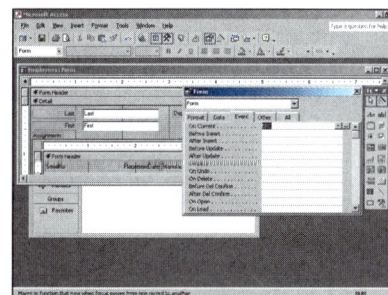

Contents

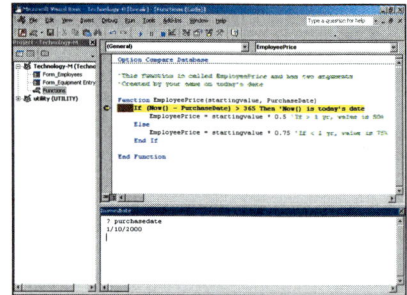

Examining Access Objects

To become proficient with Access, you should understand the purpose of the seven Access objects. Fred reviews key Access terminology and the seven Access objects.

Details

▶ A **database** is a collection of data associated with a topic. The smallest piece of information in a database is called a **field**, or category of information, such as an employee's name, e-mail address, or department. A **primary key field** is a field that contains unique information for each record such as an employee's Social Security Number. A group of related fields, such as all descriptive information for one employee, is called a **record**. A collection of records for a single subject, such as all of the employee records, is called a **table**. When a table is opened, the fields and records are displayed as a **datasheet**, as shown in Figure I-1. Several related tables form a **relational database**. Click the **Expand button** ⊞ to the left of a record in a datasheet to see related records from another table.

▶ Tables are the most important **objects** in an Access database because they contain the data. An Access database can also contain six other object types: **queries**, **forms**, **reports**, **pages**, **macros**, and **modules**. They are summarized in Table I-1.

▶ Query objects are based on tables; form, page, and report objects can be based on either tables or queries. You can enter and edit data in four of the objects—tables, queries, pages, and forms—*but the data is physically stored in only one place: tables*. The relationships among database objects are shown in Figure I-2. The macro and module objects can provide additional database productivity and automation features such as **GUI** (**graphical user interface**) screens and buttons, which mask the complexity of the underlying objects. All of the objects (except for Web pages created by the page object) are stored in one database file.

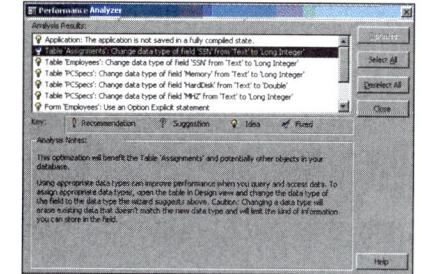

Read This Before You Begin

Software Information and Required Installation
This book was written and tested using Microsoft Office XP - Professional Edition, with a typical installation on Microsoft Windows 2000, with Internet Explorer 5.0 or higher.

What are Project Files?
To complete many of the units in this book, you need to use Project Files. You begin with a Project File so you don't have to type in all the information you need in the database. Your instructor will either provide you with a copy of the Project Files or ask you to make your own copy. Detailed instructions on how to organize your files, as well as a complete listing of all the files you'll need and will create, can be found in the back of the book (look for the yellow pages) in the Project Files List.

Why is my screen different from the book?
1. Your Desktop components and some dialog box options might be different if you are using an operating system other than Windows 2000.
2. Depending on your computer hardware capabilities and the Windows Display settings on your computer, you may notice the following differences:
   - Your screen may look larger or smaller because of your screen resolution (the height and width of your screen)
   - The colors of the title bar in your screen may be a solid blue
3. Depending on your Office settings, your toolbars may display on a single row and your menus may display with a shortened list of frequently used commands. Office menus and toolbars can modify themselves to your working style by displaying only the most frequently used buttons and menu commands.

To view buttons not currently displayed, click a Toolbar Options button ⁑ at the end of either the Standard or Formatting toolbar. To view the full list of menu commands, click the double arrow at the bottom of the menu.

This book assumes you are displaying toolbars on two rows and full menus. To view, modify or reset the toolbar and menu options, click Tools on the menu bar, then click Customize, and select the option best suited for your working style.

Important Information if you are using floppy disks

Compact on Close?
If you are storing your Access databases on floppy disks, you should NOT use the Compact on Close option (available from the Tools menu). While the Compact on Close feature works well if your database is stored on your hard drive or on another large storage device, it can cause problems if your database is stored on a floppy when the size of your database is greater than the available free space on the floppy. Here's why: When you close a database with the Compact on Close feature turned on, the process creates a temporary file that is just as large as the original database file. In a successful compact process, this temporary file is deleted after the compact procedure is completed. But if there is not enough available space on your floppy to create this temporary file, the compact process never finishes, which means that your original database is never closed properly. And if you do not close an Access database properly before attempting to use it again, you can easily corrupt it beyond repair. *Therefore, if you use floppies to complete these exercises, please follow the guidelines on how to organize your databases on floppies in the **Project Files List** so that you do not run out of room on a floppy. Also, please **do not use the Compact on Close feature for databases stored on floppies***.

Closing a Database Properly
It is extremely important to close your databases properly before copying, moving, e-mailing the database file, or before ejecting the Project Files floppy disk from the disk drive. Access database files are inherently multi-user, which means that multiple people can work on the same database file at the same time. To accomplish this capability, Access creates temporary files to keep track of which record you are working on while the database is open. These temporary files must be closed properly before you attempt to copy, move, or e-mail the database. They must also be closed before you eject a floppy that contains the database. If these temporary files do not get closed properly, the database can easily be corrupted beyond repair. Fortunately, Access closes these temporary files automatically when you close the Access application window. So to be sure that you have properly closed a database that is stored on a floppy, *close not only the database window, but also **close the Access application window*** before copying, moving, or e-mailing a database file, as well as before ejecting a floppy that stores the database.

2000 vs. 2002 File Format
New databases created in Access 2002 default to an Access 2000 file format. That's why "Access 2000 file format" is shown in the database window title bar for the figures in this book. This also means that Access databases now support seamless backward compatibility with the prior version of Access like other products in the Microsoft Office suite such as Word and Excel. But while the Project Files for this book could be opened and used in Access 2000, the figures in this book represent the Access 2002 application, use the Access 2002 menus and toolbars, and highlight the new features of Access 2002, including new task panes, new quick keystrokes, PivotTables, and improved dynamic Web pages.

Sharing
Access Information with Other Office Programs

Objectives

- ► Examine Access objects
- [MOUS] ► Examine relationships
- [MOUS] ► Import XML data
- [MOUS] ► Link data
- [MOUS] ► Publish data to Word
- [MOUS] ► Analyze data with Excel
- [MOUS] ► Merge data with Word
- [MOUS] ► Export data to XML
- [MOUS] ► Use SQL Server

Access is a relational database program that can share data with many other Microsoft Office software products. Choosing the right tool for each task is important because you often need to use features from one program with data stored in another type of file. For example, you may want to analyze information in an Excel workbook using the powerful relational database capabilities of Access. Access provides tools to import or link to Excel data so that you will not need to rekey the data into the Access database. Or, you might want to send Access data to another file format. For example, you may want to merge records from an Access query into a Word document or export an Access report as a Web page. ✎ Fred Ames, coordinator of training at MediaLoft, has developed an Access database that tracks courses, employees, and course attendance for the staff training provided by MediaLoft. Fred will share Access data with other software programs so that each MediaLoft department can have the data they have requested in a format they can use.

FIGURE I-1: Table datasheet

Instructors table opened as a datasheet

Click the Expand button to show related records

Field names

Four records

FIGURE I-2: Objects of an Access database

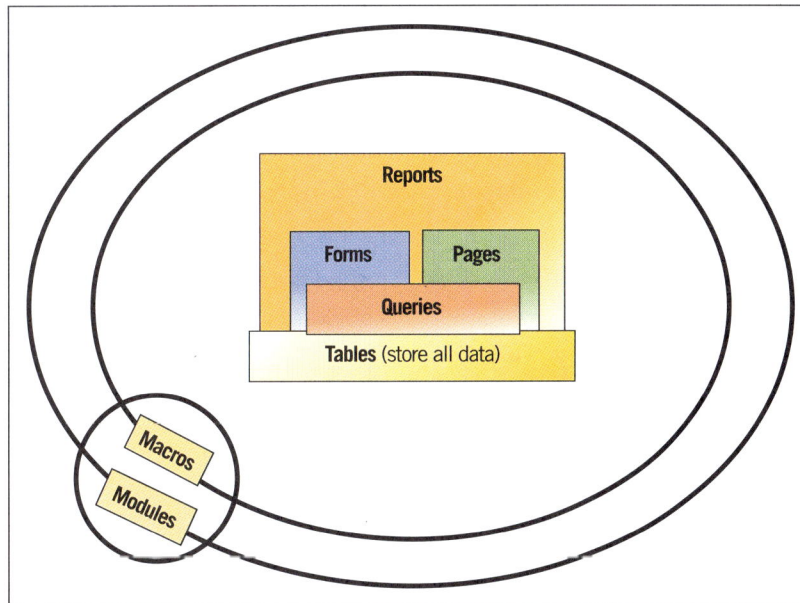

Reports

Forms

Pages

Queries

Tables (store all data)

Macros

Modules

TABLE I-1: Access objects

object	purpose
Table	Contains all of the raw data within the database in a spreadsheet-like view called a datasheet
Query	Answers a "question" a user has about the data in the database, and presents the answer in a datasheet view
Form	Provides an easy-to-use data entry screen that generally shows only one record at a time
Report	Provides a professional printout of data that may contain enhancements such as headers, footers, and calculations on groups of records; mailing labels can also be created from report objects
Page	Creates Web pages from Access objects and provides Web page connectivity features to an Access database
Macro	Stores a collection of keystrokes or commands such as printing several reports or displaying a toolbar when a form opens
Module	Stores Visual Basic for Applications programming code that extends the functions and automated processes of Access

Access 2002

Examining Relationships

An Access database is a **relational database** because more than one table can share information, or "relate." The key benefit of organizing your data into a relational database is that it minimizes redundant data. By linking separate tables of data together, you improve the accuracy of the information, and the speed and flexibility with which it can be accessed. The process of designing a relational database is called **normalization,** and involves determining appropriate fields, tables, and table relationships. Relationship types are summarized in Table I-2. ✏️ Fred develops an Instructors table to store one record for each teacher. He relates the Instructors table to the Courses table so that it participates in the relational database.

Steps 1 2 3 4

1. Start Access, open the **Training-I** database from the drive and folder where your Project Files are stored, click **Tables** on the Objects bar, then double-click the **Instructors** table
   The InstructorID field is the **primary key field** in the Instructors table and therefore contains unique data for each record. Because each instructor teaches many courses, the Instructors table should be related to the Courses table with a one-to-many relationship. The primary key field always acts as the "one" side of a one-to-many relationship.

2. Close the Instructors table, right-click the **Courses** table, then click **Design View**
   A **foreign key field** must be added to the table on the "many" side of a one-to-many relationship to link with the primary key field of the "one" table.

3. Click the **Field Name cell** just below Cost, type **InstructorID**, press **[Tab]**, press **N** to choose a Number data type, press **[Tab]**, type **Foreign Key**, as shown in Figure I-3, click the **Save button** 🖫, then close the Courses table

4. Click the **Relationships button** 🔲 on the Database toolbar
   The Employees, Attendance, Courses, and Instructors tables appear in the Relationships window. Primary key fields appear in bold. Right now, the Instructors table is not related to the rest of the tables in the database.

5. Drag the **InstructorID field** from the Instructors table to the **InstructorID field** in the Courses table, then click **Create** in the Edit Relationships dialog box
   The link between the Courses and Instructors tables has been established, but the linking line doesn't display the "one" and "many" sides of the relationship.

6. Double-click the **linking line** between the Instructors and Courses tables, then click the **Enforce Referential Integrity** check box, as shown in Figure I-4
   Checking the **Enforce Referential Integrity** option means that you cannot enter values in the foreign key field unless you first enter them in the primary key field. It also means that you cannot delete records in the "one" table if the "many" table has corresponding related records. **Cascade Update Related Field**s automatically updates the data in the foreign key field when the matching primary key field is changed. **Cascade Delete Related Records** automatically deletes all records in the "many" table if the record with the matching key field in the "one" table is deleted.

7. Click **OK** in the Edit Relationships dialog box
   Printing the Relationships window shown in Figure I-5 creates a valuable report that helps you remember what fields are in which tables.

8. Click **File** on the menu bar, click **Print Relationships**, click the **Print button** 🖨 on the Print Preview toolbar, save and close the report with the default report name **Relationships for Training-I**, then close the Relationships window

FIGURE I-3: Adding the foreign key field to the Courses table in Design View

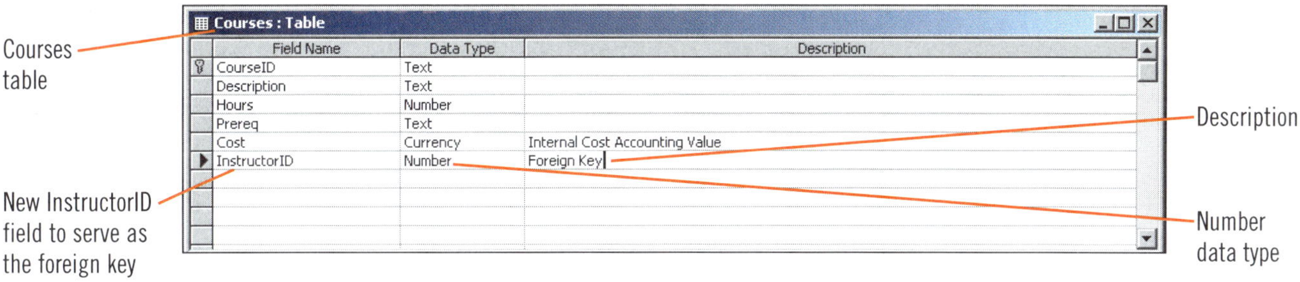

Courses table

New InstructorID field to serve as the foreign key

Field Name	Data Type	Description
CourseID	Text	
Description	Text	
Hours	Number	
Prereq	Text	
Cost	Currency	Internal Cost Accounting Value
InstructorID	Number	Foreign Key

Courses : Table

Description

Number data type

FIGURE I-4: Edit Relationships dialog box

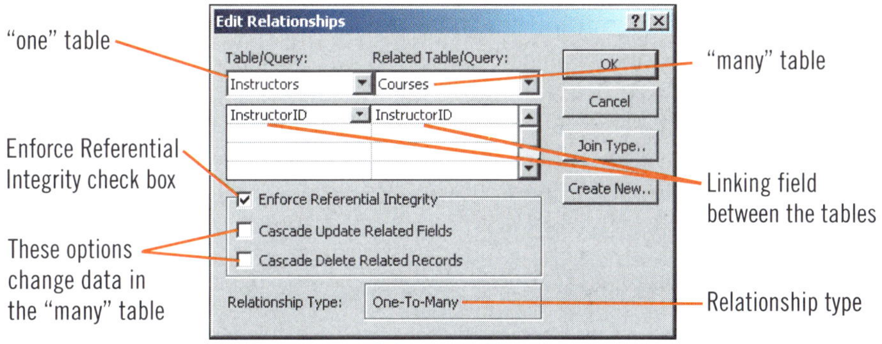

"one" table

"many" table

Enforce Referential Integrity check box

Linking field between the tables

These options change data in the "many" table

Relationship type

Edit Relationships

Table/Query: Instructors — Related Table/Query: Courses

InstructorID — InstructorID

OK / Cancel / Join Type.. / Create New..

☑ Enforce Referential Integrity
☐ Cascade Update Related Fields
☐ Cascade Delete Related Records

Relationship Type: One-To-Many

FIGURE I-5: Relationships window

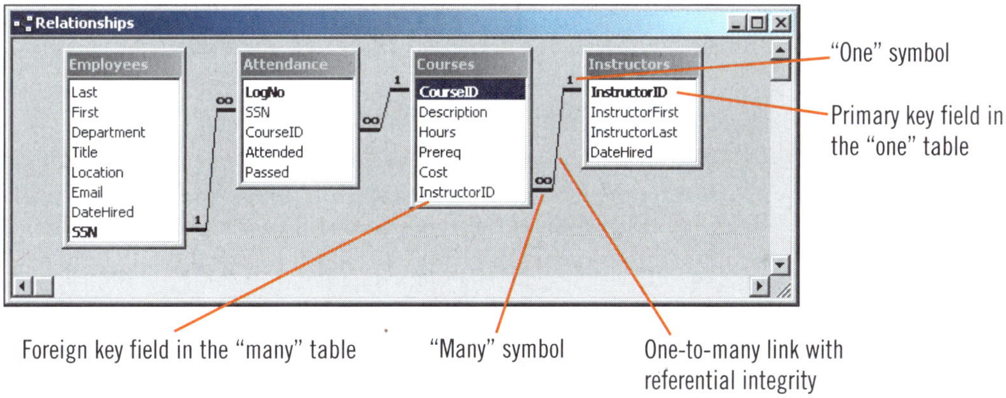

Relationships

Employees: Last, First, Department, Title, Location, Email, DateHired, **SSN**

Attendance: **LogNo**, SSN, CourseID, Attended, Passed

Courses: **CourseID**, Description, Hours, Prereq, Cost, InstructorID

Instructors: **InstructorID**, InstructorFirst, InstructorLast, DateHired

"One" symbol

Primary key field in the "one" table

Foreign key field in the "many" table

"Many" symbol

One-to-many link with referential integrity

TABLE I-2: Relationship types

relationship	description	example	notes
One-to-One	A record in Table X has no more than one matching record in Table Y	A student table has no more than one matching record in a graduation table	This relationship is not common, because all fields related this way could be stored in one table.
One-to-Many	A single record in Table X has many records in Table Y	One product can be sold many times, one customer can make many purchases, or one student can enroll in many courses	The one-to-many relationship is by far the most common relationship type
Many-to-Many	A record in Table X has many records in Table Y, and a record in Table Y has many records in Table X	One employee can take several courses, and the same course can be attended by several employees. (In the MediaLoft database, the Attendance table serves as the	To create a many-to-many relationship in Access, you must first establish a third table, called a **junction table**, between two original tables. The junction table contains foreign key fields that link to the primary key fields of each of the original junction table between the Courses tables, and establishes separate one-to-many and Employees tables.) relationships with them.

Access 2002

Importing XML Data

Importing is a process to quickly convert data from an external source into an Access database. You can import data from one Access database to another, or from many other data sources such as data files created by Excel, dBase, Paradox, and FoxPro, or text files in an HTML, XML, or delimited text file format. In the past, you might have used a delimited text file to import information from one program to another. A delimited text file typically stores one record on each line, with the field values separated by a common character such as a comma, tab, or dash. Now, a more powerful way to share data is by using an XML file. An XML file is a text file that contains Extensible Markup Language (XML) tags that identify fields and contain data. XML has become a common method to deliver data from one application to another over the World Wide Web. You may be familiar with Hypertext Markup Language (HTML), which adds tags to a text file to determine how content such as text and pictures should be formatted and positioned on a Web page. An XML file is similar to an HTML file because each uses tags, the programming codes defined by each language that transform a text file into a file that can be used to pass or present information when opened with browser software such as Internet Explorer. Think of an XML file not as a Web page itself, but as a container for storing and passing data from one computer to another via the World Wide Web. ◆▬▬ Karen Rosen, director of the Human Resources department, has asked the Training department to also track self-study materials for each course. This information is stored in an XML file called study.xml.

Steps 1 2 3 4

Trouble?

Import the study.xml file that contains the data rather than the study.xsd file that contains information about the structure of the data.

1. Click **File** on the menu bar, point to **Get External Data**, click **Import**, navigate to the drive and folder where your Project Files are stored, click the **Files of type list arrow**, click **XML Documents**, then double-click **study.xml**
The Import XML dialog box opens.

2. Click **Options**
The expanded Import XML dialog box is shown in Figure I-6. The upper portion shows the name of the table of data stored within the XML file that can be imported. The options in the lower portion of the dialog box help you determine how the data will be imported.

3. Click **OK**, then click **OK** when you see a message indicating the report is finished
The study table is imported into the Training-I database.

4. Double-click the **study** table to open its datasheet, then double-click the line that separates field names using the ↔ pointer to resize the columns to show all of the data in each field
The study datasheet, with the nine records, is displayed in Figure I-7. All of the data was successfully imported.

5. Save, then close the study datasheet

FIGURE I-6: Import XML dialog box

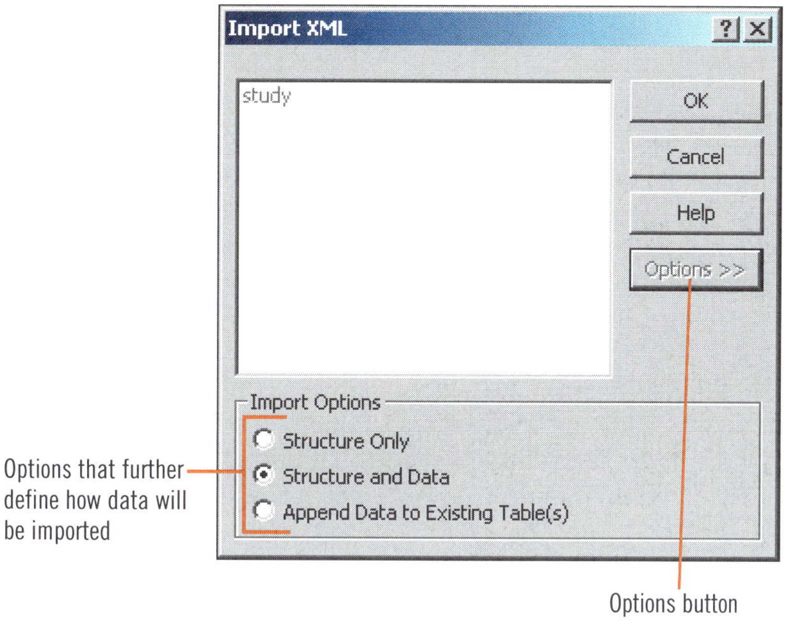
Import XML
study
OK
Cancel
Help
Options >>
Import Options
Structure Only
Structure and Data
Append Data to Existing Table(s)
Options that further define how data will be imported
Options button

FIGURE I-7: Datasheet for study table

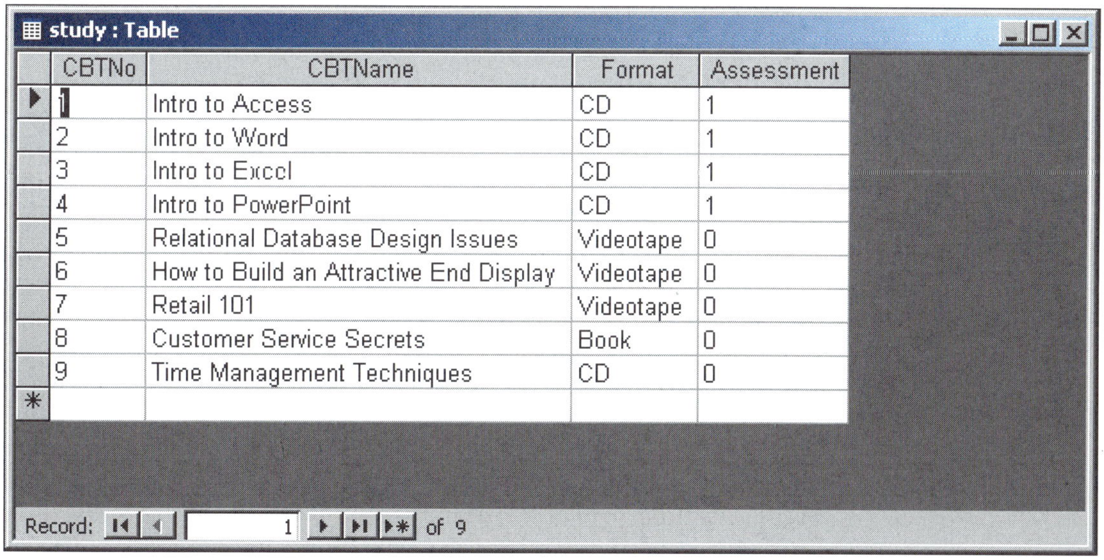
study : Table

CBTNo	CBTName	Format	Assessment
1	Intro to Access	CD	1
2	Intro to Word	CD	1
3	Intro to Excel	CD	1
4	Intro to PowerPoint	CD	1
5	Relational Database Design Issues	Videotape	0
6	How to Build an Attractive End Display	Videotape	0
7	Retail 101	Videotape	0
8	Customer Service Secrets	Book	0
9	Time Management Techniques	CD	0

Record: 1 of 9

Linking Data

Linking connects an Access database to data in an external file such as another Access, dBase, or Paradox database; an Excel or Lotus 1-2-3 spreadsheet; a text file; an HTML file; an XML file; or other data sources that support **ODBC (Open Database Connectivity)** standards. If you link, data can be entered or edited in either the original file or the Access database even though the data is only stored in the original file. Changes to data in either location are automatically made in the other. **Importing**, in contrast, makes a duplicate copy of the data in the Access database, so changes to either the original data source or the imported Access copy have no effect on the other. ◣ Fred asked the new instructors to make a list of all of their class materials. They created this list in an Excel spreadsheet, and want to maintain it there. Fred creates a link to this data from within the Training database.

Steps

1. Click **File** on the menu bar, point to **Get External Data**, then click **Link Tables**

   The Link dialog box opens, listing Access files in the current folder.

2. Navigate to the drive and folder where your Project Files are stored, click the **Files of Type list arrow**, click **Microsoft Excel**, then double-click **CourseMaterials**

   The Link Spreadsheet Wizard appears, as shown in Figure I-8. Data can be linked from different parts of the Excel spreadsheet. The data you want is on Sheet1.

3. Click **Next**, click the **First Row Contains Column Headings check box** to specify **CourseID**, **Materials**, and **Type** as field names, click **Next**, type **CourseSupplies** as the Linked Table Name, click **Finish**, then click **OK**

   The CourseSupplies table appears in the Database window with a linking Excel icon, as shown in Figure I-9. A linked table can and must participate in a one-to-many relationship with another table if it is to share data with the rest of the tables of the database.

4. Click the **Relationships button** ▦ on the Database toolbar, click the **Show Table button** ▦, double-click **CourseSupplies**, then click **Close**

   Rearranging the tables in the Relationships window can improve the clarity of the relationships.

5. Drag the **CourseSupplies field list title bar** under the Attendance table, drag the **CourseID field** in the Courses table to the **CourseID field** in the CourseSupplies table, then click **Create** in the Edit Relationships dialog box

   Your screen should look like Figure I-10. A one-to-many relationship is established between the Courses and CourseSupplies tables. You cannot establish referential integrity when one of the tables is a linked table, but the linked table can now participate in queries, forms, pages, and reports that use fields from multiple tables.

6. Click the **Save** button ▦, close the **Relationships window**, double-click the **CourseSupplies** table, click the **New Record button** ▶* on the Table Datasheet toolbar, type **Access1**, press **[Tab]**, type **MediaLoft.mdb**, press **[Tab]**, then type **File**

   You added a new record to a linked table, so the data was actually added to the original Excel workbook.

7. Close the **CourseSupplies table**, right-click the **Start button** on the taskbar, click **Explore**, navigate to the drive and folder where your Project Files are stored, double-click the **CourseMaterials Excel file** to open it in Excel, then press **[Page Down]**

   The new Access1 record was added as the last row of the Excel spreadsheet.

8. Close Excel, then close Explorer

FIGURE I-8: Link Spreadsheet Wizard dialog box

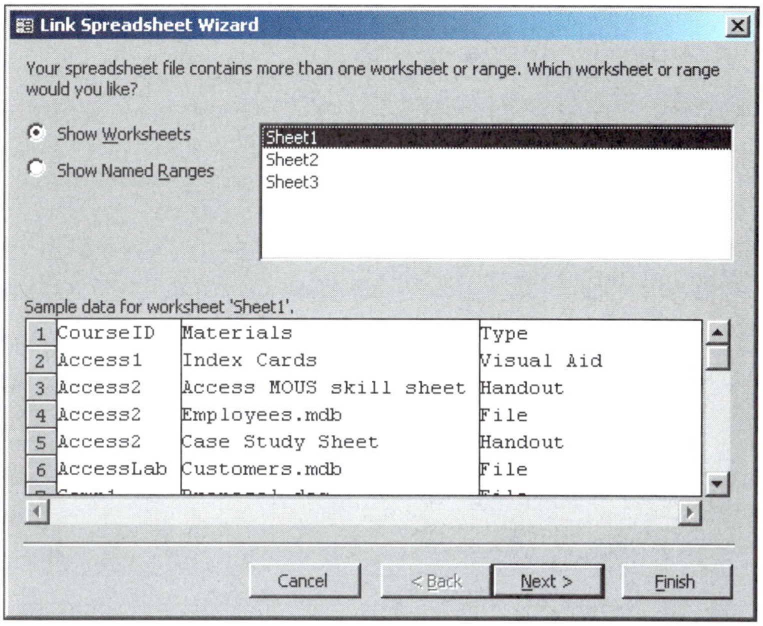

FIGURE I-9: CourseSupplies table is linked from Excel

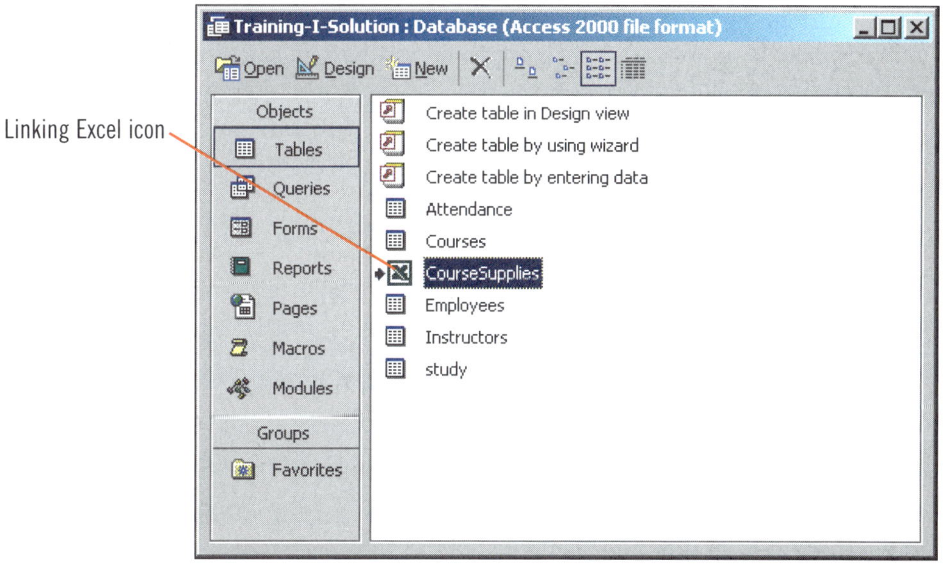

Linking Excel icon

FIGURE I-10: Relationships window with CourseSupplies table

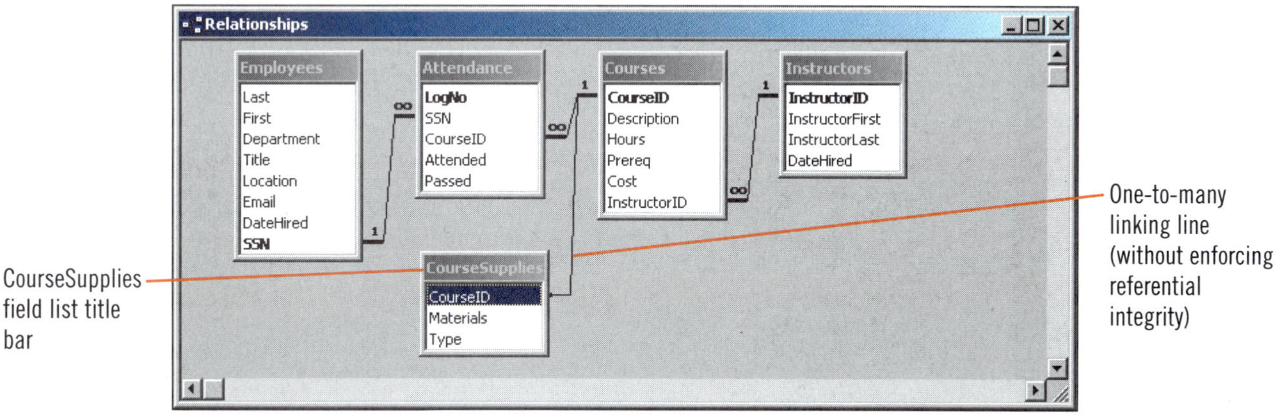

CourseSupplies
field list title
bar

One-to-many
linking line
(without enforcing
referential
integrity)

Access 2002

Publishing Data to Word

Word, the word processing program in the Microsoft Office Suite, is the premier tool for entering, editing, and formatting large paragraphs of text. You can copy data from an Access table, query, form, or report into a Word document to integrate the Access data with a larger word-processed document. You can use the **Publish It with Microsoft Word** feature to quickly copy Access data to Word which automatically copies the **recordset** (the fields and records) of a table, query, form, or report object to Word using the **Publish It with Microsoft Word button** . Publish It with Microsoft Word is one of three **OfficeLink** tools used to quickly send Access data to another Microsoft Office program. Table I-3 lists a variety of other techniques for copying Access data to Word. ▁ Fred has been asked to comment on the Access courses his department has provided. He will use the OfficeLink buttons to send the Access Courses Report to Word, then summarize his thoughts about the classes in a paragraph of text in the Word document.

Steps 123⁴

1. Click **Reports** on the Objects bar, click **Access Courses Report** (if not already selected), click the **OfficeLinks button list arrow** on the Database toolbar, click **Publish It with Microsoft Word**, then maximize the Word window

The records from the Access Courses Report object appear in a Word document in an **RTF** (**rich text format**) file format, as shown in Figure I-11. The RTF format does not support all advanced Word features, but it does support basic formatting embellishments such as multiple fonts, colors, and font sizes. The RTF file format is commonly used when two different word processing programs need to use the same file.

2. Press **[Enter]** three times to increase the space between the top of the document and the Access information, press **[Ctrl][Home]** to position the insertion point at the top of the document, then type the following:

To: **Management Committee**
From: **your name**
Re: **Analysis of Access Courses**
Date: **today's date**

The following information shows the recent demand for Access training. The information is sorted by department, and shows that the Accounting Department has had the greatest demand for Access courses.

3. Proofread your document, which should now look like Figure I-12, then click the **Print button** on the Standard toolbar

Word's **word wrap** feature determines when a line of text extends into the right margin of the page, and automatically forces the text to the next line without you needing to press Enter. This allows you to enter and edit large paragraphs of text in Word very efficiently.

4. Click the **Save button** on Word's Standard toolbar to save the Access Courses Report document, then exit Word

Files saved through the Publish It with Microsoft Word and Analyze It with Microsoft Excel feature are saved in the My Documents folder by default for most typical Microsoft Office installations.

FIGURE I-11: Publishing an Access report to Word

Access Courses
Report.rtf

Access Courses Report

Attended	CourseID	Description	Hours	Cost	Department
02/27/2003	AccessLab	Access Case Problems	12	$200	Accounting
02/20/2003	Access2	Intermediate Access	24	$400	Accounting
02/13/2003	Access1	Introduction to Access	16	$400	Accounting
02/13/2003	Access1	Introduction to Access	16	$400	Accounting
02/27/2003	AccessLab	Access Case Problems	12	$200	Book
02/20/2003	Access2	Intermediate Access	24	$400	Book

FIGURE I-12: Using Word to enter text

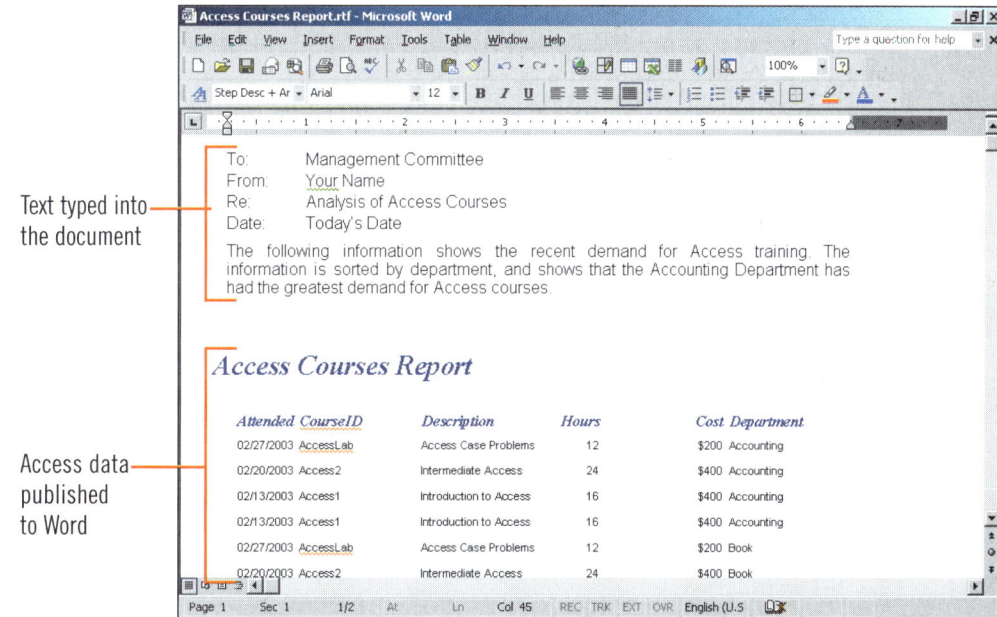

Text typed into
the document

To: Management Committee
From: Your Name
Re: Analysis of Access Courses
Date: Today's Date

The following information shows the recent demand for Access training. The information is sorted by department, and shows that the Accounting Department has had the greatest demand for Access courses.

Access Courses Report

Access data
published
to Word

Attended	CourseID	Description	Hours	Cost	Department
02/27/2003	AccessLab	Access Case Problems	12	$200	Accounting
02/20/2003	Access2	Intermediate Access	24	$400	Accounting
02/13/2003	Access1	Introduction to Access	16	$400	Accounting
02/13/2003	Access1	Introduction to Access	16	$400	Accounting
02/27/2003	AccessLab	Access Case Problems	12	$200	Book
02/20/2003	Access2	Intermediate Access	24	$400	Book

Access 2002

TABLE I-3: Techniques to copy Access data to other applications

technique	button or menu option	description
OfficeLinks	Analyze It with Microsoft Excel	Sends a selected table, query, form, or report object's records to Excel
	Publish It with Microsoft Word	Sends a selected table, query, form, or report object's records to Word
	Merge It with Microsoft Word	Helps merge the selected table or query recordset with a Word document
Office Clipboard	Copy and Paste	Click the Copy button to copy selected data to the Office Clipboard. The Office Clipboard can hold up to 24 different items. Open a Word document or Excel spreadsheet, click where you want to paste the data, then click the Paste button.
Exporting	File on the menu bar, then Export	Copies information from an Access object into a different file format
Drag and drop	Right-click an empty space on the taskbar, then click Tile Windows Horizontally or Tile Windows Vertically	With the windows tiled, drag the Access table, query, form, or report object icon from the Access window to the target (Excel or Word) window.

Analyzing Data with Excel

Excel, the spreadsheet software program in the Microsoft Office Suite, is an excellent tool for projecting numeric trends into the future. For example, you can analyze the impact of a price increase on budget or income projections by applying several different numbers. This reiterative analysis is sometimes called "what-if" analysis. **What-if analysis** allows you to change values in an Excel worksheet and watch related calculated formulas update instantly. This is a very popular use for Excel. You can use the **Analyze It with Microsoft Excel** feature to quickly copy Access data to Excel with the **Analyze It with Microsoft Excel button** . ✎ The Accounting department asked Fred to provide some Access data in an Excel spreadsheet so they can analyze how different increases in the cost of the Access classes would affect each of the departments. Fred has gathered the raw data into a report, called Access Courses Report, and uses Excel to analyze the effect of increased costs.

Steps 1 2 3 4

Trouble?

If a dialog box opens indicating that the file already exists, click Yes to replace the existing file.

1. Click **Reports** on the Objects bar, click the **Access Courses Report**, click the **OfficeLinks button list arrow** on the Database toolbar, then click **Analyze It with Microsoft Excel**

   The report data is automatically exported into an Excel workbook, as shown in Figure I-13. When you use the Analyze It with Microsoft Excel or Publish It with Microsoft Word buttons, the workbook or document you create has the same name as the Access object, and it is usually saved in the My Documents folder of your C: drive. You can send the recordset of a table, query, form, or report object to Excel using the Analyze It with Microsoft Excel button.

2. Click cell **G1** (column G, row 1), type **Cost Per Hour**, press **[Enter]**, type **=E2/D2** (in cell G2), and then press **[Enter]**

   Cell G2 contains a formula that divides the cost in cell E2 by the hours in cells D2, or 200/12.

3. Click cell **G2**, then click the **Currency Style button** on the Formatting toolbar

   You can quickly and easily copy Excel formulas to other cells using the **AutoFill** pointer ✛.

4. Point to the bottom right corner of cell G2 so that the pointer changes to ✛, then drag to cell G14

   The copied formulas are shown in Figure I-14. The workbook is now ready to perform what-if analysis by changing assumption values.

5. Click cell **E2**, type **400**, press **[Enter]**, type **500** (in cell E3), and then press **[Enter]**

   Your spreadsheet should look like Figure I-15. By changing any value in column E or D, Excel updates all formulas that depend on those values. In this case, Excel recalculated the formulas in cells G2 and G3.

6. Click the **Save button** on Excel's Standard toolbar to save the Access Courses Report workbook, then exit Excel

FIGURE I-13: Access Courses Report workbook

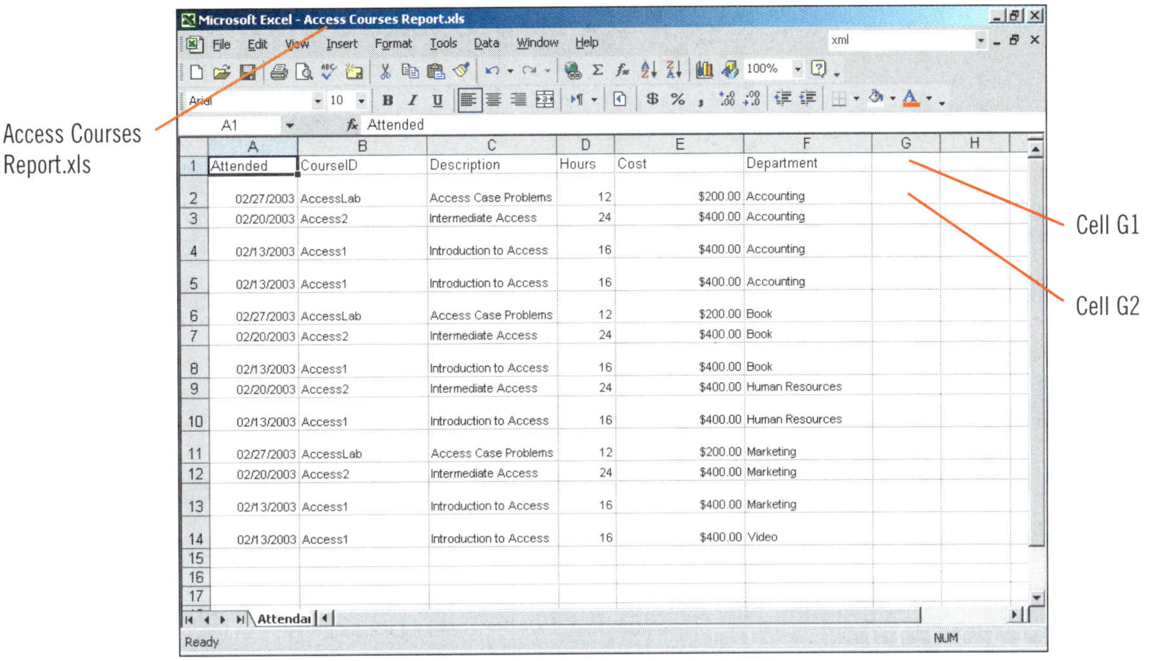

Access Courses
Report.xls

Cell G1

Cell G2

FIGURE I-14: Copying a formula in the workbook

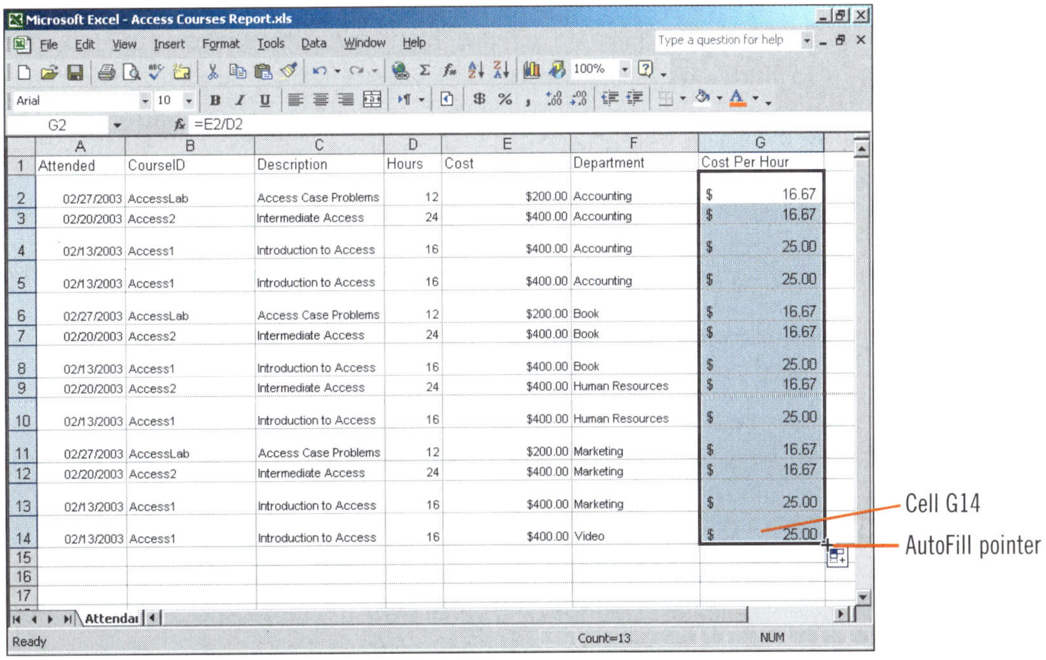

Cell G14

AutoFill pointer

FIGURE I-15: Performing "what-if" analysis

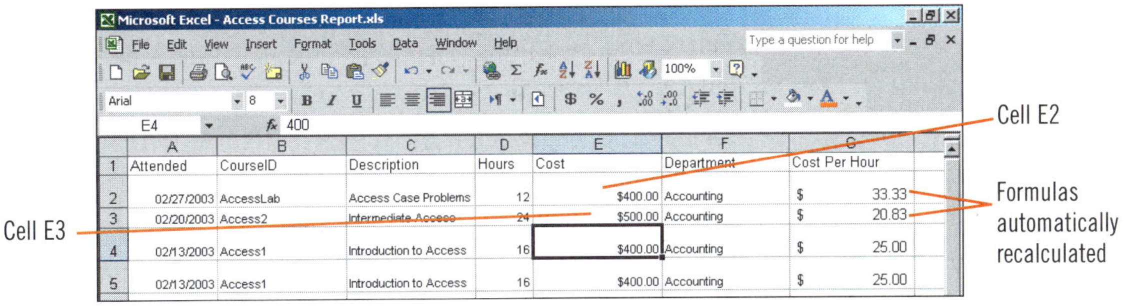

Cell E2

Cell E3

Formulas
automatically
recalculated

Access 2002

Merging Data with Word

Another OfficeLink tool called **Merge It with Microsoft Word** merges Access records with a Word form letter, label, or envelope to create mass mailing documents. You use the **Merge It with Microsoft Word button** to send records from a table, query, form, or report to Word for a mail merge. Fred wants to send the MediaLoft employees a letter announcing two new courses. He uses the Merge It with Microsoft Word feature to customize a standard form letter to each employee.

Steps 1 2 3 4

1. **Click Tables on the Objects bar, click Employees, click the OfficeLinks button list arrow on the Database toolbar, then click Merge It with Microsoft Word**
   The Microsoft Word Mail Merge Wizard starts, requesting information about the merge process.

2. **Click Create a new document and then link the data to it, then click OK**
   Word starts and opens the **Mail Merge task pane** on the right side of the window and the **Mail Merge toolbar** at the top of the window. Both offer tools to help you with the mail merge process. The next important step, however, is to create the **main document**, the document used to determine how standard text and Access data will be combined.

3. **Maximize the Word window, then type the text shown in Figure I-16**
   This is the standard text that will be consistent for each letter created in the mail merge process.

4. **Click to the right of To:, press [Tab] to align the insertion point at the same position as Your Name, click the Insert Merge Fields button on the Mail Merge toolbar, click First, then click Insert**
   Your document should look like Figure I-17. The **Insert Merge Field** dialog box lists all of the fields in the Employees table. You use the Insert Merge Field dialog box to insert **merge fields**, codes that will be replaced with the values in the field that the code represents when the mail merge is processed.

5. **Double-click Last, then click Close**
   You used the Insert Merge Field dialog box to add two merge fields to a Word document—you cannot type them directly from the keyboard—but you can insert the same merge field into one letter multiple times. Once the merge fields are entered in the main document, you can edit the main document before you merge it with the data.

Trouble?

If your final merged document contains a mistake, close it without saving, edit the main document to correct the mistake, and click the Merge to New Document button again.

6. **Click between the First and Last codes, press [Spacebar] to insert a space between the codes, click the Merge to New Document button on the Mail Merge toolbar, then click OK to merge all records**
   The mail merge process combines field values from the Employees table with the Word form letter, and creates a letter for each record in the Employees table. The first letter is to Shayla Colletti, as shown in Figure I-18. "Shayla" is the field value for the First field in the first record, and "Colletti" is the field value for the Last field in the first record. The status bar of the Word document shows that this document contains 21 pages, one page for each of the 21 records in the Employees table.

7. **Click the Next Page button below the vertical scroll bar to view the next page, and then keep clicking to view all of the pages in the document**

8. **Click File on the menu bar, click Print, click the Current page option button, click OK to print only the last page, then close Word without saving any documents**

FIGURE I-16: Main document

Insert Merge
Fields button

Mail Merge toolbar

Mail Merge
task pane

FIGURE I-17: Inserting merge fields

Inserted
merge field

Merge to New
Document button

First merge field

FIGURE I-18: Final merged document

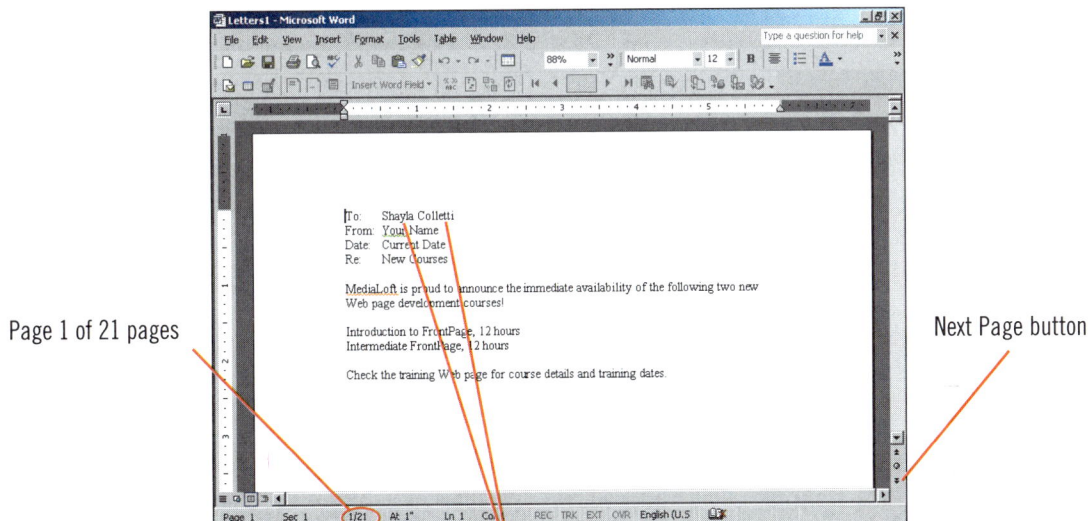

Page 1 of 21 pages

Next Page button

Field values

Access 2002

Exporting Data to XML

Exporting is a way to send Access information to another database, spreadsheet, or file format. Exporting is the opposite of importing. You can export data from an Access database to other proprietary file types such as those used by Excel, Lotus 1-2-3, dBase, Paradox, and FoxPro, and in several general file formats including HTML, XML, and various text file formats. Unlike linking, data you import or export retains no connection between its original source and the imported or exported copy. ✎ ▬▬ The Information Systems department has requested that Fred export training activity for the Accounting department into an XML file that they can use to develop a Web-based application.

Steps 123 4

1. Click **Queries** on the Objects bar, click **Accounting History**, click **File** on the menu bar, then click **Export**

The Export Query 'Accounting History' To… dialog box opens, requesting the location and format for the exported information.

2. Navigate to where your Project Files are located, type **acct** in the File name text box, click the **Save as type list arrow**, click **XML Documents**, then click **Export**

The Export XML dialog box opens, as shown in Figure I-19. The **schema** of the data represents how the tables of the database are related. If you select this check box, Access creates and exports an accompanying **XSD (Extensible Schema Document)** file to store structural information about the database. The **presentation** of the data refers to formatting characteristics such as bold and font size. If you select this check box, Access creates and exports an accompanying **XSL (Extensible Stylesheet Language)** file to store presentation information.

3. Click **OK**

Access exports the data and its schema to your Project Files folder.

4. Click **Start**, point to **Programs**, point to **Accessories**, then click **Notepad**

Notepad is a text editing program that is provided with all versions of Windows. When you want to work with an HTML or XML file that is really just a text file with embedded tags, Notepad works well because it doesn't insert extra formatting features that the HTML or XML file cannot use, or which could potentially corrupt the file.

5. Click **File** on the menu bar, click **Open**, navigate to the drive and folder where your Project Files are located, click the **Files of type list arrow**, click **All Files**, double-click **acct.xml** in the file list, then maximize Notepad

Your screen should look like Figure I-20. A less than symbol, <, and greater than symbol, >, surround each of the XML tags, and are a distinguishing characteristic of markup languages such as HTML and XML. XML data is positioned between two tags, also called the **start tag** and **end tag**. You can quickly find and change data using the Replace feature.

6. Click **Edit** on the menu bar, click **Replace**, type **Fernandez** into the Find what text box, type your last name into the Replace with text box, click **Replace All**, then click **Cancel**

All occurrences of "Fernandez" have now been replaced with your last name. Since this file has been *exported* from Access, it is a separate copy of the data in the original Accounting History query; therefore, changes to this file do not affect the data in the Training-I database.

7. Click **Edit** on the menu bar, click **Find**, type your last name into the Find what text box, then click **Find Next** three times to find three occurrences of your last name inserted as data into this XML file, as shown in Figure I-21

By examining how field values are stored, you better understand XML.

8. Click **Cancel**, click **File** on the menu bar, click **Print**, click **Print** in the Print dialog box, click **File** on the menu bar, click **Save**, then close Notepad

FIGURE I-19: Export XML dialog box

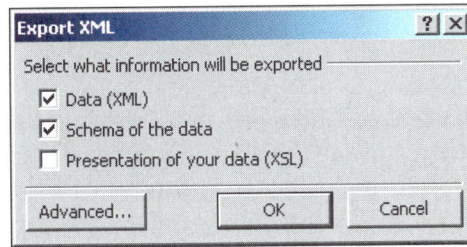

FIGURE I-20: Opening an XML file within Notepad

Acct.xml

Notepad

XML tags

XML data is positioned between XML tags

FIGURE I-21: Finding XML data

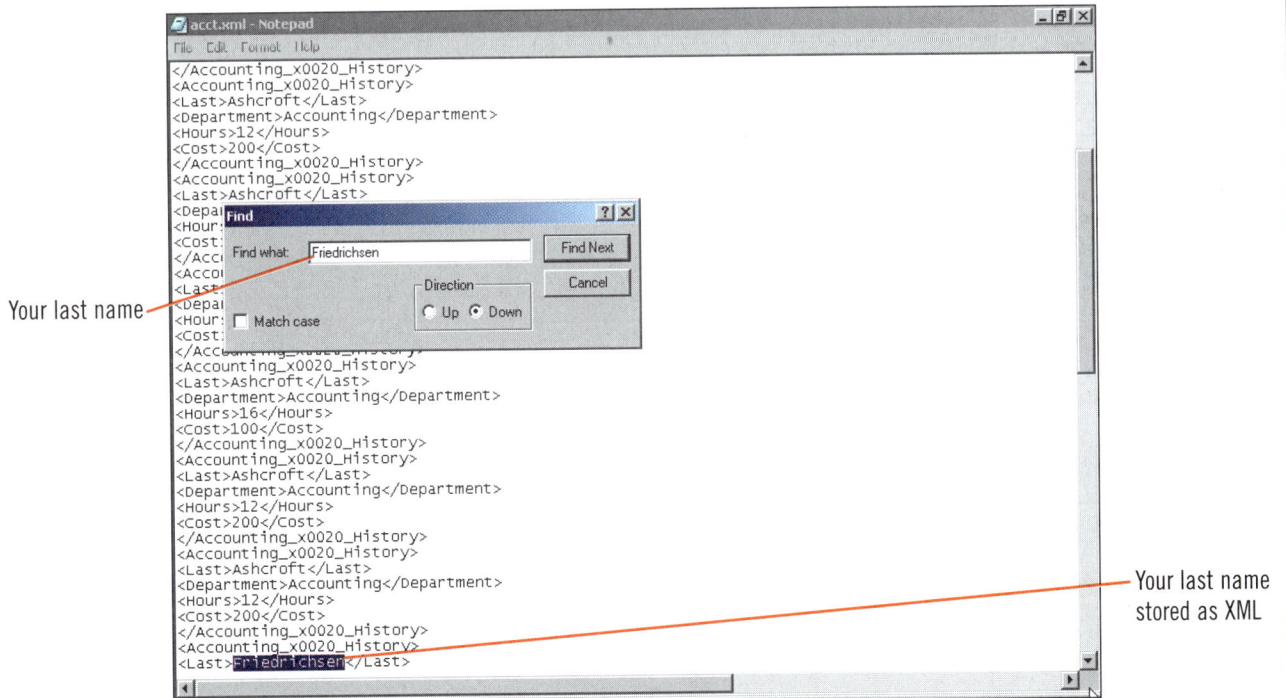

Your last name

Your last name stored as XML

Using SQL Server

SQL Server is another database program provided by Microsoft. You use SQL Server for databases that are larger and more complex than those typically maintained in Access. If your Access database is growing rapidly, you can **upsize**, or convert, to SQL Server to handle more users or process large amounts of data more efficiently. Microsoft provides the sample **NorthwindCS** database as part of the full Access 2002 installation to illustrate how an Access database can connect to an SQL Server database. The NorthwindCS database is actually an Access **project**, a special Access file that contains no data. Rather, it contains form and report objects for the end user. All of the data used by those forms and reports is stored in an SQL Server database that is typically located on a shared file server. In this manner, you can use Access projects and an SQL server database to create efficient **client/server applications** which employ a server to manage shared data and clients to process the user interface. ✐ Fred anticipates the Training database may need to be upsized to SQL Server. He decides to open the sample NorthwindCS database to start learning about client/server computing.

Steps 1234

Trouble?

If the sample databases were not previously installed on your computer, you are prompted to insert the Office CD.

1. Click **Help** on the menu bar, point to **Sample Databases**, then click **Northwind Sample Access Project**

Although you can have multiple copies of Access running at any single time, you can only have one database open in an Access window. If the Training-I database was open when you clicked Northwind Sample Access Project, Access closed the Training-I database, and then opened the NorthwindCS database. You see a dialog box for connecting the project to an SQL Server database.

2. Click **OK**

The Data Link Properties dialog box opens, as shown in Figure I-22. In this dialog box, you would enter all of the information required to make a successful connection to an SQL Server database such as the server name, database name, and any other information required by the firewall that protects the SQL Server. A **firewall** is a combination of hardware and software that adds a layer of security to corporate data. In its simplest form, a firewall consists of software that requires a valid user name and password before access to information is granted.

3. Click **Cancel**

Although you can't make the physical connection between the NorthwindCS client database and an SQL Server database unless you have access to one, you can still explore the NorthwindCS database that is used by the client.

4. Click **OK** on the Northwind Traders welcome screen, then click each of the Objects buttons on the Objects bar

You see that there are no tables in this file. Rather, this project contains only form, report, macro, page, and module objects used by the client.

5. Click **Forms** on the Objects bar

Your screen should look like Figure I-23. Notice that the title bar of the Database window indicates that the database is disconnected from an SQL Server. Therefore, you could work in the Design View of any of the existing objects, but if you tried to open any view that presents data, you'd see a message indicating that the software cannot perform that action.

6. Close the NorthwindCS database, then exit Access

FIGURE I-22: Data Link Properties dialog box

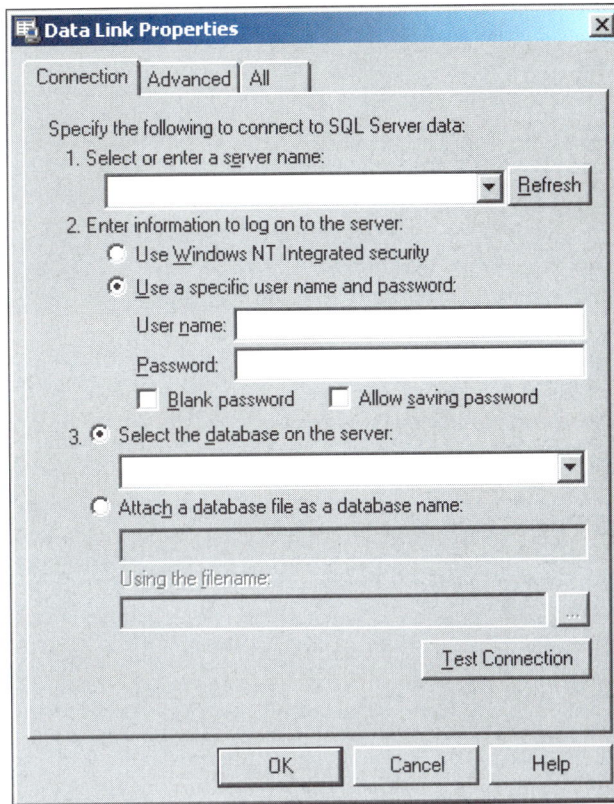

FIGURE I-22: Data Link Properties dialog box

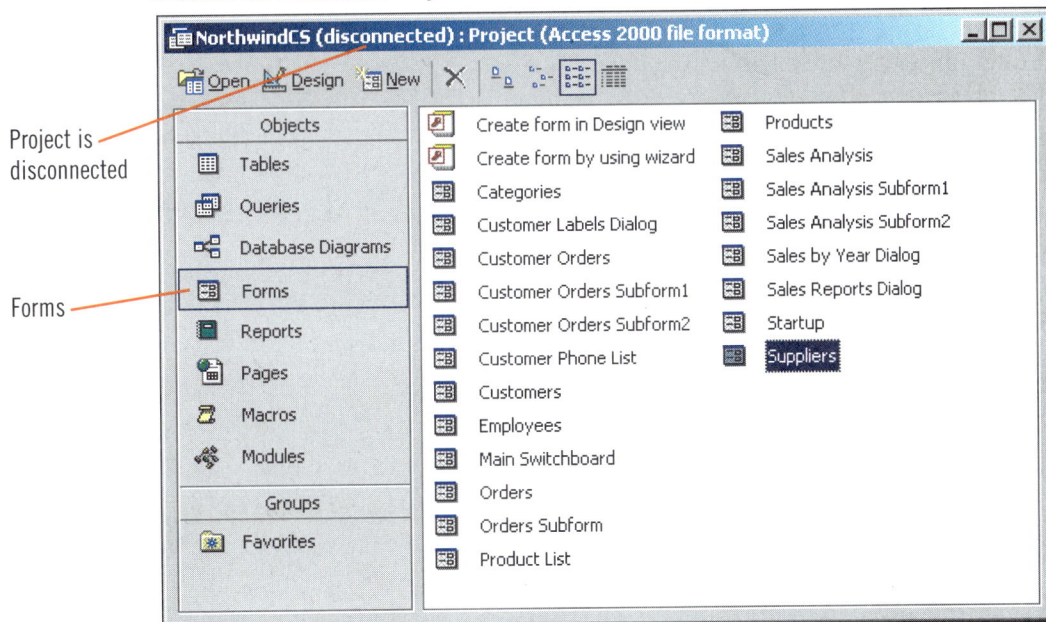

FIGURE I-23: NorthwindCS Project window

Project is disconnected

Forms

Access 2002

Practice

▶ Concepts Review

Identify each element of the Database window as shown in Figure I-24.

FIGURE I-24

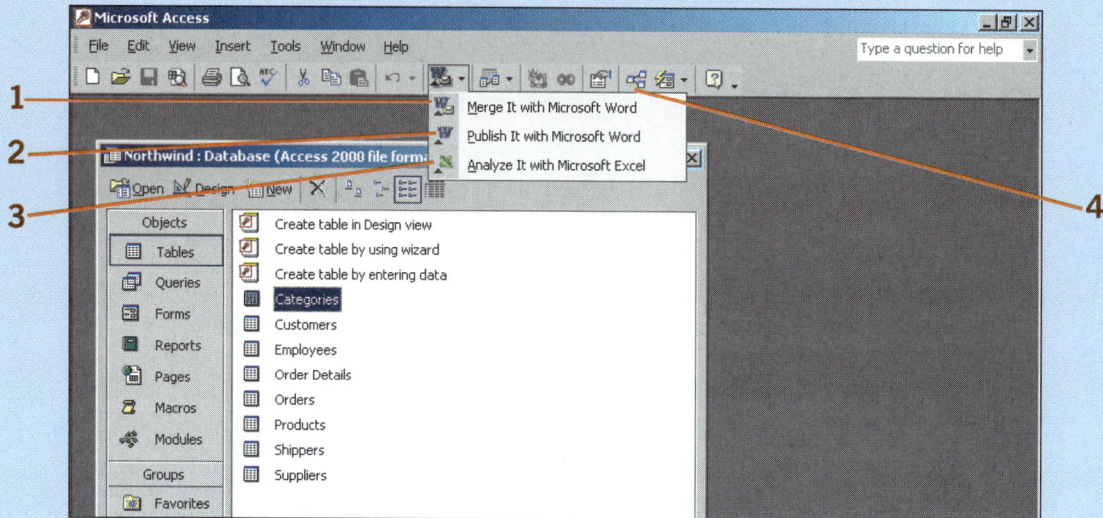

Match each term with the statement that describes its function.

5. XML
6. foreign key field
7. junction table
8. linking
9. what-if analysis
10. primary key field
11. normalization

a. A field that contains unique information for each record
b. Testing different assumptions in a spreadsheet
c. Contains foreign key fields that link to primary key fields
d. The process of determining the appropriate fields, records, and tables when designing a relational database
e. A way to connect to data in an external source without copying it
f. A field added to the table on the "many" side of a one-to-many relationship to link with the primary key field of the "one" table
g. A text file that contains tags that identify fields and contain data

Select the best answer from the list of choices.

12. Which of the following is NOT an Access object?
 a. Spreadsheet
 b. Report
 c. Table
 d. Query

13. Which of the following is NOT part of the normalization process?
 a. Determining the appropriate fields
 b. Identifying the correct number of tables
 c. Establishing table relationships
 d. Creating database hyperlinks

14. Which of the following is NOT true about XML?
 a. It is a popular format for sharing data over the Internet.
 b. It uses tags to define fields.
 c. Access cannot export data to an XML format.
 d. It is similar to HTML.

15. Which of the following software products would most likely be used to analyze the effect on future sales and profits based on the change to several different assumptions?
    - **a.** Word
    - **b.** Excel
    - **c.** Access
    - **d.** PowerPoint
16. Which of the following is NOT an OfficeLinks button?
    - **a.** Analyze It with Microsoft Excel
    - **b.** Publish It with Microsoft Word
    - **c.** Present It with Microsoft PowerPoint
    - **d.** Merge It with Microsoft Word

▶ Skills Review

1. **Examine Access objects.**
   - **a.** Start Access, then open the **Machinery-I** database from the drive and folder where your Project Files are located.
   - **b.** On a separate piece of paper, list the seven Access objects and the number of each type that exist in the Machinery-I database.
   - **c.** Use Table Datasheet View to determine the number of records in each table. Write down your answers.
   - **d.** Use Table Design View to determine the number of fields in each table. Write down your answers.
2. **Examine relationships.**
   - **a.** Click the Relationships button on the Database toolbar.
   - **b.** Drag the ProductID field from the Products table to the ProductID field of the Inventory Transactions table to create a one-to-many relationship between those tables.
   - **c.** Click Enforce Referential Integrity in the Edit Relationships dialog box, then click Create.
   - **d.** Drag the PurchaseOrderID field from the Purchase Orders table to the PurchaseOrderID field of the Inventory Transactions table to create a one-to-many relationship between those tables.
   - **e.** Click Enforce Referential Integrity in the Edit Relationships dialog box, then click Create.
   - **f.** Click File on the menu bar, click Print Relationships, then view the relationships report in Design View.
   - **g.** Add your name as a label to the Report Header section, print the report, then close report without saving it.
   - **h.** Save the changes to the Relationships window, then close it.
3. **Import XML data.**
   - **a.** Click File on the menu bar, point to the Get External Data option, then click Import.
   - **b.** In the Import dialog box, change the Files of type list to XML Documents, then import the **employ** XML file stored on the drive and folder location where your Project Files are located.
   - **c.** Open the datasheet for the new employ table, change the name in the first record to your own, then print it.
   - **d.** Click the Design View button, then examine the data types for all of the fields. On the back of your paper, identify the data type that each field was automatically assigned, then close Table Design View.
4. **Link data.**
   - **a.** Click File on the menu bar, point to the Get External Data option, then click Link Tables.
   - **b.** In the Link dialog box, change the Files of type list to Microsoft Excel, then link to the **Vendors** Excel file stored on the drive and folder where your Project Files are located.
   - **c.** In the Link Spreadsheet Wizard, be sure to specify that the first row contains column headings and that five data records are linked.
   - **d.** Name the new table **Vendors**, then finish the wizard and close the Vendors table.
5. **Publish data to Word.**
   - **a.** Click the Reports button on the Objects bar, click the Every Product We Lease report, click the Office Links list arrow, then click the Publish It with Microsoft Word button to send the information to Word.
   - **b.** Press [Ctrl][Home] to go to the top of the document if the insertion point is not already positioned at the top of the page, press [Enter] twice, then press [Ctrl][Home] to return to the top of the document.

c. Type the following at the top of the document:

INTERNAL MEMO
From: [your name]
To: **Sales Staff**
Date: [today's date]
Do not forget to mention the long lead times on the Back Hoe and Thatcher to customers. We usually do not keep these expensive items in stock.

d. Proofread the document, save, then print it. Close the document, then exit Word.

6. **Analyze data with Excel.**
   a. Click the Tables button on the Objects bar, then click the Products table.
   b. Click the OfficeLinks button list arrow, then click Analyze It with Microsoft Excel.
   c. Click cell D12, type **=AVERAGE(D2:D11)**, then press [Enter]. This formula calculates the average Unit Price for all values in the range of cells from D2 through D11.
   d. Click cell A13, type your name, press [Enter], then click the Print button on the Standard toolbar.
   e. Click cell D7, type **499.75**, then press [Enter]. Changing the value of the most expensive product should make a big difference in the calculated average Unit Price.
   f. Save, print, and close the workbook, then exit Excel.

7. **Merge data with Word.**
   a. Click the Employees table. Click the OfficeLinks button list arrow, then click Merge It with Microsoft Word.
   b. Click the "Create a new document and then link the data to it" option button, then click OK.
   c. In the Word document, enter the following standard text to serve as the main document for the mail merge:
   Date: **February 9, 2003**
   To:
   From: **your name**
   Re: **CPR Training**
   The annual CPR Training session will be held on Monday, February 17, 2003. Please sign up for this important event in the lunch room. Friends and family over 18 years old are also welcome.
   d. Click to the right of To: and press [Tab] to position your cursor at the location for the first merge field.
   e. Click the Insert Merge Fields button on the Mail Merge toolbar, double-click FirstName and LastName, then click Close. Click between the FirstName and LastName codes, then press [Spacebar].
   f. Click the Merge to New Document button on the Mail Merge toolbar, then merge all records.
   g. Print the last page of the merged document, close both the merged document and the main document without saving them, then exit Word.

8. **Export data to XML.**
   a. Click the Products table. Click File on the menu bar, then click Export.
   b. Click the Save as type list arrow, click XML Documents, double-click Products in the File name and type **prod**, click Export, then export both the data and schema.
   c. Start Notepad, then open the **prod.xml** file in Notepad.
   d. Find the SerialNumber data for the Bird House (78999), then modify it so that your initials are added to the SerialNumber such as **78999LLF**.
   e. Save, then print the prod.xml document from within Notepad. Close Notepad, then close the Machinery-I database.

9. **Use SQL Server.**
   a. Click the Help menu, point to Sample Databases, then click Northwind Sample Access Project.
   b. When prompted to connect to an SQL Server, click OK.
   c. Write down four pieces of information from the Data Link Properties dialog box that you would probably have to supply if you were physically connecting to an SQL Server, then click Cancel.

d. Click OK on the Northwind welcome screen, click the Forms button, then double-click Orders. Click OK when prompted.

e. In a Word or Notepad document, explain why Access could not perform this operation, using the words client, server, data, Orders form, NorthwindCS, and SQL Server in your answer.

f. Close the NorthwindCS database, then exit Access.

▶ Independent Challenge 1

As the manager of a college women's basketball team, you have created a database called Basketball-I that tracks the players, games, and player statistics. You need to complete the table relationships.

a. Start Access and open the database **Basketball-I** from the drive and folder where your Project Files are located.

b. Click the Relationships button and create a one-to-many relationship using the GameNo field between the Games table and the Stats table. Enforce referential integrity.

c. Similarly, create a one-to-many relationship using the PlayerNo field between the Players and Stats table. Note that the Stats table should be the "many" side of both relationships.

d. Click File on the menu bar, click Print Relationships, and then view the relationships report in Design View.

e. Add a label to the Report Header section with your name as the caption, then close the report without saving it.

f. Save the changes to the Relationships window, and close it.

g. Click the Queries button on the Objects bar, then double-click the Players Query.

h. Change the first instance of Lindsey Swift to your name, press [Page Down], then print the first page of the datasheet. On the back of the printout, explain why every occurrence of Lindsey Swift changed to your name. Also explain why your name is listed 10 times on this datasheet.

i. Close the Basketball-I database, then exit Access.

▶ Independent Challenge 2

As the manager of a women's college basketball team, you have created a database called Basketball-I that tracks the players, games, and player statistics. You want to link to an Excel file that contains information on the player's course load. On a form, you also want to create a hyperlink to a Word document.

a. Start Access and open the database **Basketball-I** from the drive and folder where your Project Files are stored.

b. If relationships between the tables have not yet been established, complete Steps b. through f. of Independent Challenge 1.

c. Click the Reports button on the Objects bar, click the Player Statistics report, click the OfficeLinks button list arrow, then click the Publish It with Microsoft Word button.

d. Press [Enter] three times, then press [Ctrl][Home] to position the insertion point at the top of the document.

e. Type your name on the first line of the document, then save, print, and close the Player Statistics document. Exit Word. Close the Basketball-I database, then exit Access.

▶ Independent Challenge 3

As the manager of a women's college basketball team, you have created a database called Basketball-I that tracks the players, games, and player statistics. You want to export some information in the Basketball-I database to an Excel worksheet to analyze the data.

a. Start Access and open the database **Basketball-I** from the drive and folder where your Project Files are located.

b. Click the Games table, then choose the Analyze It with Microsoft Excel option from the OfficeLinks button on the Database toolbar. If prompted, click Yes to replace the existing file.

c. Click cell H1, type **Margin**, click cell H2, type **=E2-F2**, and then press [Enter].

d. Click cell H2 and then use the AutoFill handle to copy the formula down the entire column, through cell H23.

e. Click cell A25, type your name, change the print settings (use the Page Setup option on the File menu) to a landscape orientation, then print the spreadsheet.

f. Save and close the workbook, then exit Excel. Close the Basketball-I database, then exit Access.

ⓔ Independent Challenge 4

You are the coordinator for the foreign studies program at your college. You have created a database that documents the primary and secondary languages used by foreign countries. The database also includes a table of common words and phrases, translated into various languages.

a. Start Access, open the **Languages-I** database from the drive and folder where your Project Files are located, then click Tables on the Objects bar.

b. Open the table datasheets to observe the entries. The Language1 and Language2 fields in the Countries table represent the primary and secondary languages for that country.

c. Click the Relationships button and create a one-to-many relationship using the LanguageID field in the Languages table and the Language1 field in the Countries table. Enforce referential integrity.

d. Similarly, create a one-to-many relationship using the LanguageID field in the Languages table and the Language2 field in the Countries table. Click No when prompted, and be sure to enforce referential integrity. The Languages table's field list will appear twice in the Relationships window with Languages_1 as the title for the second field list. The Words table is used for reference, and does not have a direct relationship to the other tables.

e. Click File on the menu bar, click Print Relationships, then view the relationships report in Design View.

f. Add a label to the Report Header section with your name as the caption, then close the report without saving it.

g. Connect to the Internet, and then go to www.ask.com, www.about.com, or any search engine. Your goal is to find a Web site that translates English to other languages, and to print one page of that Web site.

h. Add three new words or phrases to the Words table, making sure that the translation is made in all five of the represented languages: French, Spanish, German, Italian, and Portuguese.

i. Print the updated datasheet for the Words table, then close the Words table, close the Languages-I database, then exit Access.

▶ Visual Workshop

Start Access and open the **Basketball-I** database from the drive and folder where your Project Files are stored. Use the Merge It with Microsoft Word feature to merge information from the Players table to a form letter. The final page of the merged document is shown in Figure I-25. Notice that the player's first and last names have been merged to the first line, and that the player's first name is merged a second time in the first sentence of the letter. Print the last page of the merged document, then close both documents without saving them.

FIGURE I-25

```
To:     Jamie Johnson
From:   Your Name
Date:   Current Date
Re:     Big 13 Champions!

Congratulations, Jamie, for an outstanding year at State University! Your hard work and
team contributions have clinched the Big 13 Championship for State University for the
third year in a row!

Thank you for your dedication!

Keep the faith,
Coach
```

Creating
Data Access Pages

Objectives

► **Understand the World Wide Web**
► **Create Hyperlink fields**
MOUS ► **Create pages for interactive reporting**
MOUS ► **Create pages for data entry**
MOUS ► **Create pages for data analysis**
MOUS ► **Work in Page Design View**
► **Add hyperlinks**
► **Publish Web pages to Web servers**

The Internet connects a vast amount of information, provides unlimited business opportunities, and supports fast, global communication. Most content provided via the Internet is accessed through a **Web page**, a hyperlinked document that makes the Internet easy to navigate. Web pages and their underlying infrastructure are referred to as the **World Wide Web**. Now, Web page technology has evolved to also include dynamic content. **Dynamic Web pages** are connected to a database, and are re-created with up-to-date data each time the Web page is opened. You can use dynamic Web pages to view, enter, or update data stored in an underlying database. Access 2002 provides the **page** object to create dynamic Web pages. ✎ Fred Ames, coordinator of training, wants to let MediaLoft employees access the Training-J database via the Internet. He will use the page object to create dynamic Web pages.

Understanding the World Wide Web

Creating Web pages that dynamically interact with an Access database is an exciting process that involves many underlying technologies. Understanding how the Internet, the World Wide Web, and Web pages interact helps you successfully connect a Web page to an underlying Access database. ✎ Fred reviews some of the history and key terminology of the Internet and World Wide Web to better prepare himself for the task of connecting a Web page to an Access database.

Details

► The **Internet** is a worldwide network of computer networks that sends and receives information through a common communications **protocol** (set of rules) called **TCP/IP** (Transmission Control Protocol/Internet Protocol).

► The Internet supports many services, including:

- **E-Mail**: electronic mail

- **File Transfer**: uploading and downloading files containing anything from text to pictures to music to software programs

- **Newsgroups**: similar to e-mail, but messages are posted in a "public mailbox" that is available to any subscriber, rather than sent to one individual

- **World Wide Web (WWW)**: a vast number of linked documents stored on thousands of Web servers that support a wide range of activities including research, education, advertising, entertainment, news, and e-commerce

► The Internet experienced tremendous growth in the past decade partly because of the following three major factors:

- In the early 1990s, the U.S. government lifted restrictions on commercial Internet traffic, causing explosive growth in electronic commerce activities.

- Technological breakthroughs resulted from innovations in hardware such as faster computer processors and storage devices, and in networking media such as fiber-optics and satellite transmission.

- Less expensive and easier-to-use Internet systems and program software were developed for both **clients** (your computer) and **servers** (the computer that "serves" the information to you from the Internet).

► Behind all of these innovations are many amazing people. The World Wide Web was pioneered by a group of scientists who saw the need to easily share real-time information with colleagues, and started linking documents with similar content to one another. Table J-1 introduces more Internet and World Wide Web terminology. Figure J-1 shows how hyperlinks work on a Web page.

URL

Hyperlinks can be clip art, text, or pictures

TABLE J-1: Internet and World Wide Web terminology

term	definition
Web page	A special type of file created with HTML code that contains hyperlinks to other files
Web server	A computer that stores Web pages
Hyperlink	Text (usually underlined), an image, or an icon on a Web page that when clicked, presents another Web page. Hyperlinks can jump to another part of the same Web page, a different page on the same Web server, or to a different Web server in another part of the world.
HTML (Hypertext Markup Language)	A special programming language used in Web pages. An HTML programmer writes HTML code to create a Web page. Nonprogrammers create HTML Web pages using FrontPage or by converting files such as Word, Excel, and PowerPoint into HTML Web pages using menu options within those programs.
Browser	Software such as Microsoft's Internet Explorer (IE) or Netscape Navigator used to find and display Web pages (HTML files created through the Access page object are best displayed with IE version 5 or later)
ISP (Internet Service Provider)	To access the Internet from a home computer, your computer first must connect to an ISP that then connects your computer with the Internet. National ISPs include America Online, the Microsoft Network, and Sprint's Earthlink. Hundreds of regional and local ISPs exist as well.
Modem	Short for *mod*ulate-*dem*odulate. A modem is hardware (usually located inside the computer) that converts digital computer signals to analog telephone signals to allow a computer to send and receive information across ordinary telephone lines. New and faster communication technologies such as DSL, satellite systems, and cable modems that can also connect your computer to the Internet without using the existing analog telephone systems are making traditional modems obsolete.
URL (Uniform Resource Locator)	Each resource on the Internet (including Web pages) has an address so that other computers can accurately and consistently locate and view it. For example, http://www.course.com/products/ is a URL for the Web page that displays information about Course Technology, Inc. (the publisher of this textbook). A URL never includes a space.
Domain name	The middle part of a URL, such as www.course.com. The middle part of the domain name is often either the company's name or words that describe the information you find at that site. The last part of the domain name indicates the type of site, such as commercial (com), educational (edu), military (mil), organizational (org), or governmental (gov).
Home page	The first page displayed on a Web server

Creating Hyperlink Fields

A **Hyperlink field** is a field defined with the Hyperlink data type in Table Design View. The entry in a Hyperlink field can be a **Universal Naming Convention (UNC) path** or a **Uniform Resource Locator (URL) address** used to locate a file on a network. Table J-2 gives more information about networks. URLs may also specify a newsgroup address, an FTP server location, an intranet Web page address, or a file on a local area network. ✎ Fred creates a Hyperlink field called OnlineResources to store the URL for a Web page that contains up-to-date information on the subject of each class.

Steps 1234

1. Start **Access**, open the **Training-J** database from the location where your Project Files are stored, click **Tables** on the Objects bar, right-click the **Courses table**, then click **Design View** on the shortcut menu
   The Courses table opens in Design View, where you can add fields and specify their properties.

2. Click the first empty **Field Name cell** below InstructorID, type **OnlineResources**, press **[Tab]**, type **h**, click the **Save button** 🖫, then click the **Datasheet View button** 🖽
   The Courses table with the new OnlineResources field opens in Datasheet View.

   > **QuickTip**
   > You can omit the first part of an Internet Web address (http://) when entering a URL into a Hyperlink field.

3. Press **[Tab]** six times to move to the new OnlineResources field, type **www.microsoft.com/access**, press **[↓]**, point to the right edge of the **OnlineResources field name** so that the mouse pointer changes to ↔, then double-click to expand the column
   Your screen should look like Figure J-2. Hyperlink data in a datasheet appears underlined and in a bright blue color just like most text hyperlinks on Web pages.

   > **QuickTip**
   > [Ctrl]['] copies the entry in the field of the previous record to the same field of the current record.

4. Press **[Ctrl][']**, then press **[↓]**

5. Point to **www.microsoft.com/access** in either record so that the pointer changes to ⟨🖑⟩, then click **www.microsoft.com/access**
   If you are currently connected to the Internet and have Microsoft Internet Explorer browser software, your screen should look similar to Figure J-3. Netscape Navigator is another popular browser program that will also open and display Web pages. Web pages are continually updated, so the content of the Web page itself may vary. If you are not already connected to the Internet, your **dialer** (software that helps you dial and connect to your Internet Service Provider, or ISP) may appear. Once connected to your ISP, the Microsoft Access Web page should appear.

   > **QuickTip**
   > Visited links change to the color purple.

6. Click the **Courses : Table button** in the taskbar, click the **OnlineResources field** for record **5** (Introduction to Excel), type **www.microsoft.com/excel**, click the **OnlineResources field** for record **11** (Introduction to Netscape), type **www.netscape.com**, then press **[Enter]**

7. Right-click the **Courses : Table button** on the taskbar, click **Close**, click **Yes** (if prompted) to save the changes to the layout of the table, then close any open browser windows

CLUES TO USE

Understanding the Universal Naming Convention (UNC)

The **Universal Naming Convention (UNC)** is another naming convention (in addition to URL) for locating a file on a network. The structure of a UNC is \\server\sharedfoldername\filename. UNCs are used for local resources, such as a file stored on a local area network. URL addresses are used for Web pages on the Internet or a company intranet.

FIGURE J-2: A hyperlink entry

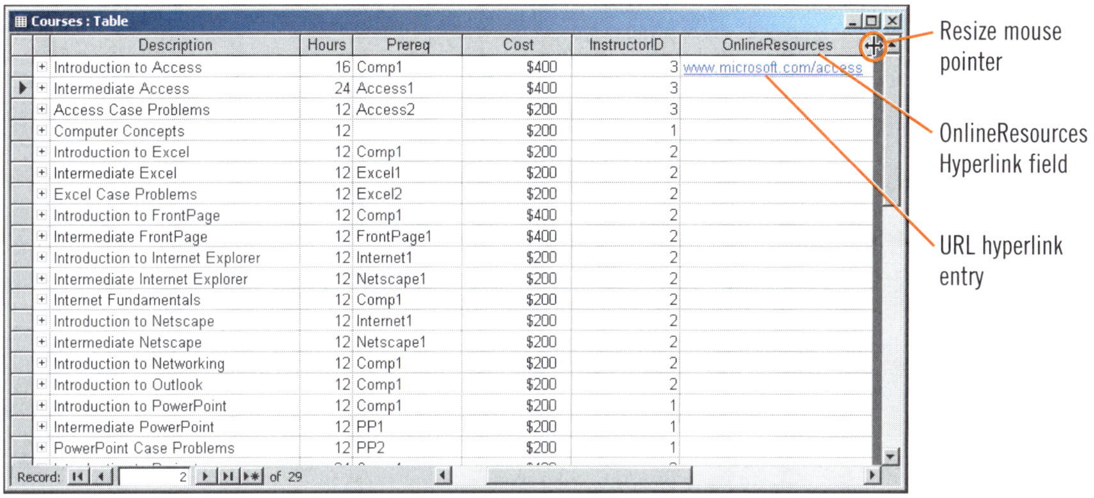

- Resize mouse pointer
- OnlineResources Hyperlink field
- URL hyperlink entry

FIGURE J-3: Access home page

- Microsoft Internet Explorer (browser software)
- URL
- Web page

TABLE J-2: Types of networks

type of network	description
LAN (local area network)	Connects local resources such as file servers, user computers, and printers by a direct cable; LANs do not cross a public thoroughfare such as a street because of distance and legal restrictions on how far and where cables can be pulled
WAN (wide area network)	Created when a LAN is connected to an existing telecommunications network, such as the phone system, to reach resources across public thoroughfares such as streets and rivers
Internet	Largest WAN in the world, spanning the entire globe and connecting many diverse computer architectures
Intranet	WANs that support the same services as the Internet (i.e., e-mail, Web pages, and file transfer) and are built with the same technologies (e.g., TCP/IP communications protocol, HTML Web pages, and browser software), but are designed and secured for the internal purposes of a business

Access 2002

Creating Pages for Interactive Reporting

The **page** object, also called the **data access page (DAP)**, is a special Access object that creates dynamic Web pages used for viewing, editing, entering, and analyzing data stored in a Microsoft Access database. **Dynamic** means that the Web page is automatically reconnected with the database to display the most current data each time it is opened or refreshed by a browser such as Internet Explorer. You can also create static Web pages that display Access data by using the export to HTML feature after selecting any table, query, form, or report. **Static** Web pages retain no connection to the Access database and therefore do not change once they have been created. They can be viewed using any browser. The page object, however, is used to develop *dynamic* Web pages that work best using Microsoft Internet Explorer (IE) as the browser. Links to existing DAPs appear when you click the Pages button on the Objects bar. Table J-3 describes three major purposes for a DAP. ✏️ Fred uses the page object to create an interactive report from the Training-J database as a Web page so it can be viewed using Internet Explorer.

Steps 1234

1. Click **Pages** on the Objects bar, then double-click **Create data access page by using wizard**

2. Click the **Tables/Queries list arrow**, click **Query: Attendance Details**, click the **Select All Fields button** ⏩, click **Next**, double-click **Department** to select it as the grouping level field, then click **Next**

Trouble?

Click the Page View button if you are viewing Page Design View instead of Page View.

3. Click **Next** to bypass sorting options, type **Department Training Information** as the page title, click the **Open the page option button**, click **Finish**, then maximize the page
Your screen should look like Figure J-4. **Page View** presents the Web page as it will appear within Internet Explorer. The **Expand button** indicates that detail records are grouped by that field. You can click the Expand button to view the detail records.

4. Click the **Expand button** ⊞, click **02/13/2003** in the Attended text box, then click the **Sort Ascending button** on the Attendance Details 1 of 16 navigation toolbar
The upper navigation toolbar works with the detail records (the records within each department), and the lower navigation toolbar controls the grouping field itself, Department. Your screen should look like Figure J-5. The Expand button has become the **Collapse button**. When clicked, the Collapse button hides the detail records within that group.

Trouble?

You will not see the insertion point inside a text box that cannot be used for data entry.

5. Click the **Last button** ▶▮ on the lower Attendance Details-Department 1 of 11 navigation toolbar to display the Video group, click ⊞, click **Lee** in the Last field, then click the **Filter by Selection button** on the Attendance Details 1 of 20 navigation toolbar
Your screen should look like Figure J-6.

QuickTip

Naming Web pages using one to eight lowercase letters helps ensure that the Web server operating system will be able to manage the file.

6. Click the **Filter Toggle button** on the Attendance Details 1 of 10 navigation toolbar to remove the filter, click the **Save button** 💾 on the Page View toolbar, navigate to the drive and folder where your Project Files are located, type **dept** in the File name text box, click **Save**, then click **OK** when prompted
By saving the page, a Web page named dept.htm has been saved to the specified drive and folder.

QuickTip

Point to a DAP icon to display a ScreenTip that shows the path to the associated Web page.

7. Close the dept page
The DAP icon contains a small linking symbol in the lower-left corner. When you double-click the DAP link, you open the external Web page in Access and use Page View as a browser to view this file. You could delete the DAP icon without disturbing the physical Web page file, but it's much easier to open the Web page in Access (for later modification) if the link to the Web page is available in the database window.

FIGURE J-4: Department Training Information data access page

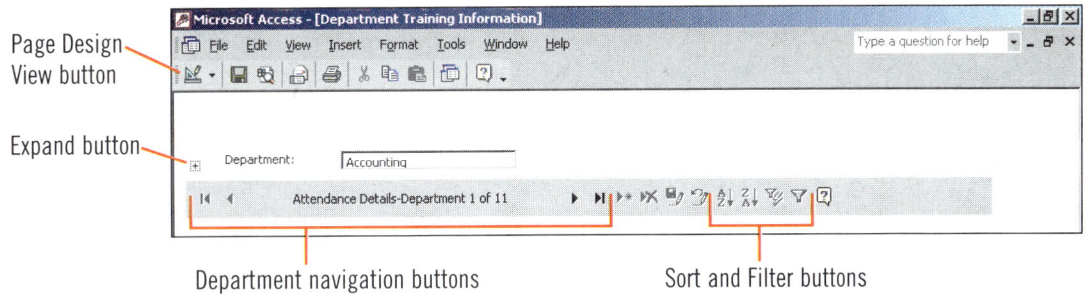

Page Design View button

Expand button

Department navigation buttons

Sort and Filter buttons

FIGURE J-5: Expanded and sorted data access page

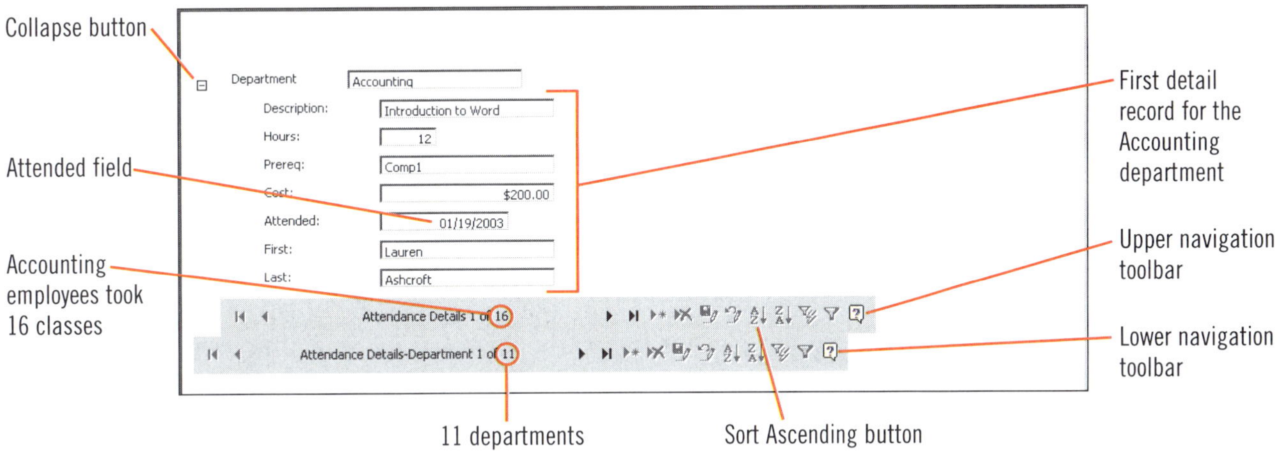

Collapse button

Attended field

Accounting employees took 16 classes

First detail record for the Accounting department

Upper navigation toolbar

Lower navigation toolbar

11 departments

Sort Ascending button

FIGURE J-6: Filtered data access page

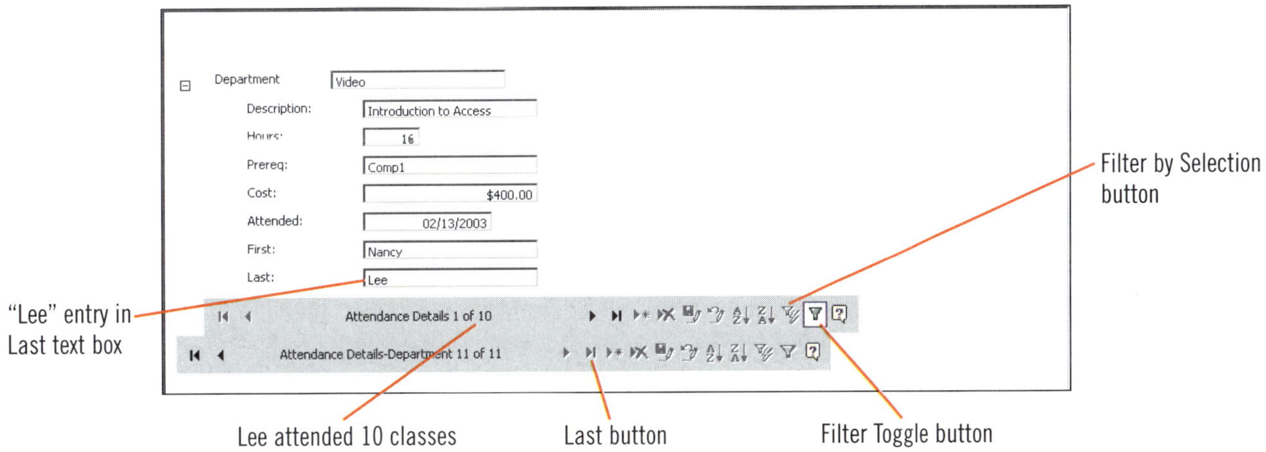

"Lee" entry in Last text box

Lee attended 10 classes

Last button

Filter by Selection button

Filter Toggle button

TABLE J-3: Purposes for data access pages

purpose	description
Data entry	Web pages that work as forms that can be used to view, add, or edit records
Interactive reporting	Web pages that work as reports that can be used to further sort, group, or filter data
Data analysis	Web pages that work as reports that can be used to analyze data using PivotTables and charts

Access 2002

Creating Pages for Data Entry

Using a DAP for data entry is similar to using an Access form. The big difference, of course, is that a dynamic Web page created by a page object can be opened with Internet Explorer (IE), whereas a user must have direct access to the actual database file to open a form object. Therefore, DAPs not only make a database more accessible, but can add a layer of database security because you can provide data entry and update features to other users without giving them direct access to the actual database file. ✎ The Human Resources department has offered to help Fred find, enter, and update information on instructors. Fred creates a data access page that works like a form to let the Human Resources department update data using the Internet Explorer browser.

Steps 1234

1. Double-click the **Create data access page by using wizard**, click the **Tables/Queries list arrow**, click **Table: Instructors**, click the **Select All Fields button** >>, click **Next**, then click **Finish** to accept the rest of the default options
   The data access page opens in **Page Design View**, as shown in Figure J-7. The **Field List** window, which organizes database objects in a folder hierarchy, is open. Each item on the Page object is called a control just as it is in Report Design View or Form Design View.

2. Click the **Page View button** 🗔 on the Page Design toolbar to view the data access page, click the **Save button** 🖫 on the Page View toolbar, navigate to the drive and folder where your Project Files are located, type **instruct** in the File name text box, click **Save**, then click **OK** when prompted with a message about the connection string
   The instruct data access page shows the first of four records in the Instructors table. You *could* use this page object within Access to enter or edit data, but the purpose of a data access page isn't data entry if you can open the actual database file. (Forms are much more powerful data entry tools if you have direct access to the database file.) The real power of the data access page object is its ability to create dynamic Web pages that can be used to enter and update data by people who *do not* have direct access to the database, but who *do* have Internet Explorer browser software.

3. Click the **Design View Button list arrow** 🖉, then click **Web Page Preview**
   The instruct.htm file opens in Internet Explorer, as shown in Figure J-8.

> **Trouble?**
> If you see #Name? errors on the Web page, click File on the IE menu bar, and then click Work Offline.

4. Click the **New button** ▶* on the navigation toolbar, click the **InstructorFirst** text box, type **Delores**, press [Tab], type **Hanneman**, press [Tab], type **9/1/03**, click the **Previous button** ◄, then click the **Next button** ▶
   Moving between records helps verify that the record for Delores Hanneman was entered successfully.

> **Trouble?**
> The [Page Up] and [Page Down] keys will not move the focus from record to record when viewing records through a Web page.

5. Close **Internet Explorer**, click the **Training-J: Database button** on the taskbar, click **Tables** on the Objects bar, then double-click the **Instructors table** to open it in Datasheet View
   Your screen should look like Figure J-9. The new record appears in the table. You used a Web page opened in Internet Explorer to dynamically update an underlying Access database!

6. Close the **Instructors** datasheet, then close the **instruct** DAP

FIGURE J-7: Page Design View

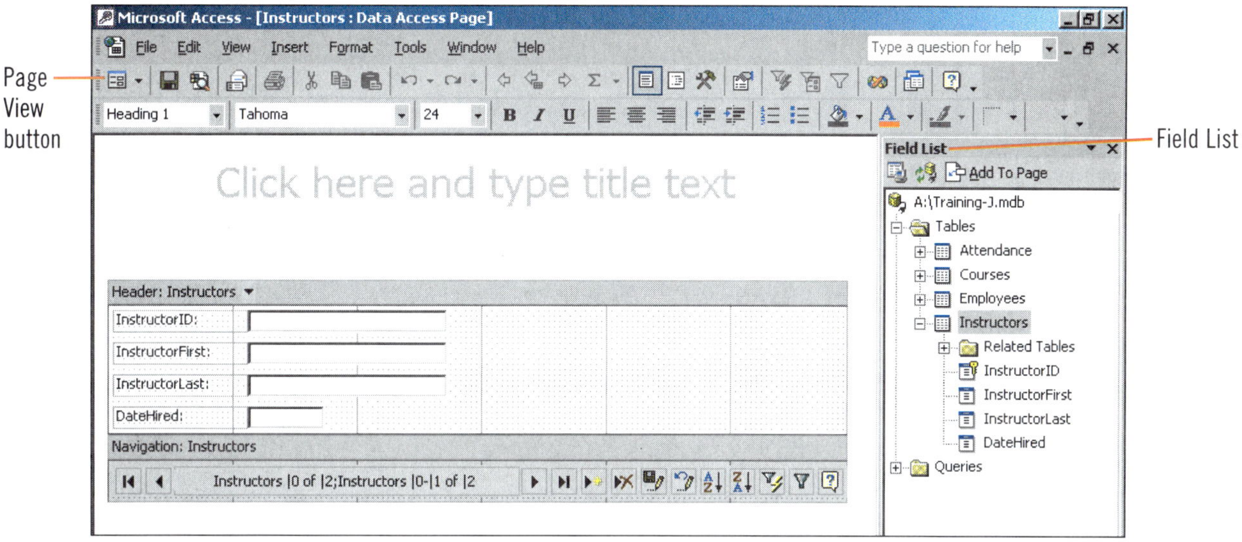

Page View button

Field List

FIGURE J-8: instruct.htm Web page opened in Internet Explorer

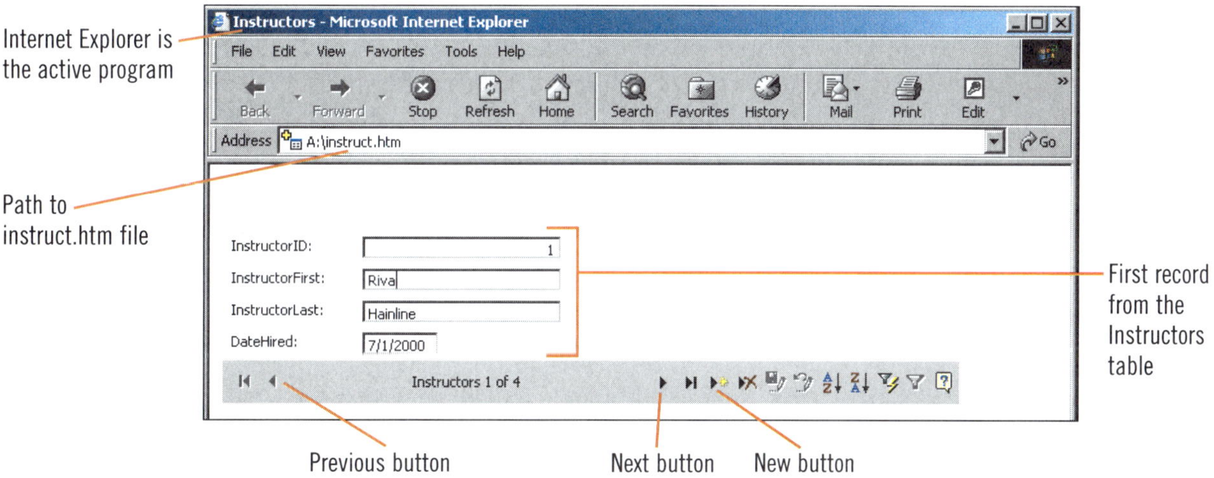

Internet Explorer is the active program

Path to instruct.htm file

First record from the Instructors table

Previous button   Next button   New button

Access 2002

FIGURE J-9: Updated Instructors table

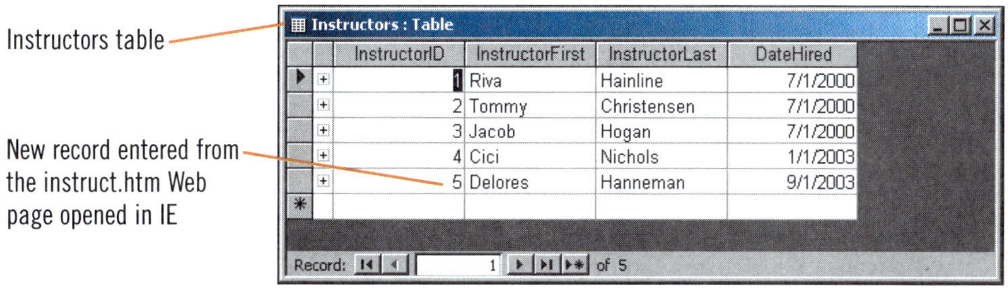

Instructors table

New record entered from the instruct.htm Web page opened in IE

Creating Pages for Data Analysis

A **PivotTable List** control displays data as a PivotTable—a table that summarizes data by columns and rows to make it easy to analyze. A typical **PivotTable** uses one field as the column heading, another field for the row heading, and summarizes a third field in the body of the PivotTable. For example, you could use a PivotTable to arrange data by summarizing sales (the field used within the body of the PivotTable) by product category (the field used as the row heading) and by state (the field used as the column heading). You cannot use the PivotTable List control to edit, delete, or add new data. Fred creates a data access page using the PivotTable List control so that he can view, summarize, and analyze information about course attendance in different ways.

Steps 1234

QuickTip

Double-click the title bar of any window to maximize it.

1. Click **Pages** on the Objects bar (if not already selected), double-click **Create data access page in Design view**, click **OK** when prompted with a message about Access 2000, then maximize the Design View window

   Page Design View is very similar to that of Form Design View or Report Design View. Table J-4 summarizes some of the key terminology used in Page Design View.

2. Click the **Queries Expand button** ⊞ in the Field List, then drag the **Department Charges** query into the upper-left area of the **Drag fields from the Field List and drop them on the page** area

   When you are dragging tables, queries, or fields from the Field List to Page Design View, a blue outline identifies the **drop zone**, the area on the page where you can successfully add that item. If the Control Wizards button ⬚ is selected on the Toolbox toolbar, the **Layout Wizard** opens to guide you through the rest of the process of dynamically adding data to a DAP.

Trouble?

If the Layout Wizard dialog box doesn't open, delete the controls that were added to the page, click the Control Wizards button ⬚ on the Toolbox toolbar, then redo Step 2.

3. Click the **PivotTable option button**, then click **OK**

   Your screen should look like Figure J-10. The fields within the Department Charges query are the column headings in the PivotTable control.

4. Point to the **middle sizing handle** on the right edge of the PivotTable control, drag ↔ to the right so that all four fields are visible as column headings within the PivotTable, then click the **Page View button** 🖳 on the Page Design toolbar

   The data access page appears within Access, and the field names display list arrows.

5. Click the **Department list arrow**, click the **(All) check box** to clear all of the check marks, click the **Accounting check box**, then click **OK**

   Only the records with "Accounting" in the Department field appear.

QuickTip

To make a change to a PivotTable permanent, you must make the change in Page Design View, then save the page.

6. Click the **Department list arrow**, click the **(All) check box** to select all departments again, click **OK**, right-click the **Description field name**, then click **Move to Row Area**

   Your screen should look like Figure J-11. The Description field entries are now organized as row headings. The PivotTable List control's major benefit is that it quickly rearranges data so you can analyze it in many ways. Any change made to a PivotTable in Page View is temporary, so this arrangement of the fields will not affect the way the PivotTable is presented the next time it is opened in a browser.

7. Click the **Save button** 🖬, navigate to the drive and folder where your Project Files are located, type **pivot**, click **Save**, then click **OK** when prompted with a message about the connection string

   The new page link is stored in the Training-J database window and the pivot.htm file is stored in the location where your Project Files are stored.

Page View button

Field List

Click here and type title text

Department Charges query

Sizing handle

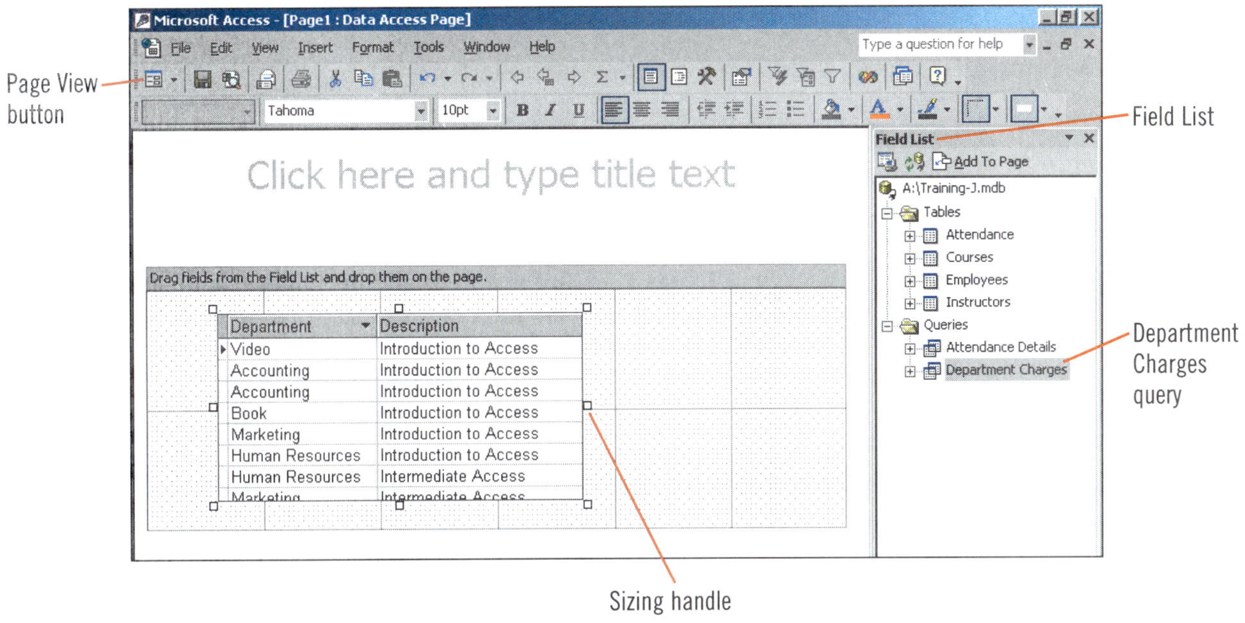

FIGURE J-11: Modified PivotTable in Page View

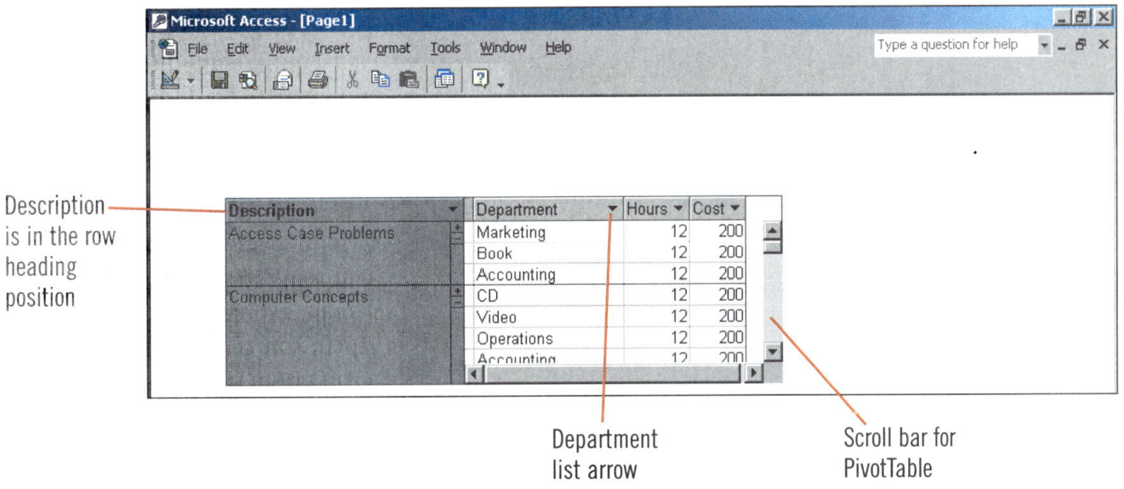

Description is in the row heading position

Department list arrow

Scroll bar for PivotTable

TABLE J-4: Design View terminology

term	definition
Field list	List that contains all of the field names that can be added in Design View
Toolbox toolbar	Toolbar that contains all of the bound and unbound controls that can be added in Design View
Control	Each individual element that can be added, deleted, or modified in Design View
Bound controls	Controls that display data from an underlying recordset; common bound controls are text boxes, list boxes, and PivotTable lists
Unbound controls	Controls that do not display data from an underlying recordset; common unbound controls for a page are labels, lines, and toolbars
Sections	Areas of the object that contain controls; sections determine where and how often a control will appear or print
Properties	Characteristics that further describe the selected object, section, or control

Working in Page Design View

You use Page Design View to modify the structure of the Web page and modify the controls that are used on the Web page. Page Design View closely resembles Form Design View and Report Design View, with some key differences, identified in Table J-5. A **PivotChart** control is used to graphically display data that is presented by a PivotTable control. You use Page Design View to add new controls or modify the existing characteristics of the page. ✒️ Fred works in Page Design View to modify the pivot Web page.

Steps 123 4

1. Click the **Design View button** 🖉 on the Page View toolbar, click **Click here and type title text**, then type **your name's Department PivotTable**
   Making an entry in the "Click here and type title text" area adds a title to a Web page.

Trouble?

If you double-click the PivotTable control instead of single-clicking it twice, you open its property sheet. Close the property sheet and try again.

2. Click the **PivotTable control** to select it, click the **PivotTable control** a second time to edit it, right-click the **Hours** field, click **Remove Field** on the shortcut menu
   Your screen should look like Figure J-12. The first click selects the control and the second click opens it for editing. You know that a PivotTable is open for editing when it displays a hashed border. Changes made and saved to the PivotTable in Page Design View permanently change how it appears when the Web page is opened in Page View or within Internet Explorer.

3. Click the **Save button** 🖫, close the page, double-click **Create data access page in Design View**, then click **OK** when prompted with a message about Access 2000

4. Click the **Queries Expand button** ➕ in the Field List, then drag the **Department Charges** query into the upper-left area of the **Drag fields from the Field List and drop them on the page** area
   The Layout Wizard allows you to choose between many presentations of the data.

5. Click the **PivotChart option button**, then click **OK**

Trouble?

If you drag the wrong field to the PivotChart, or drag a field to the wrong location, remove the field from the PivotChart by dragging it off the PivotChart, then try again.

6. Click the **Department Charges Expand button** ➕ in the Field List, drag the **Department field** to the Drop Category Fields Here, drag the **Cost field** to the Drop Data Fields Here area, drag the **Description field** to the Drop Filter Fields Here area, then click outside the PivotChart
   Your screen should look like Figure J-13. Depending on the amount of data, and how it is organized, you may have to spend some time resizing the control to display the data effectively.

QuickTip

Right-click the PivotChart and click Toolbar on the shortcut menu to toggle the PivotChart toolbar on or off.

7. Click the **PivotChart** to select it, drag the lower-right sizing handle using the ↘ mouse pointer to the lower-right corner of the screen to enlarge the chart, then click the **Page View button** 🖽 to observe the final PivotChart
   The final PivotChart should look like Figure J-14. You can work with the fields on the PivotChart to filter and reorganize the data just as you could with a PivotTable.

8. Click 🖫, navigate to the drive and folder where your Project Files are located, type **chart** as the File name, click **Save**, click **OK** when prompted with a message about the connection string, then close the page

FIGURE J-12: Modifying a PivotTable in Page Design View

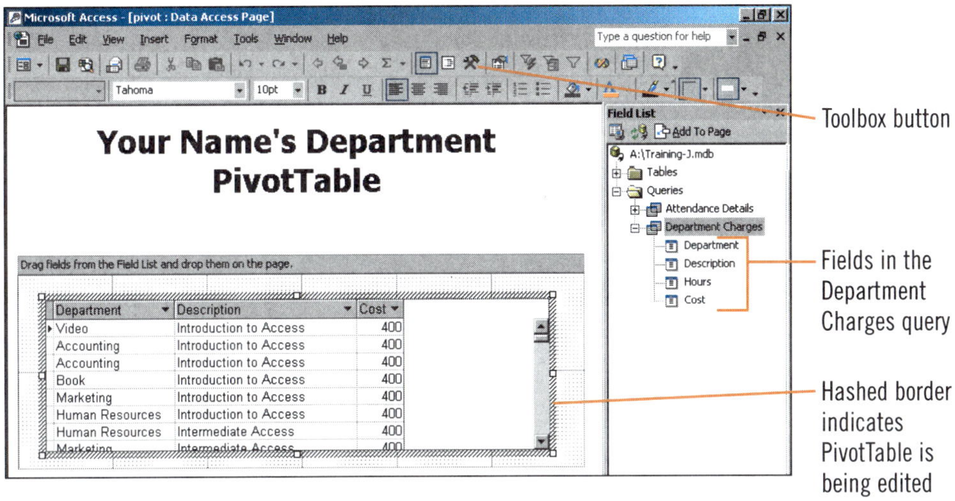

Toolbox button

Fields in the Department Charges query

Hashed border indicates PivotTable is being edited

FIGURE J-13: Building a PivotChart

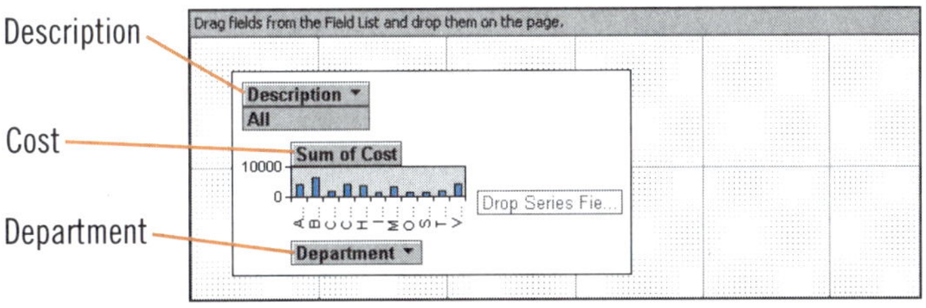

Description

Cost

Department

FIGURE J-14: Viewing the updated Web page in Internet Explorer

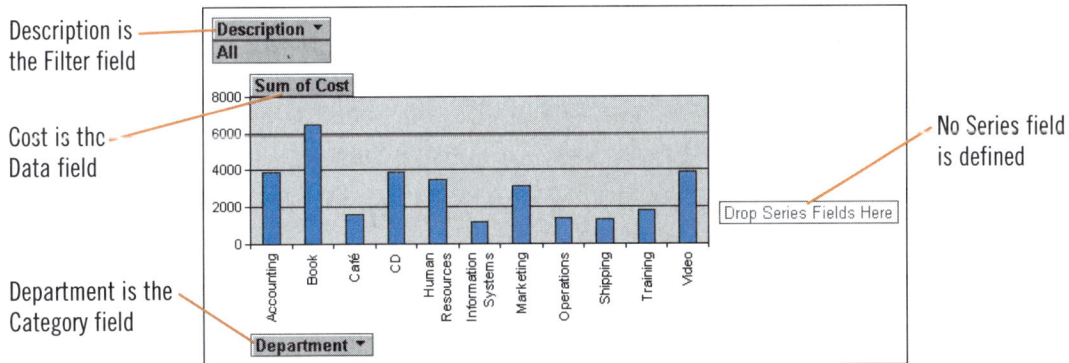

Description is the Filter field

Cost is the Data field

No Series field is defined

Department is the Category field

TABLE J-5: New features in Page Design View

item	description
Body	The area that displays text, controls, and sections
Sections	The record navigation section is used to display the navigation toolbar and the caption section is used to display text
Positioning	By default, the position of controls in the body of a page; by default, controls are positioned relative to one another
Toolbox	The Office PivotTable, Expand, and Record Navigation controls are new buttons on the Toolbox toolbar
Field List	The Field List window displays all tables, queries, and their fields

Adding Hyperlinks

A **hyperlink** is a single label, button, or image that when clicked opens another object, document or graphic file, e-mail message, or World Wide Web page. Once the Access page objects are finished, you can connect them using hyperlinks. Hyperlinks allow the user to access one Web page from another with a single click, just like World Wide Web pages reference other Web pages throughout the Internet. You add hyperlinks to pages in Page Design View. Then, when you browse through the pages, you can jump between them by clicking the hyperlinks. Fred wants to create a hyperlink between the chart and pivot Web pages so that one page can be accessed from the other. He uses Page Design View to add the hyperlinks to both pages.

Steps

1. Right-click the **pivot** page link, then click **Design View** on the shortcut menu
   Hyperlinks are added to page objects by using the **Hyperlink control**.

2. Click the **Toolbox button** to toggle on the Toolbox toolbar (if it is not already visible), click the **Hyperlink button** on the Toolbox, then click the **body** of the page about 0.5" below the PivotTable
   The Insert Hyperlink dialog box opens, as shown in Figure J-15. You can create hyperlinks to existing files, Web pages, pages in this database, new pages, or e-mail addresses.

3. Click the **Page in This Database** button, click **chart** from the Select a page in this database list, click **OK**, then click the **Page View button** on the Page Design toolbar
   The pivot Web page displays the new hyperlink.

Trouble?

If Netscape opens the Web page, it means that the .htm file extension is associated with Netscape Navigator on your computer instead of Internet Explorer. To open the Web page in Internet Explorer, copy the Web page address from the Location bar within Netscape and paste it into the Address bar of an Internet Explorer window.

4. Click the **chart hyperlink** to test the link
   The chart Web page opens within an Internet Explorer window.

5. If prompted with a message about making the page available offline, click **OK** in the message box, click **File** on the Internet Explorer menu bar, click **Work Offline**, then click the **Refresh button** on the Internet Explorer Standard buttons toolbar

6. Close the Internet Explorer window, click the **Save button**, close the **pivot** page, right-click the **chart** page, then click **Design View** from the shortcut menu

7. Click on the Toolbox, then click the **body** of the page about 0.5" below the PivotChart control

8. Click **Page in This Database** in the Insert Hyperlink dialog box (if not already selected), click the **pivot** page in the Select a page in this database list, click **OK**, click, then click

QuickTip

To make sure that Internet Explorer is displaying the latest version of a Web page, click the Refresh button on the Internet Explorer Standard Buttons toolbar.

9. Click the **pivot hyperlink** in Page View, then click the **Print button** on the Internet Explorer Standard Buttons toolbar to print the final pivot Web page
   The pivot page should open in Internet Explorer, as shown in Figure J-16. Now you can move between the two related Web pages by clicking their hyperlinks.

10. Close Internet Explorer, save and close any open page objects, close the Training-J database, then exit Access

FIGURE J-15: Insert Hyperlink dialog box

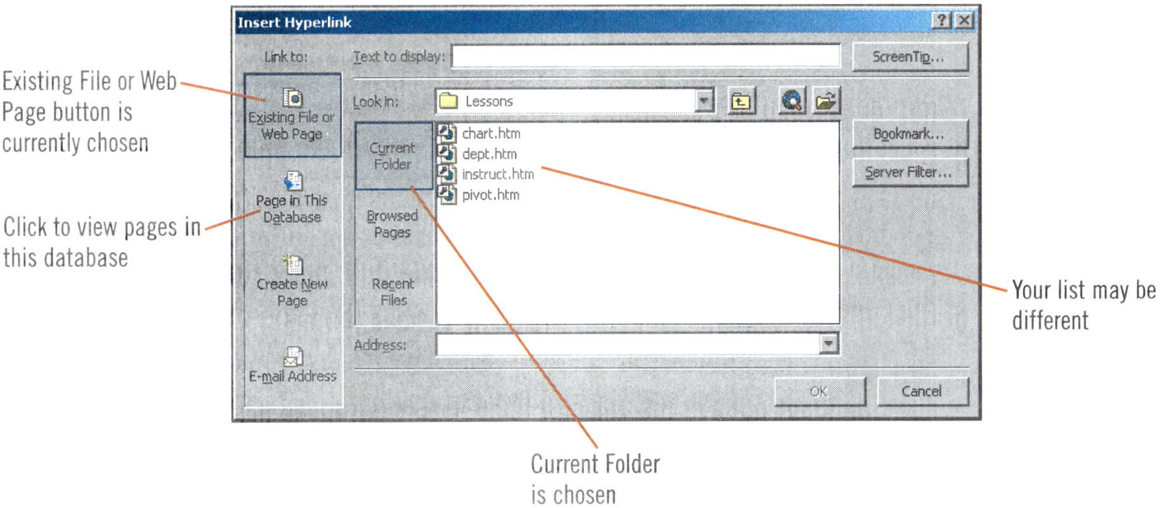

Existing File or Web Page button is currently chosen

Click to view pages in this database

Your list may be different

Current Folder is chosen

FIGURE J-16: Pivot Web page open in IE with hyperlink

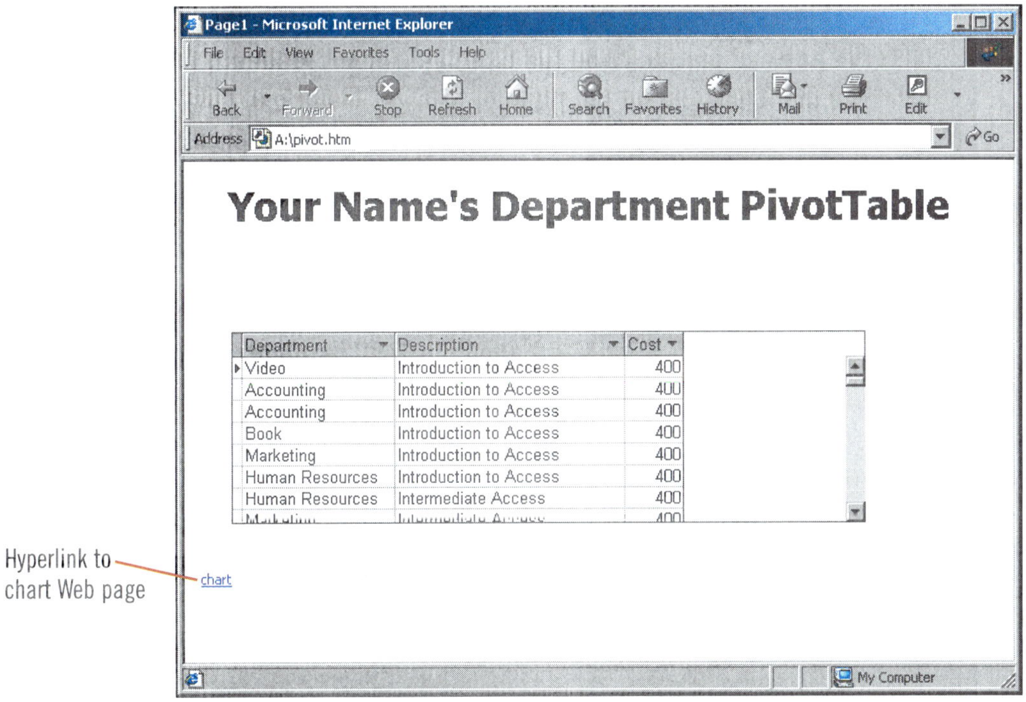

Your Name's Department PivotTable

Department	Description	Cost
▶ Video	Introduction to Access	400
Accounting	Introduction to Access	4UU
Accounting	Introduction to Access	400
Book	Introduction to Access	400
Marketing	Introduction to Access	400
Human Resources	Introduction to Access	400
Human Resources	Intermediate Access	400
Marketing	Intermediate Access	400

Hyperlink to chart Web page — chart

CLUES TO USE

Creating a hyperlink from an image

Once an image is added to a form or a DAP, you can convert it to a hyperlink by using its property sheet to modify the image's **Hyperlink Address** property. Depending on what you enter for the Hyperlink Address property, clicking the hyperlinked image in Form View or Page View (or clicking the hyperlinked image as it appears on the Web page when opened in Internet Explorer) opens another file, Access object, or Web page. For example, C:\Colleges\JCCC.doc is the Hyperlink Address property to link to the JCCC.doc Word document on the C: drive in the Colleges folder. A Hyperlink Address property of http://www.jccc.net creates a link to that Web address.

Access 2002

Publishing Web Pages to Web Servers

Making Web pages available over the Internet or a company intranet requires publishing your Web pages to a **Web server**, a computer devoted to storing and downloading Web pages. Web servers contain **Web folders**, which are special folders dedicated to organizing Web pages. Once your Web page files are stored appropriately, **clients**, computers with appropriate browser and communication software that have access to the Web folder, may download and use those files. Fred reviews the steps necessary to publish the Web pages for use over MediaLoft's intranet.

Details

► Store the Access database in a shared network folder on the Web server

On a network, most folders are not available to everyone, so be sure to put the Access database in a folder that the appropriate people have permission to use (**shared network folder**). Access databases are inherently **multi-user**, so that many people can enter and update information at the same time, provided they are given permission to use the files inside that folder. Two people cannot, however, update the same record at the same time (**record locking**).

► Use the page object within Access to create dynamic Web pages

As you have experienced, you can use the page object to create dynamic Web pages to enter and edit data, to create interactive reports, and to support sophisticated data analysis tools including PivotTables and PivotCharts.

► Save the Web page files in a shared Web folder

You must have access to a Web server with Web folders to save your Web files in these locations. Saving Web files to Web folders on a server is usually called **publishing**. Publishing is more complex than merely saving the file to your hard drive because any time you intend to share a Web page with others, you must have a compatible and secure network infrastructure already in place.

► Give the users the URL or UNC address to access the Web pages using Internet Explorer

URLs are used to access Internet Web pages. UNCs can be used when the file is located on the same local area network as the client computer.

► Use professional networking resources as necessary

Publishing a Web page to a Web folder on a Web server usually requires the knowledge and skills of professionals dedicated to the field of computer networking. People who build and maintain networks are often called **network administrators**. Those who work with Web servers, Web folders, and supporting Internet technologies are often called **Webmasters**. Table J-6 provides more tips and information about working with Web pages and Access. Figure J-17 illustrates the infrastructure involved with publishing a Web page to a Web server.

Web files created from DAPs in the Access database are located in a shared Web folder on a company's Web server

Web Server

World Wide Web

Remote user can update the Access database by accessing Web files with Internet Explorer

File Server

ISP

Client   Client   Client   Client

Remote User

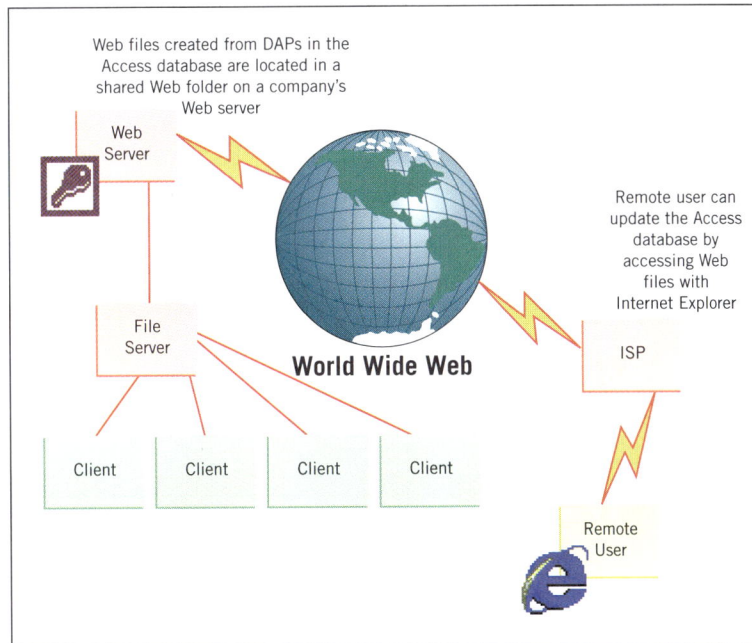

TABLE J-6: Tips for working with Web pages and Access

to...	do this...
Create DAPs from existing Access forms and reports	Select the form or report, click File on the menu bar, click Save As, then choose Data Access Page in the As list.
Open dynamic HTML files created by Access in a browser other than Internet Explorer	Use the Export option on the File menu to create server-generated Web pages from tables, queries, and forms. (Use the ASP file type for Microsoft Active Server Pages.) Server-generated HTML files pages are dynamic (and therefore change as your database changes).
Create static Web pages based on Access data	Use the Export option on the File menu to create static Web pages from tables, queries, forms, and reports. The files display a snapshot of the data at the time the static HTML file was created and can be viewed equally well in Internet Explorer and Netscape Navigator.
Open a Web page created by another program in Access	Right-click the file in the Open dialog box, then click Open in Microsoft Access on the shortcut menu.

CLUES TO USE

The connection between the Web page and database file

The Web pages you create in this unit are linked to the database with path information that specifies the current drive, folder, and filenames for both the Web page and database files. Therefore, if you change the location or name of either the Web page or database file after the Web page is initially created, the link between the two may not work. However, it's not difficult to reestablish the connection. If you open a page in Page View and see the message "The HTML file associated with this link has been moved, renamed, or deleted," it means that the Web page file has been moved or renamed. To correct this, click the Update Link button in the error message dialog box, then locate the appropriate Web page associated with

that page. If you open a page in Page View or view a Web page in Internet Explorer and see the message "Microsoft Office Web Components could not open the database drive:\path\databasename.mdb," #Name errors on the Web page, or any other errors indicating that the database cannot be found, it means that the database file has been moved or renamed. To correct this, open the page in Page Design View, open the Field List, right-click the name of the database at the top of the Field List, click Connection on the shortcut menu, click the Build button to the right of the database name on the Connection tab, then locate the appropriate database associated with that page.

Practice

► Concepts Review

Identify each element of the Web page shown in Figure J-18.

FIGURE J-18

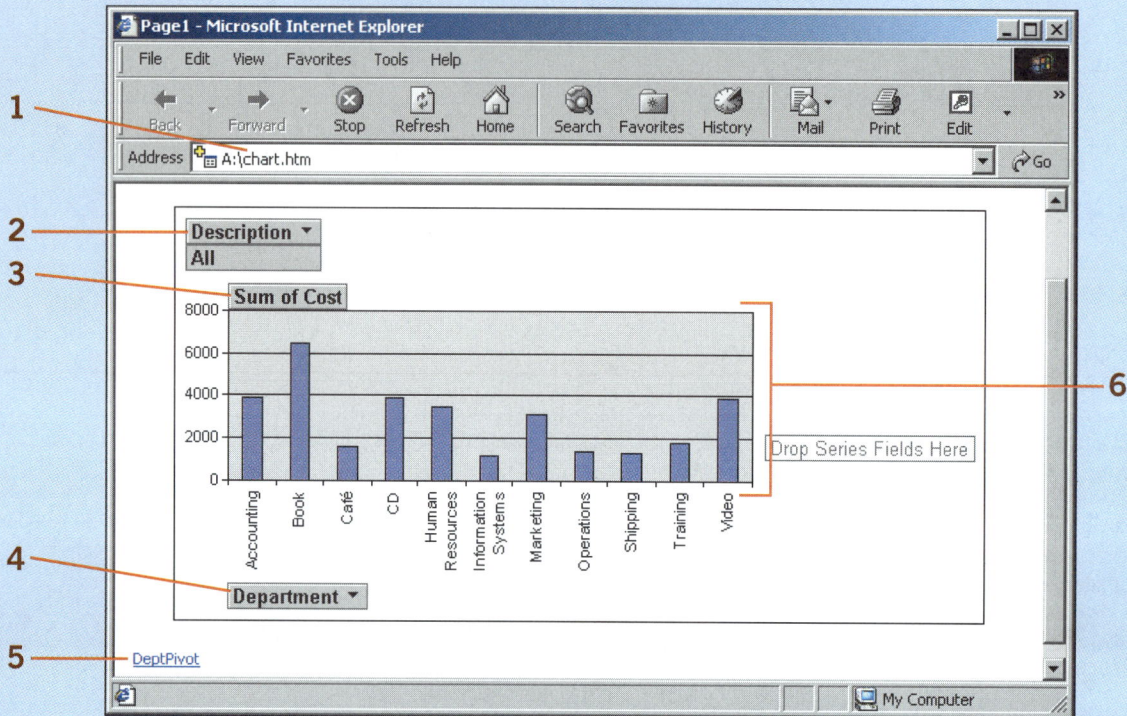

Match each term with the statement that describes its function.

7. URL

8. HTML

9. World Wide Web pages

10. browser

11. data access page

12. Internet

a. Programming language used in Web pages

b. Software loaded on a client used to find and display Web pages

c. Access 2002 object that creates dynamic Web pages

d. Worldwide network of computer networks

e. Hyperlinked documents that make the Internet easy to navigate

f. Web page address

13. The communications protocol for the Internet is:
   a. TCP/IP.
   b. HTML.
   c. URL.
   d. ISP.

14. To connect to the Internet through your home computer, you must first connect to a(n):
   a. URL.
   b. ISP.
   c. Home page.
   d. Webmaster.

15. Which of the following is NOT a service provided by the Internet?
   a. E-mail
   b. File transfer
   c. World Wide Web
   d. Electrical power

16. **Which of the following is browser software?**
    a. Windows NT
    b. Internet Explorer
    c. Microsoft Access
    d. Microsoft Excel
17. **Which of the following is a special type of Web page designed for viewing, editing, and entering data stored in a Microsoft Access database?**
    a. Browser
    b. Home page
    c. Data access page
    d. PivotTable
18. **Making Web pages created through Access available to other users is called:**
    a. Publishing.
    b. Uploading.
    c. Transferring.
    d. Rendering.
19. **DAPs create Web pages that are always:**
    a. Dynamic.
    b. Static.
    c. Used for data entry.
    d. Based on forms.
20. **Which of the following objects can NOT be converted to a DAP using the Save As option on the File menu?**
    a. Table
    b. Query
    c. Form
    d. Macro

▶ Skills Review

1. **Understand the World Wide Web.**
   a. Interview five people and ask them to identify a Web site address where they have recently experienced the following activities:
      • To sell or purchase a product or service
      • For entertainment
      • To index or reference other Internet resources (search engines)
      • To gather information about a specific topic
      • To take a class
   b. Through interviews or research, identify five ISPs in your area, and write down their names. Identify which two ISPs appear to be the most popular. Research the costs and services for these two ISPs.
2. **Create Hyperlink fields.**
   a. Open the **Machinery-J** database from the drive and folder where your Project Files are located, then open the Products table in Design View.
   b. Add a new field named **HomePage** with a Hyperlink data type.
   c. Save the Products table, open it in Datasheet View, then enter the following home page URLs into the new field for the first six records:
      1) www.toro.com
      2) www.caseih.com
      3) www.snapper.com
      4) www.deere.com
      5) www.troybilt.com
      6) www.stihl.com
   d. Click the link for www.deere.com, then print the first page of the John Deere Web site. If you are not already connected to the Internet, your dialer may appear, prompting you to connect with your chosen ISP. Once connected to your ISP, the John Deere home page should appear.
   e. Close your browser, then close the Products datasheet.
3. **Create pages for interactive reporting.**
   a. Click Pages on the Objects bar, then double-click Create data access page by using wizard.
   b. Select the ProductName and the ReorderLevel fields from the Products table, then select the TransactionDate and UnitPrice fields from the Inventory Transactions table.
   c. Group the records by ProductName, then sort the records in ascending order by TransactionDate.

d. Type **ProductActivity** for the page title, then open the new page in Page View.

e. Open Page Design View, maximize the Design View window, click in the title area of the body of the page, then type the title **your name's Garden Shop Orders**.

f. Click the Page View button, click the ProductName text box, sort the ProductName in descending order, expand the ProductName group, navigate to the record with a 7/1/2003 TransactionDate entry within the Weed Wacker ProductName group, then print that page.

g. Save the HTML file with the name **garden** to the drive and folder where your Project Files are located, then close the page.

4. Create pages for data entry.

a. Click Pages on the Objects bar, then double-click Create data access page by using the wizard.

b. Select all of the fields in the Products table.

c. Do not add any grouping levels, but sort the records in ascending order on ProductName.

d. Title the page **Products**.

e. In Design View, click in the title area of the body of the page, then type the title **your name's Products**.

f. Save the Web page as **products** to the drive and folder where your Project Files are located, click OK when prompted about the connection string, then click the View button list arrow and choose Web Page Preview to view the new Web page in Internet Explorer. If you receive #Name? errors on the Web page, click File on the IE menu bar, then click Work Offline to toggle off that option.

g. Find the Mulcher record, change the price of the mulcher from $69.50 to **$79.50**, then print the Web page within Internet Explorer in which you made this change.

h. Navigate to the next record within Internet Explorer, then back to the Mulcher record to make sure that the price change was saved. Close Internet Explorer.

i. Open the Products table in the Machinery-J database, then make sure the Mulcher record now displays $79.50 as the Unit Price. Add your initials to the end of the Serial Number entry for the Mulcher record, then print the Products datasheet in landscape mode.

j. Close the Products table, then save and close the products Web page.

5. Create pages for data analysis.

a. Click Pages on the Objects bar, double-click Create data access page in Design view, then click OK.

b. Open the Field List window if not already visible, then click the Expand button to the left of the Queries folder.

c. Drag the Products Query to the upper-left corner of the "Drag fields from the Field List and drop them on the page" area, click the PivotTable option button in the Layout Wizard dialog box, then click OK.

d. Click the PivotTable control to edit it, right-click the ProductName field in the PivotTable control, then click Move to Row Area on the shortcut menu.

e. Resize the control so that all three columns are clearly visible.

FIGURE J-19

f. Click in the title area of the body of the page, type the title **your name's Orders**, then display the page in Page View.

g. Use the TransactionDate list arrow to select only the **7/1/03** dates, then print that page, as shown in Figure J-19.

h. Save the page as **units** to the drive and folder where your Project Files are located, click OK when prompted about the connection string, then close the page.

Your Name's Orders

ProductName ▾	TransactionDate ▾	UnitsOrdered ▾
Back Hoe	7/1/2003	15
Garden Wagon	7/1/2003	14
Mulcher	7/1/2003	10
Thatcher	7/1/2003	1
Trimmer	7/1/2003	25
Weed Wacker	7/1/2003	12
Grand Total		

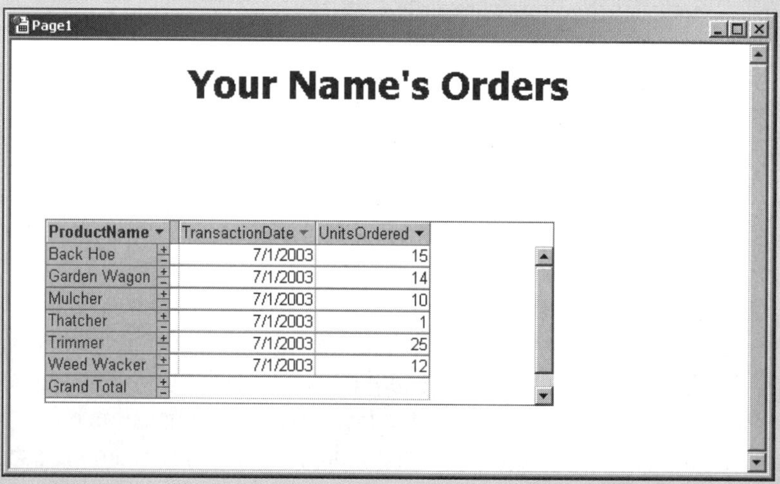

6. **Work in Page Design View.**
   a. Click the Pages button on the Objects bar, then double-click Create data access page in Design view.
   b. Expand the Queries folder in the Field List, and then drag the Products Query to the "Drag fields from the Field List and drop them on the page" area.
   c. Click PivotChart in the Layout Wizard dialog box, then click OK.
   d. Expand the Products Query in the Field List, then drag the ProductName field to the Drop Category Fields Here area of the PivotChart.
   e. Drag the TransactionDate field to the Drop Series Fields Here area of the PivotChart.
   f. Drag the UnitsOrdered field to the Drop Data Fields Here area of the PivotChart.
   g. Click in the title area of the body of the page, then type **your name's PivotChart of Orders**. Resize the PivotChart to clearly display the data.
   h. Save the page as **uchart** to the drive and folder where your Project Files are located, click OK when prompted about the connection string, open it in Page View, then print it.
   i. Close the uchart page.

7. **Add hyperlinks.**
   a. Open the products page in Design View, then use the Hyperlink button on the Toolbox toolbar to add a hyperlink to the units page. Place the hyperlink in the lower-left corner of the page.
   b. Save the products page, then close it.
   c. Open the units page in Design View, then use the Hyperlink button on the Toolbox toolbar to add a hyperlink to the products page. Place the hyperlink in the lower-left corner of the page.
   d. Save the units page, then open it in Page View.
   e. Click the products link, sort the products in descending order based on the UnitPrice field, then print that page.
   f. Close all Internet Explorer windows, close any open page objects within the Machinery-J database, then exit Access.

8. **Publish Web pages to Web servers.**
   a. Call your ISP and ask for information about the requirements to publish Web pages to their Web server. (If you are not currently connected to the Internet from home, research any ISP of your choice. You may also be able to find this information on the ISP's Web site.)
   b. If your ISP does not allow members to publish Web pages, continue researching ISPs until you find one that allows members to publish Web pages.
   c. Print or copy the documentation on how to publish Web pages to the ISP's Web server.
   d. Open Internet Explorer and type **www.geocities.com** in the Address list box.
   e. Follow the links on the Web page to determine how to create your own Web page at the geocities Web site, then print the documentation.

▶ Independent Challenge 1

As the manager of a college women's basketball team, you want to enhance the Basketball-J database to include hyperlink field entries for opponents. You also want to develop a Web page to report information on player statistics.
   a. Start Access, then open the **Basketball-J** database from the drive and folder where your Project Files are located.
   b. Open the Games table in Design View, then add a field named **WebSite** with a Hyperlink data type.
   c. Save the Games table, then open it in Datasheet View.
   d. For the second record, enter **www.creighton.edu** in the WebSite field.
   e. For the fifth record, enter **www.drake.edu** in the WebSite field.
   f. Click the www.drake.edu link to display the Web page for Drake University, then print the first page.
   g. Close the Drake Web page, close the Games table, click Pages on the Objects bar, then double-click Create data access page by using wizard.

h. Add all of the fields in the Players Query, group the information by the Last field, do not specify any sort fields, then title the page **pstats**.

i. In Design View, click in the title text area of the body of the page, then type the title **Iowa State Women's Basketball**. Include your initials in the title if you want them displayed on the printed solution.

j. Save the Web page as **pstats** to the drive and folder where your Project Files are stored, then open the Web Page Preview of the page (which opens the Web page in Internet Explorer).

k. Find and expand the details for the player with the last name of Hile, sort the detail records in descending order on the values in the TotalPts field, then print that record.

l. Close Internet Explorer, save and close the pstats DAP, close the Basketball-J database, then exit Access.

▶ Independent Challenge 2

As the manager of a college women's basketball team, you want to enhance the Basketball-J database by developing a Web page to enter new game information.

a. Start Access, then open the **Basketball-J** database from the drive and folder where your Project Files are located.

b. Click Pages on the Objects bar, then double-click Create data access page by using wizard.

c. Add all of the fields from the Games table, do not add any grouping levels, sort the records in ascending order by Date, then accept **Games** as the title for the page.

d. In Design View, click in the title area of the body of the page, then type the title **ISU Games**. Include your initials in the title to include them on the printed solution.

e. Save the Web page with the name **games** to the drive and folder location where your Project Files are stored, then display Web Page Preview to view the Games Web page in Internet Explorer.

f. Enter the following new record as record 23:

Date:	**3/1/03**
GameNo:	(The AutoNumber entry for the new record, 23, is automatically entered.)
Opponent:	**Kansas State**
Mascot:	**Wildcats**
Home-Away:	**H**
Home Score:	**100**
Opponent Score:	**52**
Web Site:	**www.ksu.edu**

g. Navigate to the first record, then back to the last.

h. Print this new record, which should look like Figure J-20, then close Internet Explorer.

i. Open the datasheet for the Games table to verify the entry in the Basketball-J database.

FIGURE J-20

j. Close the Games datasheet, close the games Web page, close the Basketball-J database, then exit Access.

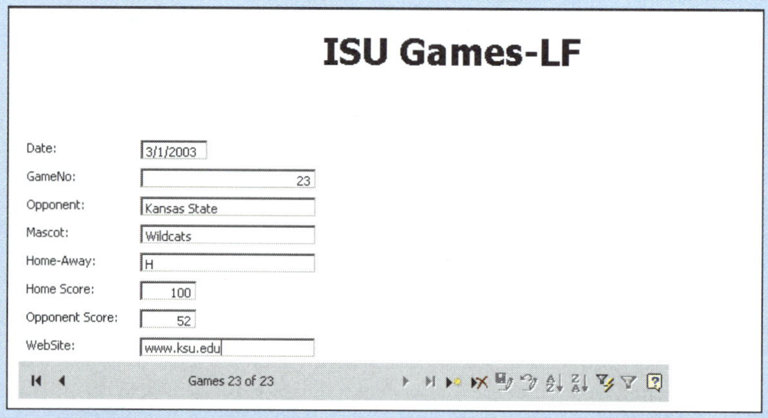

▶ Independent Challenge 3

As the manager of a college women's basketball team, you want to enhance the Basketball-J database by developing a Web page to display player statistical information as a PivotTable.

a. Start Access, then open the **Basketball-J** database from the drive and folder where your Project Files are located.

b. Click Pages on the Objects toolbar, double-click Create data access page in Design View, then click OK.

c. Expand the Queries folder in the Field List, then drag the Players Query to the upper-left corner of the "Drag fields from the Field List and drop them on the page" area.

d. Choose the PivotTable option, then click OK.

e. Widen the PivotTable control so that all of the seven fields are clearly displayed.

f. Click in the title area of the body of the Page, then type the title **Game Stats**. Include your initials in the title to include them on the printed solution.

g. Select the PivotTable to select it, click it again to edit it, right-click the Opponent field, then choose Move to Row Area on the shortcut menu.

h. Save the Web page as **gstats** to the drive and folder where your Project Files are located, then view the page in Web Page Preview so that it loads into Internet Explorer.

i. Click the Last list arrow in the PivotTable, click the All check box (to clear it), then click the Franco and Tyler check boxes to display only Denise Franco and Morgan Tyler's statistics.

j. Print this Web page, then close Internet Explorer.

k. Close the gstats Web page, close the Basketball-J database, then exit Access.

ⓔ Independent Challenge 4

You are the coordinator of the foreign studies program at your college. You help place students in foreign college study programs which have curriculum and credits that are transferable back to your college. You have started to build a database that documents the primary and secondary language used by the foreign countries for which your college has developed transfer programs. The database also includes a table of common words and phrases, translated into various languages that you use in correspondence with the host colleges.

a. Start Access, then open the **Languages-J** database from the drive and folder where your Project Files are located.

b. Open the Words table, observe the field names that represent various languages, then click the Design View button to switch to Table Design View.

c. Add a field to the database that represents a language that doesn't currently exist in the database, then save the table and display its datasheet.

d. Connect to the Internet, then go to www.yahoo.com, www.msn.com, or any general search engine to conduct some research for your database. Your goal is to find a Web page that translates English to the new language that you added to the database, then to print one page of that Web page.

e. Using the features provided by the Web page, translate the existing six words in the English field of the Words table to the new language you added as a field, then print the Words datasheet in landscape mode.

f. Use the Page Wizard to create a Web page with all of the fields in the Words table. Do not add any grouping levels, but sort the records in ascending order based on the values in the English field.

g. Title the page **Translations**.

h. In Page Design View, type the title **Translations**. Include your initials in the title to include them on the printed solution.

FIGURE J-21

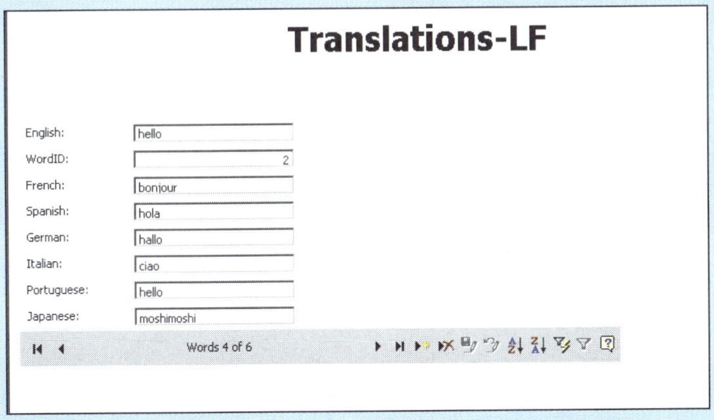

Translations-LF

English:	hello
WordID:	2
French:	bonjour
Spanish:	hola
German:	hallo
Italian:	ciao
Portuguese:	hello
Japanese:	moshimoshi

Words 4 of 6

i. Save the Web page with the name **trans** to the drive and folder where your Project Files are stored, then display Web Page Preview to view the Translations Web page in Internet Explorer.

j. Navigate to the record for the English word "hello," then print that page, as shown in Figure J-21.

k. Close Internet Explorer, close the trans Web page, close Languages-J, then exit Access.

▶ Visual Workshop

As the manager of a college women's basketball team, you need to enhance the **Basketball-J** database by developing a Web page to display player scoring information as a PivotTable. In Page Design View, use the Scoring query as the basis of the PivotTable. Move the Home-Away field and the Last field to the Row Area. Figure J-22 shows the final data access page, titled ISU Scoring. Include your initials in the title area if desired. Save the Web page with the name **scoring** to the drive and folder where your Project Files are located. Open, view, and print the page within Internet Explorer, then close all open applications.

FIGURE J-22

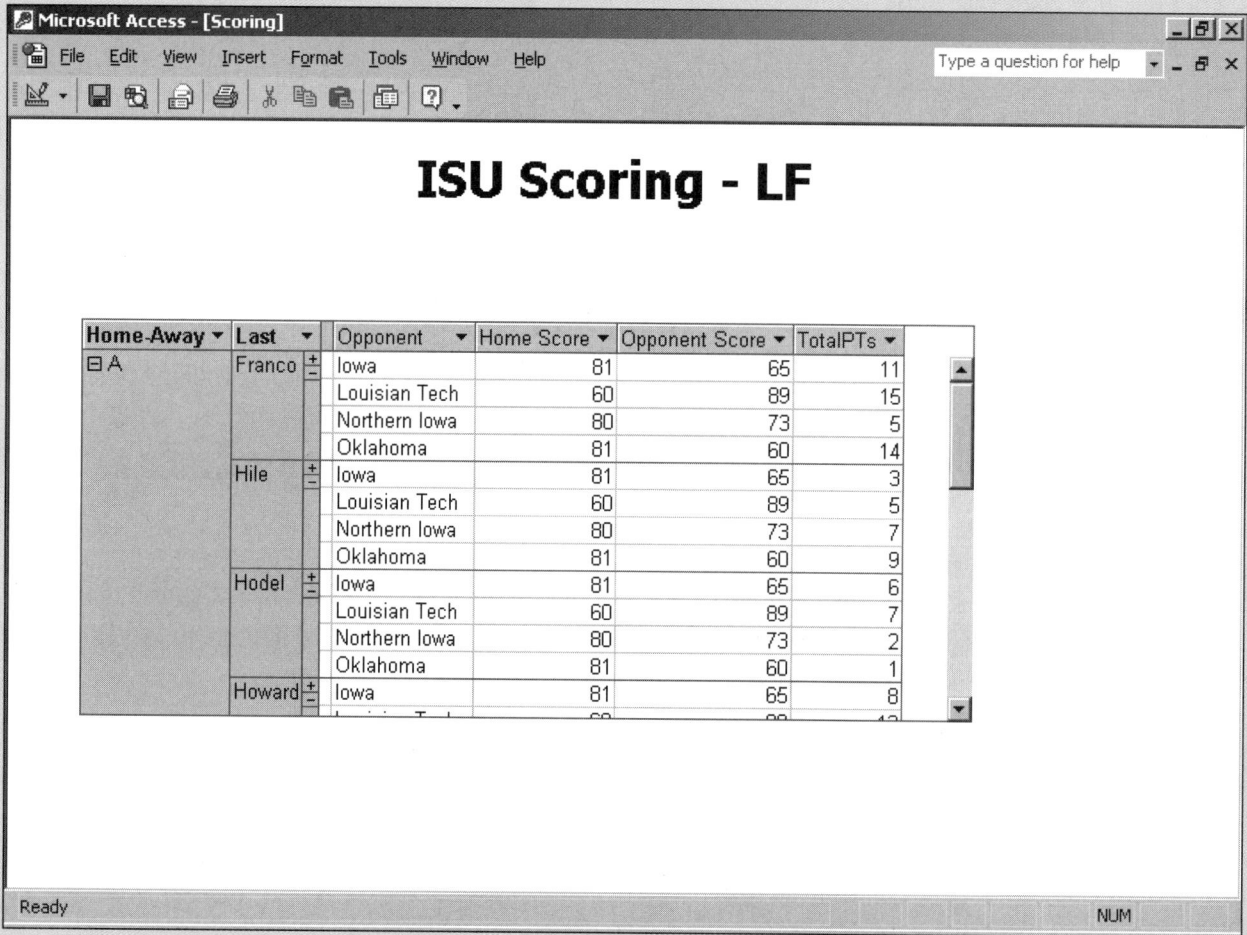

Creating
Advanced Queries

► **Query for top values**
[MOUS] ► **Create a parameter query**
► **Modify query properties**
[MOUS] ► **Create an update query**
[MOUS] ► **Create a make-table query**
[MOUS] ► **Create an append query**
[MOUS] ► **Create a delete query**
► **Specify join properties**

Queries are database objects that answer questions about the data. The most common query is the **select query**, which creates a single datasheet to display the fields and records that match specific criteria. Other types of queries, such as top value, parameter, and action queries, are powerful tools for displaying, analyzing, and updating data. An **action query** is one that makes changes to the data. There are four types of action queries: delete, update, append, and make-table. Fred Ames, coordinator of training at MediaLoft, has become very familiar with the capabilities of Access. Database users come to Fred with extensive data-analysis and data-update requests, confident that Fred can provide the information they need. Fred uses query features and new query types to handle these requests.

Querying for Top Values

Once a large number of records are entered into a table of a database, it is less common to query for all of the records, and more common to list only the most significant records by choosing a subset of the highest or lowest values from a sorted query. Use the **Top Values** feature in Query Design View to specify a number or percentage of records that you want to display in the query's datasheet. Employee attendance at MediaLoft classes has grown. To help plan future classes, Fred wants to print a datasheet listing the names of the top five classes, sorted by number of students per class. Fred creates a summarized Select Query to find the total number of attendees for each class, then uses the Top Values feature to find the five most attended classes.

Steps

1. Start Access, open the **Training-K** database, click **Queries** on the Objects bar, then double-click **Create query in Design view**
   You need fields from both the Attendance and Courses tables.

Trouble?

If you add a table's field list to Query Design View twice by mistake, click the title bar of the extra field list, then press [Delete].

2. Double-click **Attendance**, double-click **Courses**, then click **Close** in the Show Table dialog box
   Query Design View displays the field lists of the two related tables in the upper portion of the screen.

3. Double-click **LogNo** in the Attendance field list, double-click **Description** in the Courses field list, then click the **Datasheet View button** on the Query Design toolbar
   The datasheet shows 153 total records with the LogNo and Description for each course taken at MediaLoft. You want to count the LogNo entries for the records grouped by values in the Description field so that you know how many people took each course.

QuickTip

Click the at any time during the query design development process to view the resulting datasheet.

4. Click the **Design View button**, click the **Totals button** Σ on the Query Design toolbar, click **Group By** for the LogNo field, click the **Group By list arrow**, then click **Count**
   Your screen should look like Figure K-1. Sorting helps you further analyze the information and prepare for finding the top values.

5. Click the **LogNo field Sort cell**, click the **LogNo field Sort list arrow**, then click **Descending**
   Choosing a descending sort order will put the courses with the highest values in the LogNo field, those most attended by MediaLoft employees, at the top of the resulting datasheet.

6. Click the **Top Values list arrow** on the Query Design toolbar
   The number or percentage specified in the Top Values list box determines which records will be displayed, starting with the first one on the datasheet. Therefore, the Top Values feature works best when the records are also sorted. See Table K-1 for more information on how to use the Top Values feature.

7. Click **5**, then click on the Query Design toolbar
   Your screen should look like Figure K-2. The datasheet shows the five most popular MediaLoft courses. For example, the Computer Fundamentals course had 19 attendees. If more than one course had 10 attendees (a summarized value of 10 in the CountOfLogNo field), then all courses that tied for fifth place would have been displayed, too.

8. Click the **Save button** on the Query Datasheet toolbar, type **Top 5 Courses**, click **OK**, then close the datasheet
   The Top 5 Courses query appears as a query object in the database window. The last Top Value entered (5) is saved with the query.

FIGURE K-1: Designing a summary query for top values

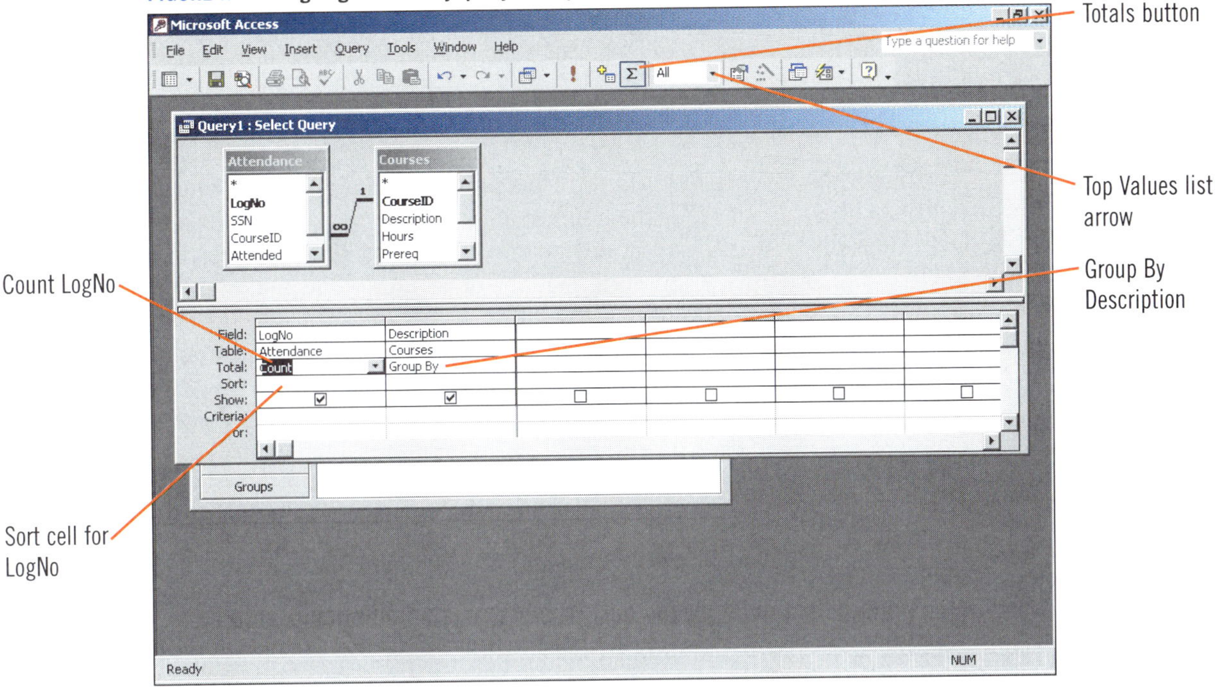
Totals button
Top Values list arrow
Group By Description
Count LogNo
Sort cell for LogNo
Microsoft Access
Query1 : Select Query
Attendance
Courses
Field: LogNo Description
Table: Attendance Courses
Total: Count Group By
Sort:
Show:
Criteria:
or:
Ready
NUM

FIGURE K-2: Top values datasheet

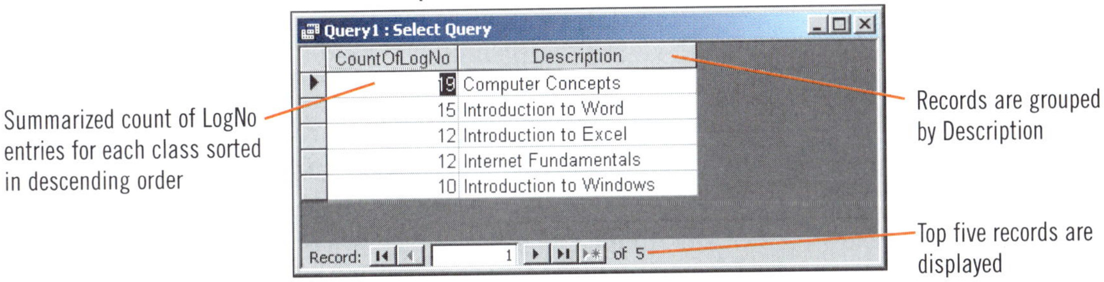
Summarized count of LogNo entries for each class sorted in descending order
Records are grouped by Description
Top five records are displayed
Query1 : Select Query
CountOfLogNo Description
19 Computer Concepts
15 Introduction to Word
12 Introduction to Excel
12 Internet Fundamentals
10 Introduction to Windows
Record: 1 of 5

TABLE K-1: Top Values options

action	to display
Click 5, or 25, or 100 from the Top Values list	Top 5, 25, or 100 records
Enter a number such as 10 in the Top Values text box	Top 10, or whatever value is entered, records
Click 5% or 25% from the Top Values list	Top 5 percent or 25 percent of records
Enter a percentage, such as 10%, in the Top Values text box	Top 10%, or whatever percentage is entered, of records

Creating a Parameter Query

A **parameter query** displays a dialog box that prompts you for an entry. Your entry is used as criteria for the query, and narrows the number of records that appear on the final datasheet just like criteria entered directly in the query design grid. You can build a form or report based on a parameter query, too. Then, when you open the form or report, the parameter dialog box appears. The entry in the dialog box determines which records are collected by the query that become the recordset for the form or report. ✎ Fred wants to enhance the Top 5 Courses query to display the top five courses for a specific department and within a specific date range. He adds parameter prompts to the Top 5 Courses query so that the resulting datasheet only shows the top five courses for the department and dates he specifies.

Steps 123 4

You can drag the title bars of the field lists to rearrange them in a way that more clearly shows their relationships.

1. Right-click the **Top 5 Courses query**, click **Design View** on the shortcut menu, click the **Show Table button** 📇, double-click **Employees**, then click **Close**
   The Employees table contains the Department field needed for this query.

2. Double-click the **Department field** in the Employees field list, then double-click the **Attended field** in the Attendance field list
   The Attended field contains the date that the course was taken. Both the Department and Attended fields will contain parameter prompts.

3. Click the **Department field Criteria cell**, type **[Enter department name:]**, and then click the **Datasheet View button** 📇
   Your screen should look like Figure K-3. Parameter criteria must be entered within [square brackets]. The entry you make in the Enter Parameter Value dialog box is used as criteria for the field that contains the parameter criteria.

Query criteria are not case sensitive so "accounting" is the same as "Accounting."

4. Type **accounting** in the Enter department name: text box, then click **OK**
   Twelve records are displayed. Though this query still selects the top five values in the LogNo field, several records have the same value in the sort field, CountOfLogNo. (Four records tied for first place and eight records tied for fifth place.)

Right-click the Criteria cell, then click Zoom or press [Shift][F2] to open the Zoom dialog box, which clearly displays a long entry.

5. Click the **Design View button** 📐, click the **Attended field Criteria cell**, type **Between [Enter start date:] And [Enter end date:]**, then click 📇
   The **Between ... And** operator will help you find all records on or between two dates. The criteria >= [Enter start date:] and <= [Enter end date:] is equivalent to Between [Enter start date:] And [Enter end date:].

6. Type **book** in the Enter department name: text box, press **[Enter]**, type **1/1/03** in the Enter start date: text box, press **[Enter]**, type **3/31/03** in the Enter end date: text box, then press **[Enter]**
   Your screen should look like Figure K-4. Once again, a tie for the fifth place record caused the query to display more than five top records.

7. Click **File** on the menu bar, click **Save As**, type **Top 5-Department-Date-Your Name** then click **OK**
   Because the object name always appears in the header of a printed datasheet, descriptive query names can help identify the information or creator of the information.

8. Click the **Print button** 🖨, then close the query
   The new query also appears as an object in the database window.

Parameter prompt   Parameter criteria

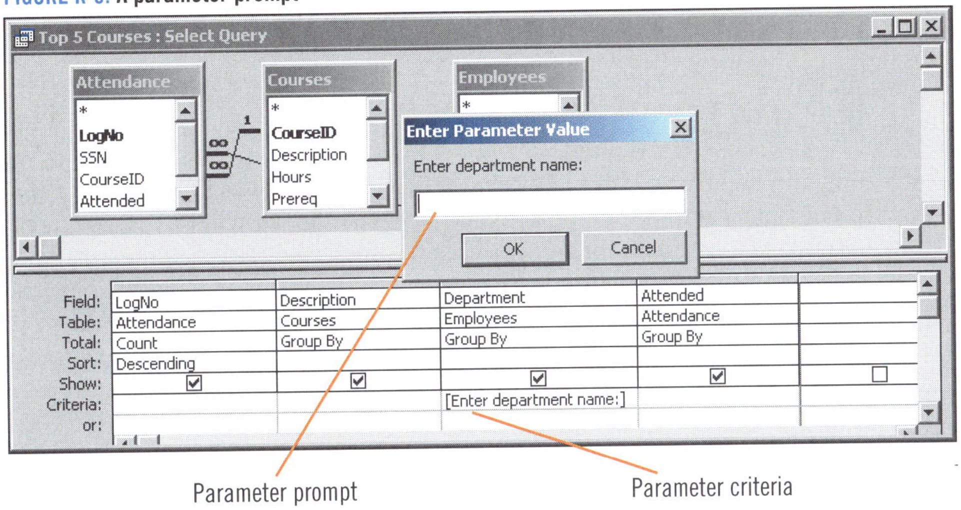

FIGURE K-4: Final datasheet for top 5 records between 1/1/03 and 3/31/03 in the Book department

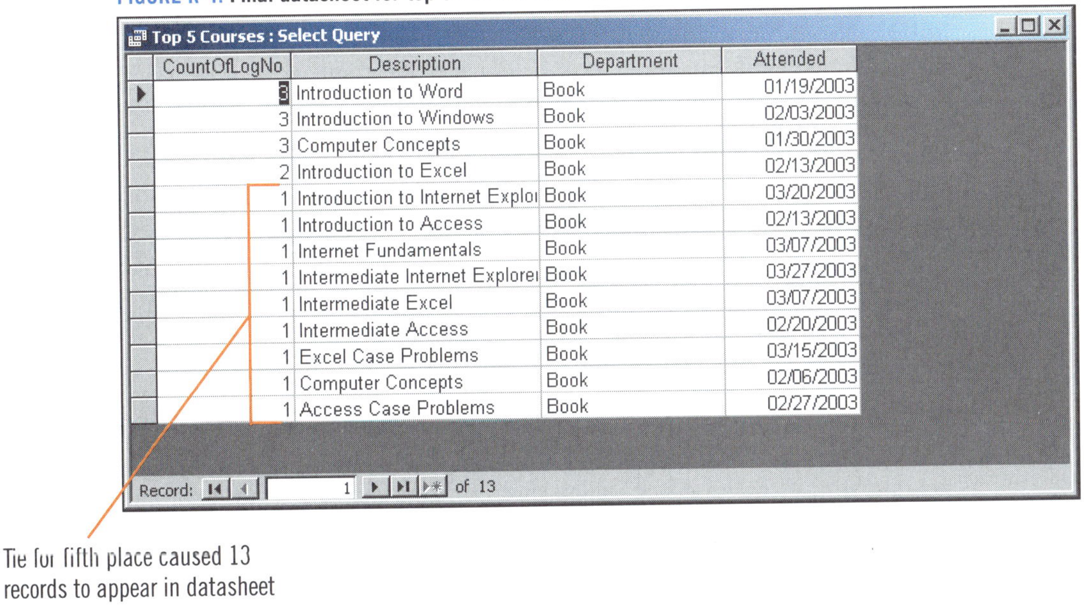

Tie for fifth place caused 13
records to appear in datasheet

Access 2002

CLUES TO USE

Concatenating a parameter prompt to a wildcard character

You can concatenate (or combine) parameter prompts with a wildcard character such as the asterisk (*) to create more flexible queries. For example, the entry: LIKE [Enter the first character of the company name:] & "*"
placed in the Criteria cell of the Company field searches for companies that begin with a specified letter. The
entry: LIKE "*" & [Enter any character(s) to search by:] & "*" placed in the Criteria cell of the Company field
searches for words that contain the specified characters anywhere in the field. The ampersand (&) is used to
concatenate items in an expression and quotation marks (" ") are used to surround text criteria.

Modifying Query Properties

Properties are characteristics that define the appearance and behavior of the database objects, fields, sections, and controls. You can view the properties for an item by opening its property sheet. To open the property sheet for an item, click the item, then click the Properties button ⊞. You can also right-click an item, and then click Properties on the shortcut menu to open the property sheet. The title bar of the property sheet always indicates which item's properties are shown. If you change field properties in Query Design View, they are modified for that query only (as opposed to changing the field properties in Table Design View, which affects that field's characteristics throughout the database). ✒️ Fred modifies the query and field properties of the Department Charges query.

Steps

1. Right-click the **Department Charges** query, then click **Properties**
The Department Charges Properties dialog box opens, providing information about the query and a text box where you can enter a description for the query.

QuickTip

Click the object column headings to sort the objects in ascending or descending order.

2. Type **Lists the department, description, hours, and cost**, click **OK**, click the **Details button** ⊞ in the Training-K database window, then maximize the database window
Five columns of information about each query object appear, as shown in Figure K-5. The Description property you entered appears in the Description column.

3. Click the **Design button** ⊞, click the **Properties button** ⊞ on the Query Design toolbar, click to the **right of the Employees field list**, click **Dynaset** in the Recordset Type property, click the **Recordset Type list arrow**, then click **Snapshot**
Your screen should look like Figure K-6. Viewing the query property sheet from within Query Design View gives a complete list of the query's properties. The **Snapshot** entry in the Recordset Type property locks the recordset (prevents it from being updated). The **Recordset Type** property determines if and how records displayed by a query are locked.

Trouble?

If the calculated field did not work correctly, return to Design View and make sure that you entered the expression PerHour:[Cost]/[Hours] accurately.

4. Move the Query Properties dialog box by dragging its **title bar** (if it covers the first blank column in the query grid), click the **blank Field cell** for the next column in the query grid, type **PerHour:[Cost]/[Hours]**, click the **Datasheet View button** ⊞, double-click **12** in the Hours field for the first record, then try to type **15**
The datasheet appears with the new calculated PerHour field in the last column. Because the query Recordset Type property was set to Snapshot, you can view the records but not update them.

5. Click the **Design View button** ⊞, click the **PerHour field** (if it's not already selected), click the **Format text box**, click the **Format list arrow**, click **Currency**, click the **Decimal Places text box**, click the **Decimal Places list arrow**, then click **2**
When you click a property in a property sheet, a short description of the property appears in the status bar. You can press [F1] to open Microsoft Access Help for a longer description of the selected property.

6. Click to the **right of the Employees field list** to display the property sheet for the query, click **Snapshot**, click the **Recordset Type list arrow**, then click **Dynaset**
Dynaset is the default property for the Recordset Type property, and allows updates to data.

7. Click ⊞ to close the property sheet, click ⊞ on the Query Design toolbar, double-click **12** in the Hours field for the first record, type **24**, then press **[Enter]** twice
Your screen should look like Figure K-7. Not only are the values in the PerHour field now formatted with a currency symbol and two digits to the right of the decimal point, but you can update the recordset again.

8. Save, then close the Department Charges query

FIGURE K-5: Details view of objects

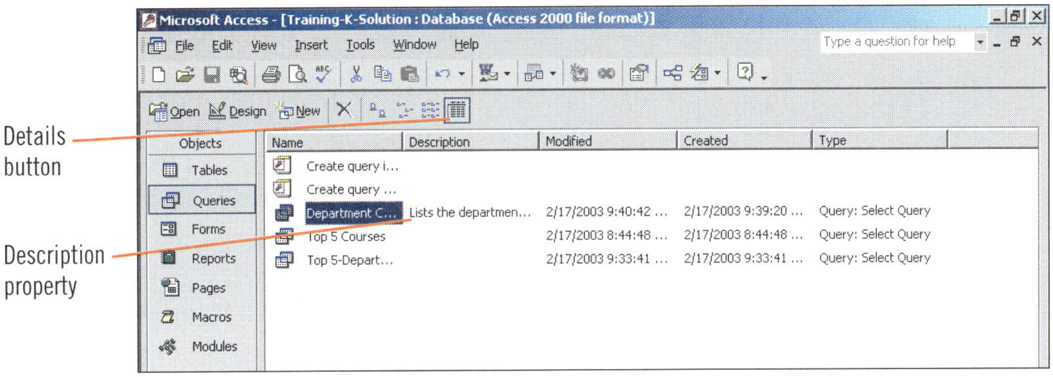

Details button

Description property

FIGURE K-6: Query property sheet

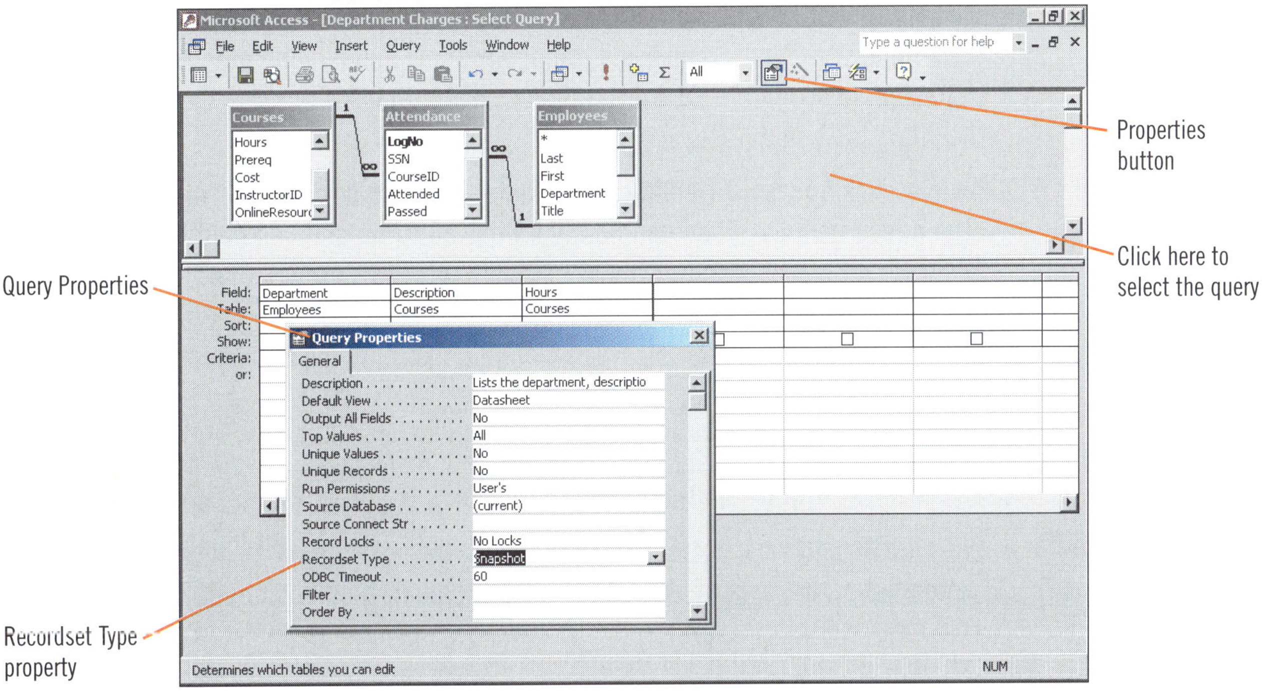

Properties button

Click here to select the query

Query Properties

Recordset Type property

FIGURE K-7: Final datasheet

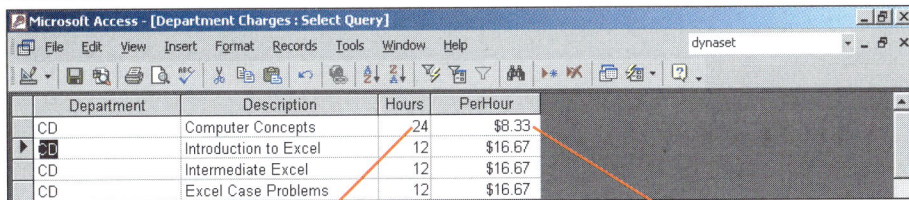

Hours value changed to 24

Formatted PerHour field recalculates when changes are made to the Hours or Cost fields

Access 2002

Creating an Update Query

An **action query** changes many records in one process. There are four types of action queries: delete, update, append, and make-table. In order for an action query to complete its action, you must run an action query using the Run button ![Run]. Because you cannot undo this action, it is always a good idea to create a backup of the database before using an action query. See Table K-2 for more information on action queries. An **update query** is a type of action query that updates the values in a field. For example, you may want to increase the price of product in a particular category by 5%. Or you may want to update the value of an area code for a subset of customers. ◢━━ The Training Department upgraded their equipment on April 1, and Fred has received approval to increase by 5% the internal cost of all courses offered after that date. He creates an update query to quickly calculate and enter the new values.

Steps

1. Click the **List button** ![List] on the database window toolbar, double-click **Create query in Design view**, double-click **Attendance**, double-click **Courses**, then click **Close** in the Show Table dialog box

2. Double-click **CourseID** from the Attendance field list, double-click **Attended** from the Attendance field list, then double-click **Cost** from the Courses field list
   The three fields are added to the query design grid. You want to change the Cost value for only those courses offered on or after April 1.

3. Click the **Attended Criteria cell**, type **>=4/1/03**, then click the **Datasheet View button** ![Datasheet] on the Query Design toolbar
   Every action query starts as a select query, as reflected in the title bar of the query window. Always look at the datasheet of the select query before initiating any action that changes data to double-check which records will be affected. In this case, 51 records are selected.

   Trouble?
   Double-click the Query Type button list arrow to immediately display the entire list of menu options.

4. Click the **Design View button** ![Design] on the Query Datasheet toolbar, click the **Query Type button list arrow** ![QueryType] on the Query Design toolbar, then click **Update Query**
   The Query Type button displays the Update Query icon ![icon] and the Update To: row appears in the query design grid, as shown in Figure K-8. All action query icons include an exclamation point to warn you that data will be changed when you click the Run button ![Run] on the Query Design toolbar.

   Trouble?
   Be sure to enter the [Cost]*1.05 update criteria for the Cost field, *not* for the CourseID or Attended fields.

5. Click the **Cost field Update To cell**, type **[Cost]*1.05**, click ![Run] on the Query Design toolbar, then click **Yes** to indicate that you want to update 51 rows
   When you run an action query, Access prompts you with an "Are you sure?" message before actually updating the data. The Undo button cannot undo changes made by action queries.

6. Click ![Datasheet] on the Query Design toolbar
   Your screen should look like Figure K-9. The datasheet of an update query shows only the updated field.

7. Close the update query without saving the changes
   You rarely need to save an update query, because once the data has been updated, you don't need the query object anymore. Also, if you double-click an action query from the database window, you run the query (as opposed to double-clicking a select query, which opens its datasheet). Therefore, don't save any queries that you won't need again, especially action queries that could inadvertently change data.

FIGURE K-8: Creating an update query

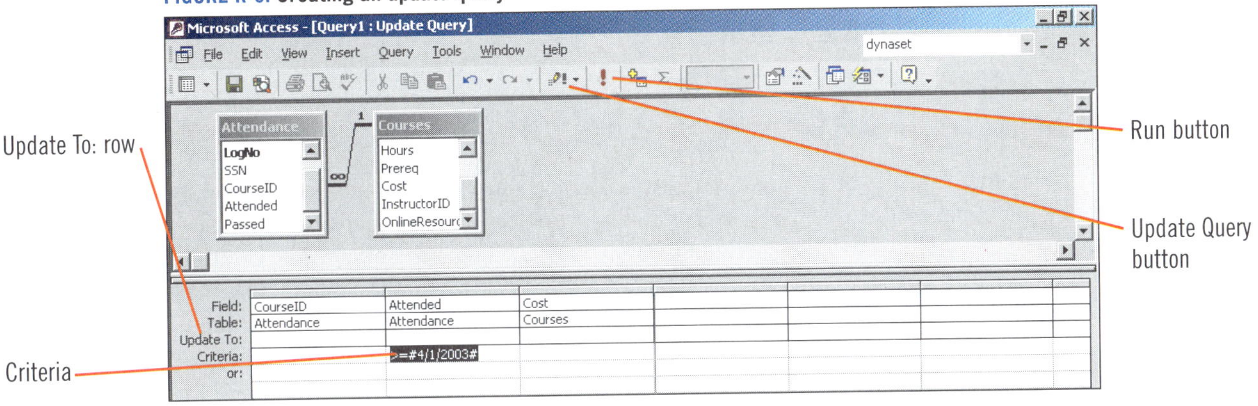

Update To: row

Run button

Update Query button

Criteria

FIGURE K-9: Updated Cost values

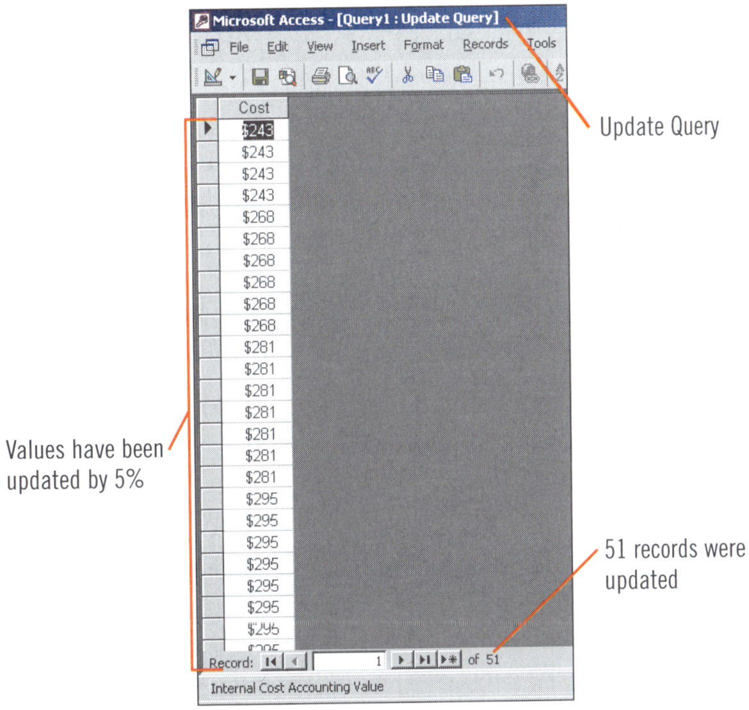

Update Query

Values have been updated by 5%

51 records were updated

TABLE K-2: Action queries

type of action query	query icon	description	example
Delete		Deletes a group of records from one or more tables	Remove products that are discontinued or for which there are no orders
Update		Makes global changes to a group of records in one or more tables	Raise prices by 10 percent for all products
Append		Adds a group of records from one or more tables to the end of a table	Append the employee address table from one division to the address table from another
Make-Table		Creates a new table from data in one or more tables	Export records to another Access database or make a back-up copy of a table

Access 2002

Creating a Make-Table Query

A **make-table query** creates a new table of data based on the recordset defined by the query. The make-table query works like an export feature in that it creates a copy of the selected data and pastes it into a new table in a database specified by the query. The location of the new table can be the current or any other Access database. Sometimes the make-table query is used to back up a subset of data. ◢◣◤ Fred uses a make-table query to archive the 1/1/2003 through 3/31/2003 records currently stored in the Attendance table.

Steps

1. Double-click **Create query in Design view**, double-click **Attendance** in the Show Table dialog box, then click **Close**

2. Double-click the *** (asterisk)** at the top of the Attendance table's field list
   Adding the asterisk to the query design grid puts all of the fields in that table in the grid. Later, if fields are added to this table, they also will be added to this query because the asterisk represents all fields in the table.

3. Double-click the **Attended field** to add it to the second column of the query grid, click the **Attended field Criteria cell**, type **<4/1/03**, then click the **Attended field Show check box** to uncheck it
   Your screen should look like Figure K-10. Before changing this select query into a make-table query, it is always a good idea to view the datasheet.

QuickTip

The sort and filter buttons work on a query datasheet in exactly the same way that they work in a table datasheet or form.

4. Click the **Datasheet View button** 🔲 on the Query Design toolbar, click any entry in the **Attended field**, then click the **Sort Descending button** 🔽 on the Query Datasheet toolbar
   Sorting the records in descending order based on the values in the Attended field allows you to confirm that no records on or after 4/1/03 appear in the datasheet.

5. Click the **Design View button** 📝, click the **Query Type list arrow** 🔽, click **Make-Table Query**, type **First Quarter 2003 Attendance Log** in the Table Name text box, then click **OK**
   Your screen should look like Figure K-11. The Query Type button displays the Make-Table icon 📋. The make-table query is ready, but the new table has not yet been created. Action queries do not delete, update, append, or make data until you click the Run button ❗.

6. Click ❗ on the Query Design toolbar, click **Yes** when prompted that you are about to paste 102 records, then close but do not save the query
   Once you've made a table of data, you do not need to save or run the make-table query again.

7. Click **Tables** on the Objects bar, then double-click **First Quarter 2003 Attendance Log** to view the new table's datasheet
   All 102 records were pasted into the new table, as shown in Figure K-12. Field properties such as the Input Mask for the SSN field and the Display Control for the Passed field were not duplicated, but you could modify the Design View of this table to change the appearance of the fields just like you could for any other table. (*Note*: −1 is used to designate "yes" and 0 is used to designate "no" when the Display Control property for a Yes/No field is set to Text Box.)

8. Close the First Quarter 2003 Attendance Log table

FIGURE K-10: Using the asterisk in a query grid

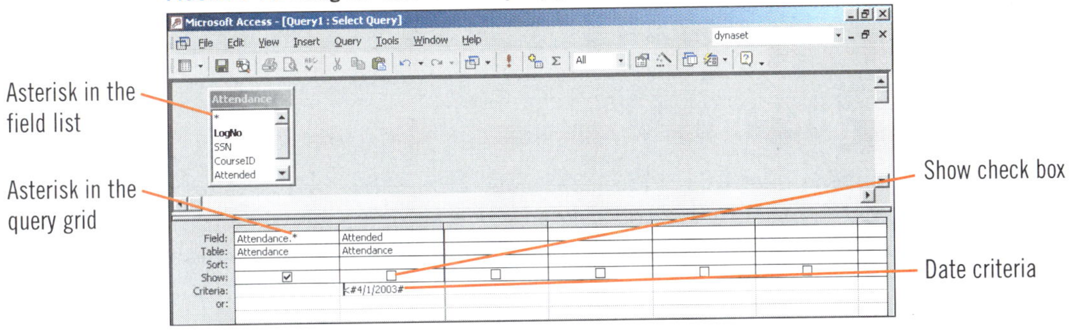

Asterisk in the field list

Asterisk in the query grid

Show check box

Date criteria

FIGURE K-11: Creating a make-table query

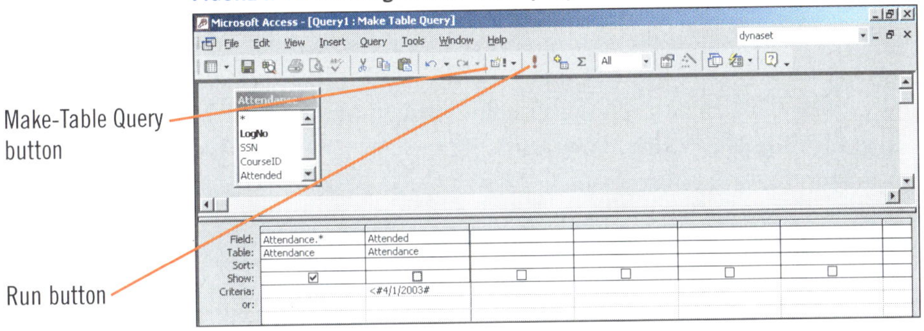

Make-Table Query button

Run button

FIGURE K-12: First Quarter 2003 Attendance Log datasheet

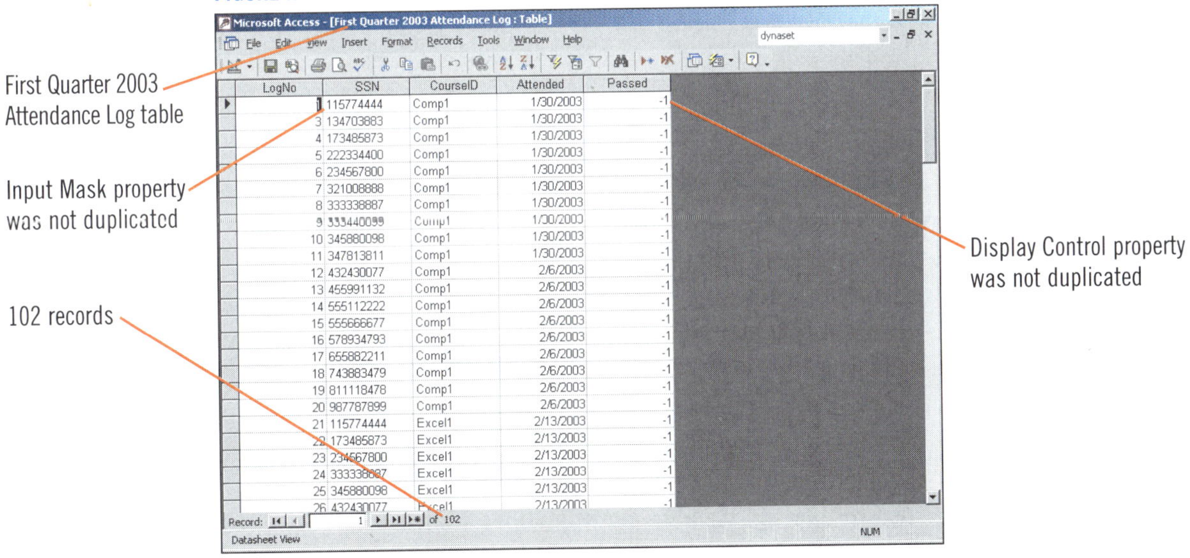

First Quarter 2003 Attendance Log table

Input Mask property was not duplicated

102 records

Display Control property was not duplicated

CLUES TO USE

1900 versus 2000 dates

If you type only two digits of a date, Access assumes that the digits 00 through 29 are for the years 2000 through 2029. If you type 30 through 99, Access assumes the years refer to 1930 through 1999. If you want to specify years outside these ranges, you must type all four digits of the year.

Creating an Append Query

An **append query** adds a selected recordset defined by a query to an existing table called the **target table**. The append query works like an export feature because the records are copied from one location and a duplicate set is pasted to another location. The target table can be in the current or in any other Access database. The most difficult thing about an append query is making sure that all of the fields you have selected in the append query match the fields of the target table where you want to append (paste) them. If the target table has more fields than those you want to append, the append query will append the data in the matching fields and ignore the other fields. If the target table lacks a field that the recordset of the append query contains, an error message will appear indicating that the query has an unknown field name which will cancel the append action. ✎ Fred would like to append April's records to the First Quarter 2003 Attendance Log table. He uses an append query to do this, then he renames the table to accurately reflect its contents.

Steps 1234

1. Click **Queries** on the Objects bar, double-click **Create query in Design view**, double-click **Attendance** in the Show Table dialog box, then click **Close**

2. Double-click the **Attendance table's field list title bar**, then drag the **highlighted fields** to the first column of the query design grid
   Double-clicking the title bar of the field list selects all of the fields, allowing you to add all the fields to the query grid quickly. To successfully complete the append process, the append query's Query Design View cannot have more fields than in the target table. Therefore, the technique of adding all of the fields to the query grid by using the asterisk in the field list and then adding the Attendance field again in order to enter the date criteria would not work for the append operation.

3. Click the **Attended field Criteria cell**, type **>=4/1/03 and <=4/30/03**, then click the **Datasheet View button** 🖩 on the Query Design toolbar
   The datasheet should show 29 records with an April date in the Attended field.

4. Click the **Design View button** 📐 on the Query Datasheet toolbar, click the **Query Type button list arrow** 🔲 on the Query Design toolbar, click **Append Query**, click the **Table Name list arrow** in the Append dialog box, click **First Quarter 2003 Attendance Log**, then click **OK**
   Your screen should look like Figure K-13. The Query Type button displays the Append Query icon ➕ and the Append To row was added to the query design grid. You would use the Append To row to choose fields in the target table if they were different from the query fields. The append action is ready to be initiated by clicking the Run button.

5. Click the **Run button** ❗ on the Query Design toolbar, click **Yes** to indicate that you want to append 29 rows, then close the query without saving the changes

6. Click **Tables** on the Objects bar, double-click the **First Quarter 2003 Attendance Log**, click any entry in the **Attended** field, then click the **Sort Descending button** 🔽 on the Table Datasheet toolbar
   The April records were appended to the table for a total of 131 records, as shown in Figure K-14.

7. Close the First Quarter 2003 Attendance Log datasheet without saving changes, right-click **First Quarter 2003 Attendance Log** in the database window, click **Rename** on the shortcut menu, type **Jan-April 2003 Log**, then press **[Enter]**
   The backup table with attendance records from January through April 2003 has been renamed.

FIGURE K-13: Creating an append query

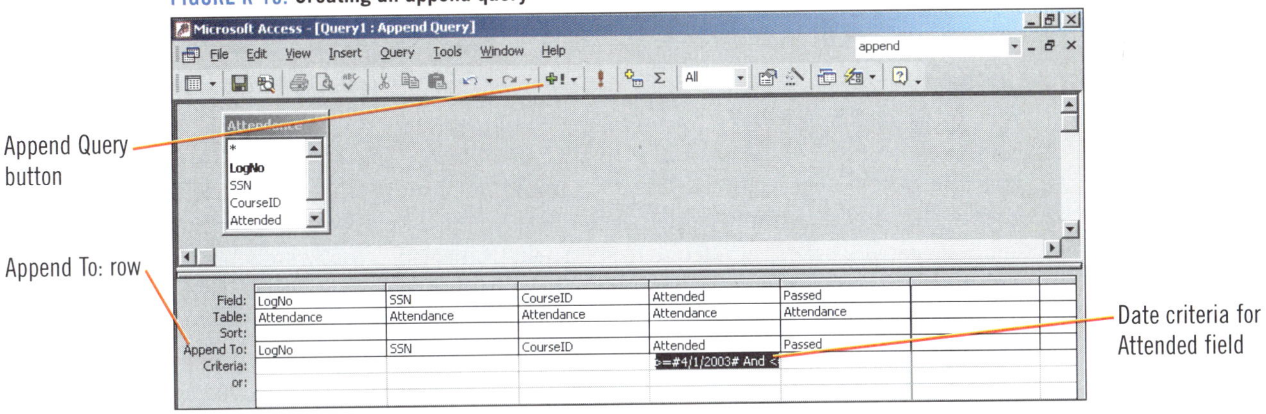

Append Query button →

Append To: row

Date criteria for Attended field

FIGURE K-14: Updated table with appended records

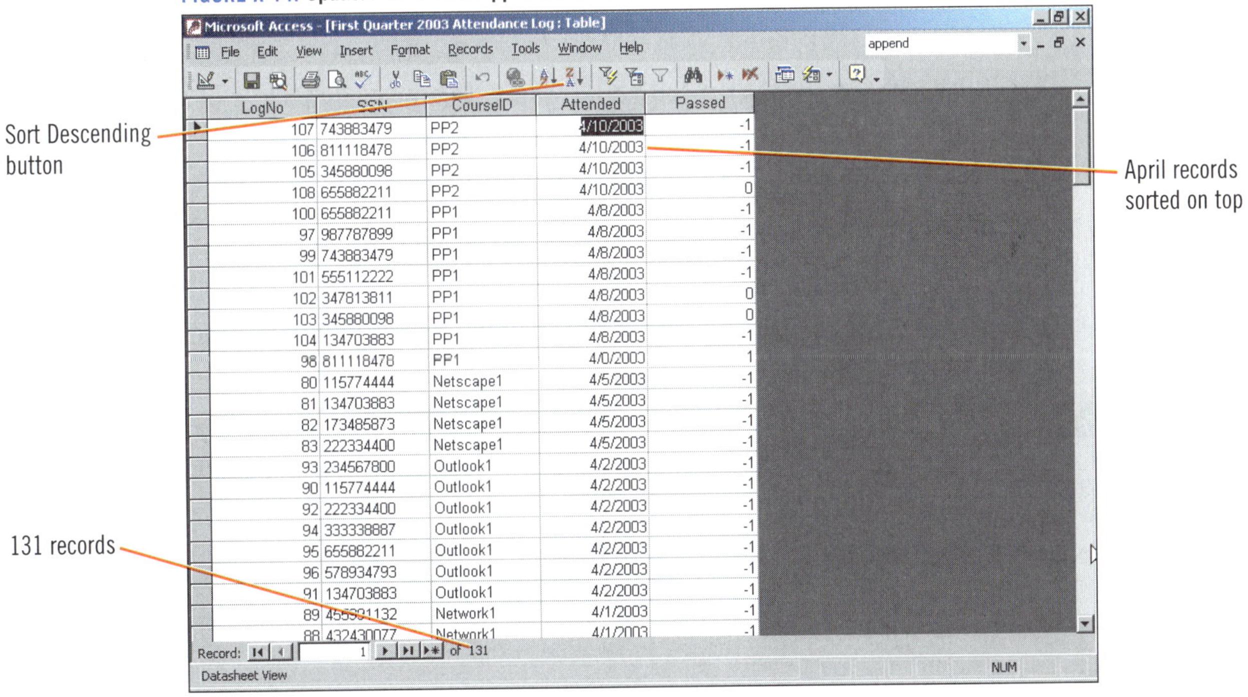

Sort Descending button

April records sorted on top

131 records

Access 2002

Creating a Delete Query

A **delete query** deletes a group of records from one or more tables as defined by a query. Delete queries always delete entire records, and not just selected fields within records, so they should be used very carefully. If you wanted to delete a field from a table, you would open Table Design View, click the field name, then click the **Delete Rows button** 🔁. Because the delete query deletes all selected records without letting you undo the action, it is wise to always have a current backup of the database before running any action query, especially the delete query. 🥕 Now that Fred has the first four months of attendance records archived in the Jan-April 2003 Log table, he wants to delete them from the Attendance table. He uses a delete query to accomplish this task.

Steps 1 2 3 4

1. Click **Queries** on the Objects bar, double-click **Create query in Design view**, double-click **Attendance** in the Show Table dialog box, then click **Close**

2. Double-click the *** (asterisk)** at the top of the Attendance table's field list, then double-click the **Attended** field

   All the fields from the Attendance table are added to the first column of the query design grid by using the asterisk. The Attended field is added to the second column of the query design grid so you can enter limiting criteria for this field.

3. Click the **Attended field Criteria cell**, type **<=4/30/03**, then press **[Enter]**

   Before you initiate the delete action, check the datasheet to make sure that you have selected the same 131 records that were added to the Jan-April 2003 Log table.

4. Click the **Datasheet View button** 🔳 on the Query Design toolbar to confirm that the datasheet has 131 records, click the **Design View button** 📐 on the Query Datasheet toolbar, click the **Query Type button list arrow** 🔲▾, then click **Delete Query**

   Your screen should look like Figure K-15. The Query Type button displays the Delete Query icon ✖, and the Delete row was added to the query design grid. The delete action is ready to be initiated by clicking the Run button ❗.

5. Click the ❗ on the Query Design toolbar, click **Yes** to confirm that you want to delete 131 rows, then close the query without saving the changes

6. Click **Tables** on the Objects bar, double-click **Attendance**, click **any entry in the LogNo field** (if it's not already selected), then click the **Sort Ascending button** 🔼 on the Table Datasheet toolbar

   Sorting in ascending order by LogNo places the oldest records on top since LogNos are assigned in sequential order based on the date that the employee attends the actual course. The oldest records should start in May, as shown in Figure K-16. All records with dates earlier than 5/1/2003 were deleted by the delete query.

7. Close the Attendance datasheet without saving changes

FIGURE K-15: Creating a delete query

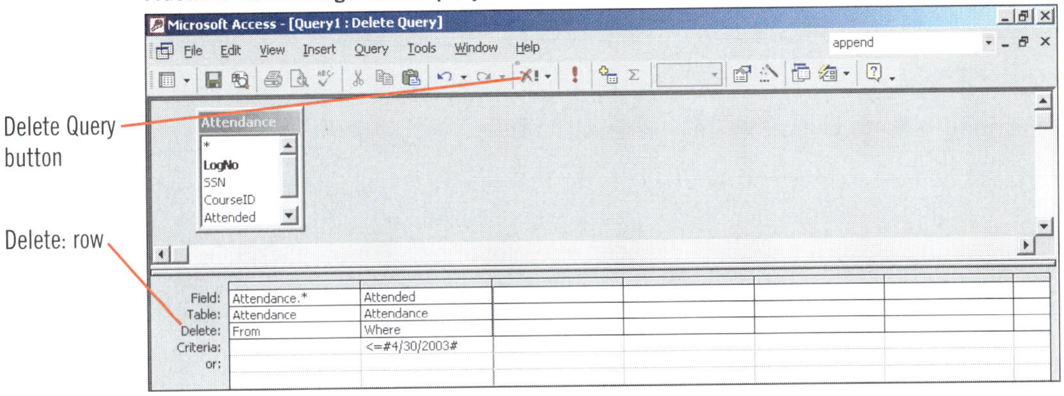

Delete Query button

Delete: row

FIGURE K-16: Attendance table without January–April records

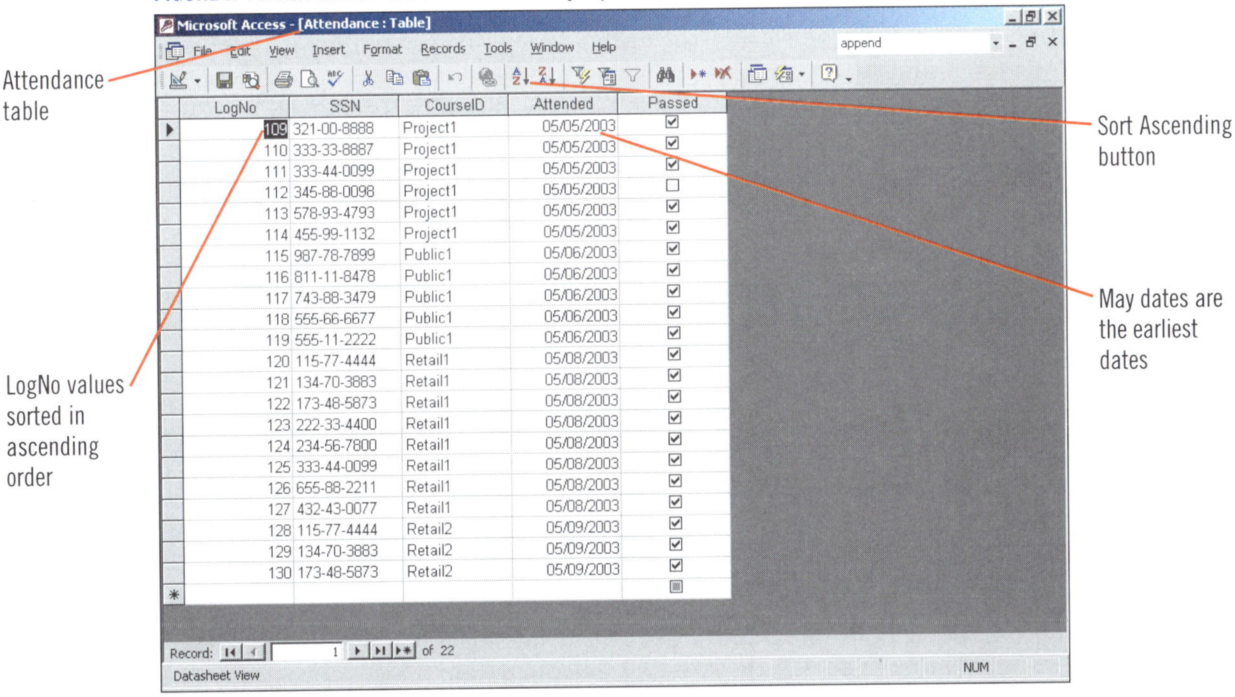

Attendance table

LogNo values sorted in ascending order

Sort Ascending button

May dates are the earliest dates

CLUES TO USE

Reviewing referential integrity

Referential integrity between two tables is established when tables are joined in the Relationships window. Referential integrity ensures that no orphaned records currently exist or are added to the database. Related tables have an **orphan record** when information in the foreign key field of the "many" table doesn't have a matching entry in the primary key field of the "one" table. An orphan record is sometimes called an **unmatched record**. The term "orphan" corresponds to general database terminology which often refers to the "one" table as containing **parent records**, and the "many" table as containing **child records**. Using this analogy, referential integrity means that a child record cannot be created without a corresponding parent record.

Specifying Join Properties

When more than one table's field list is used in a query, the tables are joined as defined in the Relationships window for the database. If referential integrity was enforced, a "1" appears next to the field that serves as the "one" side of the one-to-many relationship, and an infinity sign (∞) appears next to the field that serves as the "many" side. The "one" field is usually the primary key field for its table, and the "many" field is always called the foreign key field. If no relationships have been established, Access automatically creates join lines in Query Design View if the linking fields have the same name and data type in two tables. You can edit table relationships for an individual query in Query Design View by double-clicking the join line. ✐ Fred would like to create a query to find out which courses have never been attended. He modifies the join properties between the Attendance and Courses table to find this answer.

Steps 1 2 3 4

1. Click **Queries** on the Object bar, double-click **Create query in Design view**, double-click **Courses**, double-click **Attendance**, then click **Close**

   Because the Courses and Attendance tables already have a one-to-many relationship with referential integrity enforced in the Relationships window, the join line appears, linking the two tables using the CourseID field common to both.

2. Double-click the **one-to-many join line** between the field lists

   The Join Properties dialog box opens and displays the characteristics for the join, as shown in Figure K-17. The dialog box shows that option 1 is chosen, which means that the query will display only records where joined fields from *both* tables are equal. That means that if the Courses table has any records for which there are no matching Attendance records, those courses would not appear in the resulting datasheet.

3. Click the **2** option button

   By choosing option 2, you are specifying that you want to see ALL of the records in the Courses table, even if the Attendance table does not contain matching records. Because referential integrity is enforced, option 3 would be the same as option 1—referential integrity makes it impossible to enter records in the Attendance table that do not have a corresponding record in the Courses table.

4. Click **OK**

   The join line's appearance changes, as shown in Figure K-18.

5. Double-click **CourseID** from the Courses field list, double-click **Description** from the Courses field list, double-click **Attended** from the Attendance field list, then click the **Datasheet View button** 🔲

   All courses are now listed in the datasheet, regardless of whether anyone attended them. The courses without an entry in the Attended field are those that have never been taken. By using a filter, you can quickly isolate those courses.

6. Click the **Access1 Attended field** (it is null), then click the **Filter by Selection button** 🔽 on the Query Datasheet toolbar

   The 25 filtered records represent the courses shown in Figure K-19. They contain a **null** (nothing) value in the Attended field, and represent the courses that have not been taken since May 1, 2003. (Recall that all records prior to this date were deleted from the Attendance table and added to the Jan-April 2003 Log table.)

7. Click the **Save button** 🔳 on the Query Datasheet toolbar, type **No Attendance Since 5/1/03 – Your Initials** in the Query Name text box, click **OK**, click the **Access1 Attended field value**, click 🔽 (to refilter for null values), then click the **Print button** 🖨

   If you wanted to permanently save the "is null" criteria for the Attended field, you would add it to Query Design View.

8. Close the datasheet without saving changes, then close the Training-K database

FIGURE K-17: Join Properties dialog box

Double-click join line to open the Join Properties dialog box

Default join property

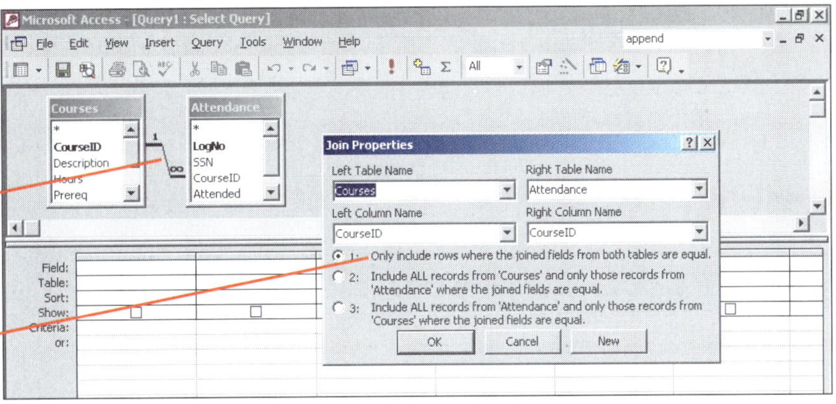

FIGURE K-18: The join line's appearance changes when its properties are changed

Join line's appearance shows that *all* records from the Courses table will be included in the datasheet

FIGURE K-19: Filtering for courses with no attendance records

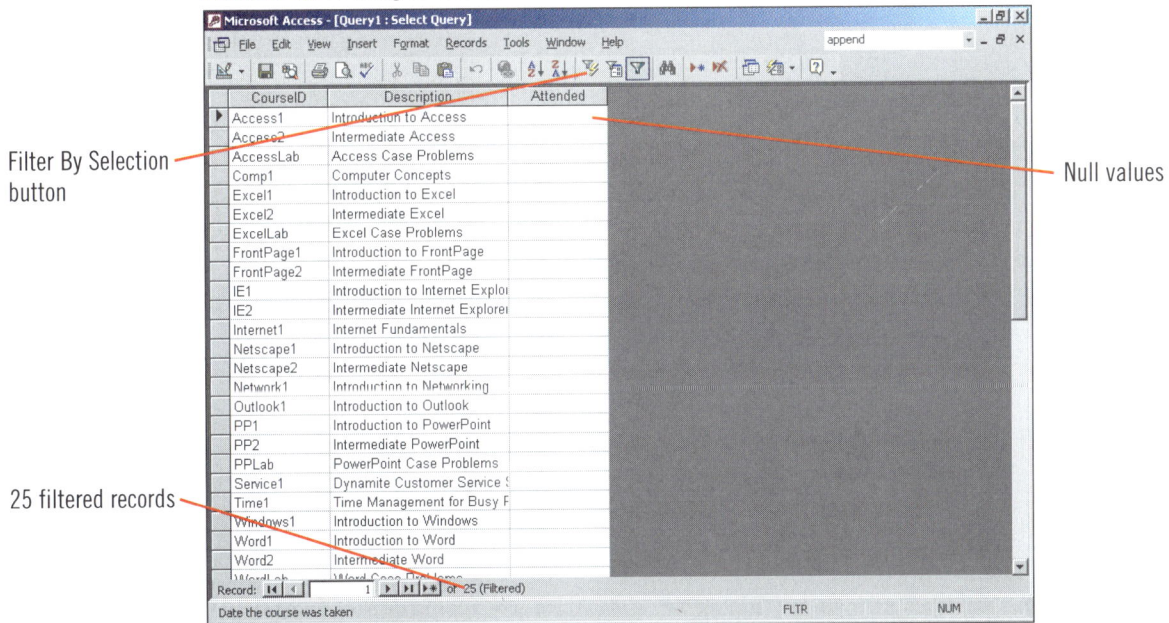

Filter By Selection button

Null values

25 filtered records

Finding duplicate and unmatched records

When referential integrity is enforced on a relationship before data is entered into a database, no one can enter a foreign key field value in the "many" table that doesn't already exist in a record on the "one" side of the relationship. Sometimes, though, you inherit a database in which referential integrity was not imposed from the beginning, and unmatched and duplicate records already exist in the database. Or, you may be asked to scrub, a database term for "find and correct," unmatched and duplicate records that are imported into your database from another source. The **Find Duplicates Query Wizard** and **Find Unmatched Query Wizard** can help you solve these database problems.

Practice

► Concepts Review

Identify each element of the Query Design View shown in Figure K-20.

FIGURE K-20

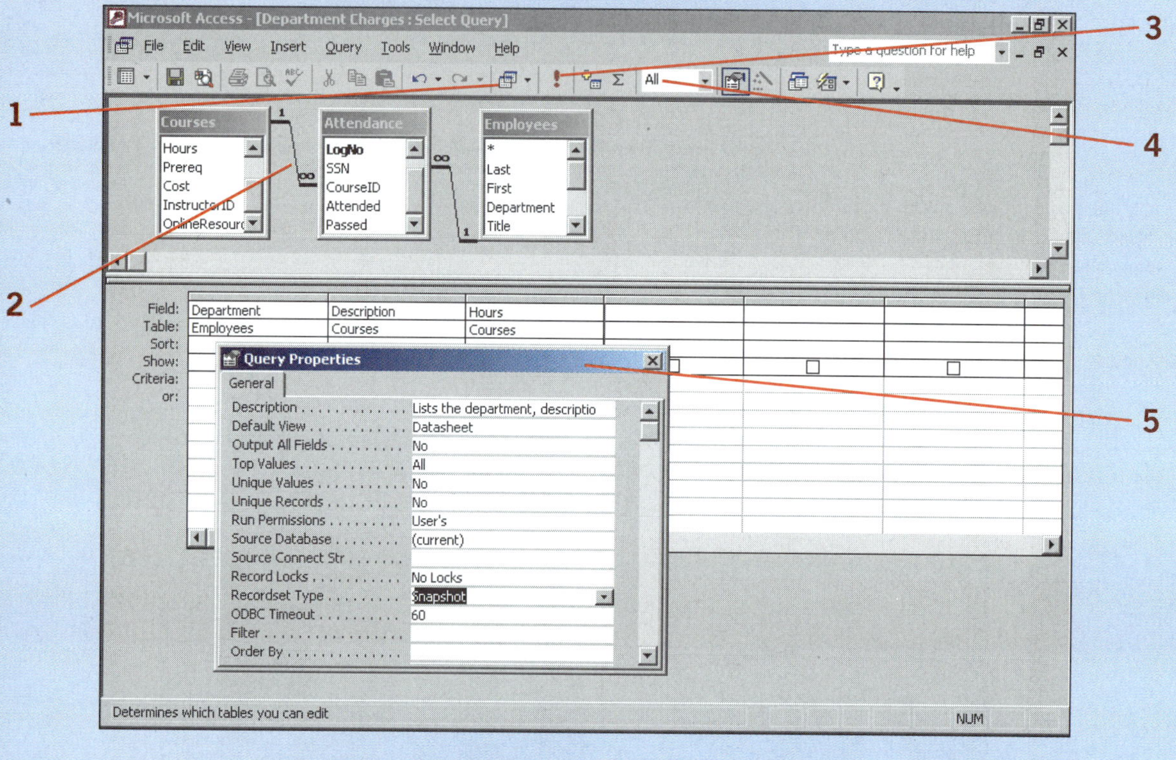

Match each term with the statement that describes its function.

6. Top values query
7. Select query
8. Action query
9. Properties
10. Snapshot
11. Parameter query

a. Displays a dialog box prompting you for criteria
b. Makes changes to data
c. Displays only a number or percentage of records from a sorted query
d. Displays fields and records that match specific criteria in a single datasheet
e. Makes the recordset not updateable
f. Characteristics that define the appearance and behavior of items within the database

Select the best answer from the list of choices.

12. **Which entry for the Recordset Type query property will not allow you to modify the recordset?**
    a. No Updates
    b. Snapshot
    c. Referential Integrity
    d. Dynaset (No Nulls)

13. **Which of the following is a valid parameter criteria entry in the query design grid?**
    a. >=(Type minimum value here:)
    b. >=Type minimum value here: }
    c. >=[Type minimum value here:]
    d. >=Type minimum value here:

14. **You cannot use the Top Values feature to:**
    a. Display a subset of records.
    b. Show the top 30 records.
    c. Update a field's value by 10 percent.
    d. Show the bottom 10 percent of records.

15. **Which of the following is not an action query?**
    a. Union query
    b. Delete query
    c. Make-table query
    d. Append query

16. **Which of the following precautions should you take before running a delete query?**
    a. Check the resulting datasheet to make sure the query selects the right records.
    b. Have a current backup of the database
    c. Understand the relationships between the records you are about to delete in the database.
    d. All of the above

17. **When querying tables in a one-to-many relationship with referential integrity enforced, which records will appear (by default) on the resulting datasheet?**
    a. Only those with matching values in both tables
    b. All records from the "one" table, and only those with matching values from the "many" side
    c. All records from the "many" table, and only those with nonmatching values from the "one" side
    d. All records from both tables will appear at all times

18. **The process defined by an action query doesn't happen until you click which button?**
    a. Properties 🔲
    b. Design View 📐
    c. Save 💾
    d. Run ❗

19. **Which of the following queries is most often used to create a back-up copy of a table?**
    - **a.** Update
    - **b.** Delete
    - **c.** Top Values
    - **d.** Make-Table

20. **Where does an append query append the selected records?**
    - **a.** To the first table in the current database
    - **b.** To the last table in the current database
    - **c.** To a new table in a new database
    - **d.** To the target table which can be in the current or a different database

▶ Skills Review

1. **Query for top values.**
    - **a.** Start Access, then open the **Seminar-K** database from the drive and folder where your Project Files are located.
    - **b.** Create a new select query with the EventName field from the Events table and the RegistrationFee field from the Registration table.
    - **c.** Add the RegistrationFee field a second time, then click the Totals button on the Query Design toolbar. In the Total row of the query grid, Group By the EventName field, Sum the first RegistrationFee field, then Count the second Registration Fee field.
    - **d.** Sort in descending order by the summed RegistrationFee field.
    - **e.** Enter **2** in the Top Values list box to display the top two seminars in the datasheet.
    - **f.** Save the query as **Top 2 Seminars – Your Initials**, view, print, then close the datasheet without saving it.

2. **Create a parameter query.**
    - **a.** Create a new select query with the AttendeeLastName field from the Attendees table the RegistrationDate field from the Registration table, and the EventName field from the Events table.
    - **b.** Add the parameter criteria **Between [Enter Start Date:] And [Enter End Date:]** in the Criteria cell for the RegistrationDate field.
    - **c.** Specify an ascending sort order on the RegistrationDate field.
    - **d.** Click the Datasheet View button, then enter **5/1/03** as the start date and **5/31/03** as the end date in order to find everyone who has attended a seminar in May of the year 2003. You should view 6 records.
    - **e.** Save the query as **May Registration – Your Initials**, then print the datasheet.

3. **Modify query properties.**
    - **a.** Open the May Attendance – Your Initials query in Query Design View, open the property sheet for the query, change the Recordset Type property to Snapshot, then close the Query Properties dialog box.
    - **b.** Right-click the RegistrationDate field, then click Properties from the shortcut menu to open the Field Properties dialog box. Enter **Date of Registration** for the Caption property, change the Format property to Medium Date, then close the Field Properties dialog box.
    - **c.** View the datasheet for records between **5/1/03** and **5/31/03**. Print, save, then close the datasheet.

4. **Create an update query.**
    - **a.** Create a new select query, and select all the fields from the Registration table by double-clicking the Registration field list's title bar and dragging the selected fields to the query design grid.
    - **b.** Enter **>=5/1/03** in the Criteria cell for the RegistrationDate field to find those records in which the

RegistrationDate is on or after 5/1/03. View the datasheet. Observe and note the values in the RegistrationFee field. There should be six records.

c. In Query Design View, change the query to an update query, then enter **[RegistrationFee]+5** in the RegistrationFee field Update To cell in order to increase each value in that field by $5.

d. Run the query to update the six records.

e. Using the Query Type button, change the query back to a select query, then view the datasheet to make sure that the RegistrationFee fields were updated properly.

f. Save the query as **Registration Fee Update – Your Initials**, print, then close the datasheet.

5. Create a make-table query.

a. Create a new select query, and select all the fields from the Registration table by double-clicking the Registration field list's title bar and dragging the selected fields to the query design grid.

b. Enter **<=3/31/03** in the Criteria cell for the RegistrationDate field to find those records in which the RegistrationDate is on or before 3/31/00.

c. View the datasheet. There should be 15 records.

d. In Query Design View, change the query into a make-table query that creates a new table in the current database. Give the new table the name **1Qtr2003 – Your Initials**.

e. Run the query to paste 15 rows into the 1Qtr2003 – Your Initials table.

f. Close the make-table query without saving it, click Tables on the Objects bar, open the 1Qtr2003 – Your Initials table, view the 15 records, print the datasheet, then close it.

6. Create an append query.

a. Create a new select query, and select all the fields from the Registration table by double-clicking the Registration field list's title bar and dragging the selected fields to the query design grid.

b. Enter **>=4/1/03 and <=4/30/03** in the Criteria cell for the RegistrationDate field to find those records in which the RegistrationDate is in April, 2003.

c. View the datasheet. There should be one record.

d. In Query Design View, change the query into an append query that appends to the 1Qtr2003 – Your Initials table.

e. Run the query to append the row into the 1Qtr2003 – Your Initials table by clicking the Run button on the Query Design toolbar.

f. Close the append query without saving it.

g. Rename the 1Qtr2003 – Your Initials table to **Jan-Apr2003 –ß Your Initials**, open the datasheet (there should be 16 records), print it, then close it.

7. Create a delete query.

a. Create a new select query, and select all the fields from the Registration table by double-clicking the Registration field list's title bar and dragging the selected fields to the query design grid.

b. Enter **<5/1/03** in the Criteria cell for the RegistrationDate field to find those records in which the RegistrationDate is before May 1, 2003.

c. View the datasheet. There should be 16 records.

d. In Query Design View, change the query into a delete query.

e. Run the query to delete 16 records from the Registration table.

f. Close the query without saving it.

g. Open the Registration table in Datasheet View to confirm that there are only six records, then close it.

8. **Specify join properties.**
   a. Create a new select query with the following fields: AttendeeFirstName and AttendeeLastName from the Attendees table, and RegistrationFee from the Registration table.
   b. Double-click the link between the Attendees and Registration tables to open the Join Properties dialog box. Click the option button to include ALL records from Attendees and only those records from Registration where the joined fields are equal.
   c. View the datasheet, add your own first and last name as the last record, but do not enter anything in the RegistrationFee field for your record.
   d. Print the datasheet, save the query with the name **Registration Fee List**, then close the datasheet.
   e. Close the Seminar-K database, then exit Access.

▶ Independent Challenge 1

As the manager of a college women's basketball team, you want to create several queries using the Basketball-K database.
   a. Start Access, then open the **Basketball-K** database from the drive and folder where your Project Files are located.
   b. Open the Player Stats query in Query Design View, then enter **Between [Enter start date:] and [Enter end date:]** in the Criteria cell for the Date field.
   c. View the datasheet for all of the records between **1/1/2003** and **12/31/2003**. There should be 18 records.
   d. Use the Save As option on the File menu to save the query with the name **2003 – Your Initials**, then print the datasheet.
   e. In Query Design View of the 2003 – Your Initials query, sort the records in descending order on the TotalPts field, then use the **5%** Top Values option.
   f. View the datasheet for all of the records between **1/1/2003** and **12/31/2003**. There should be two records.
   g. Use the Save As option on the File menu to save the query with the name **2003 – Top 5% – Your Initials**. Print, then close the datasheet.
   h. Open the Victories query in Query Design View, then add a new calculated field as the fifth field with the following field name and expression: **Win%:[Home Score]/[Opponent Score]**
   i. View the datasheet to make sure that the Win% field calculates properly. Because the home score is generally greater than the opponent score, most values will be greater than 1.
   j. In Query Design View, click the Win% field, click the Properties button, change the Format property of the Win% field to Percent and the Decimal Places property to **0**.
   k. View the datasheet, use the Save As feature to save the query as **Victories – Your Initials**, print, then close it.
   l. Close Basketball-K database, then exit Access.

▶ Independent Challenge 2

As the manager of a college women's basketball team, you want to enhance the Basketball-K database and need to create several action queries using the Basketball-K database.
   a. Start Access, then open the **Basketball-K** database from the drive and folder where your Project Files are located.
   b. Create a new select query, and select all the fields from the Stats table by double-clicking the field list's title bar and dragging the selected fields to the query design grid.
   c. Add criteria to find all of the records with the GameNo field equal to **1**, **2**, or **3**, then view the datasheet. There should be 18 records.
   d. In Query Design View, change the query to a make-table query to paste the records into a table in the current database called **123 – Your Initials**.

e. Run the query to paste the 18 rows, then close the query without saving it.

f. Open the datasheet for the 123 – Your Initials table, then print it.

g. Create another new select query that includes all of the fields from the Stats table by double-clicking the field list's title bar and dragging the selected fields to the query design grid.

h. Add criteria to find all of the statistics for those records with the GameNo field equal to 4 or 5, then view the datasheet. There should be 12 records.

i. In Query Design View, change the query to an append query to append the records to the 123 – Your Initials table.

j. Run the query to append the 12 rows, then close the query without saving it.

k. Rename the 123 – Your Initials table to **12345 – Your Initials**, open the datasheet, then print it. There should be 30 records.

l. Close the 12345 – Your Initials table, close the Basketball-K database, then exit Access.

► Independent Challenge 3

As the manager of a college women's basketball team, you want to query the Basketball-K database to find specific information about each player.

a. Start Access, then open the **Basketball-K** database from the drive and folder where your Project Files are located.

b. Create a new select query in Query Design View using the Players and Stats tables.

c. Double-click the linking line to open the Join Properties dialog box, then change the join properties to include ALL records from Players and only those from Stats where the joined fields are equal.

d. Add the First and Last fields from the Players table, and the Assists fields from the Stats table.

e. Type **is null** in the Criteria cell for the Assists field, then view the datasheet to find those players who have never recorded an Assist value in the Stats table. There should be seven records.

f. Add your name as the last record, but do not enter an Assists value for this record.

g. Print the datasheet, save the query as **Redshirts**, then close the datasheet.

h. Close Basketball-K, then exit Access.

Ⓔ Independent Challenge 4

Your culinary club is collecting information on international chocolate factories and museums, and has asked you to help build a database to organize the information.

a. Start Access, then open the **Chocolate-K** database from the drive and folder where your Project Files are located.

b. Open the Places of Interest report, then print it.

c. Connect to the Internet, then go to a search engine such as www.google.com or www.about.com to search for information about international chocolate factories and museums. Or, you might look for information by going directly to a chocolate company's home page and searching for places to visit from there. Your goal is to find a Web page with information about an international chocolate factory or museum to add to the existing database, and to print that Web page.

d. Using the Countries form, add the record you found on the World Wide Web to the database, then close the Countries form.

e. Open the Places of Interest query in Query Design View, double-click the link line between the Countries and ChocolatePlaces tables, then choose option 2, which includes ALL records from the Countries table.

f. Open the Places of Interest report in Report Design View, add your name as a label to the header, preview, then print the report. On the printout, circle the record you added to the database. On the printout, circle any countries that do NOT have any related records in the ChocolatePlaces table.

g. Close the Places of Interest report, close Chocolate-K, then exit Access.

Access 2002

▶ Visual Workshop

As the manager of a college women's basketball team, you want to create a query from the **Basketball-K** database with the fields from the Players and Stats tables as shown. The query is a parameter query that prompts the user for a start and end date. Figure K-21 shows the datasheet where the start date of 1/1/03 and end date of 1/31/03 are used. Save and name the query **Offense – Your Initials**, then print the datasheet.

FIGURE K-21

Query1 : Select Query

First	Last	FG	3P	FT	Date
Lindsey	Swift	3	2	1	1/2/2003
Ellyse	Howard	3	0	1	1/2/2003
Amy	Hodel	0	0	1	1/2/2003
Denise	Franco	4	1	3	1/2/2003
Megan	Hile	1	2	1	1/2/2003
Morgan	Tyler	3	0	3	1/2/2003
Lindsey	Swift	4	2	3	1/5/2003
Ellyse	Howard	4	0	4	1/5/2003
Amy	Hodel	2	0	5	1/5/2003
Denise	Franco	1	2	1	1/5/2003
Megan	Hile	1	0	1	1/5/2003
Morgan	Tyler	1	0	5	1/5/2003
Lindsey	Swift	4	2	3	1/9/2003
Ellyse	Howard	4	1	3	1/9/2003
Amy	Hodel	2	1	5	1/9/2003
Denise	Franco	5	1	1	1/9/2003

Record: 1 of 18

Unit
L

Creating
Advanced Forms and Reports

Objectives

- ▶ **Add check boxes and toggle buttons**
- ▶ **Use conditional formatting in a form**
- ▶ **Create custom Help**
- ▶ **Add tab controls**
- ▶ **Add charts**
- ▶ **Modify charts**
- ▶ **Add subreport controls**
- ▶ **Modify section properties**

Advanced controls such as tab controls, charts, and subreports are powerful communication tools. Conditional formatting allows you to highlight exceptional information within a form or report to more clearly present key information. Using these advanced features to enhance forms and reports improves the value of your database. Fred Ames, coordinator of training at MediaLoft, wants to enhance existing forms and reports to more professionally and clearly present the information. Fred will use form and report controls such as check boxes, conditional formatting, tab controls, charts, and subreports to improve the forms and reports in the Training-L database.

Adding Check Boxes and Toggle Buttons

A **check box** control is often used to display the value of a Yes/No field on a form or report. A check box can appear in only one of two ways: checked or unchecked. A check means "Yes," and the absence of a check means "No." It is much easier to answer Yes/No questions on a form by clicking a check box rather than typing the word "Yes" in a text box. A **toggle button** control can also display the value of a Yes/No field. You click a toggle button to change the value from "No" to "Yes" just like a check box. When a toggle button appears indented or pushed in, it means "Yes," and when appears raised or not pushed in, it means "No." By default, Access represents any field with a Yes/No data type as a check box control on a form, regardless of whether the field was added to the form through the Form Wizard, AutoForm options, or in Form Design View. Fred would like to improve the visual appeal of the Employee Course Attendance form and Attendance Subform.

Steps

1. Open the **Training-L** database, click **Forms** on the Objects bar, then double-click the **Employee Course Attendance form**
   The form opens in Form View. The Attendance Subform is presented as a datasheet.

2. Click the **Design View button** 📝 on the Form View toolbar, then maximize the Employee Course Attendance form
   Your screen should look like Figure L-1. To change the appearance of the controls on the subform, you must change the **Default View** property for the form from Datasheet (which allows no special formatting) to Continuous Forms.

Trouble?

If the subform appears as a white rectangle, click the Form View button 📄, then click the Design View button to refresh the screen.

3. Click the **subform** to select it, double-click the subform's **Form Selector button**, click the **Format tab** (if not already selected) on the Form property sheet, click **Datasheet** in the Default View property, click the **Default View list arrow**, then click **Continuous Forms**

4. Click the **Properties button** 📋 on the Form Design toolbar, then click the **Form View button** 📄 on the Form Design toolbar
   Because of the change to the subform's Default View property, the subform displays the records as continuous forms, the way they also appear in Form Design View, rather than as a datasheet.

5. Click 📝 on the Form View toolbar, right-click the **Passed check box** in the subform, point to **Change To**, then click **Toggle Button**
   Table L-1 provides more information on which controls are interchangeable.

6. Point to the **middle-right resize handle** on the toggle button, drag ↔ to the right edge of the form, click the **toggle button**, type **Passed the test?**, then click 📄
   Your screen should look similar to Figure L-2. You also can change the text displayed on the button using the Caption property on the Format tab in the toggle button's property sheet.

7. Click the **Save button** 💾 on the Form View toolbar
   The changes are saved to the Employee Course Attendance form and the Attendance Subform.

8. Close the Employee Course Attendance form

FIGURE L-1: Form and subform in Form Design View

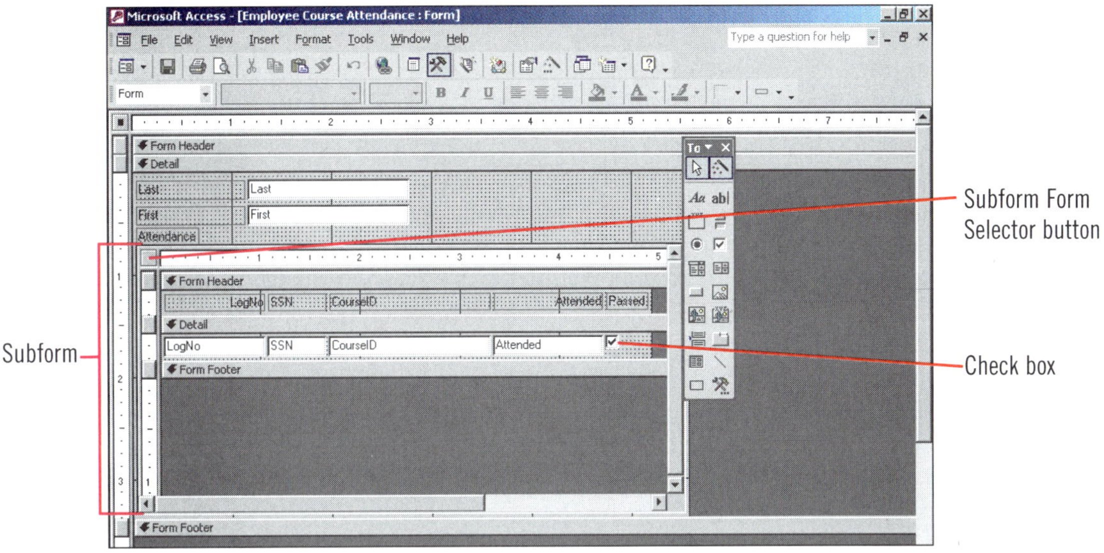

Subform Form
Selector button

Check box

Subform

FIGURE L-2: Toggle buttons displaying "Yes" and "No" values

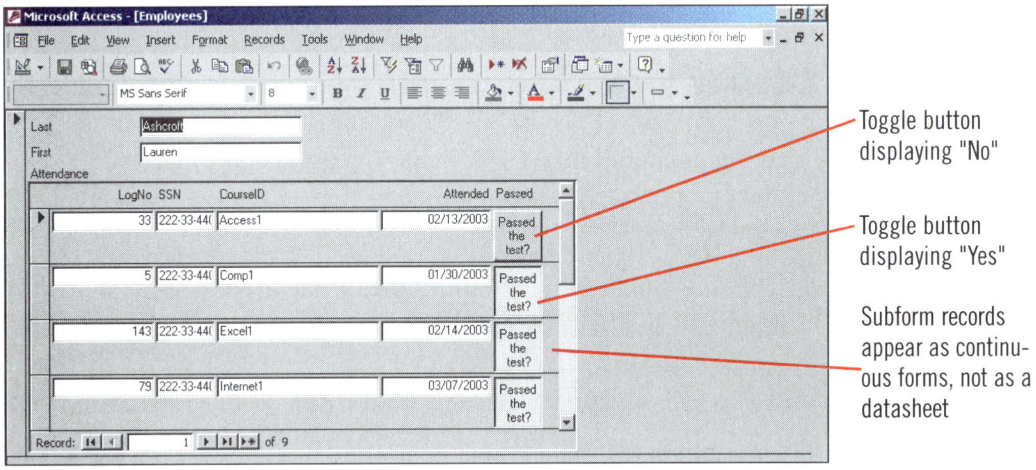

Toggle button
displaying "No"

Toggle button
displaying "Yes"

Subform records
appear as continu-
ous forms, not as a
datasheet

TABLE L-1: Interchangeable bound controls

control	Toolbox toolbar button	can be interchanged with	used most commonly when the field has
Text box	abl	List box, combo box	An unlimited number of choices such as a Price, LastName, or Street field
List box		Text box, combo box	A limited number of predefined values such as a Manager, Department, or State field
Combo box		Text box, list box	A limited number of common values, yet you still need the ability to enter a new value from the keyboard, such as a City field
Check box	✓	Toggle button, option button	Only two values, "Yes" or "No," such as a Veteran field
Option button	●	Check box, toggle button	A limited number of values, such as "female" or "male" for a Gender field; most commonly used with an option group that can contain several option buttons, each representing a possible value for the field
Toggle button		Check box, option button	Only two values, "Yes" or "No," and you want the appearance of the field to look like a button

Using Conditional Formatting in a Form

Conditional Formatting can be used to determine the appearance of a field on a form or report based on its value, a value in another field, or when the field has the focus. **Focus** is when a field can receive user input through the keyboard or mouse. Conditional formatting also provides a way to alert the user to exceptional situations as data is being entered or reported. Format changes include changing the text color, background color, or style of the control. If you conditionally format a control based on a value in another field, you must use an **expression**, which contains a combination of field names, operators, and values that calculate an answer. ✎ The users of the Courses form (which includes the Course-Employee Subform) would like Fred to modify the form so that they can quickly identify those course attendees with the title of "Salesperson." Additionally, Fred uses conditional formatting to more clearly show which text box has the focus.

Steps

Trouble?

If the subform appears as a white rectangle, click the Form View button 🖼, then click the Design View button 🖼 to refresh the screen.

1. Double-click the **Courses form**, view the overall layout of the form and subform, then click the **Design View button** 🖼 on the Form View toolbar

   The main form provides four fields of information about the course, and the subform represents each person who attended the course.

2. Click the **subform** to select it, click the **subform vertical ruler** to the left of the Last text box to select all four text boxes in the Detail section of the subform, click **Format** on the menu bar, then click **Conditional Formatting**

   The Conditional Formatting dialog box opens. The first condition will highlight the field with the focus.

3. Click the **Condition 1 Field Value Is list arrow**, click **Field Has Focus**, click the **Condition 1 Fill/Back Color list arrow** 🎨, then click **bright yellow** (fourth row, third box from the left)

   The second condition will highlight which attendees have the title of "Salesperson."

QuickTip

You can include up to three conditions in the Conditional Formatting dialog box.

4. Click **Add** in the Conditional Formatting dialog box, click the **Condition 2 Field Value Is list arrow**, click **Expression Is**, press [Tab], type **[Title]="Salesperson"**, click the **Condition 2 Bold button** 🅱, click the **Condition 2 Font/Fore Color list arrow** 🅰, then click **bright red** (third row, first box from the left)

   Your screen should look like Figure L-3. When an expression is used in the Conditional Formatting dialog box, the expression must evaluate to be either "true," which turns the formatting on, or "false," which turns the formatting off.

5. Click **OK**, click the **Form View button** 🖼 on the Form Design toolbar, then click **Lee** (the value in the Last field for the first record) in the subform

   Your screen should look like Figure L-4.

6. Press [Tab] three times to move the focus to the Salesperson entry for the first record, type **Sales Manager**, then press [Tab]

   Your screen should look like Figure L-5, in which the values in the first record in the subform are no longer red and boldface. Conditional formatting reverts to default formatting if the condition is no longer true.

7. Save, then close the Courses form

FIGURE L-3: Conditional Formatting dialog box

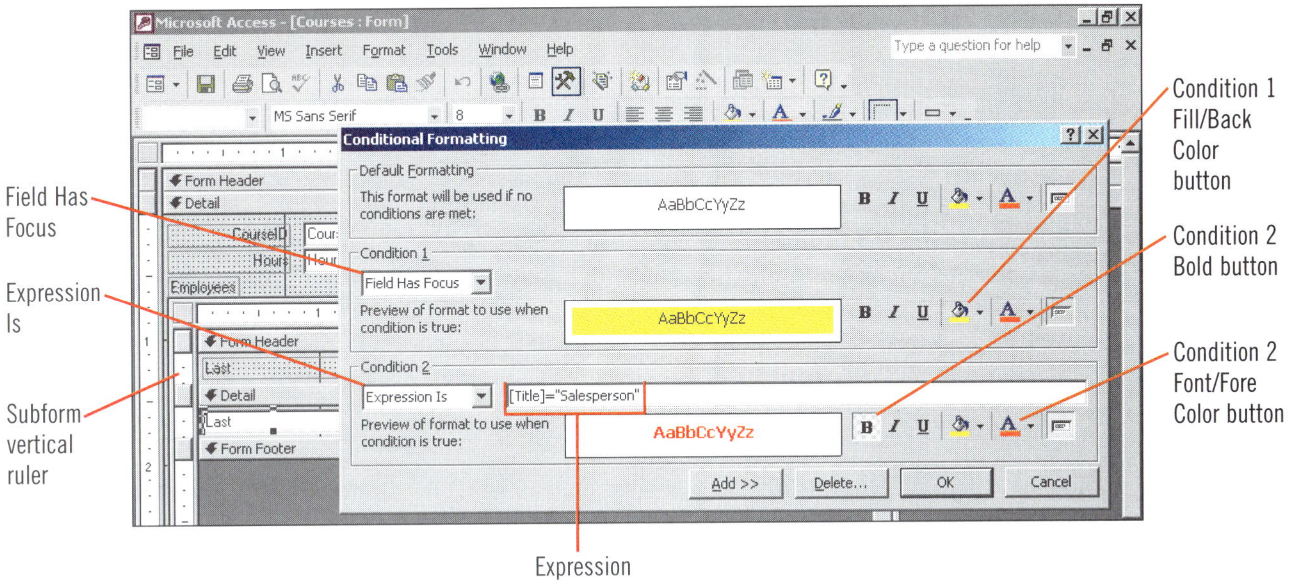

Field Has Focus

Expression Is

Subform vertical ruler

Condition 1 Fill/Back Color button

Condition 2 Bold button

Condition 2 Font/Fore Color button

Expression

FIGURE L-4: The control with the focus has a bright yellow back color

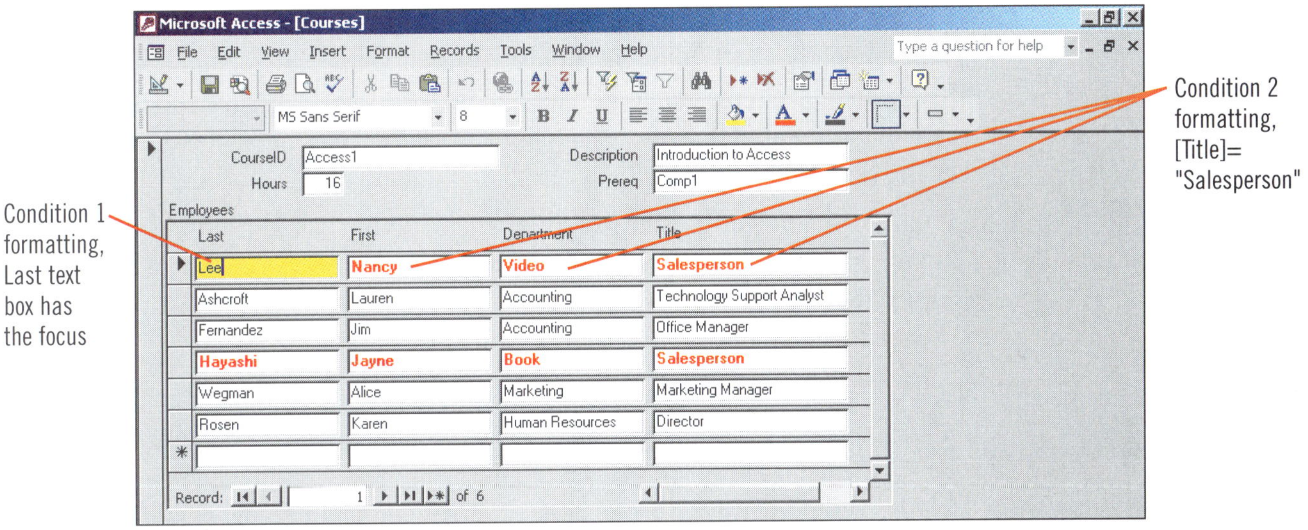

Condition 1 formatting, Last text box has the focus

Condition 2 formatting, [Title]= "Salesperson"

Last	First	Department	Title
Lee	Nancy	Video	Salesperson
Ashcroft	Lauren	Accounting	Technology Support Analyst
Fernandez	Jim	Accounting	Office Manager
Hayashi	Jayne	Book	Salesperson
Wegman	Alice	Marketing	Marketing Manager
Rosen	Karen	Human Resources	Director

FIGURE L-5: Conditional formats change as data is edited

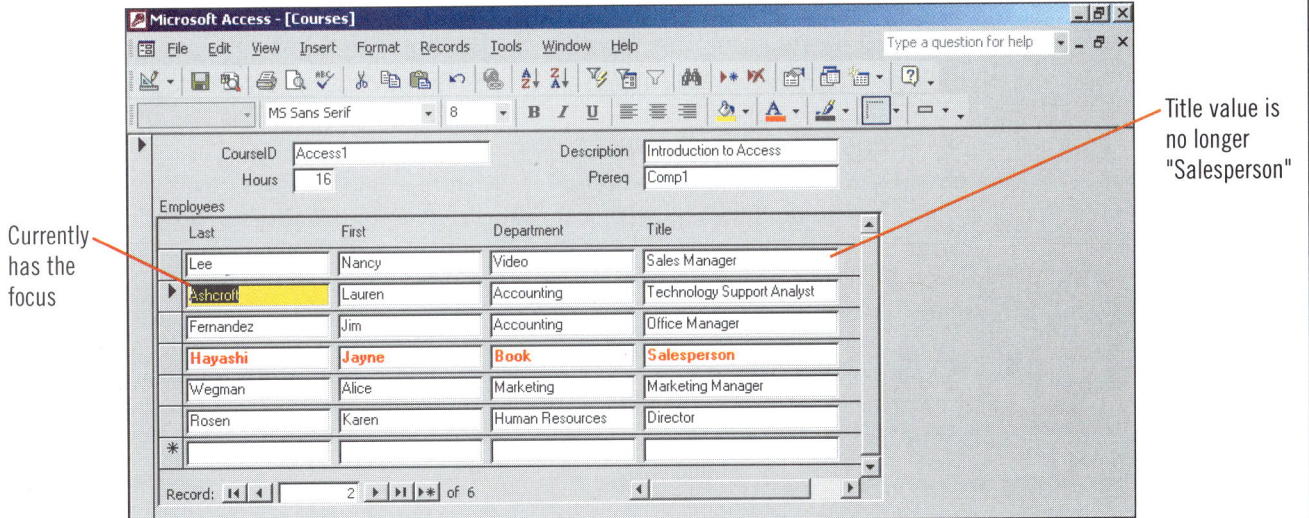

Currently has the focus

Title value is no longer "Salesperson"

Last	First	Department	Title
Lee	Nancy	Video	Sales Manager
Ashcroft	Lauren	Accounting	Technology Support Analyst
Fernandez	Jim	Accounting	Office Manager
Hayashi	Jayne	Book	Salesperson
Wegman	Alice	Marketing	Marketing Manager
Rosen	Karen	Human Resources	Director

Access 2002

Creating Custom Help

You can create several types of custom Help for a form or a control on a form. If you want to display a textual tip that pops up over a control when you point to it, use the **ControlTip Text** property for that control. Or use the **Status Bar Text** property to display helpful information about a form or control in the status bar. ✎ Fred wants to allow other users to enter new course records as those courses become available. He quickly creates a new form based on the Courses table, then adds custom Help to guide the new users as they enter the data.

Steps 1234

Trouble?

The AutoForm tool uses the same AutoFormat that was chosen during the Form Wizard process. Therefore, your form may not have a standard AutoFormat as shown in the figures.

1. Click the **New button** in the Database window toolbar, click **AutoForm: Columnar**, click the **Choose the table or query where the object's data comes from list arrow**, click **Courses**, then click **OK**
   The Courses form is created. You can modify the ControlTip Text and Status Bar Text properties for text boxes and other bound controls in Form View.

2. Click **View** on the menu bar, click **Properties**, click the **Other tab** in the Text Box: CourseID property sheet, click the **ControlTip Text property text box**, type **Use a 1 suffix for an introductory course**, press **[Enter]**, then point to the **CourseID text box**
   A control tip pops up, as shown in Figure L-6. You can view and enter long entries using the Zoom dialog box.

QuickTip

Click a property, then press [Shift][F2] to open the Zoom dialog box for that property.

3. Right-click the **ControlTip Text property**, click **Zoom**, click to the right of the word **"course"** in the Zoom dialog box, press **[Spacebar]**, then type **and a 2 suffix for an intermediate course**
   The Zoom dialog box should look like Figure L-7.

4. Click **OK**, then click **Comp1** in the Prereq text box
   The property sheet now shows the properties for the Prereq text box (even though the title bar still shows Text Box: CourseID).

QuickTip

Click a property, then press [F1] to open the Microsoft Access Help window for the specific explanation of that property.

5. Click the **Status Bar Text text box** in the Text Box: Prereq property sheet
   When the property sheet is open, a short description of the selected property appears in the status bar.

6. Type **Comp1 can be waived by achieving an 80% score on the Computers 101 test**, close the property sheet, then point to the **CourseID text box**
   Your screen should look like Figure L-8. The status bar displays the entry in the Status Bar Text property for the Prereq text box because the Prereq text box has the focus. The ControlTip Text for the CourseID text box is displayed because you are pointing to the CourseID text box. Unbound controls such as labels do not have a Status Bar Text property because they cannot have the focus, but a label can display ControlTip Text. To modify the ControlTip Text property for a label or other unbound control, you must be able to first select the control to access its property sheet. To select an unbound control, you must work in Form Design View.

7. Click the **Save button** on the Form View toolbar, type **Course Entry** in the Form Name text box, click **OK**, then close the Courses Entry form

FIGURE L-6: Using the ControlTip Text property

ControlTip Text

Other tab

Text Box: CourseID property sheet

ControlTip Text property

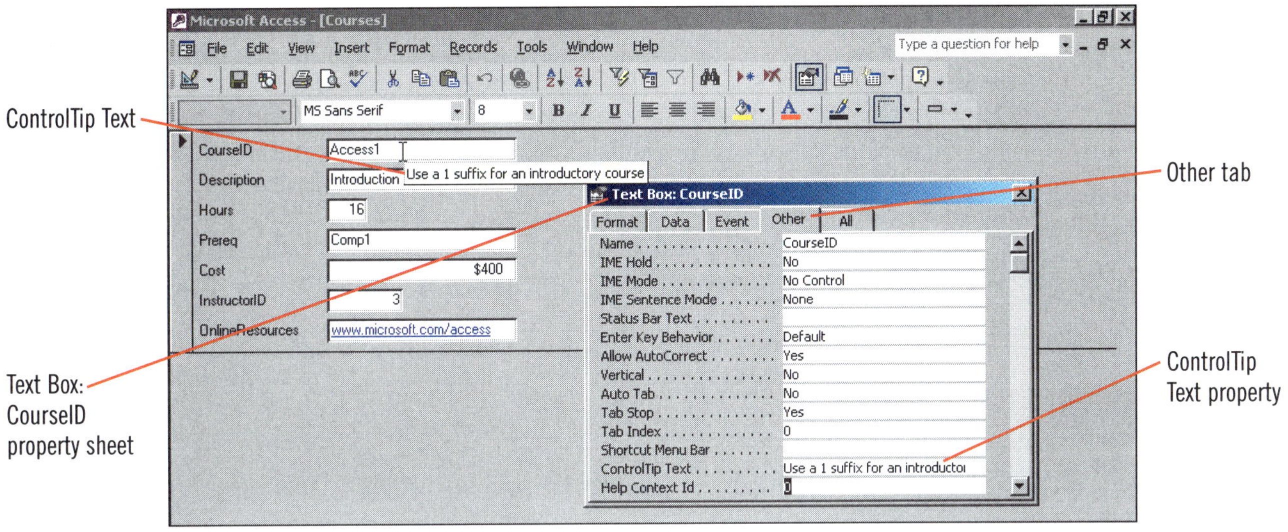

FIGURE L-7: Zoom dialog box

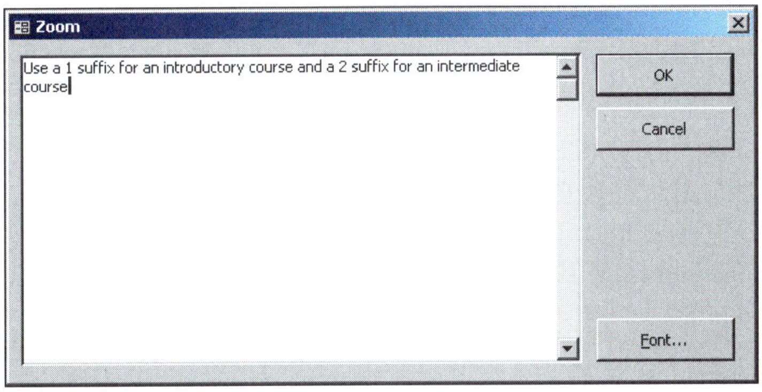

FIGURE L-8: Using the Status Bar Text property

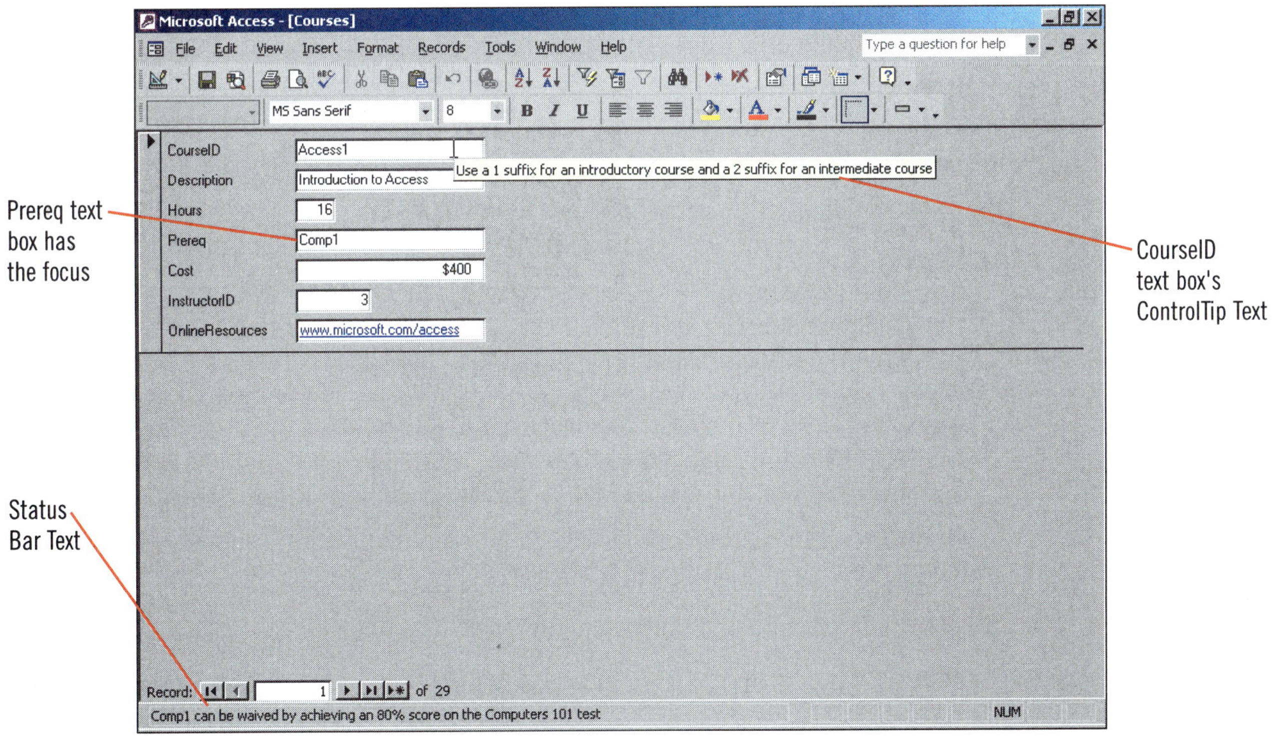

Prereq text box has the focus

CourseID text box's ControlTip Text

Status Bar Text

Access 2002

Adding Tab Controls

The **tab control** is a powerful unbound control used to organize the controls on a form and to give the form a three-dimensional look. You are already familiar with using tab controls because you have used them in many Access dialog boxes such as the property sheet. The property sheet uses tab controls to organize properties identified by their category name such as Format, Data, Event, Other, and All. ✍ Fred created a form to be used for many employee update activities called Employee Update Form. He wants to add tab controls to the form to better organize and present some of the information.

Steps 1234

1. Right-click the **Employee Update Form**, click **Design View** on the shortcut menu, click the **Toolbox button** 🔧 to toggle the Toolbox on (if it is not already visible), click the **Tab Control button** 🗔 on the Toolbox toolbar, then click immediately below the **First text box** in the Detail section of the form
   Your screen should look like Figure L-9. By default, the tab control is added with two "pages," with the default names of Page17 and Page18, on the respective tabs.

QuickTip

To add more pages, right-click the tab control in Form Design View, then click Insert Page on the shortcut menu.

2. Double-click **Page17** to open its property sheet, click the **Other tab** (if it is not already selected), double-click **Page17** in the Name property text box, type **Personnel Info**, click the **Page18 tab** on the form, double-click **Page18** in the Name text box of the property sheet, type **Course Attendance**, then close the property sheet
   The tabs now describe the information they will organize, but you still need to add the appropriate controls to each page of the tab control.

QuickTip

The page will become dark gray when you are successfully adding control(s) to that page.

3. Click the **Personnel Info tab**, click the **Field List button** 🗔 on the Form Design toolbar to toggle it on (if it is not already visible), click **Department** in the field list, press and hold **[Shift]**, click **SSN** in the field list (you may have to scroll) to select all fields between the Department and SSN, release **[Shift]**, then drag the **highlighted fields** to the top middle area of the Personnel Info page
   Your screen should look similar to Figure L-10. The six fields are added to the Personnel Info page on the tab control.

Trouble?

The Control Wizards button 🔨 must be selected before you click the Subform/Subreport button 🗔 on the Toolbox toolbar in order to use the SubForm Wizard.

4. Click the **Course Attendance tab**, click the **Subform/Subreport button** 🗔 on the Toolbox toolbar, click the **Course Attendance page**, click **Yes** if prompted to install the wizard, click the **Use existing Tables and Queries** option button in the SubForm Wizard dialog box, click **Next**, click the **Select All Fields button** >>, click **Next**, click **Show Attendance for each record in Employees using SSN** (if not already selected), click **Next**, type **Attendance Info**, then click **Finish**
   You can add any type of control, even a subform control, to a tab control page.

5. Use ↔ to drag the left-middle and right-middle sizing handles of the subform to the edges of the main form, click the **Form View button** 🗔, click the **Course Attendance tab**, then maximize the Employee Update Form window
   Your screen should look similar to Figure L-11.

6. Save, then close the Employee Update Form

FIGURE L-9: Adding a tab control

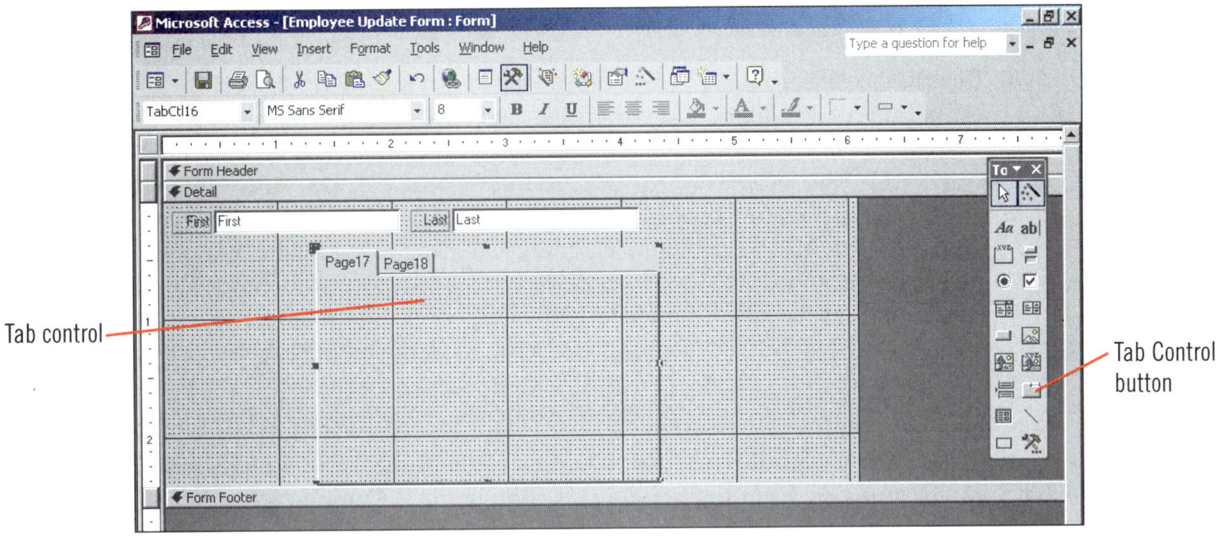

Tab control

Tab Control button

FIGURE L-10: Adding fields to a page on a tab control

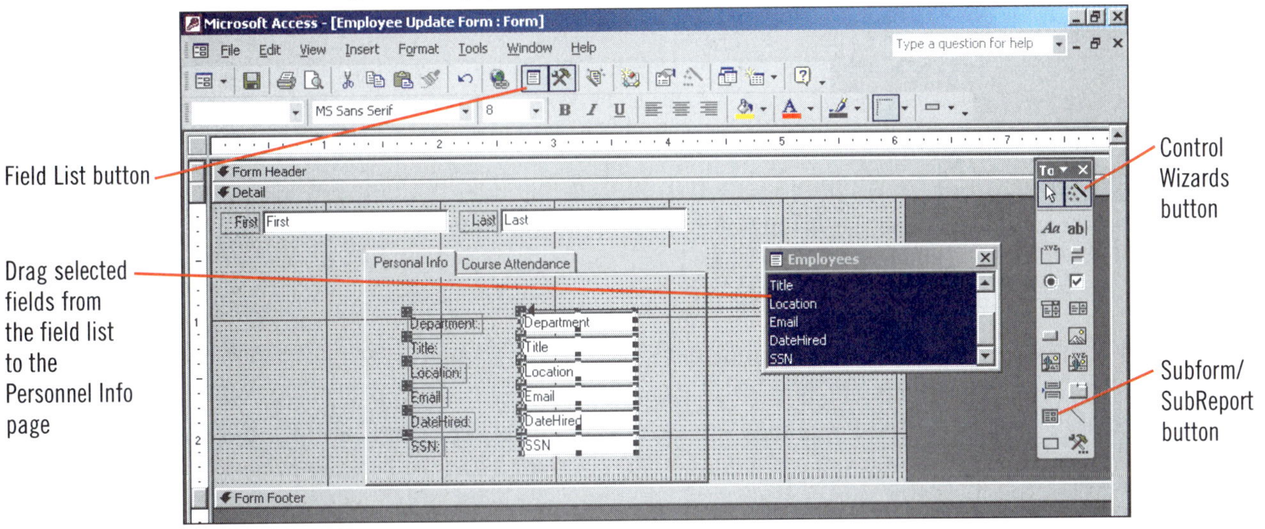

Field List button

Drag selected fields from the field list to the Personnel Info page

Control Wizards button

Subform/ SubReport button

FIGURE L-11: The tab control in Form View

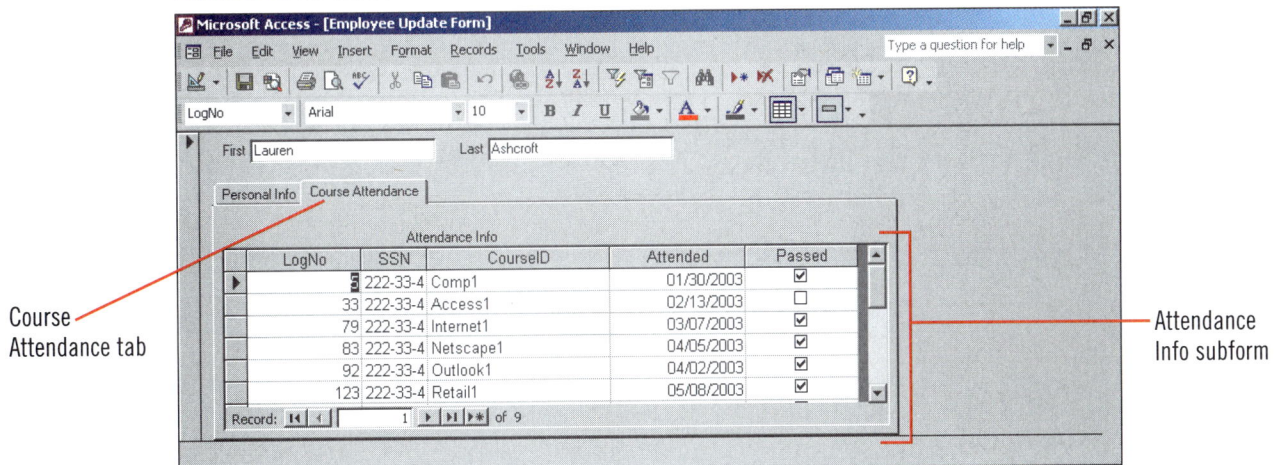

Course Attendance tab

Attendance Info subform

Access 2002

Adding Charts

Charts, also called graphs, are visual representations of numeric data that help users see comparisons, patterns, and trends in data. Charts can be inserted on a form, report, or data access page. Access provides a **Chart Wizard** that helps you with the process of creating the chart. Before using the Chart Wizard, however, you should determine what data you want the graph to show and what chart type you want to use. Table L-2 provides more information on common chart types. ✎ Fred created a Department Summary query with two fields: Attended from the Attendance table, and Department from the Employees table. Instead of reporting this information as a datasheet of values, he uses the Chart Wizard to graphically display both a total count of employees who attended internal MediaLoft courses, and a count of employees subtotaled by department.

Steps

1. Click **Reports** on the Objects bar, click the **New button** 🔳 in the database window toolbar, click **Chart Wizard**, click the **Choose the table or query where the object's data comes from list arrow**, click **Department Summary**, then click **OK**
The Chart Wizard starts and presents the fields in the Department Summary query.

QuickTip

Click any chart button to read a description of that chart in the lower-right corner of the Chart Wizard dialog box.

2. Click the **Select All Fields button** 🔳, then click **Next**
The Chart Wizard lists the chart types that you can create, as shown in Figure L-12. The Column Chart is the default chart type.

3. Click **Next**
The next dialog box determines which fields will be used for the x-axis, bar, and series (legend) areas of the chart. For this chart, you want the bars to represent a total count of number of values in the Attended field. The Department field should be used as x-axis labels.

QuickTip

Double-click a button in the Data area to change the way it is summarized.

4. Drag the **Attended field button** from the field buttons on the right to the **Data** area, then drag the **Attended by month button** from the Series area out of the chart area, as shown in Figure L-13
Because the Attended field holds date data, bars should count the number of entries.

Trouble?

Depending on the size of your chart, the scale on the y-axis, the labels on the x-axis, or the chart title may appear slightly different.

5. Click **Next**, type **Total Attendance by Department** as the title for your chart text box, then click **Finish**
Your chart should look similar to Figure L-14. The chart is difficult to read as it currently appears, but you can modify a chart in Design View to improve its appearance.

TABLE L-2: Common chart types

chart type	chart icon	most commonly used to show	example
Column	📊	Comparisons of values	Each bar represents the annual sales for a different product for the year 2003
Line	📈	Trends over time	Each point on the line represents monthly sales for one product for the year 2003
Pie 2003	🥧	Parts of a whole	Each slice represents total quarterly sales for a company for the year
Area	📉	Cumulative totals	Each section represents monthly sales by representative, stacked to show the cumulative total sales effort for the year 2003

FIGURE L-12: Chart types

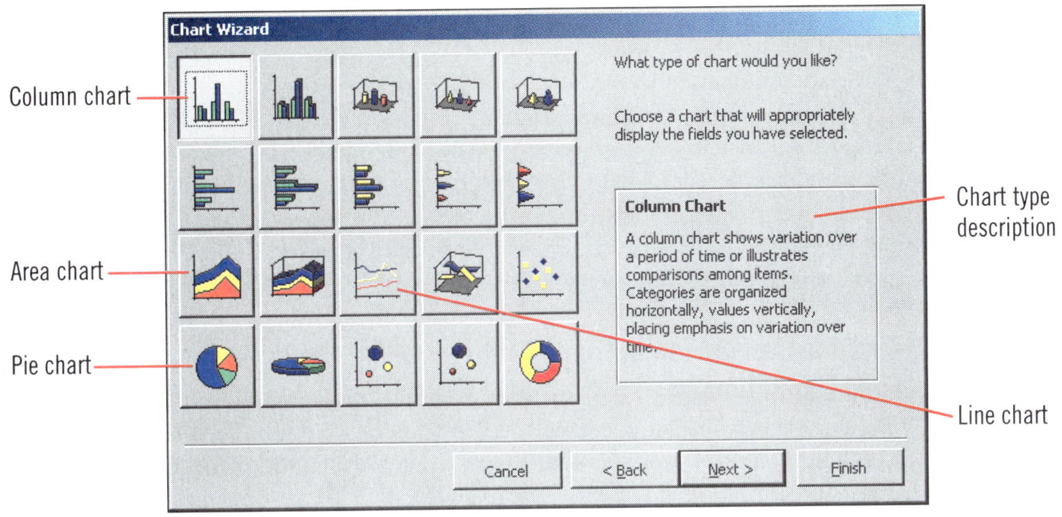

Column chart

Area chart

Pie chart

Chart type description

Line chart

FIGURE L-13: Determining chart layout

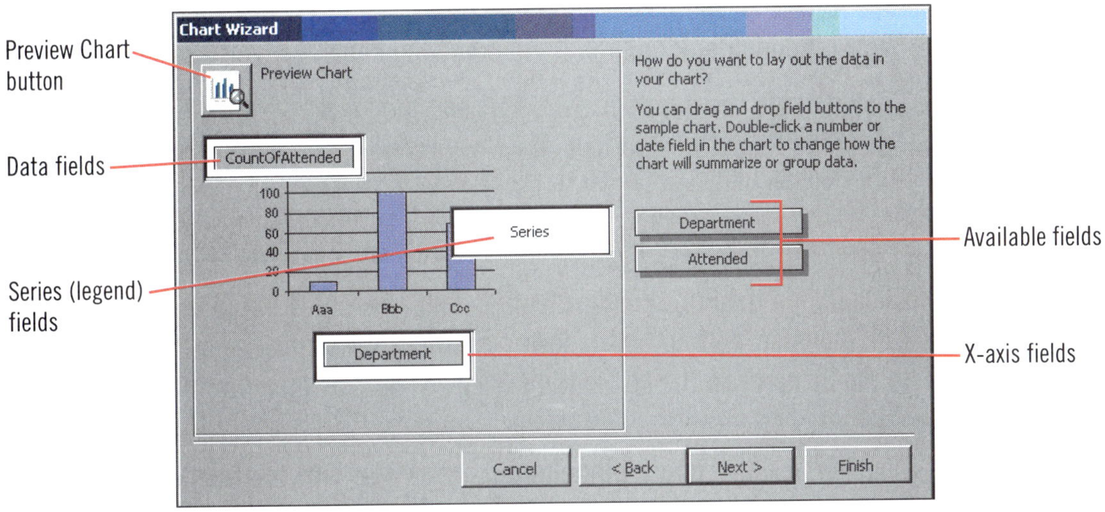

Preview Chart button

Data fields

Series (legend) fields

Available fields

X-axis fields

FIGURE L-14: Total Attendance by Department chart

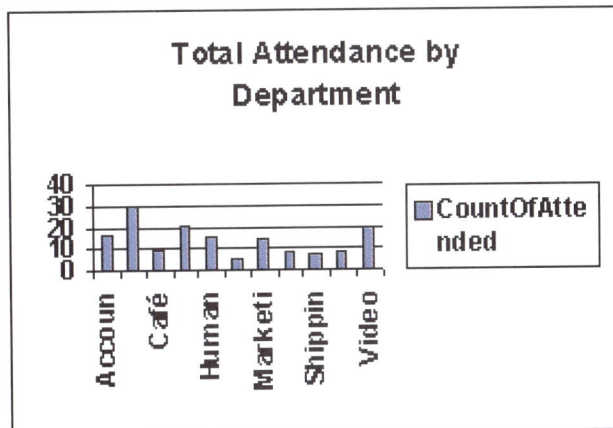

Modifying Charts

All charts are modified in Design View of the form or report that contains the chart. Modifying a chart is challenging because Design View doesn't show you the actual chart values, but instead, displays a chart placeholder that represents the embedded chart object. To modify the chart, you modify the chart placeholder. To view the changes as they apply to the real data you are charting, return to either Form View for a form, or Print Preview for a report. ✎ Fred wants to remove the legend and resize the chart to better display the values on the axes. He makes all modifications to the existing chart in Report Design View.

Steps 1 2 3 4

1. Click the **Design View button** 🖼, maximize the Report Design View window, click the **Field List button** 📋 to close it (if it's visible), then double-click the **chart** to edit it
   The chart is now ready to be edited, as shown in Figure L-15. The hashed border of the chart placeholder control indicates that the chart is in **edit mode**, and the Chart menu bar and Chart Standard toolbar appear. You can delete, move, or resize the chart object without being in edit mode, but if you want to modify any of the individual chart elements such as the title, legend, or axes, you must double-click the chart placeholder to open edit mode. In edit mode, you can select and then modify individual items within the chart. If you double-click the *edge* of the chart placeholder, you will open its property sheet instead of opening it in edit mode.

2. Click **Chart** on the menu bar, click **Chart Options**, click the **Legend tab**, click the **Show legend check box** to toggle it off, then click **OK**

3. Click **outside the chart** to exit Chart edit mode, then click the **Print Preview button** 🔍 on the Report Design toolbar
   Your chart should look similar to Figure L-16. Because the chart has only one series of bars, a clear title (rather than a legend) is used to describe the series. But most of the elements, including the x-axis labels and bars, are still too small to clearly display the information.

4. Click 🖼 on the Print Preview toolbar, click the **chart placeholder** to select the control, then use ⤡ to drag the **lower-right corner sizing handle** down and to the right to the **5"** mark on the horizontal ruler and the **3.5"** mark on the vertical ruler
   With the chart placeholder resized, you can expand the size of the chart within it.

5. Double-click the **chart placeholder**, click the **View Datasheet button** 📊 on the Chart Standard toolbar to toggle it off, then use ⤡ to drag the **lower-right corner sizing handle** of the Chart Area (identified by the hashed border) to just within the border of the chart placeholder
   Your chart should look similar to Figure L-17. You can modify any element such as the labels on the x-axis, also called the Category Axis, or the y-axis, also called the Value Axis, but you must select them before you change or format them.

6. Click the **East label** to select the entire Category Axis, click the **Font Size list arrow** ⏷, click **10**, click **outside the chart** to exit chart edit mode, then click 🔍 on the Report Design toolbar
   The final chart is shown in Figure L-18. It clearly shows that of all the departments, the Book Department has the most attendees at MediaLoft's internal training courses.

7. Click **File** on the menu bar, click **Save As**, type **Department Graph-Your Initials**, then click **OK**

8. Click the **Print button** 🖨 on the Print Preview toolbar, then close the Department Graph-Your Initials report

FIGURE L-15: Editing a chart in Design View

Chart menu bar

View Datasheet button

Hashed border

Chart datasheet

Chart Standard toolbar

Chart placeholder

FIGURE L-16: Chart still needs improvement

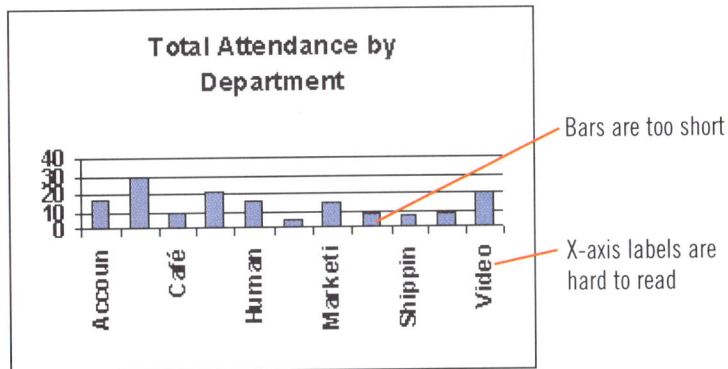

Total Attendance by Department

Bars are too short

X-axis labels are hard to read

FIGURE L-17: Increasing the chart size

View Datasheet button

3.5" mark on vertical ruler

5" mark on horizontal ruler

Sizing handle for Chart area

Sizing handle for chart object placeholder

FIGURE L-18: Final chart

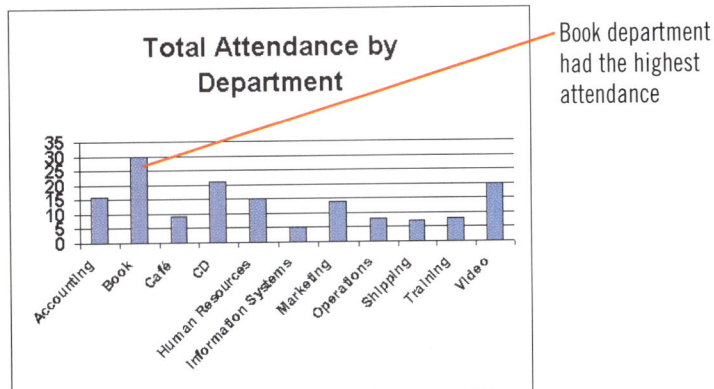

Total Attendance by Department

Book department had the highest attendance

Access 2002

Adding Subreport Controls

A **subreport** control displays a report within another report. The report that contains the subreport control is called the **main report**. You use the subreport control when you want to link two reports together to automate printing. You also can use a subreport control when you want to change the order in which information automatically prints. For example, if you want report totals (generally found in the Report Footer section, which prints on the last page) to print on the first page, you could use a subreport to present the grand total information, and place it in the main report's Report Header section, which prints first. ✎ Now that Fred has created the Department Graph report, he will add it as a subreport to the Department Enrollment report so that both reports are viewed and printed at the same time.

Steps 1 2 3 4

1. Right-click the **Department Enrollment** report, click **Design View** on the shortcut menu, scroll, point to the **bottom edge** of the report, then use ✛ to drag the bottom edge of the report down about **1"**
   You've expanded the size of the Report Footer section to make room for the subreport control.

2. Click the **Toolbox button** 🛠 on the Report Design toolbar to toggle it on (if it's not already visible), click the **Subform/Subreport button** ▦ on the Toolbox toolbar, then click below the **Grand Total label** in the Report Footer section
   The SubReport Wizard opens, as shown in Figure L-19.

3. Click the **Use an existing report or form option button**, click **Department Graph Report-Your Initials**, click **Next**, click **Finish** to accept the name **Department Graph-Your Initials** for the subreport, maximize the Report Design View window (if not already maximized), then scroll down to view the Report Footer section
   The subreport control appears in Report Design View, as shown in Figure L-20, and automatically expands the size of the Report Footer section to accommodate the large control.

4. Click the **Print Preview button** 🔍 on the Report Design toolbar, then click the **Last page button** ▶| on the navigation buttons
   Your screen should look like Figure L-21. The Report Footer section contains the subreport—the Department Graph–Your Initials report—which will now print on the last page of the Department Enrollment report.

   Trouble?

   If your report has a different total number of pages, to print the graph, replace 8 with the last page number for your report.

5. Click **File** on the menu bar, click **Print**, click the **Pages** option button, type **8** in the From: text box, press **[Tab]**, type **8** in the To: text box, then click **OK** to print the last page of the Enrollment Report

6. Close the Department Enrollment report, then click **Yes** to save the changes when prompted

FIGURE L-19: SubReport Wizard

Use an existing report or form

FIGURE L-20: Subreport in Report Design View

Report Footer section

Grand Total label

Subform/Subreport button

FIGURE L-21: Department graph displayed as a subreport

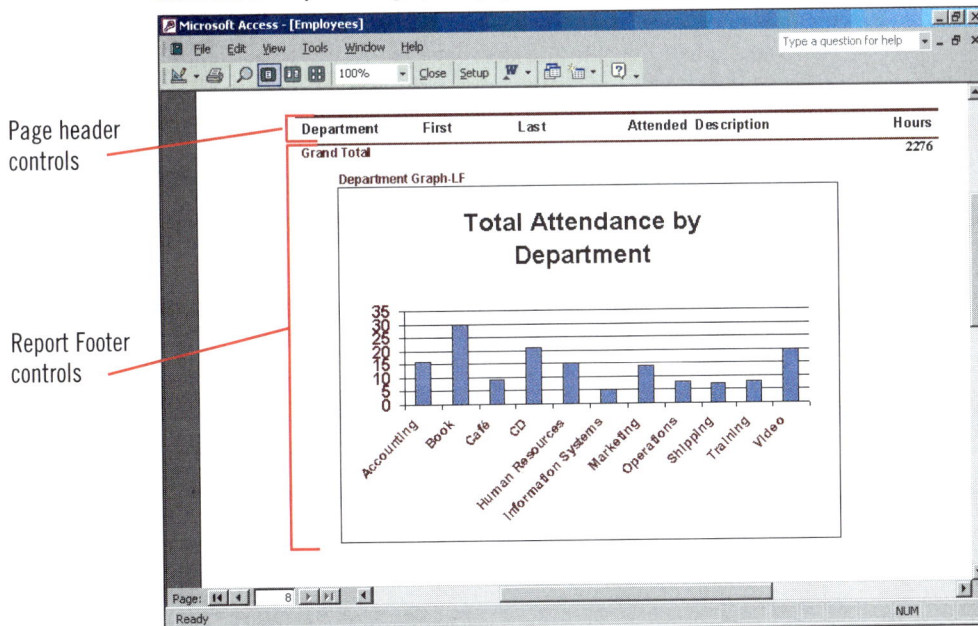

Page header controls

Report Footer controls

Access 2002

Modifying Section Properties

Report **section properties** can be modified to improve report printouts. For example, if the records on the report are grouped by the values in the Department field, you may want each new Department Header to print at the top of a new page. Or, you may want to modify section properties to format the section with color. For example, you could change the section's Back Color property to emphasize where the section appears on the printout. ✎ Fred wants to change the Department Enrollment report so that the records for each new department start at the top of a new page. He also wants to highlight Department Header and Department Footer sections by changing their Back Color property. He makes these section property changes in Report Design View.

Steps 123 4

1. Right-click the **Department Enrollment report**, click **Design View** on the shortcut menu, double-click the **Department Footer section** to open its property sheet, then click the **Format tab** in the property sheet
   The property sheet for the Department Footer section opens, as shown in Figure L-22.

2. Click the **Force New Page list arrow**, then click **After Section**
   This property change means that after the Group Footer prints, the rest of the report will continue at the top of the next page.

3. Click **16777215** in the Back Color property, click the **Back Color Build button** [...], click the **light yellow box** (second column on the top row), then click **OK**
   The Department Footer section will appear with a light yellow background color in Print Preview, as well as on the printout if a color printer is used.

4. Click the **Department Header section**, click **16777215** in the Back Color property, click [...], click the **light yellow box**, then click **OK**
   You formatted both the Department Header and Department Footer sections with the same light yellow background color.

5. Click the **Properties button** 🖭 on the Report Design toolbar to close the property sheet, click the **Print Preview button** 🔍, then click 🔍 to zoom out
   Your screen should look like Figure L-23. By modifying section color properties, you have clarified where each new department starts and stops. You have also forced the report to continue at the top of the next page after printing each Department Footer section.

6. Click the **Design View button** 🖾 on the Print Preview toolbar, click the **Label button** 🔠 on the Toolbox toolbar, click to the right of the **Department Enrollment label** in the Report Header section, type **your name**, then click the **Save button** 🖫 on the Report Design toolbar

7. Click **File** on the menu bar, click **Print**, click the **Pages option button**, type **1** in the From: text box, press **[Tab]**, type **1** in the To: text box, then click **OK**
   The first page of the Department Enrollment report is sent to the printer.

8. Close the **Department Enrollment** report, close **Training-L database**, then exit **Access**

FIGURE L-22: Using section properties

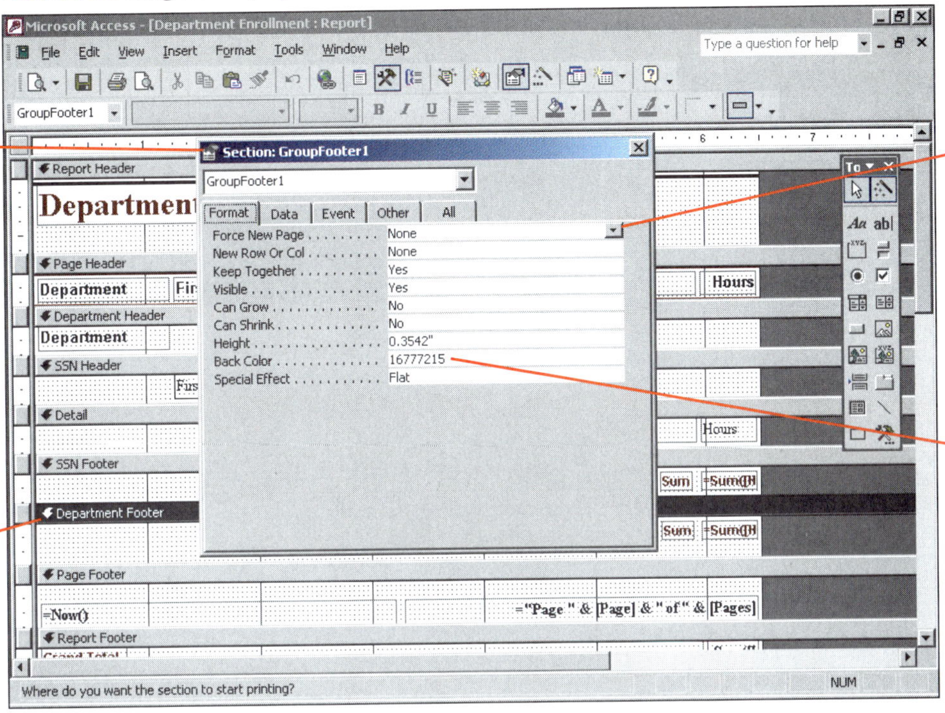
Section: GroupFooter1 property sheet
Force New Page list arrow
Back Color property
Department Footer section
Microsoft Access - [Department Enrollment : Report]
Section: GroupFooter1
Force New Page .... None
New Row Or Col .... None
Keep Together .... Yes
Visible .... Yes
Can Grow .... No
Can Shrink .... No
Height .... 0.3542"
Back Color 16777215
Special Effect .... Flat
Where do you want the section to start printing?

FIGURE L-23: Using section colors

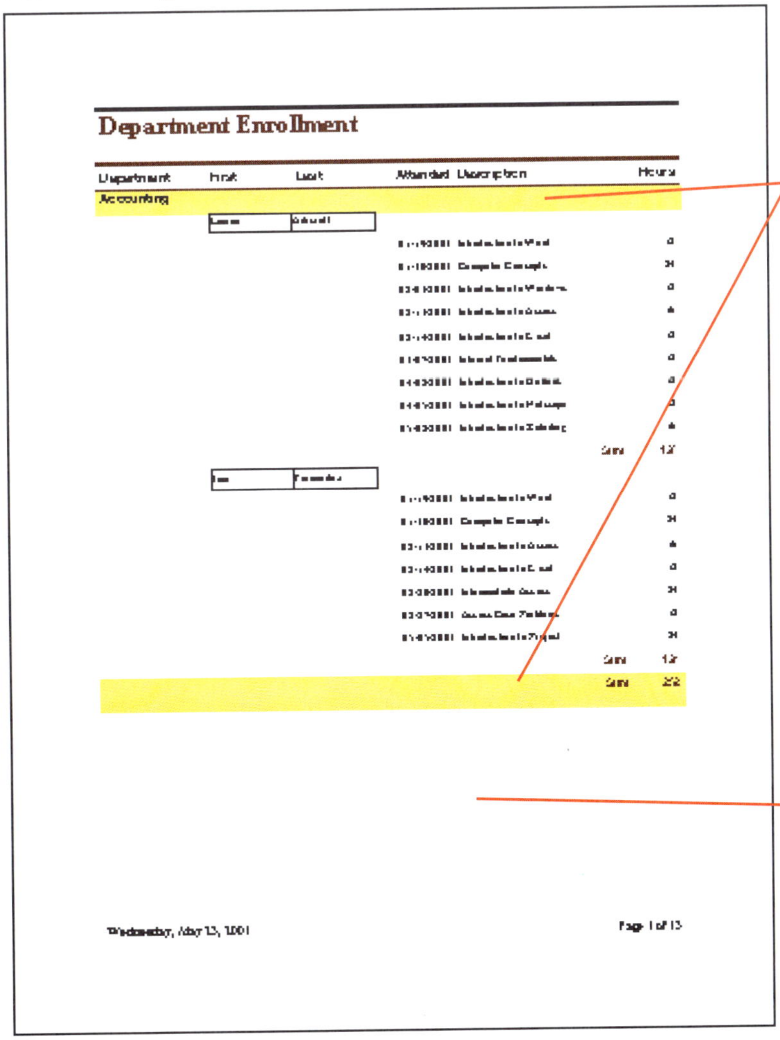
Department Enrollment
Department Header and Department Footer sections are formatted with a light yellow back color
report continues on a new page as soon as the Department Footer prints

Practice

▶ Concepts Review

Identify each element of the Report Design View shown in Figure L-24.

FIGURE L-24

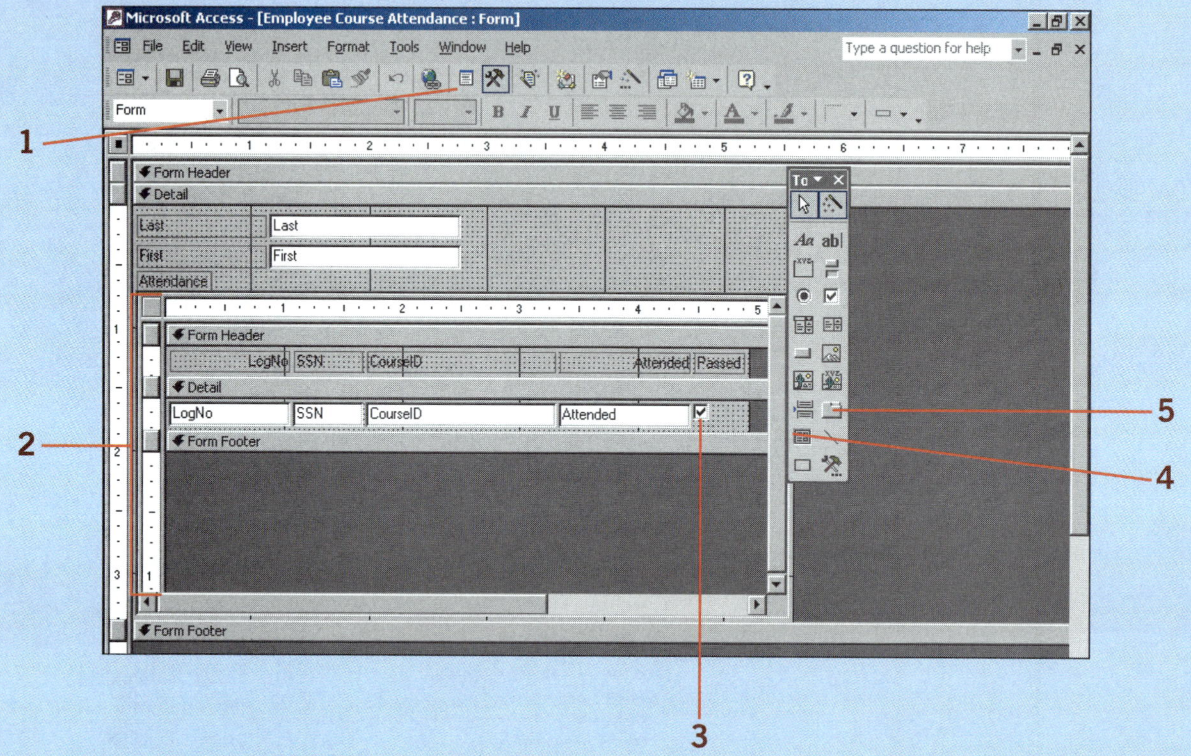

Match each term with the statement that describes its function.

6. **Focus**
7. **Tab control**
8. **Sections**
9. **Conditional formatting**
10. **Charts**
11. **Check box**

a. Allows you to change the appearance of a control on a form or report based on criteria you specify

b. Visual representations of numeric data

c. The ability to receive user input through the keyboard or mouse

d. Determine where and how controls print on a report

e. A control that is often used to display a Yes/No field on a form

f. An unbound control used to organize a form and give it a three-dimensional look

Select the best answer from the list of choices.

12. Which controls are NOT interchangeable?
  a. Text box and combo box
  b. Combo box and list box
  c. Check box and toggle button
  d. Check box and option group

13. When would you most likely use a toggle button control?
  a. For a field with a limited set of choices
  b. For a field with only two choices: Yes or No
  c. In place of a command button
  d. In place of an unbound label

14. Which control would be the best candidate for a City field?
  a. Toggle button
  b. Combo box
  c. Check box
  d. Command button

15. Which control property would you use to automatically display text when you point to a control?
  a. ControlTip Text
  b. Status Bar Text
  c. Popup Text
  d. Help Text

16. Which type of chart would be the best candidate to show an upward sales trend over several months?
  a. Pie
  b. Column
  c. Scatter
  d. Line

17. Which type of control would you use to combine two reports into one?
  a. Report Footer
  b. Subreport
  c. Calculated properties
  d. Main report

18. Which property would you use to force a new group of records to start printing at the top of the next page?
  a. Force New Page
  b. Subreport
  c. Visible
  d. Section Break

19. To modify a chart legend, you must open the chart in:
  a. Edit mode.
  b. Chart mode.
  c. Property mode.
  d. Design mode.

20. Which view do you use to add more pages to the tab control?
  a. Form Design View
  b. Form View
  c. Report Print Preview
  d. Page View

▶ Skills Review

1. Add check boxes and toggle buttons.
  a. Start Access, then open the **Seminar-L** database from the drive and folder where your Project Files are located.
  b. Open the Attendees form in Form View, then check the EarlyBirdDiscount check box for the first record in the subform of the first person, Phuong Pham.
  c. Open Design View of the Attendees form. If the subform appears as a white box, click the Form View button, then click the Design View button a second time to refresh the screen, which will display the controls within the subform.
  d. Maximize the form, then use the subform's Form Selector button to open its property sheet and change the Default View property of the subform to Continuous Forms. Close the property sheet.
  e. Change the EarlyBirdDiscount check box in the subform into a toggle button.
  f. Expand the height of the subform by dragging the lower-middle sizing handle for the subform down about two inches, then use the middle-right sizing handle for the EarlyBirdDiscount toggle button to widen it to the right edge of the subform.

g. Click the toggle button, then type the text **Early Bird Discount?**

h. View the form in Form View. The subform should be large enough to clearly display three or four records, as shown in Figure L-25. Use Form Design View to make modifications as needed.

i. Open the form in Form View, then click the toggle button to enter Yes in the EarlyBirdDiscount field for the second record in the subform for Phuong Pham.

j. Enter your own last name in place of Pham, then print only this record.

k. Save, then close the form.

FIGURE L-25

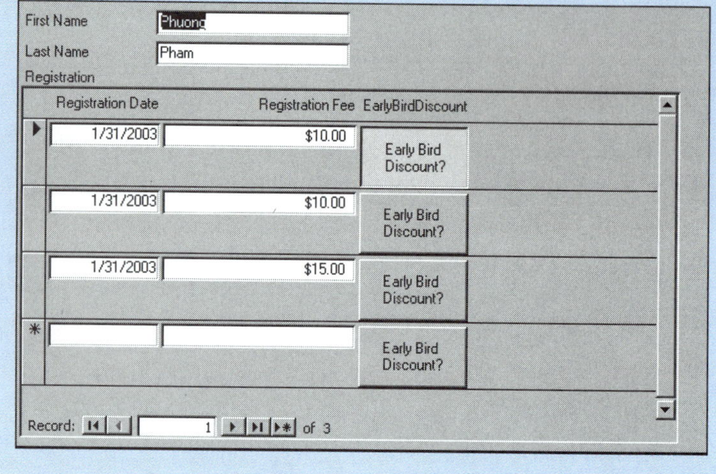

2. **Use conditional formatting in a form.**

a. Open the Attendees form in Design View. If the subform appears as a white box, click the Form View button, then click the Design View button again to refresh the screen and display the controls within the subform.

b. Click the RegistrationDate text box, then press and hold [Shift] while clicking the RegistrationFee text box to select both controls in the Detail section of the subform.

c. Click Format on the menu bar, click Conditional Formatting, set Condition 1 to Expression Is, then enter **[RegistrationFee]>10** as the criteria.

d. Apply a bold and blue Font/Fore Color for the Condition 1 format, then save the form.

e. Click the AttendeeFirstName text box, then press and hold [Shift] while clicking the AttendeeLastName text box control to select both controls in the Detail section of the main form.

f. Click Format on the menu bar, click Conditional Formatting, then set Condition 1 to Field Has Focus.

g. Apply a light blue Fill/Back color for the Condition 1 format, then save the form.

h. Display the form in Form View, then enter your own first name in place of Phuong in the first record.

i. Change the Registration Fee to **$11** for the first record in the subform, then tab through the record to make sure that both the RegistrationDate and RegistrationFee text boxes change format based on the new RegistrationFee.

j. Save the form, print the first record, then close the form.

3. **Create custom Help.**

a. Open the Attendees form in Design View.

b. Open the property sheet for the EarlyBirdDiscount toggle button, then select the Other tab.

c. Type **To qualify, registration must be one month before the event** for the ControlTip Text property. Use the Zoom dialog box to make this long entry, if desired.

d. Type **Discounts can also be given for group registrations** for the Status Bar Text property. Use the Zoom dialog box to make this long entry, if desired.

e. Close the property sheet, save the form, then open the form in Form View.

f. Point to the toggle button for the third record in the subform to make sure that the ControlTip Text property works.

g. Click the toggle button for the third record in the subform, then observe the status bar to make sure that the Status Bar Text property works.

h. Save, then close the Attendees form.

4. **Add tab controls.**
   a. Open the Events form in Design View.
   b. Add a tab control under the Event Name label.
   c. Modify the Page5 Name property of the first tab to be **Event Info**.
   d. Modify the Page6 Name property of the second tab to be **Participants**.
   e. Open the field list, then add the Location, Date, and AvailableSpaces fields from the field list to the middle of the Event Info page.
   f. Add a subform to the Participants page, using the SubForm Wizard to guide your actions. Click the Existing tables or queries option button in the SubForm Wizard, then select the RegistrationDate field from the Registration table, and the AttendeeFirstName and AttendeeLastName fields from the Attendees table.
   g. Link the main form to the subform by using the Show Registration for each record in Events using EventID option.
   h. Type **Registration** as the name of the subform.
   i. Expand the height and width of the subform control to use the existing room on the form, then view the form in Form View.
   j. Click the Participants tab to make sure both tabs work correctly, select Estate Planning and type **Your Name Seminar** (to uniquely identify your printout), then print the first record twice, once with the Event Info tab displayed and once with the Participants tab displayed.
   k. Save, then close the Events form.

5. **Add charts.**
   a. Click Reports on the Objects bar, then click the New button on the database window toolbar.
   b. Click the Chart Wizard option, and choose the Registration table for the object's data.
   c. Select the EventID and RegistrationFee as the fields from the Registration table for the chart.
   d. Choose a Column Chart type.
   e. Sum the RegistrationFee field in the Data area, and use the EventID field as the x-axis. (*Hint*: These should be the defaults, but click the Preview Chart button to verify these choices.)
   f. Type **Registration Fee Totals-Your Initials** for the chart title, then save it with the name **Registration Fee Totals**.

6. **Modify charts.**
   a. Open the Registration Fee Totals report in Design View.
   b. Double-click the chart to edit it.
   c. Remove the legend, then increase the size of both the control and the chart within it to as large as reasonably fits on your screen.
   d. Click any value in the y-axis to select it, click Format on the menu bar, then click the Number option.
   e. Click the Number tab in the Format Axis dialog box, click the Currency category, change the Decimal places text box to **0**, then click OK in the Format Axis dialog box.
   f. Click outside the chart object to return to Report Design View, preview the report, print it, save the changes, then close the Registration Fee Totals report.

7. **Add subreport controls.**
   a. Use the Report Wizard to create a report on all of the fields in the Events table.
   b. Do not add any grouping levels, but sort the records in ascending order by EventID.
   c. Use a Tabular layout, a Portrait orientation, and a Casual style.
   d. Type **Event Information** as the title for the report.
   e. Open Event Information in Report Design View, then open the Report Footer section by dragging the bottom edge of the report down about one inch.
   f. Add a subreport control to the upper-left part of the Report Footer section.
   g. Use the SubReport Wizard to guide your actions in creating the subreport. Use the existing Registration Fee Totals report for the subreport, and accept the name **Registration Fee Totals** for the subreport name.
   h. Preview the report, print it, save, then close the Event Information report.

8. Modify section properties.

    a. Use the Report Wizard to create a report on all of the fields in the Registration table, as well as the EventName field in the Events table.

    b. View the data by Events, but do not add any more grouping or sorting fields.

    c. Use an Outline 2 layout, a Landscape orientation, and a Compact style.

    d. Type **Event Details** for the report title.

    e. Open Event Details in Design View, then open the property sheet for the Events_EventID Header section.

    f. Change the Force New Page property on the Format tab to Before Section. Change the Back Color property to light blue. (*Hint*: Use the Build button to locate the color on the palette.)

    g. Close the property sheet, use a label control to add your name to the Page Header section, preview the report, then print the first two pages.

    h. Save, then close the Event Details report. Close Seminar-L, then exit Access.

▶ Independent Challenge 1

As the manager of a college women's basketball team, you want to enhance the forms within the Basketball-L database.

    a. Start Access, then open the database **Basketball-L** from the drive and folder where your Project Files are located.

    b. Click the Forms button on the Objects bar, then double-click the Create form by using wizard option.

    c. Select all of the fields in the Players table.

    d. Use a Columnar layout and a Standard style, then type **Player Information** as the title for the form.

    e. Maximize the Player Information form, open it in Design View, then change the Lettered? check box to a toggle button with the text **Varsity Letter?**

    f. Resize the toggle button so that it clearly displays the text and is as wide as the form.

    g. Open the toggle button's property sheet, then type **Must have 200 minutes of playing time to letter** for the ControlTip Text property.

    h. In the toggle button's property sheet, type **For the year 2003** for the Status Bar Text property.

    i. Close the property sheet, display the form in Form View, enter your own last name in the first record, then click the toggle button to indicate you've earned a varsity letter.

    j. Print the first record, save the form, close the Player Information form and the Basketball-L database, then exit Access.

▶ Independent Challenge 2

As the manager of a college women's basketball team, you want to enhance the forms within the Basketball-L database.

    a. Start Access, then open the database **Basketball-L** from the drive and folder where your Project Files are located.

    b. Open the Player Statistics form in Design View, then add a tab control just below the Last label.

    c. Modify the Page5 Name property of the first tab to be **Player Background**.

    d. Modify the Page6 Name property of the second tab to be **Statistics**.

    e. Add the Height, PlayerNo, Year, Position, HomeTown, and HomeState fields from the field list to the middle of the Player Background page.

    f. Add a subform to the Statistics page based on all the fields from the Stats table. Link the main form to the subform by using the "Show Stats for each record in Players using PlayerNo" option.

    g. Type **Stats** as the name of the subform.

    h. Expand the height and width of the subform control to the existing margins of the form, then view the form in Form View.

i. Click the Statistics tab to make sure both tabs work correctly, move to the second record and enter your name in the First text box, then print the second record twice to show both pages of the tab control.

j. Save, then close the Player Statistics form. Close the Basketball-L database, then exit Access.

▶ Independent Challenge 3

As the manager of a college women's basketball team, you want to create a chart from the Basketball-L database to summarize three-point goals.

a. Start Access, then open the database **Basketball-L** from the drive and folder where your Project Files are located.

b. Click the Reports button on the Objects bar, click the New button on the database window toolbar, click Chart Wizard, then base the object on the Stats table.

c. Select the PlayerNo, 3P (three pointers), and 3PA (three pointers attempted) fields for the chart.

d. Select Column Chart for the chart type.

e. Drag the 3PA field to the Data area of the chart so that both the SumOf3P and SumOf3PA fields are in the Data area, and the PlayerNo field is in the Axis area of the chart.

f. Type **3 Pointers–Your Initials** for the title of the chart.

g. Print the chart, then save the report with the name **3 Pointers**.

h. Close the 3 Pointers report, close the Basketball-L database, then exit Access.

ⓔ Independent Challenge 4

Tab controls appear in many styles and are used on many Web pages to help users navigate a Web site. In this independent challenge, surf the Internet to find Web pages that present information organized similarly to how tab controls are used on Access forms.

a. Connect to the Internet, go to www.course.com, the home page for Course Technology, the publisher of this textbook, then explore the navigation aids on the page to determine if any controls work the way tab controls work on a form. Go back to the home page and print only the first page. On the printout, identify the area of the Web page that worked like tab controls. If you didn't think that the Web page used tab controls, explain why.

b. Go to www.bta.org.uk or www.travelbritain.org, a travel guide to Britain (substitute your own favorite international travel site if desired), and explore the site to identify tab controls. Print a page that uses tab controls (they may not look exactly like tabs). On that printout, identify the area of the Web page that worked like tab controls. If you didn't think that the Web page used tab controls, explain why.

c. Go to www.soccerage.com, a Web site with international soccer information (substitute your own favorite international sports site if desired), and explore the site to identify tab controls. Print a page that uses tab controls (they may not look exactly like tabs). On the printout, identify the area of the Web page that worked like tab controls. If you didn't think that the Web page used tab controls, explain why.

d. Not all Web pages organize their content by using hyperlinks that look like tab controls. On a piece of paper, write a paragraph about the other types of hyperlinks you found that help organize and navigate a site, and identify and explain the characteristics of the controls you liked best.

▶ Visual Workshop

As the manager of a college women's basketball team, you want to create a form that highlights outstanding statistics if either scoring or rebounding totals are equal to or greater than **10** for an individual game effort. Start Access, then open the **Basketball-L** database from the drive and folder where your Project Files are located. Open the Players form in Design View, then use the conditional formatting feature to format the FG (field goals), 3P (three-point shots), and FT (free throws) text boxes in the Stats Subform1 to have bold text and a yellow background if the following expression that totals their scoring for that game is true: **2*[FG]+3*[3P]+[FT]>=10**. Conditionally format the Reb-O (offensive rebounds) and Reb-D (defensive rebounds) text boxes to have a bold text and green background if the following expression that totals rebounds is true: **[Reb-O]+[Reb-D]>=10**. Display the record for Ellyse Howard, which should look like Figure L-26. Enter your own name in the First and Last text boxes, then print that record.

FIGURE L-26

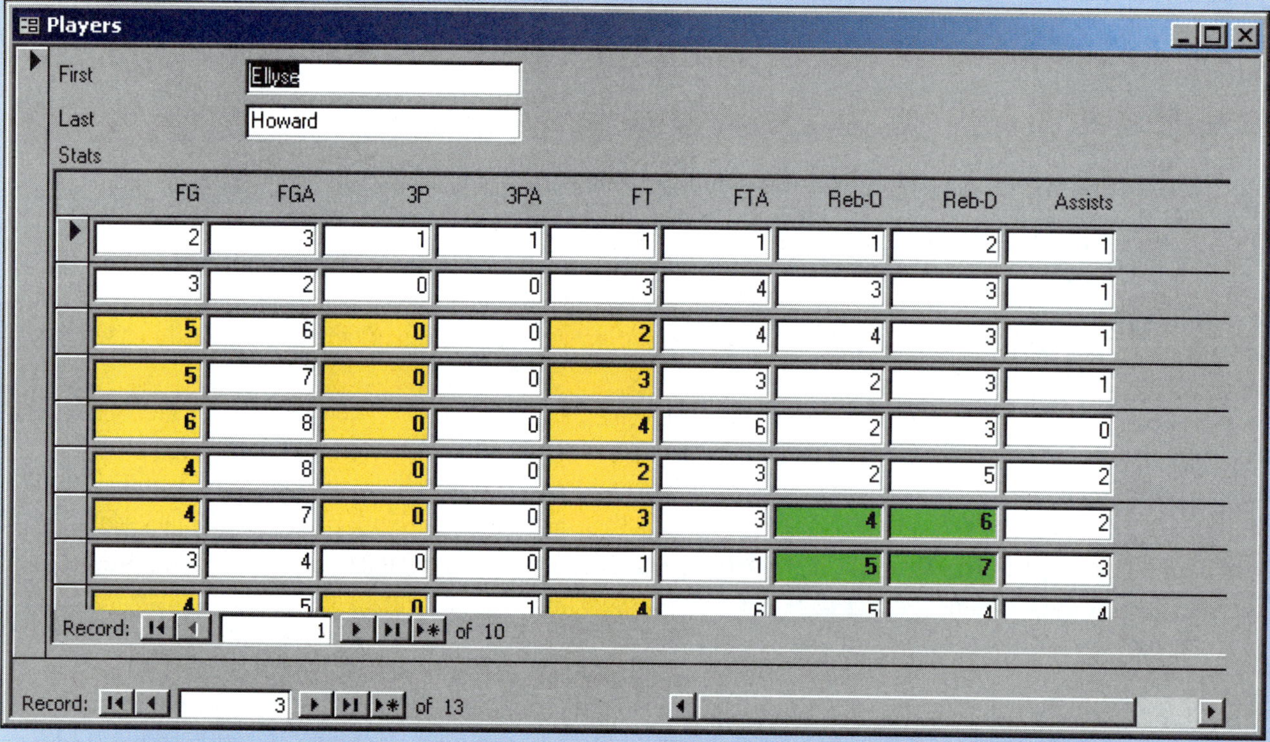

	FG	FGA	3P	3PA	FT	FTA	Reb-O	Reb-D	Assists
First: Ellyse									
Last: Howard									
Stats									
▶	2	3	1	1	1	1	1	2	1
	3	2	0	0	3	4	3	3	1
	5	6	0	0	2	4	4	3	1
	5	7	0	0	3	3	2	3	1
	6	8	0	0	4	6	2	3	0
	4	8	0	0	2	3	2	5	2
	4	7	0	0	3	3	4	6	2
	3	4	0	0	1	1	5	7	3
	4	5	0	1	4	6	5	4	4

Record: ◀◀ ◀ 1 ▶ ▶▶ ▶* of 10

Record: ◀◀ ◀ 3 ▶ ▶▶ ▶* of 13

Managing

Database Objects

Objectives

- ▶ Work with objects
- ▶ Use the Documenter
- ▶ Group objects
- ▶ Modify shortcuts and groups
- MOUS ▶ Create a dialog box
- MOUS ▶ Create a pop-up form
- MOUS ▶ Create a switchboard
- MOUS ▶ Modify a switchboard

As your database grows in size and functionality, the number of objects (especially queries and reports) grows as well. Your ability to find, rename, delete, and document objects, and your proficiency to present objects in an organized way to other database users will become important skills. ✎ Kristen Fontanelle is the network administrator at MediaLoft headquarters. She has developed a working database to document MediaLoft computer equipment. The number of objects in the database makes it increasingly difficult to find and organize information. Kristen will use powerful Access documentation, object grouping, and switchboard features to manage the growing database.

Working with Objects

Working with Access objects is similar to working with files in Windows Explorer. For example, you can use the **View buttons** (Large Icons 🔳, Small Icons 🔳, List 🔳, and Details 🔳) on the database window toolbar to arrange the objects in four different ways just as you arrange files within Windows Explorer. Similarly, you can right-click an object within Access to open, copy, delete, or rename it just as you would right-click a file within Windows Explorer. ✐ Kristen deletes, renames, sorts, and adds descriptions to several objects to make the Database window easier to use.

Steps 1 2 3 4

1. **Start Access, open the Technology-M database from the drive and folder where your Project Files are located, maximize the database window, click Queries on the Objects bar (if it is not already selected), then click the Details button 🔳 on the Database window toolbar**
   Your screen should look like Figure M-1, with five columns of information for each object: Name, Description, Modified (date the object was last changed), Created (date the object was originally created), and Type. By default, objects are sorted in ascending order by name, and the Description column is blank.

QuickTip

Point to the line between column headings, then drag ↔ left or right to resize that column.

2. **Click the Created column heading to sort the objects in ascending order on the date they were originally created, click the Created column heading again to sort the objects in descending order on the date they were originally created, then click the Name column heading**
   The query objects are now sorted in ascending order by name. You use the Description column to further describe the object.

3. **Right-click the Equipment Specs query, then click Properties on the shortcut menu**
   The Equipment Specs Properties dialog box opens, as shown in Figure M-2.

4. **Enter Includes memory, hard drive, and processor information in the Description text box, then click OK**
   Part of the description appears in the Database window and helps identify the selected object. If an object is no longer needed, you should delete it to free up disk space and keep the database window organized.

5. **Right-click the Employees Query, click Delete on the shortcut menu, then click Yes when prompted**
   Although object names can be 64 characters long and can include any combination of letters, numbers, spaces, and special characters except a period (.), exclamation point (!), accent (`), or brackets ([ ]), keep them as short, yet descriptive, as possible. Short names make objects easier to reference in other places in the database, such as in the Record Source property for a form or report.

6. **Right-click the Human Resources query, click Rename on the shortcut menu, type HR, press [Enter], right-click the Information Systems query, click Rename on the shortcut menu, type IS, then press [Enter]**
   Your final screen should look like Figure M-3. With shorter query names, you can see all of the object names in the Database window without resizing the columns.

FIGURE M-1: Viewing object details

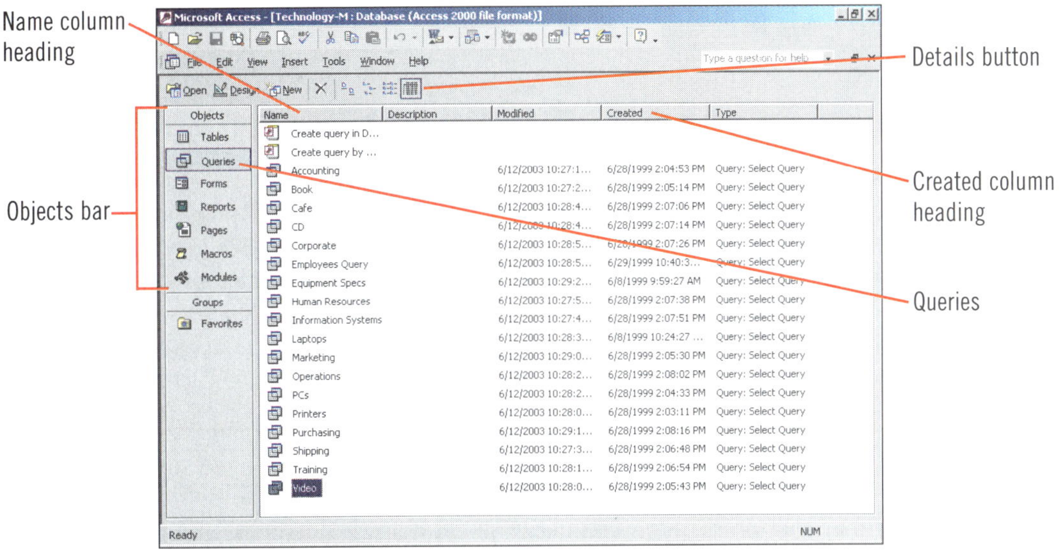

Name column heading

Details button

Objects bar

Created column heading

Queries

FIGURE M-2: Equipment Specs Properties dialog box

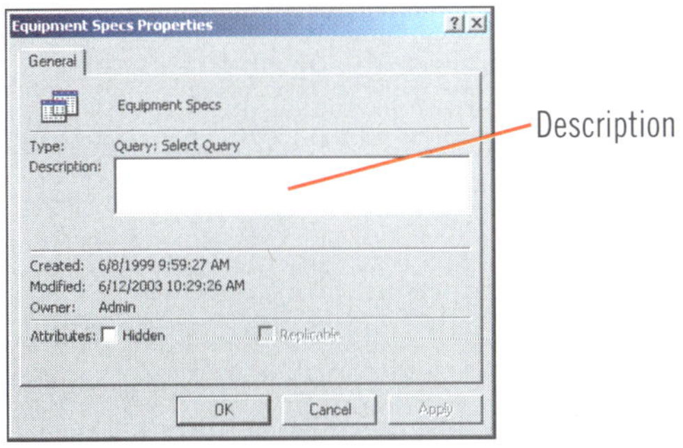

Description

FIGURE M-3: Final Database window

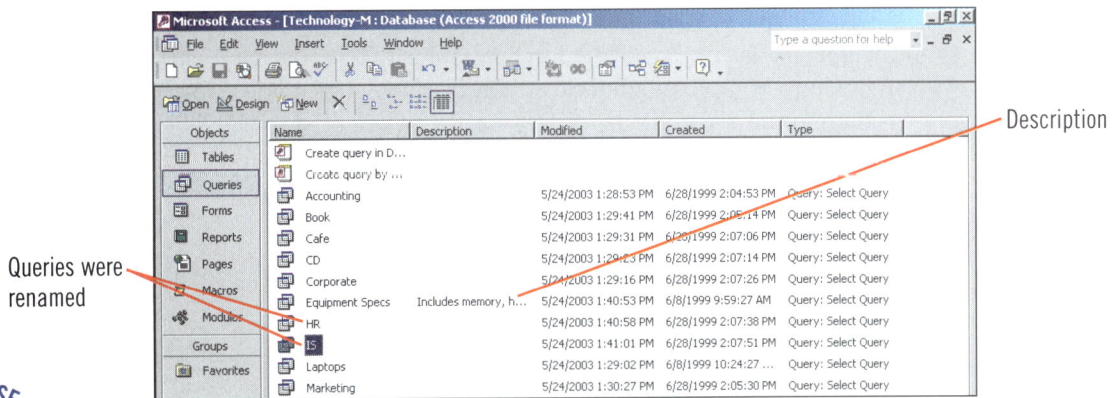

Description

Queries were renamed

Updating names with Name AutoCorrect

Name AutoCorrect fixes discrepancies between references to field names, controls on forms and reports, and object names when you change them. For example, if a query includes the field "LastName," but you change that field name to "LName" in Table Design View, the Name AutoCorrect feature will update the field name to "LName" within the query as well. Similarly, if a report is based on a query named "Department Income," and you change the query name to "Dept Inc," the Name AutoCorrect feature will automatically update the Record Source property for the report to "Dept Inc" to match the new query name. However, Name AutoCorrect will not repair references in Visual Basic for Applications code, replicated databases, linked tables, or a number of other database situations. Click Tools on the menu bar in the database window, click Options, and then click the General tab to view the Name AutoCorrect options.

Using the Documenter

As your Access database becomes more successful, users will naturally find new ways to use the data. Your ability to modify a database depends on your understanding of existing database objects. Access provides an analysis feature called the **Documenter** that creates reports on the properties and relationships among the objects in your database. This documentation is especially helpful to those who need to use the database, but did not design the original tables. ◣ Kristen uses the Documenter to create paper documentation to support the Technology-M database for other MediaLoft employees.

Steps 1 2 3 4

1. **Click Tools on the menu bar, point to Analyze, click Documenter, click Yes if prompted to install the feature, then click the Tables tab**
   The Documenter dialog box opens, displaying tabs for the object types.

2. **Click Options in the Documenter dialog box**
   The Print Table Definition dialog box, shown in Figure M-4, opens. This dialog box gives you some control over what type of documentation you will print for the table. The documentation for each object type varies slightly. For example, the documentation on forms and reports would include information on controls and sections, which are not part of table objects.

3. **Click Cancel in the Print Table Definition dialog box**
   You can also select or deselect individual objects by clicking the check box beside their name, or you can click the Select All button to quickly select all objects of that type.

QuickTip

Information about the progress of Documenter appears in the status bar.

4. **Click Select All, click the Forms tab, click Select All, click OK, then click 🔍 on the report preview to zoom in**
   Documenter is now creating a report about all of the table and form objects in the Technology-M database, and will display it as an Access report. This can be a lengthy process (taking several seconds) depending on the speed of your computer and the number of objects that Documenter is examining. After Access completes the report, your screen looks like Figure M-5, which shows a report that displays information about the first table, Assignments, on the first page.

5. **Click the Last Page button ▸▮ in the navigation toolbar, click the Previous Page button ◂▮, then scroll down so that your screen looks like Figure M-6**
   The report contains about three pages of documentation for each table, and about six pages per form. The properties for each control on the form are listed in two columns. Because most form controls have approximately 50 properties, you can quickly see why the documentation that lists each control and section property can become so long. You can print the report, or send it to a Word document using the OfficeLinks buttons, but you cannot modify the report in the Report Design View or save the report as an object within the database window.

6. **Click Close on the Print Preview toolbar**

FIGURE M-4: Print Table Definition dialog box

Print Table Definition

Include for Table
- ☑ Properties
- ☑ Relationships
- ☑ Permissions by User and Group

Include for Fields
- ○ Nothing
- ○ Names, Data Types, and Sizes
- ● Names, Data Types, Sizes, and Properties

Include for Indexes
- ○ Nothing
- ○ Names and Fields
- ● Names, Fields, and Properties

OK   Cancel

FIGURE M-5: First page of documentation

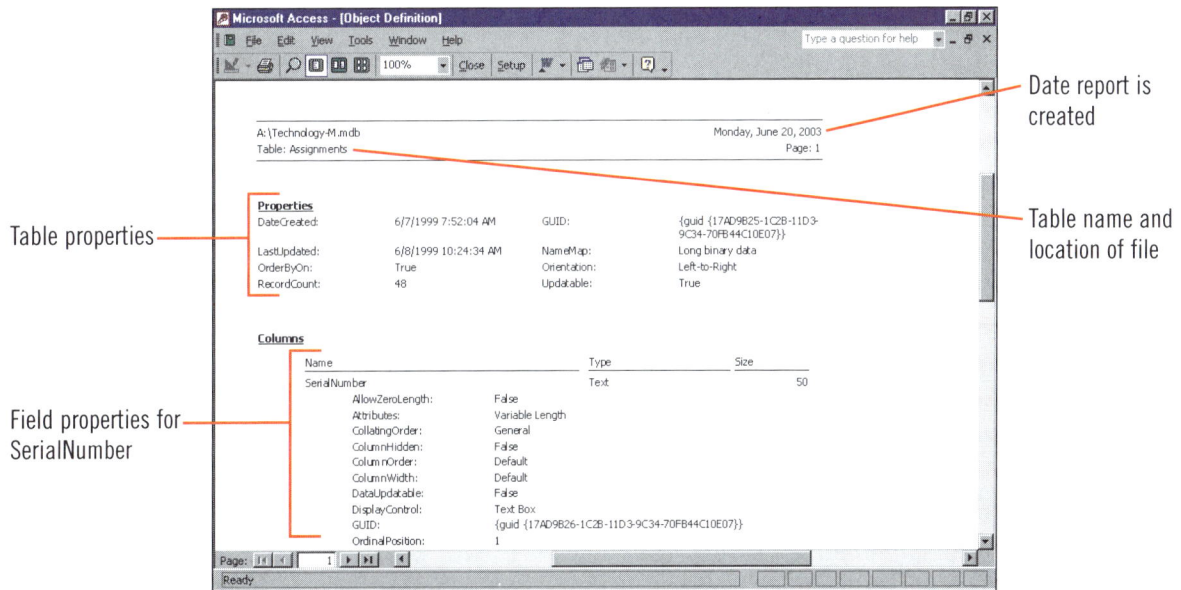

Date report is created

Table name and location of file

Table properties

Field properties for SerialNumber

A:\Technology-M.mdb   Monday, June 20, 2003
Table: Assignments   Page: 1

Properties
DateCreated: 6/7/1999 7:52:04 AM   GUID: {guid {17AD9B25-1C2B-11D3-9C34-70FB44C10E07}}
LastUpdated: 6/8/1999 10:24:34 AM   NameMap: Long binary data
OrderByOn: True   Orientation: Left-to-Right
RecordCount: 48   Updatable: True

Columns
Name   Type   Size
SerialNumber   Text   50
  AllowZeroLength: False
  Attributes: Variable Length
  CollatingOrder: General
  ColumnHidden: False
  ColumnOrder: Default
  ColumnWidth: Default
  DataUpdatable: False
  DisplayControl: Text Box
  GUID: {guid {17AD9B26-1C2B-11D3-9C34-70FB44C10E07}}
  OrdinalPosition: 1

FIGURE M-6: Second to last page of documentation

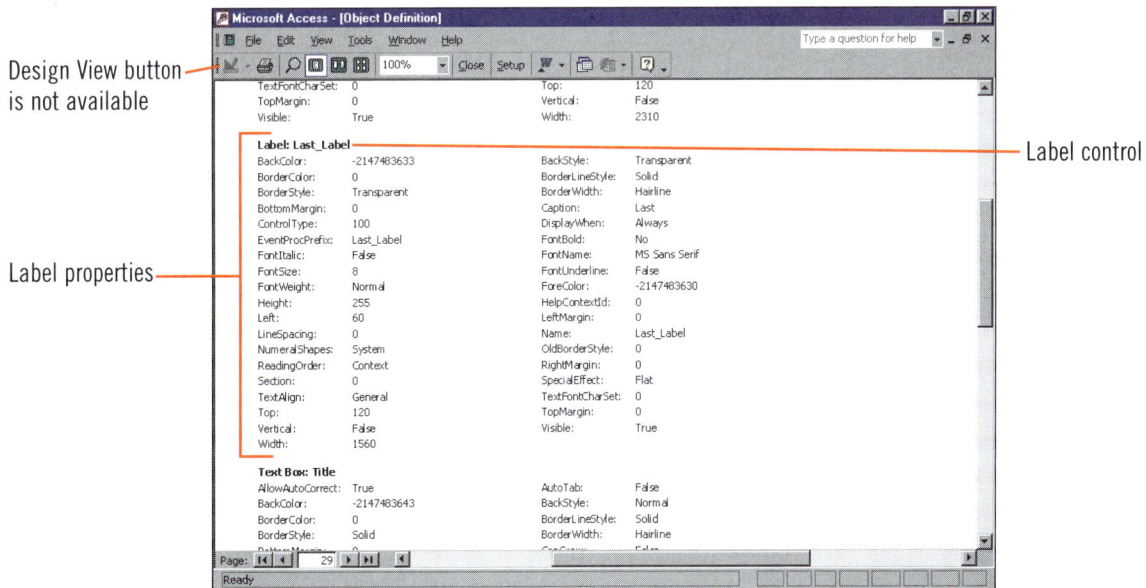

Design View button is not available

Label control

Label properties

TextFontCharSet: 0   Top: 120
TopMargin: 0   Vertical: False
Visible: True   Width: 2310

Label: Last_Label
BackColor: -2147483633   BackStyle: Transparent
BorderColor: 0   BorderLineStyle: Solid
BorderStyle: Transparent   BorderWidth: Hairline
BottomMargin: 0   Caption: Last
ControlType: 100   DisplayWhen: Always
EventProcPrefix: Last_Label   FontBold: No
FontItalic: False   FontName: MS Sans Serif
FontSize: 8   FontUnderline: False
FontWeight: Normal   ForeColor: -2147483630
Height: 255   HelpContextId: 0
Left: 60   LeftMargin: 0
LineSpacing: 0   Name: Last_Label
NumeralShapes: System   OldBorderStyle: 0
ReadingOrder: Context   RightMargin: 0
Section: 0   SpecialEffect: Flat
TextAlign: General   TextFontCharSet: 0
Top: 120   TopMargin: 0
Vertical: False   Visible: True
Width: 1560

Text Box: Title
AllowAutoCorrect: True   AutoTab: False
BackColor: -2147483643   BackStyle: Normal
BorderColor: 0   BorderLineStyle: Solid
BorderStyle: Solid   BorderWidth: Hairline

Grouping Objects

Viewing every object in the database window can be cumbersome when your database contains many objects. You can place objects in **groups** to easily organize or classify objects. For example, you might create a group for each department that uses the database so that the forms and reports used by each department are presented as a set. A group consists of **shortcuts** (pointers) to each database object that belongs to the group and does not affect the original location of the object. To work with groups, click the **Groups bar** below the Objects bar in the Database window. ✎━━━ Kristen organizes the objects in the Technology-M database by creating groups for the objects used by two different departments: Human Resources (HR) and Accounting.

Steps 1 2 3 4

1. **Right-click Favorites on the Groups bar, click New Group on the shortcut menu, type HR, click OK, then click HR on the Groups bar**
   Your screen should look like Figure M-7. Because you just created the HR group, it doesn't contain any objects. The **Favorites group** is provided for every new Access database and is similar in function to the Favorites folder used in other Microsoft programs. Within an Access database, the Favorites group organizes *objects* rather than files because it is an Access group (rather than a folder).

2. **Right-click Favorites on the Groups bar, click New Group on the shortcut menu, type Accounting, then click OK**
   After creating the new groups, you are ready to use them to organize other database objects.

3. **Click Queries on the Objects bar, drag the Accounting query to the Accounting group, drag the Equipment Specs query to the Accounting group, then drag the HR query to the HR group**
   Dragging an object to a group icon places a shortcut to that object within that group.

4. **Click Reports on the Objects bar, drag the Accounting report to the Accounting group, drag the Human Resources report to the HR group, then click the Accounting group**
   Your screen should look like Figure M-8, with three shortcut icons representing two queries and one report in the Accounting group. Because both a query and a report object were named "Accounting," Access added a "1" to the "Accounting" shortcut icon that represents the Accounting report. These shortcuts are just pointers to the original objects, and therefore do not change the name of the original object. You can open or design an object by accessing it through a shortcut icon. You also can drag an object to more than one group, thereby creating more than one shortcut to it.

QuickTip

You can resize the Groups or Objects sections by pointing to the top edge of the Objects or Groups button and dragging ↕ to resize that section of the Objects bar.

5. **Click Groups on the Groups bar three times**
   You can expand, collapse, or restore this section of the Objects bar.

6. **Click Objects on the Objects bar three times**
   Displaying all Objects and Groups buttons is a good way to arrange the database window for a new user.

FIGURE M-7: Creating groups

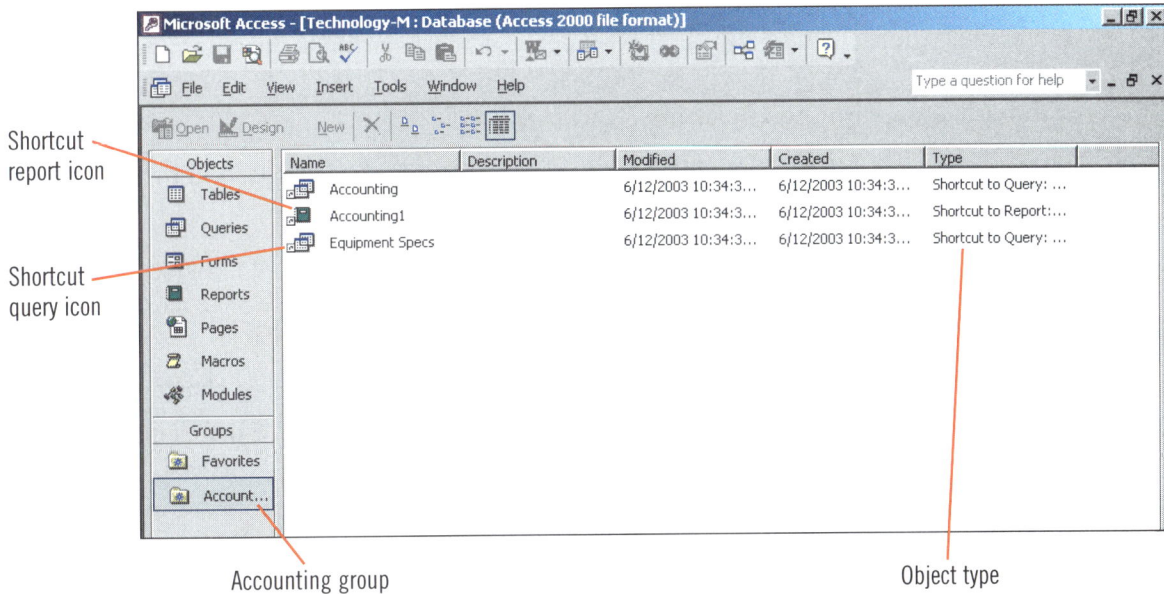

Groups button

Favorites

New HR group

Groups bar

FIGURE M-8: Dragging objects to groups

Shortcut report icon

Shortcut query icon

Accounting group

Object type

Speech recognition—interface of the future?

Speech recognition means being able to talk to your computer, and having it respond appropriately to the instruction you gave it. For example, to display the query objects in the database window, it would be faster and easier for most people to say "Queries," than to click the Queries button on the Objects bar, especially if your hand wasn't already resting on the mouse. Office XP products including Access 2002 support speech recognition, but you must have a microphone, install the speech recognition software, and train the software to recognize the sound of your unique voice. For more information on speech recognition, open Microsoft Access Help to the "About speech recognition" page.

Modifying Shortcuts and Groups

Once groups are created and object shortcuts are added to them, you work with the shortcut as if you were working directly with the original object. Any changes you make to an object by accessing it through a shortcut are saved with the object, just as if you had opened that object without using the shortcut. You can delete, rename, or copy a shortcut by right-clicking it and choosing the appropriate command from the shortcut menu. The biggest difference between working with shortcuts and actual objects is that if you delete a shortcut, you delete only that pointer, which does not affect the original object it references. If you delete an object, however, it is, of course, permanently deleted, and any shortcuts that reference it will no longer function properly. You can also rename or delete entire groups. ✎ Kristen modifies groups and shortcuts to clarify the Technology-M database.

Steps 1234

1. Right-click the **Accounting1 shortcut** in the Accounting group, click **Rename** on the shortcut menu, type **Accounting Report**, then press **[Enter]**

   A shortcut name does not have to use the same name as the object that it points to, but the shortcuts should be clearly named. The shortcut icon to the left of the shortcut indicates the type of object it represents.

2. Right-click **Accounting** on the Groups bar, click **Rename Group** on the shortcut menu, type **Acctg**, then press **[Enter]**

   The Groups bar should look like Figure M-9.

3. Right-click **Acctg**, click **New Group** on the shortcut menu, type **IS** in the New Group Name text box, then press **[Enter]**

4. Drag the **Equipment Specs shortcut** from the Acctg group to the IS group

   Dragging a shortcut from one group to another creates a copy of that shortcut in both groups. Shortcuts that point to the same object can have different names.

5. Click **IS** on the Groups bar, double-click the **Equipment Specs shortcut** in the IS group to open the query in Datasheet View, double-click **256** in the Memory field for the first record (SerialNo JK123FL3), type **512**, then close the datasheet

   Edits and entries made to Query Datasheet View through a query shortcut work exactly the same as if you had made the change in the original Query Datasheet View. Changes to data from any object view modify data that is physically stored in table objects.

6. Click **Tables** on the Objects bar, double-click the **PCSpecs table** to open its datasheet, click the **Find button** 🔍 on the Table Datasheet toolbar, type **JK123FL3** in the Find what text box, press **[Enter]**, then click **Cancel**

   The Memory field for the JK123FL3 record contains the value 512, as shown in Figure M-10.

7. Close the PCSpecs datasheet

FIGURE M-9: Modifying groups

Renamed shortcut

Renamed group

FIGURE M-10: A change made through a shortcut

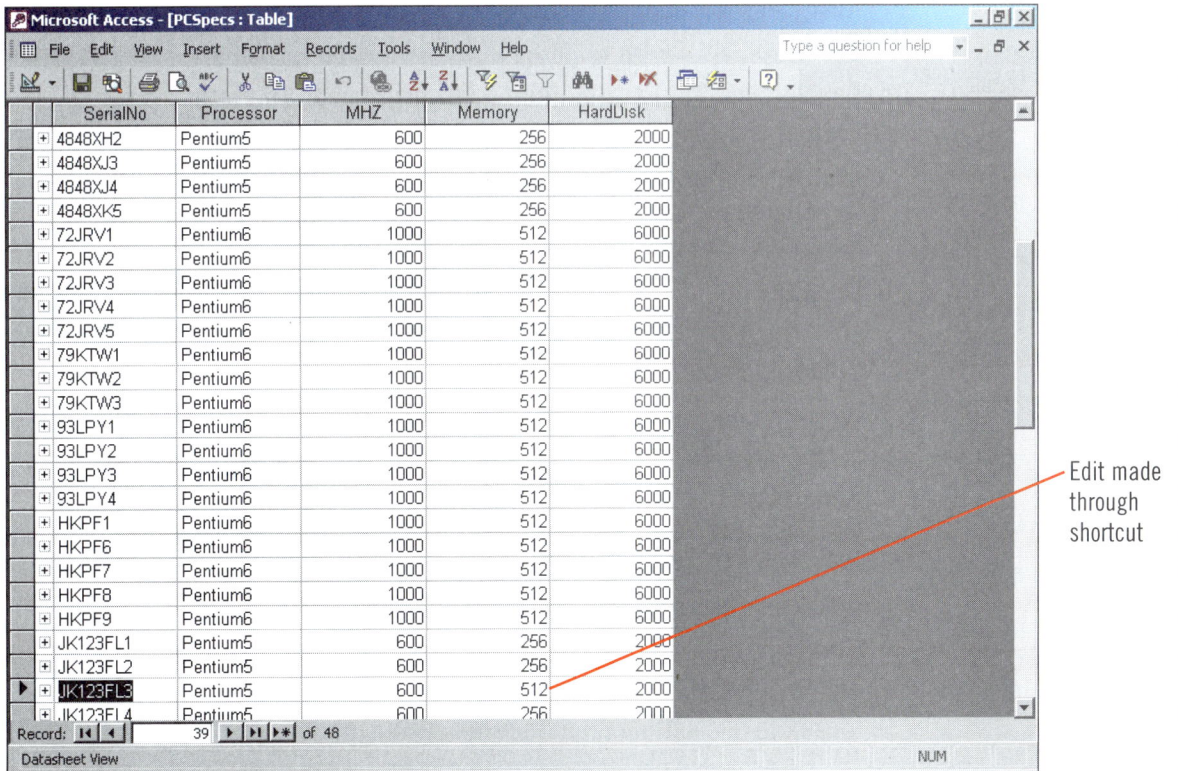

Edit made through shortcut

Creating a Dialog Box

A **dialog box** is a special form that displays information or prompts a user for a choice. For example, you might create a dialog box to give the user a list of reports to view or print. Use dialog boxes to simplify the Access interface. You use form properties such as **Border Style** and **Auto Center** to make a form look like a dialog box. Kristen wants to create a dialog box that lets database users access the three reports that the Accounting department regularly prints. She also wants to add a shortcut to the dialog box in the Accounting group to simplify the printing process.

1. Click **Forms** on the Objects bar, click the **List button** on the Database window toolbar, then double-click **Create form in Design view**

   You create a dialog box in Form Design View. A dialog box is not bound to an underlying table or query, and therefore doesn't use the Record Source property. A dialog box often contains command buttons to automate tasks.

Trouble?

Make sure that the Control Wizards button is selected on the Toolbox before you click to start the Command Button Wizard.

2. Click the **Toolbox button** on the Form Design toolbar (if the Toolbox is not already visible), click the **Command Button button** on the Toolbox, then click ⁺▭ in the upper-left corner of the form

   The **Command Button Wizard** shown in Figure M-11 assists you in creating new command buttons. The Command Button Wizard organizes over 30 of the most common command button actions within six categories.

3. Click **Report Operations** in the Categories list, click **Preview Report** in the Actions list, click **Next**, click **Accounting** as the report choice (if it is not already selected), click **Next**, click the **Text option button**, press **[Tab]**, type **Sorted by Name**, click **Next**, type **Name** in the button name text box, then click **Finish**

   The command button appears in Form Design View, as shown in Figure M-12. The name of the command button appears in the Object box on the Formatting (Form/Report toolbar).

Trouble?

Every command button must be given a unique name that is referenced in underlying Visual Basic for Applications (VBA) code. Deleting a command button from Design View does not delete the underlying code, so each new button name must be different, even if the button has been deleted.

4. Click the **Command Button button**, click ⁺▭ below the first command button, click **Report Operations** in the Categories list, click **Preview Report** in the Actions list, click **Next**, click **Accounting Manufacturer**, click **Next**, click the **Text option button**, press **[Tab]**, type **Sorted by Manufacturer**, click **Next**, type **Mfg**, then click **Finish**

5. Double-click the **Form Selector button** to open the form's property sheet, click the **Format tab** (if it is not already selected), click **Sizable** in the Border Style property, click the **Border Style list arrow**, then click **Dialog**

   The **Dialog** option for the Border Style property indicates that the form will have a thick border and may not be maximized, minimized, or resized.

6. Click **Yes** in the Navigation Buttons property, click the **Navigation Buttons list arrow**, click **No**, click **Yes** in the Record Selectors property, click the **Record Selectors list arrow**, then click **No**

7. Close the property sheet, restore, then resize the form and Form Design window so it is approximately 3" wide by 3" tall, click the **Save button**, enter **Accounting Reports** as the form name, click **OK**, then click the **Form View button**

   Restoring and resizing the form best displays the property changes you made to the Border Style, Navigation Buttons, and Record Selectors properties, as shown in Figure M-13.

8. Click the **Sorted by Manufacturer command button**

   Clicking the Sorted by Manufacturer command button displays the Accounting Manufacturer report.

9. Close the Accounting Manufacturer report, then close the Accounting Reports form

FIGURE M-11: Command Button Wizard

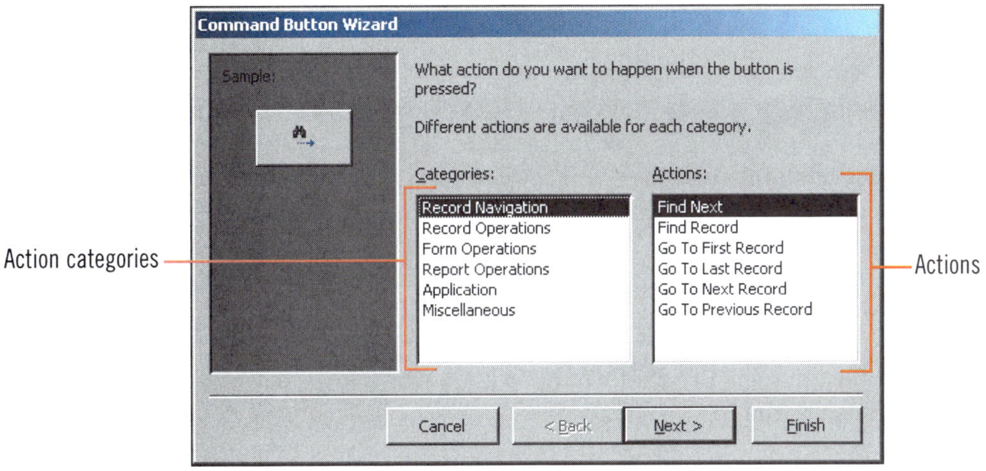

Action categories

Actions

FIGURE M-12: Adding a command button

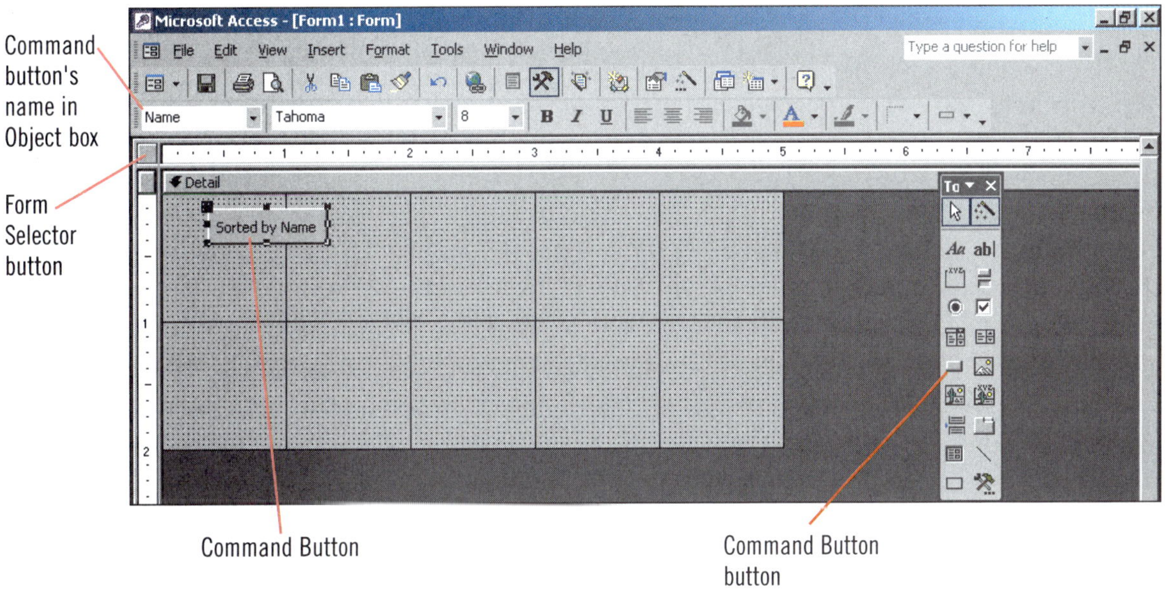

Command button's name in Object box

Form Selector button

Command Button

Command Button button

FIGURE M-13: The final dialog box in Form View

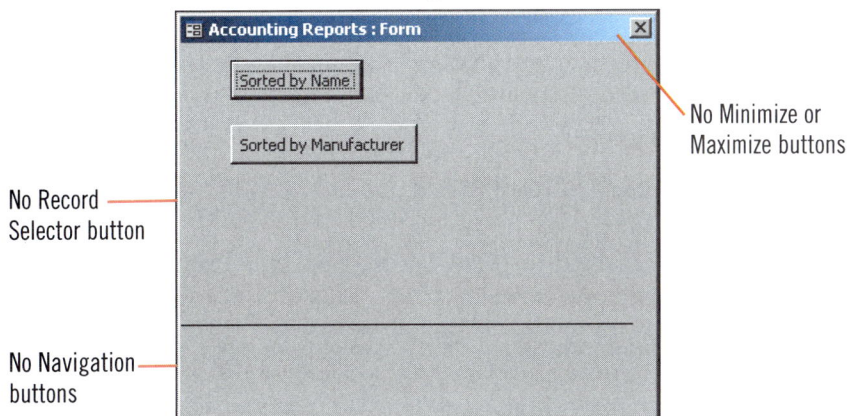

No Minimize or Maximize buttons

No Record Selector button

No Navigation buttons

Creating a Pop-up Form

A **pop-up form** is another special type of form that stays on top of other open forms, even when another form is active. For example, you might want to create a pop-up form to give the user easy access to reference lists such as phone numbers or e-mail addresses. You can open a pop-up form with a command button. ◤ Kristen creates a pop-up form to access employee e-mail information. She adds a command button on the Employees form to open the pop-up form.

Steps

1. Double-click **Create form by using wizard**, click the **Tables/Queries list arrow**, then click **Table: Employees**
   You want to add three fields to the pop-up form.

2. Double-click **First**, double-click **Last**, double-click **Email**, click **Next**, click the **Tabular option button**, click **Next**, click **Standard** for the style (if it is not already selected), click **Next**, type **Email Info** for the title of the form, then click **Finish**
   The Email Info form opens in Form View, as shown in Figure M-14. You change a form into a pop-up form by changing form properties in Form Design View.

3. Click the **Design View button** 🖳, double-click the **Form Selector button**, click the **Other tab** in the Form property sheet, click the **Pop Up property list arrow**, click **Yes**, close the property sheet, save, then close the form
   You want to open the Email Info pop-up form with a command button on the Employees form.

4. Right-click the **Employees form**, then click **Design View** on the shortcut menu
   The Employees form contains four bound fields: Last, First, Department, and Title, as well as a subform that displays the equipment assigned to that employee.

> **QuickTip**
> If the field list is in the way, drag its title bar to move it or click the Field List button 📇 on the Form Design toolbar to toggle it off.

5. Point to the **right edge of the form**, then drag ↔ to the **6.5"** mark on the horizontal ruler
   You want to put the command button in the upper-right corner of the form.

6. Click the **Command Button button** 🔲 on the Toolbox, click ⁺🔲 to the right of the Title text box, click **Form Operations** in the Categories list, click **Open Form** in the Actions list, click **Next**, click the **Email Info** form, click **Next**, click the **Open the form and show all the records option button**, click **Next**, click the **Text option button**, press **[Tab]**, type **Email**, click **Next**, type **Email** as the name of the button, then click **Finish**
   Your screen should look similar to Figure M-15.

7. Click the **Form View button** 📰, click the **Email command button**, resize the **Email Info window**, then drag the **Email Info title bar** down so that your screen looks like Figure M-16
   The power of pop-up forms is that they stay on top of all other forms and can be turned on and off as needed by the user.

8. Click **Ingraham** in the Last text box in the Employees form, click the **Sort Ascending button** 📶, double-click **Maria** in the First text box of the Employees form, type **Mary**, then press **[Tab]**
   "Maria" also changed to "Mary" in the pop-up form because both forms are tied to the underlying Employee table.

9. Close the Email Info pop-up form, save, then close the Employees form

FIGURE M-14: Creating the Email Info pop-up form

FIGURE M-15: Adding a command button to the Employees form

Form Selector button

Command Button button

New command button

FIGURE M 16: The final form and pop-up form

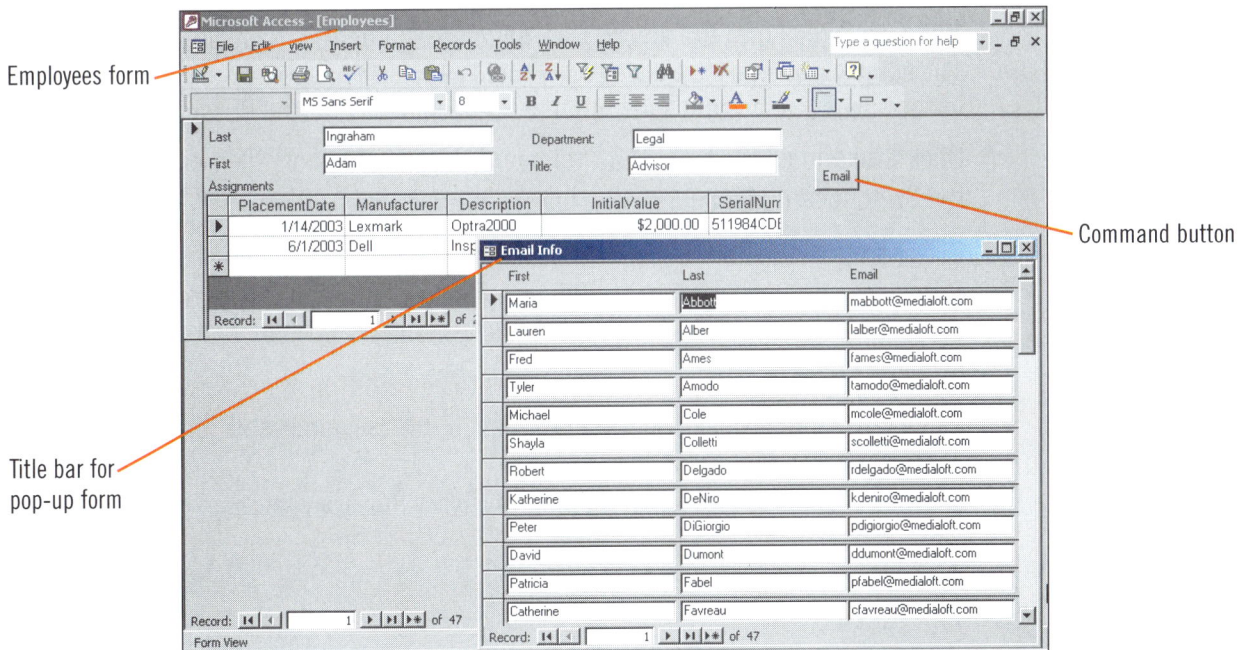

Employees form

Command button

Title bar for pop-up form

Access 2002

Creating a Switchboard

A **switchboard** is a special Access form that uses command buttons to simplify and secure the database. Switchboards are created and modified by using a special Access tool called the **Switchboard Manager**. Using the Switchboard Manager, you can create sophisticated switchboard forms without having advanced form development skills, such as how to work with controls or how to modify property settings. ✎ Kristen creates a switchboard form to make the database easier to navigate.

Steps

1. **Click Tools on the menu bar, point to Database Utilities, click Switchboard Manager, then click Yes when prompted to create a switchboard**
   The Switchboard Manager dialog box opens and presents the first switchboard page, which you can edit or delete. Each new switchboard form you create is listed in the Switchboard Pages list of this dialog box. One switchboard page must be designated as the **default switchboard**, the first switchboard in the database, and the one you use to link to additional switchboard pages.

2. **Click Edit**
   The Edit Switchboard Page dialog box opens. The switchboard form does not contain any items.

3. **Click New**
   The Edit Switchboard Item dialog box opens, prompting you for three important items: Text (a label on the switchboard form that identifies the corresponding command button), Command (which corresponds to a database action), and Switchboard (which further defines the command button action). Switchboard options depend on the action selected in the Command list.

4. **Type Open Employees Form in the Text text box, click the Command list arrow, click Open Form in Edit Mode, click the Form list arrow, then click Employees**
   The Edit Switchboard Item dialog box should look like Figure M-17.

5. **Click OK to add the first command button to the switchboard, click New, type Accounting Reports in the Text text box, click the Command list arrow, click Open Form in Edit Mode, click the Form list arrow, click Accounting Reports, then click OK**
   The Edit Switchboard Page dialog box should look like Figure M-18. Each entry in this dialog box represents a command button that will appear on the final switchboard.

6. **Click Close to close the Edit Switchboard Page dialog box, then click Close to close the Switchboard Manager dialog box**

7. **Click Forms on the Objects bar (if it is not already selected), double-click the Switchboard form, then click the Switchboard Restore Window button (if it is maximized)**
   The finished switchboard opens in Form View, as shown in Figure M-19.

8. **Click the Open Employees Form command button on the Switchboard, close the Employees form, click the Accounting Reports command button, then close Accounting Reports dialog box**
   Switchboard forms provide a fast and easy way to help users navigate a large database.

Becomes a label on the switchboard

Identifies the action for a command button on the switchboard

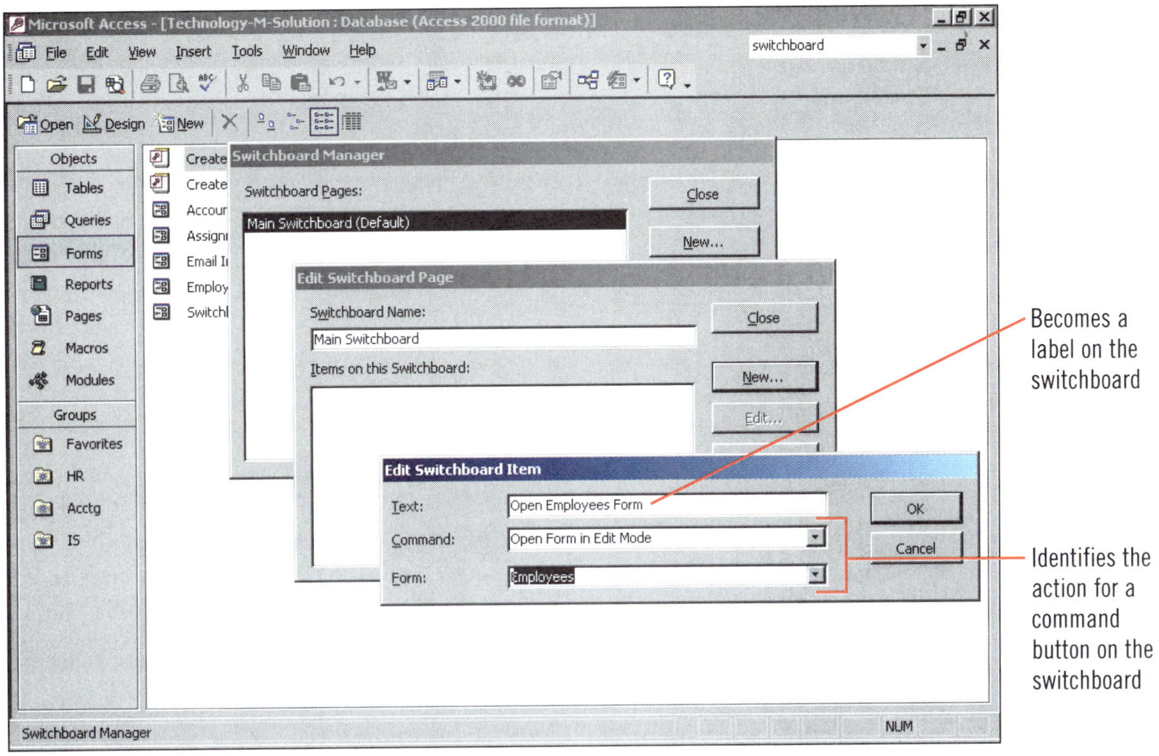

FIGURE M-18: **Edit Switchboard Page dialog box**

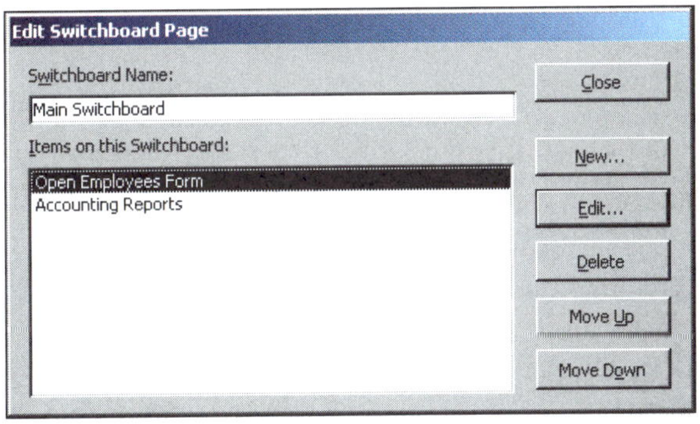

FIGURE M-19: **Switchboard**

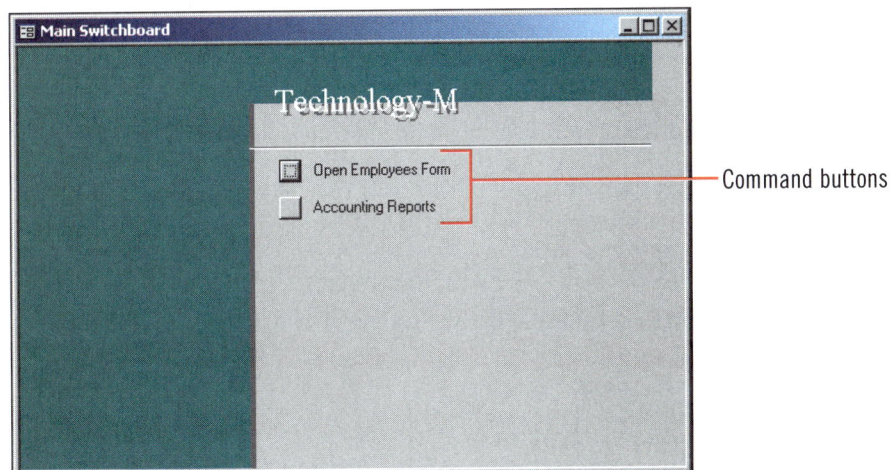

Command buttons

Modifying a Switchboard

Always use the Switchboard Manager to add, delete, move, and edit the command buttons and text that describes the command buttons on a switchboard form. Use Form Design View to make formatting modifications such as changing form colors, adding clip art, or changing the switchboard title. ~~✎~~ Kristen is happy with the initial switchboard form she created, but she would like to improve it by changing the title, colors, and order of the command buttons. She uses Form Design View to make the formatting changes and the Switchboard Manager to change the order of the buttons.

Steps 1 2 3 4

1. Click the **Design View button** 🖼 on the Form View toolbar, then click the **dark green rectangle** on the left of the Detail section
   The dark green blocks on the left and top portion of the Switchboard are actually rectangles, added to provide color. You can modify them just as you would modify any clip art object.

2. Click the **Fill/Back Color button list arrow** 🎨▾ on the Formatting (Form/Report) toolbar, click the **yellow box** (third column and fourth row from the top), click the **dark green rectangle** on the top of the Detail section, click 🎨▾, then click the **red box** (first column and third row from the top)

3. Click the **white Technology-M label** to select it, point to the edge, use ✋ to drag the white Technology-M label up into the red rectangle, click the **gray Technology-M** label to select it, then press **[Delete]**
   The modified switchboard should look like Figure M-20.

Trouble?

If you need to delete your Switchboard form and start over, you must first delete the Switchboard Items table before you can re-create the form.

4. Click the **Label button** 🔤 on the Toolbox toolbar, click the **yellow rectangle**, type **your name**, then press **[Enter]**
   You use Form Design View to modify colors, titles, and make other formatting changes. Notice that the text describing each command button does not appear in Form Design View. This text and other information about the command buttons on the Switchboard form are stored in a table called Switchboard Items.

5. Click the **Save button** 💾 on the Form Design toolbar, close the switchboard, click **Tools** on the menu, point to **Database Utilities**, click **Switchboard Manager**, then click **Edit**
   You use the Switchboard Manager to edit the text that accompanies command buttons.

6. Click **Accounting Reports**, click **Edit**, click to the left of the **A** in the Text text box, type **Preview**, press **[Spacebar]**, then click **OK**
   You can add, delete, move, or edit command buttons from the Edit Switchboard Page dialog box.

7. Click **Move Up** to make Preview Accounting Reports the first item in the switchboard, click **Close**, then click **Close**

8. Double-click the **Switchboard** form to open it in Form View, click 🖨 on the Form View toolbar to print the Switchboard, close the switchboard, then exit Access
   The modified switchboard should look like Figure M-21.

FIGURE M-20: Switchboard in Form Design View

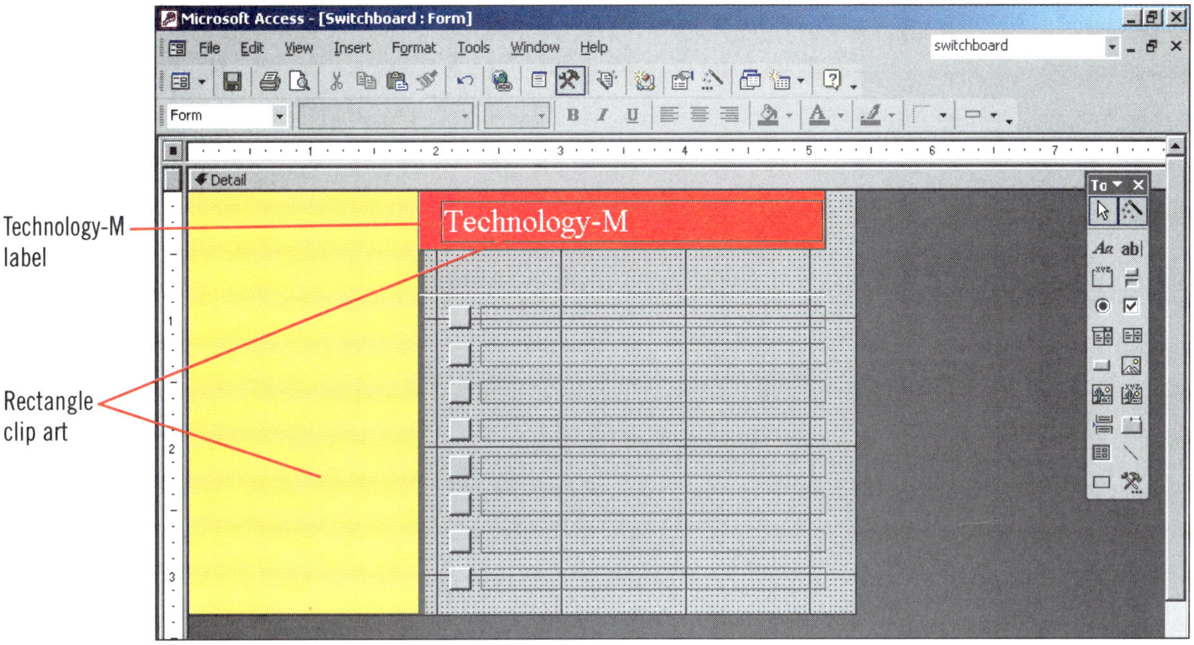

FIGURE M-21: Modified switchboard

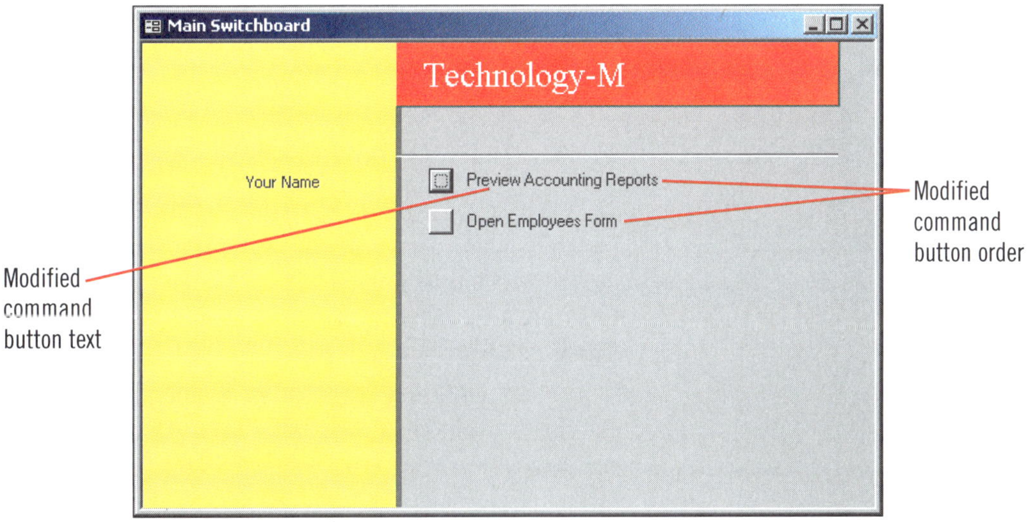

Access 2002

CLUES TO USE

The Northwind database

Microsoft provides a sample database with Access 2002 called **Northwind** that illustrates how to use Access switchboards and dialog boxes. To open the Northwind database, click Help on the menu bar, point to Sample Databases, then click Northwind Sample Database. If this is the first time the database has been opened, you will be prompted to install it. Northwind not only contains sample switchboard forms, but it is a robust relational database that provides many useful sample objects of all types.

Practice

► Concepts Review

Identify each element of the Database window shown in Figure M-22.

FIGURE M-22

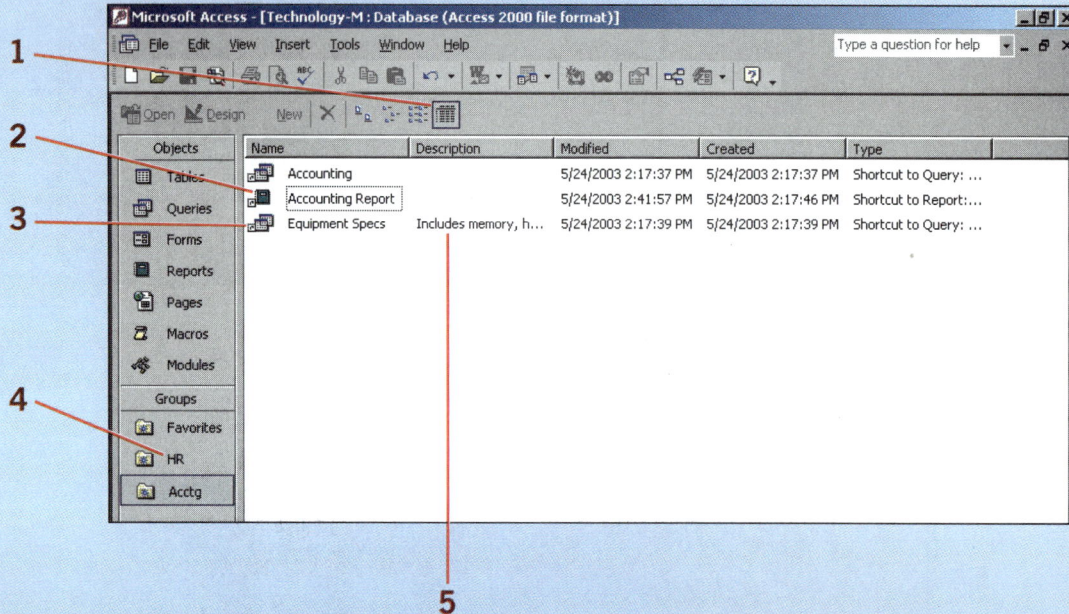

Match each term with the statement that describes its function.

6. Group
7. Pop-up form
8. Shortcut
9. Northwind
10. Documenter
11. Switchboard

a. Creates reports on the properties and relationships among the objects in your database
b. Pointer to database objects
c. Special type of form that stays on top of other open forms, even when another form is active
d. Special type of form that uses command buttons to simplify and secure access to database objects
e. Sample database used to illustrate many Access features, including switchboards
f. Helps you easily organize and classify objects

Select the best answer from the list of choices.

12. Which View button do you use to see the date that the object was created?
   a. List
   b. Small Icons
   c. Date
   d. Details
13. Which feature fixes discrepancies between references to field names, controls, and objects when you rename them?
   a. Documenter
   b. Renamer
   c. Name AutoCorrect
   d. Switchboard Manager

14. **If you wanted to add a command button to a switchboard, which view or tool would you use?**
    a. Form Design View
    b. Report Design View
    c. Switchboard Manager
    d. Switchboard Analyzer

15. **Which item would NOT help you organize the Access objects that the Human Resources (HR) Department most often uses?**
    a. A report that lists all HR employees
    b. A switchboard that provides command buttons to the appropriate HR objects
    c. A dialog box with command buttons that reference the most commonly used HR forms and reports
    d. An HR group with shortcuts to the HR objects

16. **Northwind is the name of a sample:**
    a. Switchboard form.
    b. Database.
    c. Pop-up form.
    d. Dialog box.

17. **A dialog box is which type of object?**
    a. Table
    b. Form
    c. Macro
    d. Report

18. **A switchboard is which type of object?**
    a. Table
    b. Form
    c. Macro
    d. Report

19. **If you wanted to modify the text that identifies each command button on the switchboard, which view or tool would you use?**
    a. Table Design View
    b. Form Design View
    c. Switchboard Manager
    d. Documenter

20. **If you wanted to change the clip art on a switchboard, which view or tool would you use?**
    a. Form View
    b. Form Design View
    c. Switchboard Manager
    d. Switchboard Documenter

► Skills Review

1. **Work with objects.**
   a. Open the **Basketball–M** database, then maximize the Database window.
   b. Click the Details button to view the details, then click Reports on the Objects bar.
   c. Open the property sheet for the Player Field Goal Stats report (resize the columns to view the entire report name if needed), then type **Forwards and Guards** for the Description property.
   d. Click Queries on the Objects bar, then rename the Games query with the name **Score Delta**.
   e. Open the Games Summary Report in Design View, open the report property sheet, then check the Record Source property on the Data tab. Because the Games Summary Report was based on the former Games Query object, the new query name should appear in the Record Source property.
   f. Close the property sheet, save, then close the Games Summary Report.

2. **Use the Documenter.**
   a. Click Tools on the menu bar, point to Analyze, then click Documenter.
   b. Click the Tables tab, click Select All, click the Reports tab, click the Games Summary Report check box, then click OK.
   c. Watch the status bar to track the progress of the Documenter.
   d. The final report is several pages long. Click File on the menu bar, click Print, click the Pages option button, enter **1** in the From text box, enter **1** in the To text box, then click OK to print the first page. Write your name on the printout.
   e. Close the report created by Documenter.

3. Group objects.
  a. Create a new group named **Forwards**.
  b. Create shortcuts for the Forward Field Goals query and the Forward Field Goal Stats report in the Forwards group.
  c. Create a new group named **Guards**.
  d. Create shortcuts for the Guard Field Goals query and Guard Field Goal Stats report in the Guards group.

4. Modify shortcuts and groups.
  a. Rename the Forward Field Goals query shortcut in the Forwards group to **Forward FG Query**.
  b. Rename the Forward Field Goal Stats report shortcut in the Forwards group to **Forward FG Report**.
  c. Rename the Guard Field Goals query shortcut in the Guards group to **Guard FG Query**.
  d. Rename the Guard Field Goal Stats report shortcut in the Guards group to **Guard FG Report**.
  e. Double-click the Forward FG Query shortcut in the Forwards group, then enter your name to replace Amy Hodel on any record where her name appears.
  f. Print the datasheet, save, then close the Forward Field Goals query.

5. Create a dialog box.
  a. Start a new form in Form Design View.
  b. Add a command button to the upper-left corner of the form using the Command Button Wizard. Select Report Operations from the Categories list, select Preview Report from the Actions list, then select the Games Summary Report.
  c. Type **Preview Games Summary Report** as the text for the button, then type **GamesReport** for the button name.
  d. Add a second command button below the first to preview the Player Field Goal Stats report.
  e. Type **Preview Player FG Stats** as the text for the button, then type **PlayersReport** for the button name.
  f. Below the two buttons, add a label to the form with your name.
  g. In the property sheet for the form, change the Border Style property of the form to Dialog, the Record Selectors property to No, and the Navigation Buttons property to No.
  h. Close the property sheet, restore the form (if it is maximized), resize the form and Form Design View window until it is approximately 3" wide by 3" tall, then save the form as **Team Reports**.
  i. Open the Team Reports form in Form View, test the buttons, then print the form. Your Team Reports form should be similar to Figure M-23.

FIGURE M-23

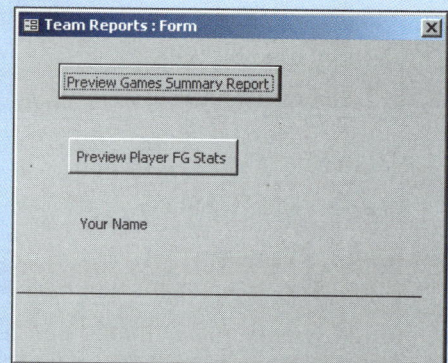

6. Create a pop-up form.
  a. Using the Form Wizard, create a form with the following fields from the Players table: First, Last, and PlayerNo.
  b. Use a Tabular layout, a Standard style, and title the form **Player Pop-up**.
  c. In Design View of the Player Pop-up form, resize the First and Last labels and text boxes to about half of their current width.
  d. Move the Last and PlayerNo labels and text boxes next to the First label and text box so that the entire form can be narrowed to no larger than 3" wide. Resize the form to 3" wide.
  e. Open the property sheet for the Player Pop-up form, change the Pop Up property to Yes, then close the property sheet.
  f. Save, then close the Player Pop-up form.
  g. Open the Team Reports form in Form Design View, then add a command button to the bottom of the form using the Command Button Wizard.
  h. In the Command Button Wizard, select the Form Operations category, the Open Form action, and the Player Pop-up form to open. The form should be opened to show all of the records.
  i. Type **Open Player Pop-up** as the text for the button, then name the button **PlayerPopup**.

j. Save the Team Reports form, then open it in Form View. Click the Open Player Pop-up command button to test it. Test the other buttons as well. The Player Pop-up form should stay on top of all other forms and reports until you close it.

k. Save, then close all open forms and reports.

7. Create a switchboard.

a. Click Tools on the menu bar, point to Database Utilities, click Switchboard Manager, then click Yes to create a new switchboard.

b. Click Edit to edit the Main Switchboard, then click New to add the first item to it.

c. Type **Select a Team Report** as the Text entry for the first command button, select Open Form in Add Mode for the Command, select Team Reports for the Form, then click OK to add the first command button to the switchboard.

d. Click New to add a second item to the switchboard. Type **Open Player Entry Form** as the Text entry, select Open Form in Add Mode for the Command, select Player Entry Form for the Form, then click OK to add the second command button to the switchboard.

e. Close the Edit Switchboard manager dialog box, then close the Switchboard Manager dialog box. Open the Switchboard form and click both command buttons to make sure they work. Notice that when you open a form in Add Mode (rather than using the Open Form in Edit Mode action within the Switchboard Manager), the navigation buttons indicate that you can only add a new record, and not edit an existing one.

f. Close all open forms including the Switchboard form.

8. Modify a switchboard.

a. Click Tools on the menu bar, point to Database Utilities, click Switchboard Manager, then click Edit to edit the Main Switchboard.

b. Click the Open Player Entry Form item, then click Edit.

c. Select Open Form in Edit Mode for the Command, select Player Entry Form for the Form, then click OK.

d. Move the Open Player Entry Form item above the Select a Team Report item, then close the Switchboard Manager.

e. In Form Design View of the Switchboard form, delete both the white and gray Basketball–M labels, add a label with the name of your favorite team's name to the top of the form, then add a label with your own name to the left side of the form. Format the labels with a color and size that makes them easy to read in Form View.

f. View the modified switchboard in Form View, as shown in Figure M-24, then test the buttons. Notice the difference in the Open Player Entry Form button (the form opens in Edit Mode versus Add Mode).

g. Save, print, then close the Switchboard form.

h. Close the Basketball–M database, then exit Access.

FIGURE M-24

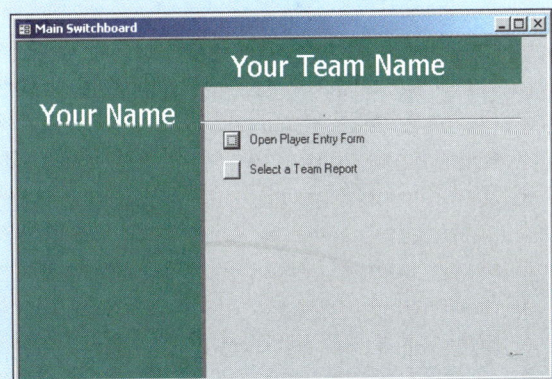

▶ Independent Challenge 1

As the manager of a doctor's clinic, you have created an Access database called Patients-M to track insurance claim reimbursements that are fixed (paid at a predetermined fixed rate), or denied (not paid by the insurance company). You want to create two groups to organize database objects. You also want to document the database's relationships.

a. Start Access, then open the database **Patients–M** from the drive and folder where your Project Files are located.

b. Create two new groups, **Fixed** and **Denied**.

c. Add shortcuts for the Monthly Query–Fixed query, the Date of Service Report–Fixed report, and the Monthly Claims Report–Fixed report to the Fixed group.

d. Add shortcuts for the Monthly Query–Denied query, the Date of Service Report–Denied report, and the Monthly Claims Report–Denied report to the Denied group.

e. Click Tools on the menu bar, point to Analyze, then click Documenter. On the Current Database tab, click Relationships, then click OK.

f. Print the Documenter's report, then close it. Write your name on the printout.

g. Close the Patients–M database, then exit Access.

► Independent Challenge 2

As the manager of a doctor's clinic, you have created an Access database called Patients–M to track insurance claim reimbursements that are fixed (paid at a predetermined fixed rate) or denied (not paid by the insurance company). You want to create a new dialog box to make it easier to preview the reports within your database.

a. Start Access, then open the database **Patients–M** from the drive and folder where your Project Files are located.

b. Start a new form in Form Design View.

c. Using the Command Button Wizard, add a command button to the form. Select Report Operations from the Categories list, select Preview Report from the Actions list, then select the Date of Service Report–Denied report.

d. Type **Preview Date of Service–Denied** as the text for the button, then type **PDOSD** for the button name.

e. Using the Command Button Wizard, add a second command button under the first. Select Report Operations from the Categories list, select Preview Report from the Actions list, then select the Date of Service Report–Fixed report.

f. Type **Preview Date of Service–Fixed** as the text for the button, then type **PDOSF** for the button name.

g. Using the Command Button Wizard, add a third command button under the second. Select Report Operations from the Categories list, select Preview Report from the Actions list, then select the Monthly Claims Report–Denied report.

h. Type **Preview Monthly Claims–Denied** as the text for the button, then type **PMCD** for the button name.

i. Using the Command Button Wizard, add a fourth command button under the third. Select Report Operations from the Categories list, select Preview Report from the Actions list, then select the Monthly Claims Report–Fixed report.

FIGURE M-25

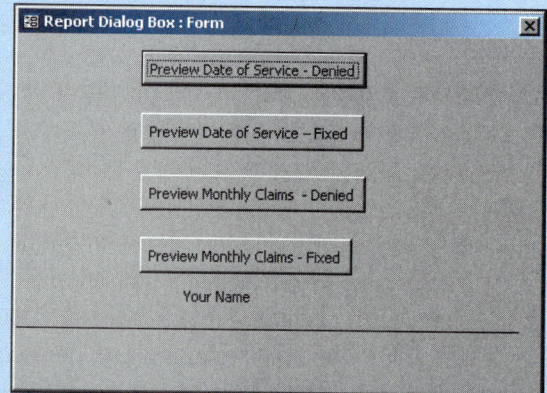

j. Type **Preview Monthly Claims–Fixed** as the text for the button, then type **PMCF** for the button name.

k. Below the buttons, add a label to the form with your name.

l. Open the property sheet for the form, change Border Style property to Dialog, the Record Selectors property to No, and the Navigation Buttons property to No.

m. Close the property sheet, restore the form (if it is maximized), resize the form and Form Design View window so they are approximately 3" wide by 3" tall, then save the form as **Report Dialog Box**.

n. Open the Report Dialog Box form in Form View, test the buttons, then print the form. It should look like Figure M-25.

o. Close the Report Dialog Box form, close the Patients–M database, then exit Access.

▶ Independent Challenge 3

As the manager of a doctor's clinic, you have created an Access database called Patients–M to track insurance claim reimbursements that are fixed (paid at a predetermined fixed rate), or denied (not paid by the insurance company). You want to create a pop-up form to provide physician information. You want to add a command button to the Claim Entry Form to open the pop-up form.

a. Start Access, then open the database **Patients–M** from the drive and folder where your Project Files are located.
b. Use the Form Wizard to create a form with all three of the fields in the Doctors table.
c. Use a Tabular layout, a Standard style, and type **Doctor Pop-up** for the form title.
d. In Form Design View of the Doctor Pop-up form, resize all three labels and text boxes to about half their current width.
e. Move the PodLastName and PodCode labels and text boxes next to the PodFirstName label and text box, then resize the form to no wider than 3".
f. Open the property sheet for the form, then change the Pop-Up property to Yes.
g. Save, then close the Doctor Pop-up form.
h. In Form Design View of the Claim Entry Form, use the Command Button Wizard to create a command button placed in the right of the Form Header section.
i. Select Form Operations from the Categories list, select Open Form from the Actions list, select the Doctor Pop-up form, then choose the option button to open the form and show all of the records.
j. Type **Open Doctor Pop-up** as the text for the button, then type **Docs** for the button name.
k. Add a label to the Form Header with your name.
l. Save the Claim Entry Form, open it in Form View, then click the Open Doctor Pop-up command button.
m. Move through the records of the Claim Entry form. The Doctor Pop-up form should stay on top of all other forms.
n. Print the first record in the Claim Entry form. Close all open forms, close the Patients–M database, then exit Access.

ⓔ Independent Challenge 4

Switchboard forms appear in many styles and are used on many Web pages to help you navigate that Web site. In this independent challenge, surf the Internet to find Web pages that present information organized similarly to how switchboards are used on Access forms.

a. Connect to the Internet, go to www.unisa.ac.za, the home page for the University of South Africa (substitute your own school or company home page, if desired), then explore the navigation aids on the page to determine if they have any controls that work similarly to how a switchboard works. Go back to the home page and print only the first page. On the printout, identify the area of the Web page that worked like a switchboard. If you didn't think that the Web page used a switchboard, explain why.
b. Go to www.google.com, a search engine (substitute your own favorite search engine, if desired), then explore the home page to determine if the page works like a switchboard. Return to the home page, then print only the first page. On the printout, identify the area of the Web page that worked like a switchboard. If you didn't think that the Web page worked like a switchboard, explain why.
c. Go to www.web100.com, a Web page that logs popular Web sites (substitute your own favorite reference or portal Web site, if desired), then explore the navigation aids on the page to determine if they have any controls that work similarly to how a switchboard works. Go back to the home page, then print only the first page. On the printout, identify the area of the Web page that worked like a switchboard. If you didn't think that the Web page used a switchboard, explain why.

d. Not all Web pages organize their content by using hyperlinks that work like switchboards. On a piece of paper, write a paragraph about the other types of hyperlinks you found that help organize and navigate a site, then identify and explain the characteristics of the controls you liked best.

▶ Visual Workshop

As the manager of a doctor's clinic, you have created an Access database called **Patients–M** to track insurance claim reimbursements that are fixed (paid at a predetermined fixed rate), or denied (not paid by the insurance company). Create a switchboard form to give the users an easy interface, as shown in Figure M-26. Both command buttons on the switchboard open forms in Edit Mode. Add and modify the labels shown at the top of the switchboard in Form Design View, and be sure to add your own name as the manager. Print the switchboard.

FIGURE M-26

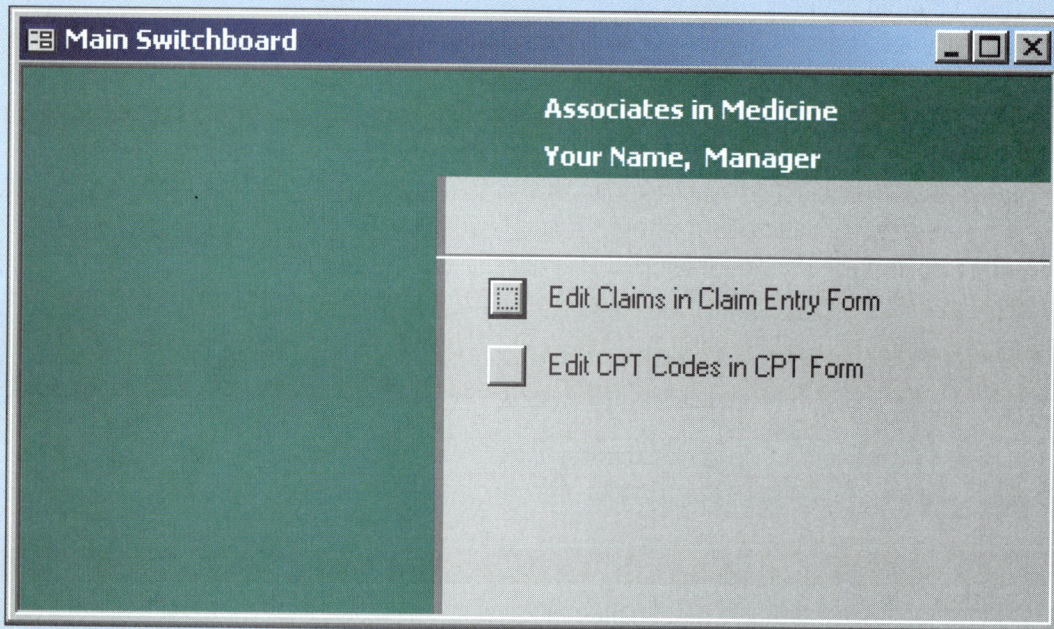

Creating

Macros

A **macro** is a database object that stores Access actions. When you **run** a macro, you execute the stored set of actions. **Actions** are the tasks that you want the macro to perform. Access provides about 50 actions from which to choose when creating a macro. Almost any repetitive Access task such as printing a report, opening a form, or exporting data is a good candidate for a macro. Automating routine and complex tasks by using a macro builds efficiency, accuracy, and flexibility into your database. ◢━ Kristen Fontanelle, a network administrator at MediaLoft, has noticed that several tasks are repeated on a regular basis and can be automated with macros.

Understanding Macros

A macro object may contain one or more actions, or tasks that you want Access to perform. When you run a macro, the actions are executed in the order in which they are listed in **Macro Design View**. Each action has a specified set of **arguments** that provide additional information on how to carry out the action. For example, the OpenForm action contains six arguments including Form Name (identifies which form to open) and View (determines whether the form should be opened in Form View or Design View). Creating macros is easy because after choosing the appropriate macro action, the associated arguments for that action automatically appear in the lower pane of Macro Design View. ⚡ Kristen studies the major benefits of using macros, macro terminology, and the components of Macro Design View before building her first macro.

Details

▶ The major benefits of using macros include:

- saving time by automating routine tasks.

- increasing accuracy by ensuring that tasks are executed consistently.

- improving the functionality and ease of use of forms by adding command buttons that execute macros.

- ensuring data accuracy in forms by using macros to respond to data entry errors.

- automating data transfers such as exporting data to an Excel workbook.

- creating your own customized environment by using macros to customize toolbars and menus.

▶ Macro terminology:

- A **macro** is an Access object that stores a series of actions to perform one or more tasks.

- Each task that you want the macro to perform is called an **action**. Each macro action occupies a single row in Macro Design View.

- **Macro Design View** is the window in which you create a macro, as shown in Figure N-1. See Table N-1 for a description of Macro Design View components.

- **Arguments** are properties of an action that provide additional information on how the action should execute.

- A **macro group** is an Access macro object that stores more than one macro. The macros in a macro group run independently of one another, but are grouped together to organize multiple macros that have similar characteristics. For example, you may want to put all of the macros that print reports in one macro group.

- An **expression** is a combination of values, fields, and operators that result in a value.

- A **conditional expression** is an expression that results in either a true or false answer that determines if a macro action will execute or not. For example, if the Country field contains a null value (nothing), you may want the macro to execute an action that sends the user a message.

- An **event** is something that happens on a form, window, toolbar, or datasheet—such as the click of a command button or an entry in a field—that can be used to initiate the execution of a macro.

Modifying Actions and Arguments

Macros can contain as many actions as necessary to complete the process that you want to auto-mate. Each action is evaluated in the order in which it appears in Macro Design View, starting at the top. A macro stops executing actions when it encounters a blank row in Macro Design View. While some macro actions manipulate data or objects, others are used only to make the database easier to use. **MsgBox** is a useful macro action because it displays an informational message. ✐ Kristen decides to add an action to the Print All Equipment Report macro to clarify what is happening when the macro runs. She adds a MsgBox action to the macro to dis-play a descriptive message for the user.

1. Click the **Design button** 📄 on the Database window toolbar
   The Print All Equipment Report macro opens in Macro Design View.

2. Click the **Action cell** for the second row, click the **Action list arrow**, press **m** to quickly scroll to the actions that start with the letter "m", then click **MsgBox**
   Each action has its own arguments that further clarify what the action will do.

   QuickTip
   Press [F1] to display Help text for the action and argu-ment currently selected.

3. Click the **Message argument text box** in the Action Arguments pane, then type **Click the Print button to print the All Equipment report**
   The Message argument determines what text appears in the message box. By default, the Beep argument is set to "Yes" and the Type argument is set to "None."

4. Click the **Type argument text box** in the Action Arguments pane, read the description in the lower-right corner of Macro Design View, click the **Type list arrow**, then click **Information**
   The Type argument determines which icon will appear in the dialog box that is created by the MsgBox action.

5. Click the **Title argument text box** in the Action Arguments pane, then type **To print this report...**
   Your screen should look like Figure N-3. The Title argument specifies what text will display in the title bar of the resulting dialog box. If you leave the Title argument empty, the title bar of the resulting dialog box will display "Microsoft Access."

6. Click the **Save button** 🖫 on the Macro Design toolbar, then click the **Run button** 🞂 on the Macro Design toolbar
   If your speakers are turned on, you should hear a beep, then the message box should appear, as shown in Figure N-4.

7. Click **OK** in the dialog box, close the All Equipment report, then close Macro Design View

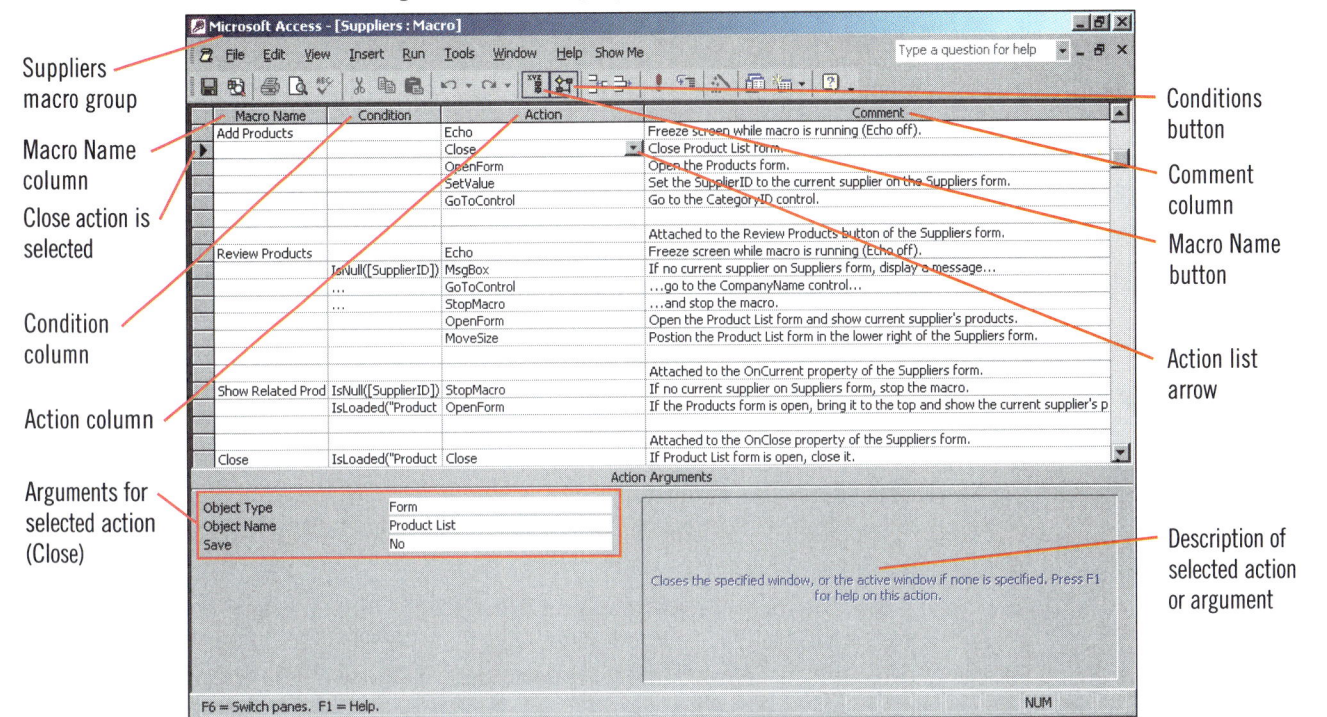

FIGURE N-1: Macro Design View of a macro group

TABLE N-1: Macro Design View components

Component	Description
Macro Name column	Contains the names of individual macros within a macro group. If the macro object contains only one macro, it isn't necessary to use this column because you can run the macro by referring to the macro by the macro object's name. View this column by clicking the Macro Names button 🞂. The Macro Names button works as a toggle to open and close the Macro Name column.
Condition column	Contains conditional expressions that are evaluated either true or false. If true, the macro action on that row is executed. If false, the macro action on that row is skipped. View this column by clicking the Conditions button 🞂. The Conditions button works as a toggle to open and close the Condition column.
Action column	Contains the actions, or the tasks, that the macro executes when it runs
Comment column	Contains optional explanatory text for each row
Action Arguments pane	Displays the arguments for the selected action
▶	Indicates which row is currently selected

Creating a Macro

In some software programs, you can create a macro by using a "macro recorder" to record, or save, the keystrokes and mouse clicks you use to perform a task. Access doesn't use that method. In Access, you create a macro by choosing a series of actions in Macro Design View that accomplish the job you want to automate. Therefore, if you are to become proficient with Access macros, you must be comfortable with macro actions. Access provides more than 50 macro actions. Some of the most common actions are listed in Table N-2. ✎ Kristen observes that time can be saved opening the All Equipment report from the Employees form, so she decides to create a macro to automate this task.

Steps

1. **Start Access, open the Technology-N database from where your Project Files are located, click Macros on the Objects bar, then click the New button 📄 on the Database window toolbar**

   Macro Design View opens, ready for your first action. The Macro Name and Condition columns are not visible by default, but can be toggled on by clicking their respective buttons on the Macro Design toolbar. They are only needed, of course, if you are creating multiple macros in the same macro object or using conditional expressions.

2. **Click the Action list arrow, press o to quickly scroll to the actions that start with the letter "o", then click OpenReport**

   The OpenReport action is added as the first line, and the arguments that further define the OpenReport action appear in the Action Arguments pane in the lower half of Macro Design View. The OpenReport action has two required arguments: Report Name and View. The Filter Name and Where Condition arguments are optional.

   > **QuickTip**
   > Press [F6] to jump between the actions and Action Arguments panes in Macro Design View.

3. **Click the Report Name argument text box in the Action Arguments pane, click the Report Name List arrow, then click All Equipment**

   All of the report objects in the Technology-N database display in the Report Name argument list.

4. **Click the View argument text box in the Action Arguments pane, click the View list arrow, then click Print Preview**

   Your screen should look like Figure N-2. Macros can be one or many actions long. In this case, the macro is only one action long and has no conditional expressions.

5. **Click the Save button 💾 on the Macro Design toolbar, type Preview All Equipment Report in the Macro Name text box, click OK, then close Macro Design View**

   The Technology-N database window shows the Print All Equipment Report object as a macro object.

6. **Click the Run button ❗ in the Database window toolbar**

   The All Equipment report opens in Print Preview.

7. **Close the All Equipment preview window**

FIGURE N-2: Macro Design View with OpenReport action

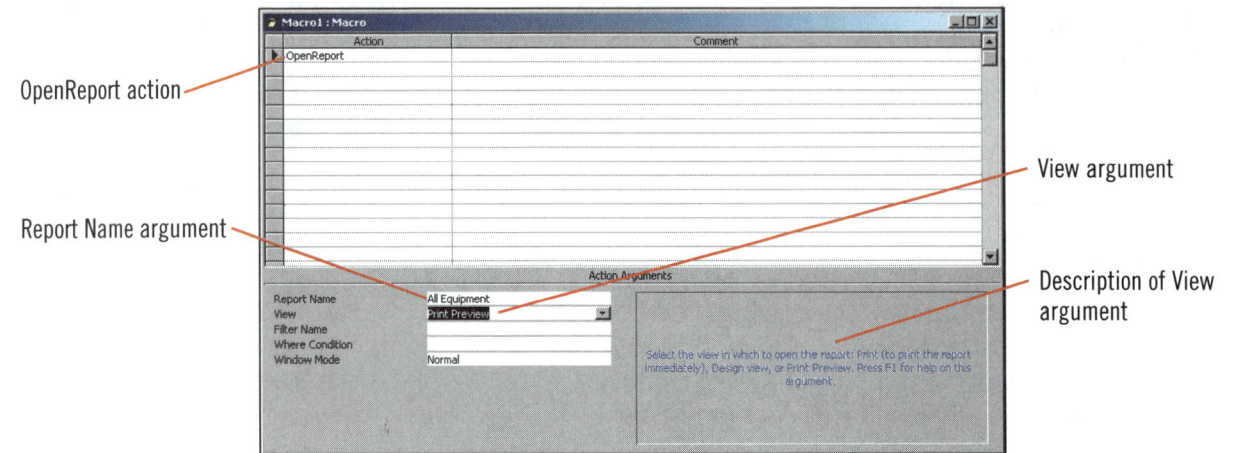

TABLE N-2: Common macro actions

subject area	macro action	description
Handling data in forms	ApplyFilter	Restricts the number of records that appear in the resulting form or report by applying limiting criteria
	FindRecord	Finds the first record that meets the criteria
	GoToControl	Moves the focus (where you are currently typing or clicking) to a specific field or control
	GoToRecord	Makes a specified record the current record
Executing menu options	RunCode	Runs a Visual Basic function (a series of programming statements that do a calculation or comparison and return a value)
	RunCommand	Carries out a specified menu command
	RunMacro	Runs a macro or attaches a macro to a custom menu command
	StopMacro	Stops the currently running macro
Importing/Exporting data	TransferDatabase TransferSpreadsheet TransferText	Imports, links, or exports data between the current Microsoft Access database and another database, spreadsheet, or text file
Manipulating objects	Close	Closes a window
	Maximize	Enlarges the active window to fill the Access window
	OpenForm	Opens a form in Form View, Design View, Print Preview, or Datasheet View
	OpenQuery	Opens a select or crosstab query in Datasheet View, Design View, or Print Preview; runs an action query
	OpenReport	Opens a report in Design View or Print Preview, or prints the report
	OpenTable	Opens a table in Datasheet View, Design View, or Print Preview
	PrintOut	Prints the active object, such as a datasheet, report, form, or module
	SetValue	Sets the value of a field, control, or property
Miscellaneous	Beep	Sounds a beep tone through the computer's speaker
	MsgBox	Displays a message box containing a warning or an informational message
	SendKeys	Sends keystrokes directly to Microsoft Access or to an active Windows-based application

FIGURE N-3: New MsgBox action

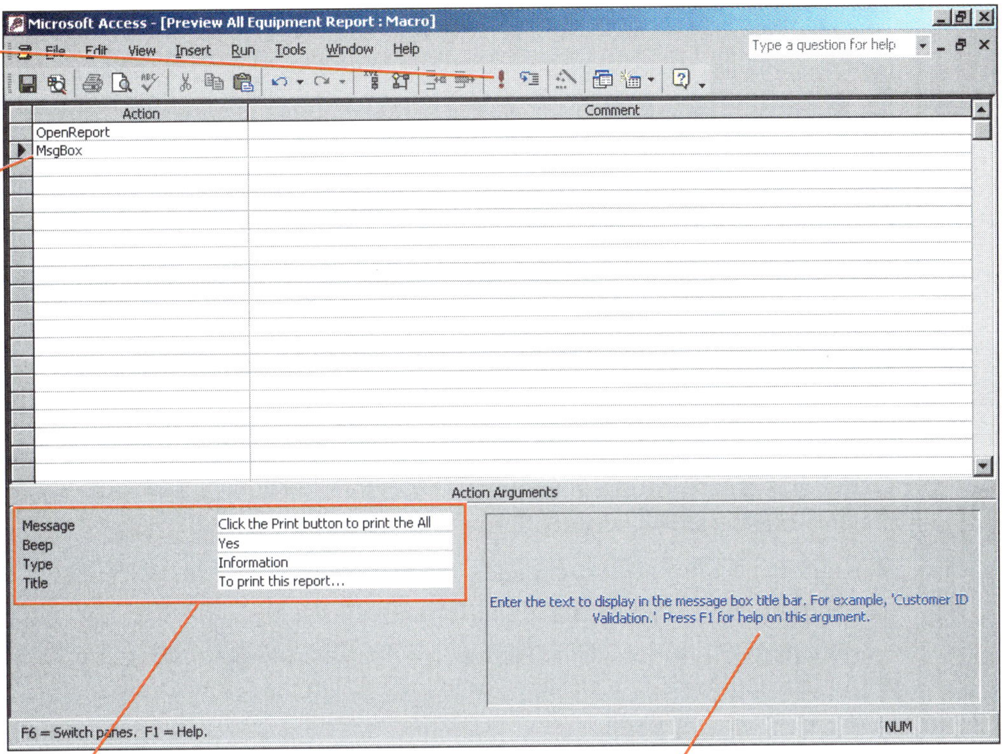

Run button

MsgBox action

Arguments for the selected action

Description of the Title argument

FIGURE N-4: Dialog box created by MsgBox action

Title argument determines the text in the title bar

Type argument determines icon

Message argument determines message text

Access 2002

Creating a Macro Group

A **macro group** is a macro object that stores more than one macro. Macro groups are used to organize multiple macros that have similar characteristics, such as all the macros that print reports or all the macros that are used by the same form through various command buttons. When you put several macros in the same macro object to create a macro group, you must enter a unique name for each macro in the Macro Name column (in the same row as the first macro action) to identify where each macro starts. ✐ Kristen adds a macro that prints the Accounting Report in an existing macro object thereby creating a macro group.

Steps

1. Right-click the **Preview All Equipment Report macro**, click **Rename**, type **Preview Reports Macro Group**, then press **[Enter]**
   Object names should identify the object as clearly as possible.

2. Right-click the **Preview Reports Macro Group**, click **Design View** on the shortcut menu, click the **Macro Names button** on the Macro Design toolbar, type **Preview All Equipment** in the Macro Name column, then press **[Enter]**
   An individual macro in a macro group is named in the Macro Name column.

3. Click the **Macro Name cell** in the fourth row, type **Preview Accounting Report**, then press **[Enter]**
   An individual macro in a macro group stops when it hits a blank row, or when a new macro name is entered in the Macro Name column. Therefore, a blank row between macros is not required, but it does help to clarify where macros start and stop even when the Macro Name column is not visible.

QuickTip

To resize the columns of Macro Design View, point between the column headings then drag ↔.

4. Click the **Action list arrow**, scroll and click **OpenReport**, click in the **Report Name argument text box** in the Action Arguments pane, click the **Report Name list arrow**, click **Accounting Report**, click the **View argument text box**, click the **View list arrow**, then click **Print Preview**
   Your screen should look like Figure N-5. One benefit of creating several macros in one macro group is that you can copy and paste actions from one macro to another.

5. Click the **row selector of the MsgBox action of the Preview All Equipment macro**, click the **Copy button** on the Macro Design toolbar, click the **record selector for the fifth row**, then click the **Paste button** on the Macro Design toolbar
   Action argument values are copied with the action, but need to be edited as necessary to work with the new macro.

6. Select **All Equipment** in the Message property text box in the Action Arguments pane, type **Accounting,** then click the **Save button** on the Macro Design toolbar
   Your screen should look like Figure N-6. To run a macro (other than the first macro) from within a macro group, you use the Tools menu.

7. Click **Tools** on the menu bar, point to **Macro**, click **Run Macro**, click the **Macro Name list arrow** in the Run Macro dialog box, click **Preview Reports Macro Group.Preview Accounting Report**, then click **OK**
   Referring to a specific macro within a macro group by separating them with a period is called **dot notation**. Dot notation is also used when developing modules with Visual Basic programming code.

8. Click **OK**, then close the Accounting report and Macro Design View
   The Preview Reports Macro Group contains two macros.

FIGURE N-5: Creating a macro group

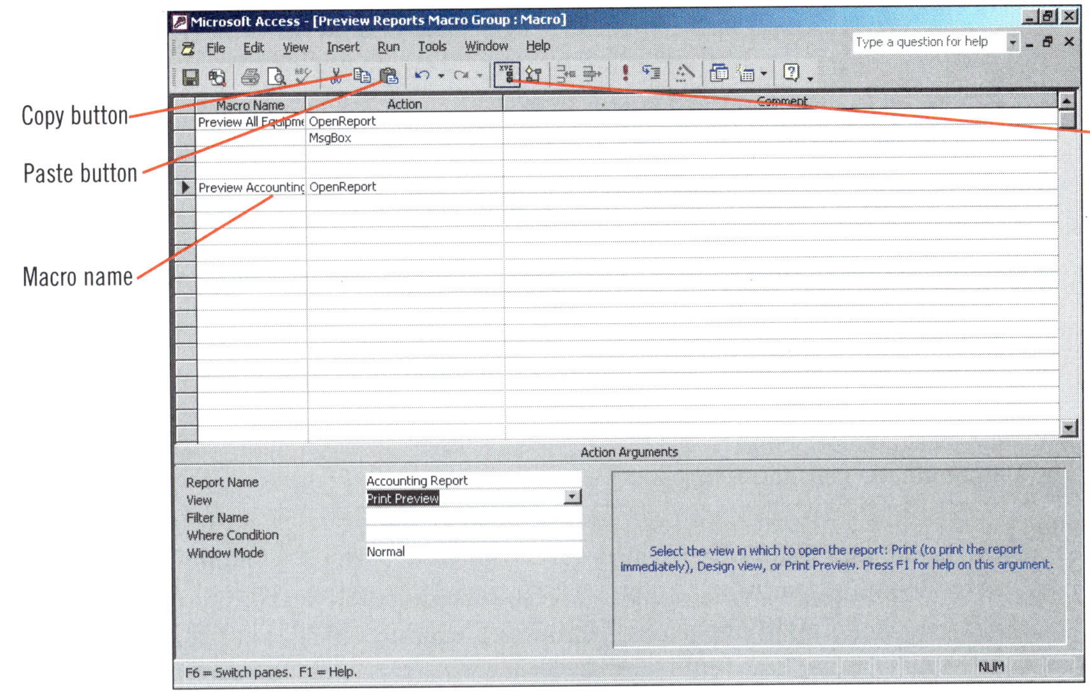

Copy button

Paste button

Macro name

Macro Names button

FIGURE N-6: Creating the Print Accounting Report macro

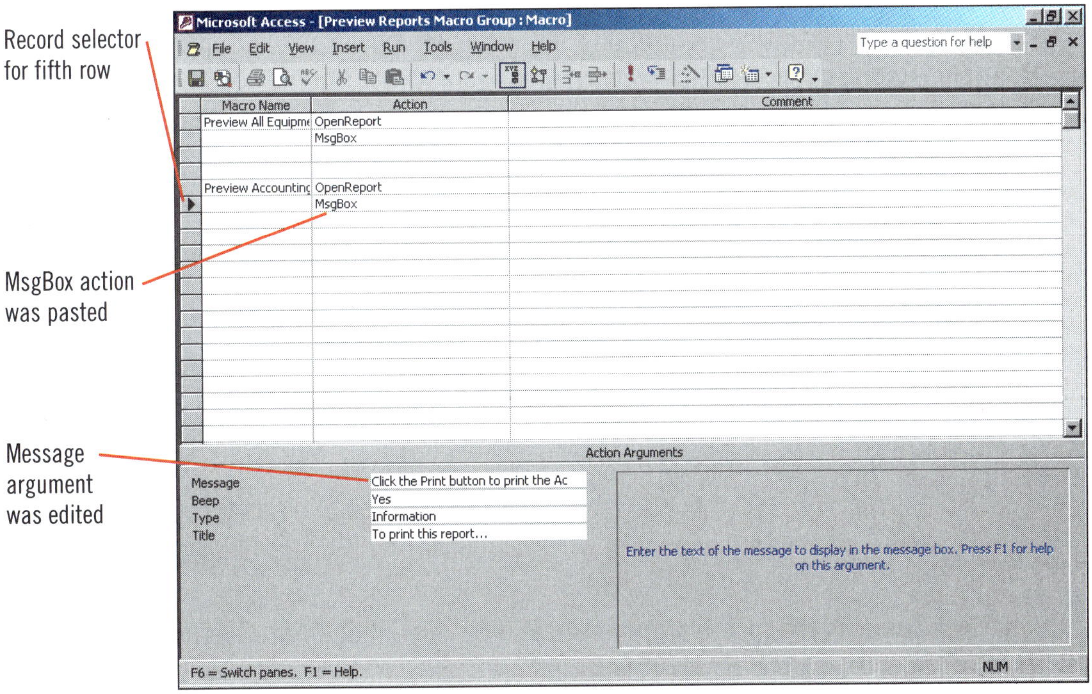

Record selector for fifth row

MsgBox action was pasted

Message argument was edited

Assigning a macro to a key combination

You can assign a key combination (such as [Ctrl][L]) to a macro by creating a macro group with the name **AutoKeys**. Enter the key combination in the Macro Names column for the first action of the associated macro. Any key combination assignments you make in the AutoKeys macro override those that Access has

already specified. Therefore, be sure to check the Keyboard Shortcuts information in the Microsoft Access Help system to make sure that the AutoKey assignment that you are creating doesn't override an Access quick keystroke that a user may already be using for another purpose.

Access 2002

Setting Conditional Expressions

Conditional expressions are entered in the Condition column of Macro Design View. They result in a true or false value. If the condition evaluates true, the action on that row is executed. If the condition evaluates false, the macro skips that row. When building a conditional expression that refers to a value in a control on a form or report, use the following syntax: [Forms]![*formname*]![*controlname*] or [Reports]![*reportname*]![*controlname*]. Separating the object type (Forms or Reports) from the object name and from the control name by using [square brackets] and exclamation points ! is called **bang notation**. At MediaLoft, everyone who has been with the company longer than five years is eligible to take their old PC equipment home as soon as it has been replaced. Kristen uses a conditional macro to emphasize this information in a form.

Steps

1. Click the **New button** in the database window, click the **Conditions button** on the Macro Design toolbar, right-click the **Condition cell** in the first row, click **Zoom**, then type **[Forms]![Employees]![DateHired]<Date()-(5*365)** in the Zoom dialog box
   The Zoom dialog box should look like Figure N-7. This conditional expression says "Check the value in the DateHired control on the Employees form and evaluate true if that value is earlier than five years from today. Evaluate false if that value is not earlier than five years ago."

2. Click **OK** to close the Zoom dialog box, drag ⟷ between the Condition and Action columns to expand the Condition column to its widest value, click the **Action cell** for the first row, click the **Action list arrow**, then scroll and click **SetValue**
   The SetValue action has two arguments.

3. Click the **Item argument text box** in the Action Arguments pane, type **[Forms]![Employees]![PCProgram]**, click the **Expression text box** in the Action Arguments panel, then type **Yes**
   Your screen should look like Figure N-8.

4. Click the **Save button** on the Macro Design toolbar, type **5PC** in the Macro Name text box, click **OK**, then close the 5PC macro
   Test the macro using the Employees form.

5. Click **Forms** on the Objects bar, then double-click the **Employees form**
   The record for Evelyn Storey, hired 1/1/92, appears. You use the 5PC macro to determine whether the PC Program check box should be checked.

6. Click **Tools** on the menu bar, point to **Macro**, click **Run Macro**, verify that **5PC** is in the Macro Name text box, then click **OK**
   After evaluating the date of this record and determining that this employee has been working at MediaLoft longer than five years, the PC Program check box was automatically checked (set to "Yes"), as shown in Figure N-9.

7. Click the **Last Record button** on the main form Navigation buttons, click **Tools** on the menu bar, point to **Macro**, click **Run Macro**, verify that **5PC** is in the **Macro Name text box**, then click **OK**
   Because Kristen Fontanelle was not hired more than five years ago, the PC Program check box was not checked (set to "yes") when you ran the macro.

8. Close the Employees form

FIGURE N-7: Zoom dialog box

Form name → `[Forms]![Employees]![DateHired]<Date()-(5*365)`

→ 5 years times 365 days per year

Control name →

→ Date function returns today's date

OK

Cancel

Eont...

FIGURE N-8: Creating a conditional expression

Microsoft Access - [Macro1 : Macro]

File Edit View Insert Run Tools Window Help

Type a question for help

Condition	Action	Comment
[Forms]![Employees]![DateHired]<Date()-(5*365)	SetValue	

Condition entry →

SetValue action →

→ Conditions button

Action Arguments

Item   `[Forms]![Employees]![PCProgram]`
Expression   `Yes`

Enter an expression that will be used to set the value for this item. You should not precede the expression with an equal sign. Click the Build button to use the Expression Builder to set this argument. Required argument. Press F1 for help on this argument.

F6 = Switch panes. F1 = Help.

NUM

FIGURE N-9: Running the 5PC macro

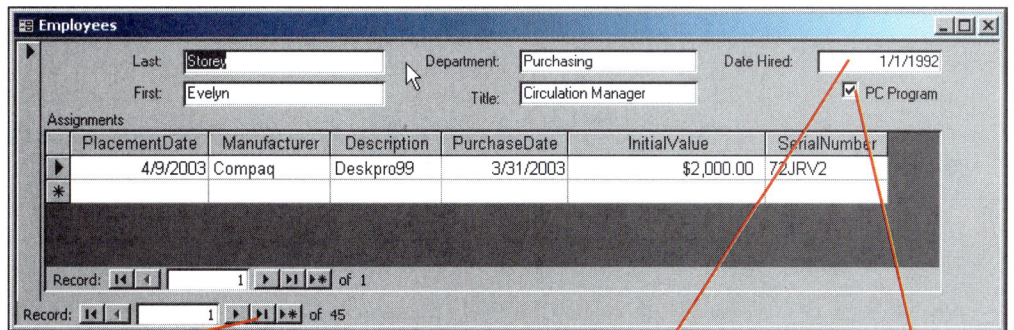

Employees

Last: Storey   Department: Purchasing   Date Hired: 1/1/1992
First: Evelyn   Title: Circulation Manager   ☑ PC Program

Assignments

PlacementDate	Manufacturer	Description	PurchaseDate	InitialValue	SerialNumber
4/9/2003	Compaq	Deskpro99	3/31/2003	$2,000.00	72JRV2

Record: 1 of 1

Record: 1 of 45

Main form Last Record button

When the hire date is over five years ago...

...the PC Program check box is set to "yes"

Working with Events

An **event** is a specific activity that occurs within the database such as clicking a command button, editing data, or opening or closing a form. Events can be triggered by the user, or by the database itself. By assigning a macro to an appropriate event, rather than running the macro from the Tools menu, you further automate and improve your database. ◀━━ Now that Kristen has developed the 5PC macro, she will attach it to an event on the Employees form so that she doesn't have to run the macro for each record.

Steps 1 2 3 4

QuickTip

In the property sheet, a short description of the current property appears in the status bar. Press [F1] for more help on that property.

1. Right-click the **Employees form**, click **Design View** on the shortcut menu, then click the **Properties button** 📋 to open the property sheet for the form
   All objects, sections, and controls have a variety of events to which macros can be attached. Most event names are self-explanatory for that item, such as the On Click event (which occurs when that item is clicked).

2. Click the **Event tab**, click the **On Current list arrow**, then click **5PC**
   Your screen should look like Figure N-10.

3. Click 📋 to close the property sheet, then click the **Form View button** 🔳 on the Form View toolbar
   The On Current event occurs when focus moves from one record to another, therefore the 5PC macro will automatically run as you move from record to record in the form.

4. Click the **Next Record button** ▶ in the main form Navigation buttons fifteen times while observing the PC Program check box
   For every Date Hired value that is earlier than five years before today's date, the PC Program check box is automatically checked (set to "yes").

5. Save, then close the Employees form

FIGURE N-10: Assigning a macro to an event

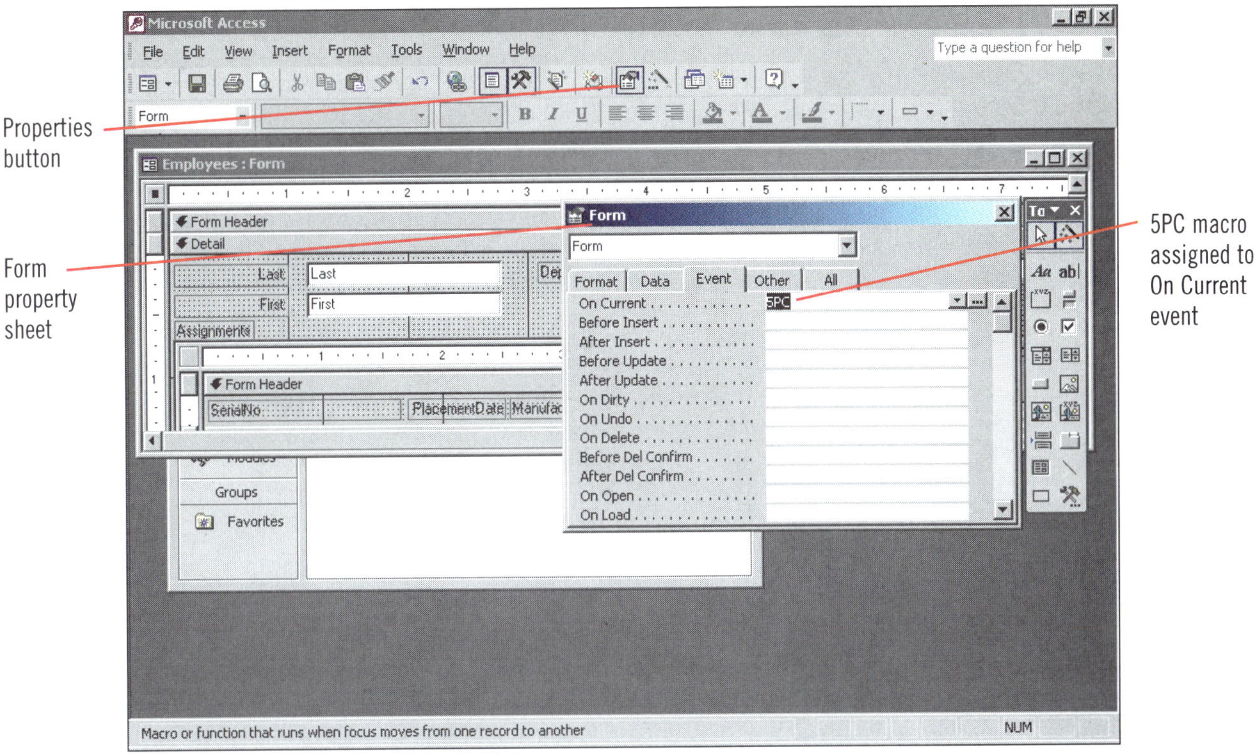

Properties button

Form property sheet

5PC macro assigned to On Current event

Macro or function that runs when focus moves from one record to another

NUM

Access 2002

CLUES TO USE

Assigning a macro to a command button

A common way to run a macro from a form is to first add a command button to the form, and then run the macro from the command button. To do this, add a command button to the form using the Command Button Wizard. Select the Run Macro action from the Miscellaneous category. The selected macro is assigned to the **On Click** event for the command button, and runs when you click the command button in Form View.

Customizing Toolbars

There are many ways to run a macro: by clicking the Run button in Macro Design View, by using commands on the Tools menu, by assigning the macro to an event on a control, or by assigning it to a toolbar, menu, or shortcut menu. The benefit of assigning a macro to a toolbar button as compared to assigning the macro to a command button on a specific form is that the toolbar can be made available to the user at all times, whereas a command button on a form is available only when that specific form is open. Macros that are run from multiple forms are great candidates for custom toolbars. Kristen decides to create a new toolbar for the print macros.

Steps 1234

1. Click **Macros** on the Objects bar, click the **Preview Reports Macro Group**, click **Tools** on the menu, point to **Macro**, then click **Create Toolbar from Macro**
The Preview Reports Macro Group toolbar appears on your screen. All of the macros in that group are automatically added to the toolbar.

2. Drag the **Preview Reports Macro Group toolbar title bar** to dock it just below the Database toolbar, as shown in Figure N-11
Because this toolbar contains buttons for only two macros (the two found in the Print Reports Macro Group), the entire name of the macro fits comfortably on the toolbar. If you wanted the toolbar to support many macros, you'd either have to shorten the text, or use icons in order to fit all of the macros on the toolbar.

3. Right-click the **Preview Reports Macro Group toolbar**, click **Customize** on the shortcut menu, right-click the **Preview All Equipment macro button** on the Preview Reports Macro Group toolbar, then point to **Change Button Image** on the shortcut menu
Your screen should look like Figure N-12. The shortcut menu that allows you to modify toolbar button images and text is available only when the Customize dialog box is open.

4. Click the **Shoes icon** 👟 on the icon palette, right-click the **Preview All Equipment macro button** again, then click **Default Style** on the shortcut menu
The Default Style for a button displays only the button image, not the text.

5. Right-click the **Preview Accounting Report macro button** on the Preview Reports Macro Group toolbar, point to **Change Button Image** on the shortcut menu, click the **Scales icon** ⚖ on the icon palette, right-click the **Preview Accounting Report macro button**, then click **Default Style** on the shortcut menu
Any image on any button on any toolbar button can be edited.

6. Right-click ⚖ on the Preview Reports Macro Group toolbar, then click **Edit Button Image**
The Button Editor dialog box opens, which allows you to change the appearance of the picture pixel by pixel.

7. Click the **green box** on the Colors palette, then click all 11 squares in the **left scale**, as shown in Figure N-13
With enough time and patience, you could create any number of unique button images.

8. Click **OK**, then click **Close** to close the Customize dialog box
The new Preview Reports Macro Group toolbar can be turned on or off from anywhere within the database, just like any other toolbar. New buttons can be added or modified at any time.

9. Point to ⚖, then point to 👟 on the Preview Reports Macro Group toolbar
Each button on the Preview Reports Macro Group toolbar has a ScreenTip like buttons on other toolbars.

FIGURE N-11: Preview Reports Macro Group toolbar

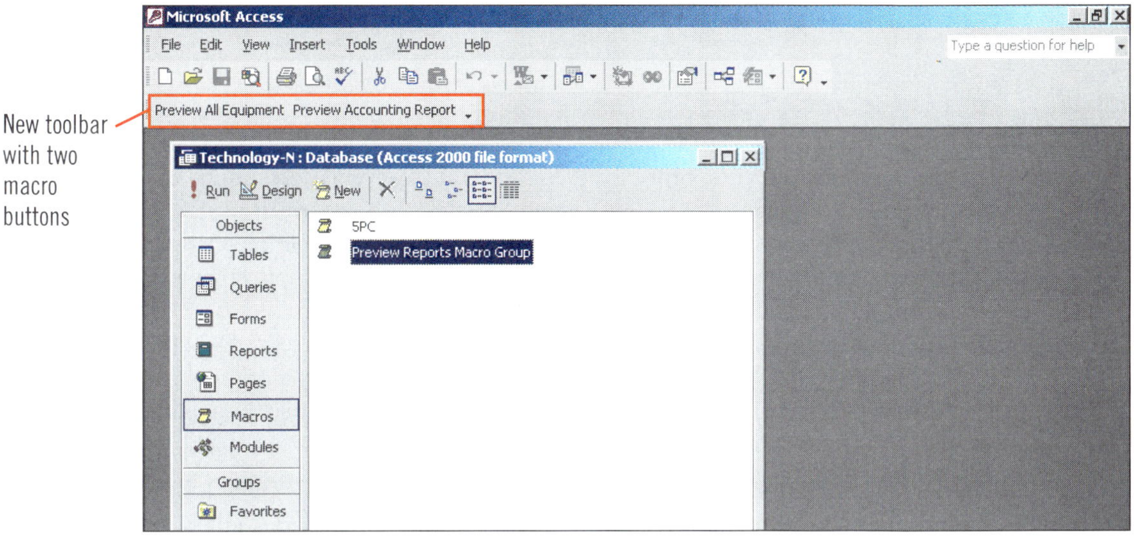

New toolbar with two macro buttons

FIGURE N-12: Customizing a button image

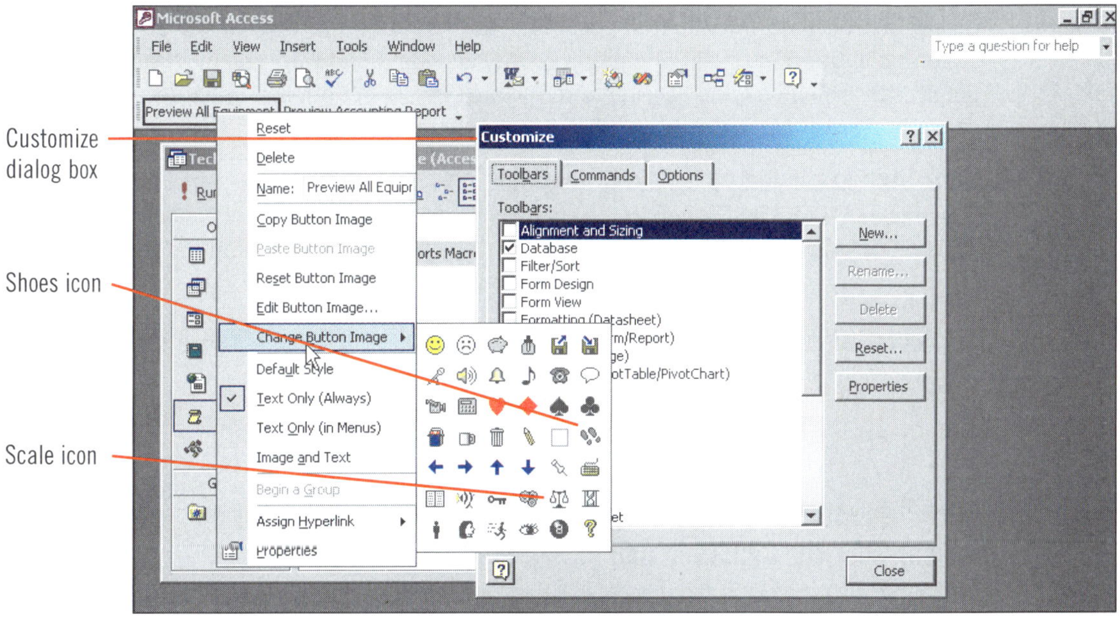

Customize dialog box

Shoes icon

Scale icon

FIGURE N-13: Button Editor dialog box

Left scale

Green box

Troubleshooting Macros

When macros don't execute properly, Access supplies several techniques to debug them. **Debugging** means to determine why the macro doesn't run properly. It usually involves breaking a dysfunctional macro down into small pieces that can be individually tested. For example, you can **single step** a macro, which means to run it one line (one action) at a time to observe the effect of each specific action in the Macro Single Step dialog box. Another debugging technique is to disable a particular macro action(s) by entering false in the Condition cell for the action(s) that you wish to temporarily skip. Before building more sophisticated macros, Kristen uses the Preview Reports Macro Group to learn debugging techniques.

1. Right-click **Preview Reports Macro Group**, click **Design View** from the shortcut menu, click the **Single Step button** on the Macro Design toolbar, then click the **Run button** on the Macro Design toolbar

   The screen should look like Figure N-14, with the Macro Single Step dialog box open. This dialog box displays information including the name of the macro, whether the current action's condition is true, the action's name, and the action arguments. From the Macro Single Step dialog box you can step into the next macro action, halt execution of the macro, or continue running the macro without single stepping.

2. Click **Step** in the Macro Single Step dialog box

   Stepping into the second action lets the first action execute, and pauses the macro at the second action. The Macro Single Step dialog box now displays information about the second action.

3. Click **Step**

   The second action, the MsgBox action, executes, displaying the message box.

4. Click **OK**, then close the All Equipment report

   You can use the Condition column to temporarily ignore an action while you are debugging a macro.

5. Click to stop single stepping, click the **Conditions button** on the Macro Design toolbar, click the **Condition cell** for the first row, then type **False**

   Your screen should look like Figure N-15.

6. Click the **Save button** on the Macro Design toolbar, then click the **Run button**

   Because the Condition value is False for the OpenReport action, it did not execute, and the macro jumped to the second action, the MsgBox action.

7. Click **OK**, double-click **False** in the Condition cell, then press **[Delete]**

   Closing the Condition column does not delete or change the values stored in that column. To change the Preview All Equipment macro so that the All Equipment report opens in Print Preview the next time you run this macro, you must delete the False entry for the OpenReport action.

8. Click **File** on the menu bar, click **Print**, then click **OK** in the Print Macro Definition dialog box

9. Save and close the Preview Reports Macro Group, close the Technology-N database, then exit Access

FIGURE N-14: Single stepping through a macro

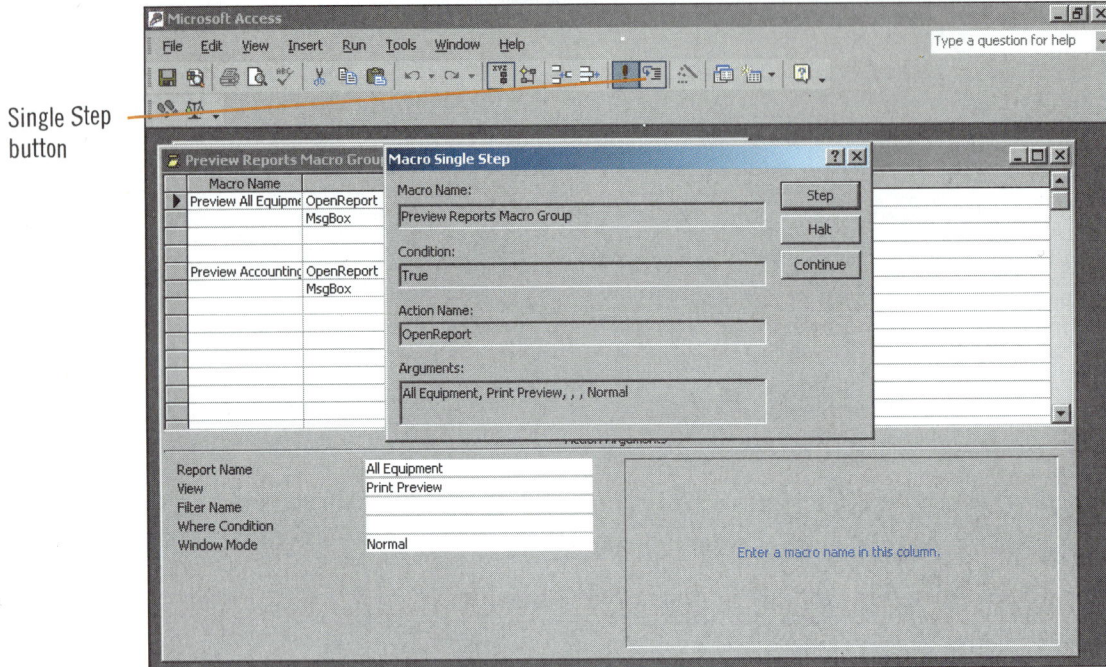

Single Step button

Microsoft Access

File Edit View Insert Run Tools Window Help

Type a question for help

Macro Single Step

Preview Reports Macro Group

Macro Name	
Preview All Equipme	OpenReport
	MsgBox
Preview Accounting	OpenReport
	MsgBox

Macro Name:

Preview Reports Macro Group

Condition:

True

Action Name:

OpenReport

Arguments:

All Equipment, Print Preview, , , Normal

Step

Halt

Continue

Enter a macro name in this column.

Action Arguments	
Report Name	All Equipment
View	Print Preview
Filter Name	
Where Condition	
Window Mode	Normal

FIGURE N-15: Using a False condition

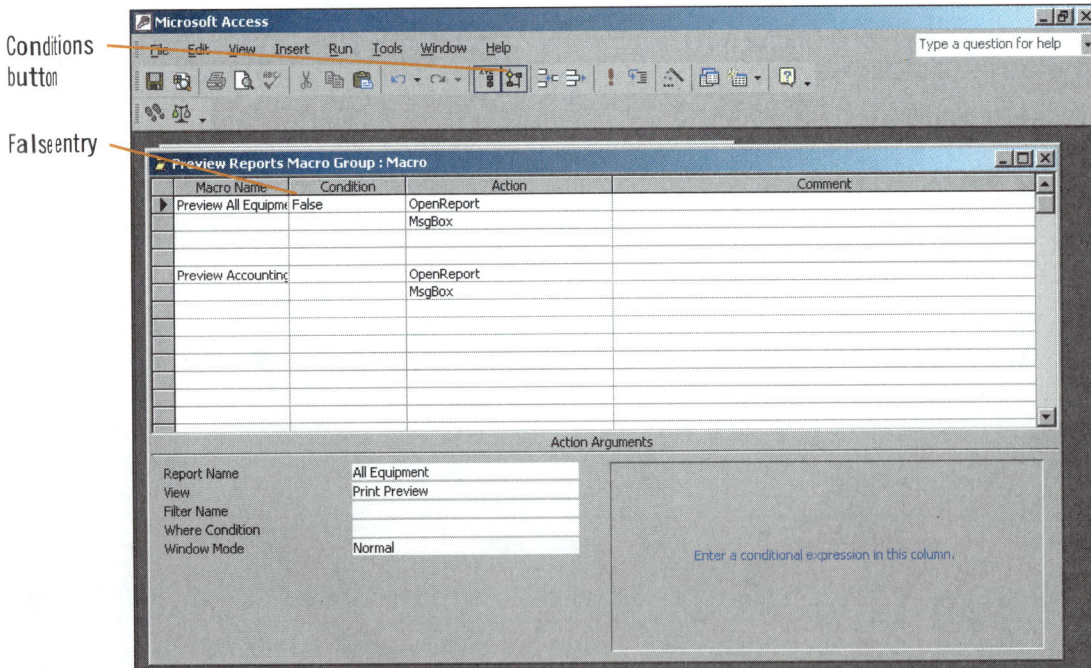

Conditions button

False entry

Microsoft Access

File Edit View Insert Run Tools Window Help

Type a question for help

Preview Reports Macro Group : Macro

Macro Name	Condition	Action	Comment
Preview All Equipme	False	OpenReport	
		MsgBox	
Preview Accounting		OpenReport	
		MsgBox	

Action Arguments

Report Name	All Equipment
View	Print Preview
Filter Name	
Where Condition	
Window Mode	Normal

Enter a conditional expression in this column.

Practice

► Concepts Review

Identify each element of Macro Design View shown in Figure N-16.

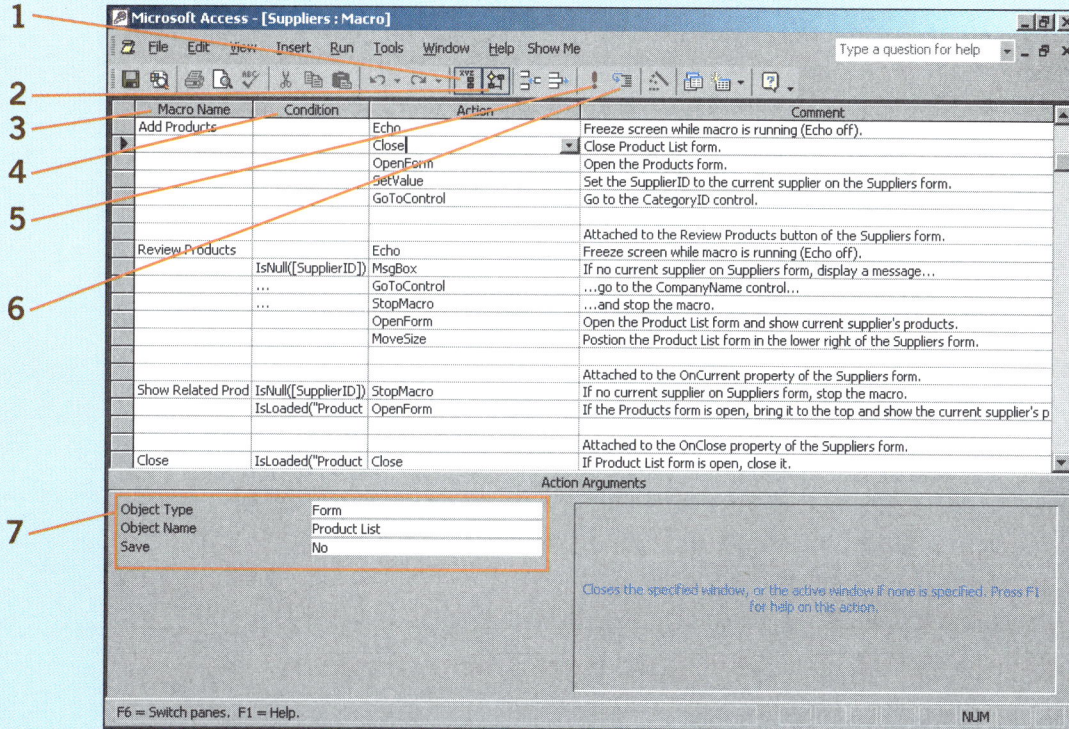

Match each term with the statement that describes its function.

8. Macro
9. Conditional expression
10. Arguments
11. Debugging
12. Actions
13. Event

a. Specific action that occurs within the database such as clicking a button or opening a form
b. Individual steps that you want the Access macro to perform
c. Access object that stores one or more actions that perform one or more tasks
d. Determining why a macro doesn't run properly
e. Provide additional information to define how an Access action will perform
f. Evaluates as either true or false, which determines whether Access executes that action or not

Select the best answer from the list of choices.

14. Which of the following is *not* a major benefit of using a macro?
    a. To save time by automating routine tasks
    b. To ensure consistency in executing routine or complex tasks
    c. To make the database more flexible or easy to use
    d. To redesign the relationships among the tables of the database

15. Which of the following *best* describes the process of creating an Access macro?
    a. Use the macro recorder to record clicks and keystrokes as you complete a task.
    b. Use the single-step recorder to record clicks and keystrokes as you complete a task.
    c. Use the Macro Wizard to determine which tasks are done most frequently.
    d. Open Macro Design View and add actions, arguments, and conditions to accomplish the desired task.

16. Which of the following would *not* be a way to run a macro?
    a. Click the Run button on the Database window toolbar.
    b. Assign the macro to an event of a control on a form.
    c. Add the macro as a button on a toolbar, then click the button.
    d. Add the macro as an entry on the title bar, then click the title bar.

17. Which is *not* a reason to run a macro in single-step mode?
    a. You want to change the arguments of a macro while it runs.
    b. You want to observe the effect of each macro action individually.
    c. You want to debug a macro that isn't working properly.
    d. You want to run only a few of the actions of a macro.

18. Which is *not* a reason to use conditional expressions in a macro?
    a. More macro actions are available when you are also using conditional expressions.
    b. Conditional expressions allow you to skip over actions when the expression evaluates as false.
    c. You can enter false in the Conditions column for an action to skip it.
    d. Conditional expressions give the macro more power and flexibility.

19. Which example illustrates the proper syntax to refer to a specific control on a form?
    a. {Forms}!{*formname*}!(*controlname*)
    b. (Forms)!(*formname*)!(*controlname*)
    c. Forms!*formname.controlname*
    d. [Forms]![*formname*]![*controlname*]

20. Which event executes every time you move from record to record in a form?
    a. New Record
    b. On Current
    c. On Move
    d. Next Record

▶ Skills Review

1. **Understand macros.**
    a. Start Access, then open the **Basketball-N** database from where your Project Files are stored.
    b. Open the Print Macro Group in Macro Design View, then record your answers to the following questions on a sheet of paper:
       • How many macros are in this macro group?
       • What are the names of the macros in this macro group?

- What actions does the first macro in this macro group contain?
- What arguments does the first action contain? What values were chosen for those arguments?
  - **c.** Close Macro Design View for the Print Macro Group object.

2. **Create a macro.**
   - **a.** Start a new macro in Macro Design View.
   - **b.** Add the OpenQuery action to the first row of Macro Design View.
   - **c.** Select Score Delta as the value for the Query Name argument of the OpenQuery action.
   - **d.** Select Datasheet for the View argument of the OpenQuery action.
   - **e.** Select Edit for the Data Mode argument for the OpenQuery action.
   - **f.** Save the macro object with the name **View Score Delta**.
   - **g.** Run the macro to make sure it works, then close the Score Delta query and the View Score Delta Macro Design View.

3. **Modify actions and arguments.**
   - **a.** Open the View Score Delta macro in Macro Design View.
   - **b.** Add a MsgBox action in the second row of Macro Design View.
   - **c.** Type **We had a great season!** for the Message argument in the Action Arguments pane of the MsgBox action.
   - **d.** Select Yes for the Beep argument of the MsgBox action.
   - **e.** Select Warning! for the Type argument of the MsgBox action.
   - **f.** Type **Iowa State Cyclones** for the Title argument of the MsgBox action.
   - **g.** Save the macro, then run it to make sure the MsgBox action works as intended.
   - **h.** Click OK in the dialog box created by the MsgBox action, then close the Score Delta query and the View Score Delta macro.

4. **Create a macro group.**
   - **a.** Rename the View Score Delta macro, changing it to **Query Macro Group**.
   - **b.** Open Query Macro Group in Macro Design View.
   - **c.** Open the Macro Name column, then type the name **View Score Delta** on the first line for the first macro.
   - **d.** Start another macro by typing **View Forward FG** in the Macro Name cell of the fourth row.
   - **e.** Add an OpenQuery action for the first action of the Forward FG Macro.
   - **f.** Select Forward Field Goals for the Query Name argument of the OpenQuery action, and use the default entries for the other two arguments.
   - **g.** Add a MsgBox action for the second action of the View Forward FG macro.
   - **h.** Type **Forward Field Goals** as the Message argument for the MsgBox action.
   - **i.** Select Yes for the Beep argument of the MsgBox action.
   - **j.** Select Critical for the Type argument of the MsgBox action.
   - **k.** Type **2002-2003 Season** for the Title argument of the MsgBox action, then save the macro.
   - **l.** Click Tools on the menu bar, point to Macro, click Run macro, then run the View Forward FG macro.
   - **m.** Click OK, close the query datasheet, then close the Query Macro Group.

5. **Set conditional expressions.**
   - **a.** Start a new macro in Macro Design View.
   - **b.** Click the Conditions button on the Macro Design toolbar to open the Condition column.
   - **c.** Enter the following condition in the Condition cell of the first row: **[Forms]![Game Summary Form]![Home Score]>[Opponent Score]** (*Hint:* Use the Zoom dialog box or widen the column to more clearly view the entry.)
   - **d.** Add the SetValue action to the first row.
   - **e.** Type the following entry in the Item argument value for the SetValue action: **[Forms]![Game Summary Form]![Victory]**
   - **f.** Type **Yes** for the Expression argument for the SetValue action.
   - **g.** Save the macro with the name **Victory Calculator**, then close Macro Design View.

6. **Work with events.**
   a. Open the Game Summary Form in Form Design View.
   b. Open the property sheet for the form.
   c. Assign the Victory Calculator macro to the On Current event of the form.
   d. Close the property sheet, save the form, then open the Game Summary Form in Form View.
   e. Navigate through the first four records. The Victory check box should be marked for the first three records, but not the fourth.
   f. Print the third and fourth records, then close the Game Summary Form.

7. **Customize toolbars.**
   a. Click Macros on the Objects bar, click the Print Macro Group, click Tools on the menu bar, point to Macro, then click Create Toolbar from Macro.
   b. Dock the toolbar with the three text buttons just below the Database toolbar in the database window.
   c. Right-click the new toolbar, then click Customize on the shortcut menu to open the Customize dialog box.
   d. Change the button image for each of the three macros to the question mark icon and a default style (image only).
   e. Edit the button images so that the second macro question mark button is red (instead of yellow) and the third is blue (instead of yellow).
   f. Close the Customize dialog box, then point to each icon to make sure that the ScreenTip relates to the three macro names in the Print Macro Group.

8. **Troubleshoot macros.**
   a. Open the Print Macro Group in Macro Design View.
   b. Click the Single Step button on the Macro Design toolbar, then click the Run button on the Macro Design toolbar.
   c. Click Step twice to step through the two actions of this macro, then click OK in the resulting message box.
   d. Open the Condition column by clicking the Conditions button on the Macro Design toolbar (if it's not already opened).
   e. Enter the value **False** as a condition to the first row, the OpenReport action of the Games Summary macro.
   f. Save the macro, then click the Run button.
   g. Click the Step button twice to move through the actions of the macro. This time the Games Summary report should *not* be printed. Click OK when prompted.
   h. Delete the False condition in the first row, save the macro, then click the Single Step button to toggle it off.
   i. Click File on the menu bar, click Print, click OK in the Print Macro Definition dialog box, then close Macro Design View.
   j. Close the Basketball-N database, then exit Access.

► Independent Challenge 1

As the manager of a doctor's clinic, you have created an Access database called Patients-N to track insurance claim reimbursements. You will use macros to help automate the database.

   a. Start Access, then open the database **Patients-N** from the drive and folder where your Project Files are located.
   b. Open Macro Design View of the CPT Form Open macro. (CPT stands for Current Procedural Terminology, which is a code that describes a medical procedure.) If the Single Step button is toggled on, click it to toggle it off.
   c. On a separate sheet of paper, identify the macro actions, arguments for each action, and values for each argument.
   d. In two or three sentences, explain in your own words what tasks this macro automates.
   e. Close the CPT Form Open macro.
   f. Open the Claim Entry Form in Form Design View. Maximize the window.
   g. In the footer of the Claim Entry Form are several command buttons. (*Hint:* Scroll the main form to see these buttons.) Open the property sheet of the Add CPT Code button, then click the Event tab.
   h. On your paper, write the event to which the CPT Form Open macro is assigned.

i. Open the Claim Entry Form in Form View, then click the Add CPT Code button in the form footer.

j. On your paper, write the current record number that is displayed for you.

k. Scroll up the CPT form, then find the record for CPT Code 99243. Write the RBRVS value for this record, then close the CPT form and Claim Entry form. (RBRVS stands for Resource Based Relative Value System, a measurement of relative value between medical procedures.)

l. Close the Patients-N database, then exit Access.

▶ Independent Challenge 2

As the manager of a doctor's clinic, you have created an Access database called Patients-N to track insurance claim reimbursements. You will use macros to help automate the database.

a. Start Access, then open the database **Patients-N** from the drive and folder where your Project Files are located.

b. Start a new macro in Macro Design View, then click the Macro Names button on the Macro Design toolbar to open the Macro Name column. If the Single Step button is toggled on, click it to toggle it off.

c. Type **Preview DOS-Denied** as the first macro name, then add the OpenReport macro action in the first row.

d. Select Date of Service Report—Denied for the Report Name argument, then select Print Preview for the View argument of the OpenReport action. Leave the other two arguments blank.

e. In the third row, type **Preview DOS-Fixed** as a new macro name, then add the OpenReport macro action in the third row.

f. Select Date of Service Report—Fixed for the ReportName argument, then select Print Preview for the View argument of the second OpenReport action. Leave the other two arguments blank.

g. Save the object with the name **Preview Group**, close Macro Design View, then click the Preview Group macro object to select it.

h. Click File on the menu bar, click Print, then click OK in the Print Macro Definition dialog box.

i. Run the Preview DOS-Denied macro to test it, then close Print Preview.

j. Run the Preview DOS-Fixed macro to test it, then close Print Preview.

k. Close the Patients-N database, then exit Access.

▶ Independent Challenge 3

As the manager of a doctor's clinic, you have created an Access database called Patients-N to track insurance claim reimbursements. You will use macros to help automate the database.

a. Start Access, then open the **Patients-N** database from the drive and folder where your Project Files are located.

b. Start a new macro in Macro Design View, then click the Conditions button on the Macro Design toolbar to open the Condition column. If the Single Step button is toggled on, click it to toggle it off.

c. Enter the following in the Condition cell of the first row: **[Forms]![CPT Form]![RBRVS]=0**

d. Select the SetValue action for the first row.

e. Enter the following as the Item argument value for the SetValue action: **[Forms]![CPT Form]![Research]**

f. Type **Yes** as the Expression argument value for the SetValue action.

g. Save the macro with the name **Value Research**, close Macro Design View, then click the Value Research macro object to select it.

h. Click File on the menu bar, click Print, then click OK in the Print Macro Definition dialog box.

i. Open the CPT Form in Form Design View, and open the property sheet for the form.

j. Assign the Value Research macro to the On Current event of the form.

k. Close the property sheet, save the form, then open the CPT Form in Form View.

l. Use the Next Record button to move quickly through all 64 records in the form. Notice that the macro places a check mark in the Research check box only when the RBRVS value is equal to zero.

m. Save and close the CPT Form, then close the Patients-N database.

ⓔ Independent Challenge 4

Your culinary club is collecting information on international chocolate factories, museums, and stores, and has asked you to help build a database to organize the information. You collect some information on the World Wide Web to enter into the database, then tie the forms together with macros attached to command buttons.

a. Go to www.godiva.com. Your goal is to determine if there is a Godiva Boutique store in Toronto, Canada, where some members of your group will be visiting. Because Web sites change often, the links to find the Godiva Boutique stores in Toronto from the Godiva home page may vary from those provided. Therefore, if you cannot find the following links, or if the links don't work, use the Search text box to find the stores.

b. Click the links from the Godiva home page to locate the Godiva Boutique stores in Toronto, Canada.

c. Once you find the page that lists the Godiva store locations in Toronto, Canada, select that information on the Web page, then print the selection.

d. Open the **Chocolate-N** database from the drive and folder where your Project Files are stored, then open the Countries form in Form View.

e. Click the New Record button for the main form, then type **Canada** in the Country text box.

f. In the subform for the Canada record, enter **Godiva Boutique** in the Name field, **S** in the Type field (S for store), the address information that you found on the Web site in the Street field, **Toronto** in the City field, and **Ontario** in the StateProvince field.

g. Open Macro Design View for a new macro, then add the PrintOut action to the first row. If the Single Step button is toggled on, click it to toggle it off. Modify the Print Range argument to Selection, save the macro with the name PrintRecord, then close it.

h. In Form Design View of the Countries form, add a label with your name to the left section of the Form Header section, then add a command button to the right section. If the Command Button Wizard starts, click Cancel.

i. In the property sheet for the Command button, click the On Click property on the Event tab. Click the list arrow for the On Click property, then click PrintRecord. You attached the PrintRecord macro to the On Click property for this command button. Therefore, when the command button is clicked in Form View, the PrintRecord macro should run.

j. Double-click the text on the command button, then type **Print Current Record**.

k. Save the form, then view it in Form View.

l. Find the Canada record, then click the Print Current Record command button. Only that record should print.

m. Close the Countries form, then exit Access.

▶ Visual Workshop

As the manager of a doctor's clinic, you have created an Access database called **Patients-N** to track insurance claim reimbursements. Develop a new macro called **Query Group** with the actions and argument values shown in Figure N-17 and Table N-3. Run both macros to test them, and debug them if necessary. Print the macro by clicking File on the menu bar. Click Print, and then click OK in the Print Macro Definition dialog box.

TABLE N-3: Macro actions and arguments for the Query Group

macro name	action	argument	argument value
Denied	OpenQuery	Query Name	Monthly Query – Denied
		View	Datasheet
		Data Mode	Edit
	Maximize		
	MsgBox	Message	These claims were denied
		Beep	Yes
		Type	Information
		Title	Denied
Fixed	OpenQuery	Query Name	Monthly Query – Fixed
		View	Datasheet
		Data Mode	Edit
	Maximize		
	MsgBox	Message	These claims were fixed
		Beep	Yes
		Type	Information
		Title	Fixed

FIGURE N-17

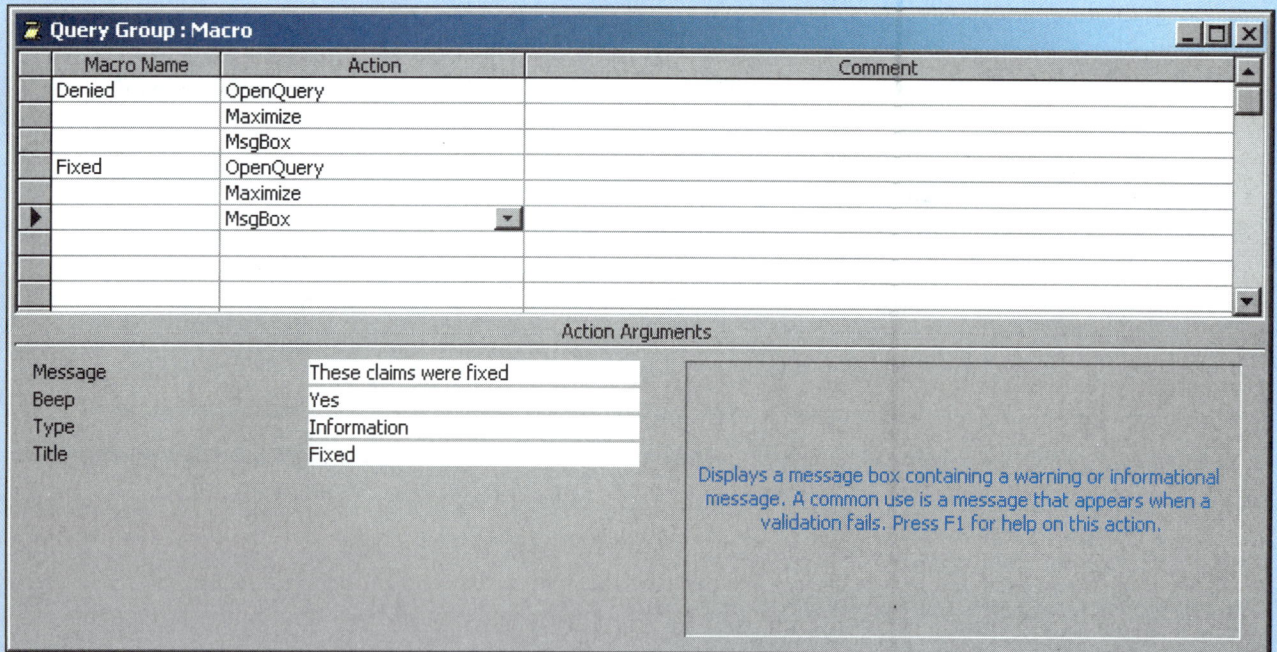

Macro Name	Action	Comment
Denied	OpenQuery	
	Maximize	
	MsgBox	
Fixed	OpenQuery	
	Maximize	
	MsgBox	

Action Arguments

Message — These claims were fixed
Beep — Yes
Type — Information
Title — Fixed

Displays a message box containing a warning or informational message. A common use is a message that appears when a validation fails. Press F1 for help on this action.

Creating

Modules

Objectives

- ► **Understand modules**
- ► **Compare macros and modules**
- [MOUS] ► **Create functions**
- [MOUS] ► **Use If statements**
- [MOUS] ► **Document procedures**
- [MOUS] ► **Examine class modules**
- [MOUS] ► **Create sub procedures**
- ► **Troubleshoot modules**

Access is a robust and easy-to-use relational database program. End users can quickly create reports and forms that previously took programmers hours to build. Because Access provides so many user-friendly tools such as wizards and graphical Design Views to accomplish complex tasks, many Access database administrators don't need to work with the Microsoft Office programming language, **Visual Basic for Applications (VBA)**, to meet most user needs. When programming *is* required, however, Access provides the VBA development environment to write the programming code. The Access **module** object stores VBA code. Kristen Fontanelle, network administrator for MediaLoft, uses VBA to enhance the capabilities of the database.

Understanding Modules

A **module** is an Access object that stores Visual Basic for Applications (VBA) programming code. VBA is written in the **Visual Basic Editor Code window** (**Code window**), shown in Figure O-1. The components and text colors of the Code window are described in Table O-1. An Access database has two kinds of modules: **class modules**, which contain VBA code used only within a form or report, and store the code within the form or report object itself; and **standard modules**, which contain global code that can be executed from anywhere in the database. Standard modules are displayed as module objects in the database window when you click the Modules button on the Objects bar. Kristen asks some questions about VBA.

Details

▶ **What does a module contain?**

A module contains VBA programming code organized in **procedures**. A procedure is several lines of VBA code, each of which is called a **statement**. Modules may also contain **comments** that help explain the code.

▶ **What is a procedure?**

A **procedure** is a series of VBA statements that perform an operation or calculate an answer. There are two types of procedures: Functions and Subs. **Declaration statements** precede procedure statements and help set rules for how the statements in the module are processed.

▶ **What is a function?**

A **function** is a procedure that returns a value. Access supplies many built-in statistical, financial, and date functions, such as Sum, Pmt, and Now, that can be used in an expression in a query, form, or report to calculate a value. You might need to create a new function, however, to help perform calculations unique to your database. For example, you could create a new function called StockOptions, to calculate the date an employee is eligible for stock options.

▶ **What is a sub?**

A **sub** (also called **sub procedure**) performs a series of VBA statements, but does not return a value and cannot be used in an expression like a function procedure. You use subs to manipulate controls and objects. They are generally executed based on an event, such as clicking a command button or check box.

▶ **What are arguments?**

Arguments are constants, variables, or expressions passed to a procedure (usually a function procedure) that are required for it to execute. For example, the full syntax for the Sum function is Sum(*expr*), where *expr* represents the argument for the Sum function, the item that is being summed. Arguments are specified immediately after a procedure's name and are enclosed in parentheses. Multiple arguments are separated by commas.

▶ **What is an object?**

In VBA, an **object** is any item that can be identified or manipulated, including the traditional Access objects (table, query, form, report, page, macro, module), and smaller pieces of the traditional objects including controls, sections, and existing procedures.

▶ **What is a method?**

A **method** is an action that *an object can perform*. Procedures are often written to invoke methods in response to user actions. For example, you could invoke the GoToPage method when the user clicks a command button to move the focus to a specific control.

▶ **What is an event?**

An **event** is a specific action that occurs *on or to an object*, and is usually the result of a user action. Clicking a command button, editing data, or closing a form, are examples of events.

Visual Basic
window title bar

Object list

Declaration
statements

Project Explorer
Window

Visual Basic
window buttons

Code window
buttons

Procedure list

VBA code in
Code window

Procedure
View button

Full Module
View button

Utility Functions
module is selected

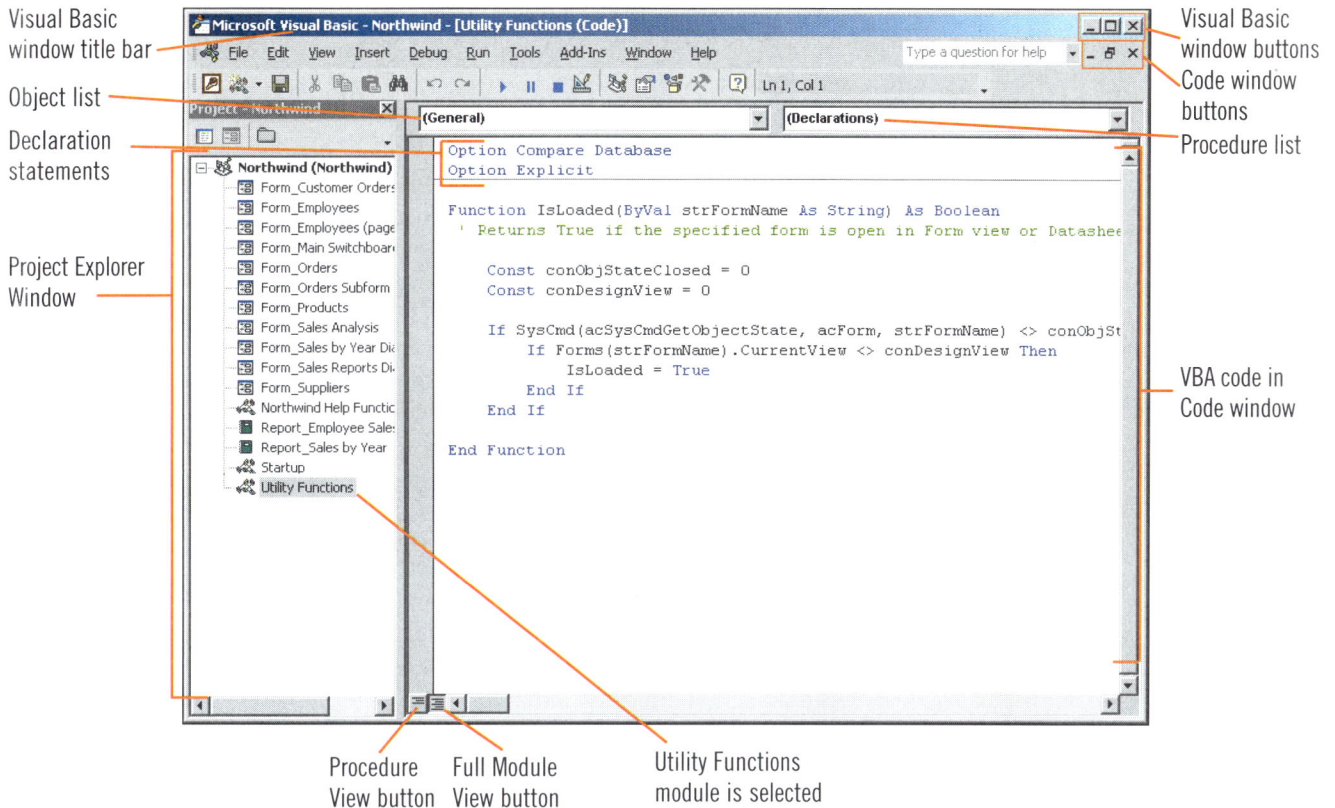

TABLE O-1: Components and text colors for the Visual Basic window

component or color	description
Visual Basic window	The entire Microsoft Visual Basic program window that contains smaller windows including the Code window and Project Explorer window
Code window	Contains the VBA for the project selected in the Project Explorer window
Project Explorer window	Displays a hierarchical list of the projects in the database; a **project** can be a module itself, or an object that contains class modules such as a form or report
Procedure View button	Shows the statements that belong only to the current procedure
Full Module View button	Shows all the lines of VBA (all of the procedures) in the current module
Declaration statements	Statements that apply to every procedure in the module such as declarations for variables, constants, user-defined data types, and external procedures in a dynamic link library
Object list	In a class module, lists the objects associated with the current form or report
Procedure list	In a standard module, lists the procedures in that module; in a class module, lists the events (such as Click or Dblclick) that the item selected in the Object box can use
Blue	Keyword text—blue words are reserved by VBA and are already assigned specific meanings
Black	Normal text—black words are the unique VBA code developed by the user
Red	Syntax error text—a line of code in red indicates that it will not execute correctly because there is a syntax error (perhaps a missing parenthesis or a spelling error)
Green	Comment text—any text after an apostrophe is considered documentation, and is therefore ignored in the execution of the procedure

Access 2002

Comparing Macros and Modules

Both macros and modules help run your database more efficiently (faster) and effectively (with fewer errors). To create either a macro or a module requires some understanding of programming concepts, an ability to follow a process through its steps, and patience. Some tasks can be accomplished by using either an Access macro or with VBA, and there are guidelines to help guide your choice of which object is best for the task. Also, note that creating macros in the other Microsoft Office products (Excel, Word, and PowerPoint) actually creates VBA code. ➤ Kristen learns how macros and modules compare by asking more questions.

Details

▶ **For what types of tasks are macros best suited?**

Macros are an easy way to handle repetitive, simple tasks such as opening and closing forms, showing and hiding toolbars, and printing reports.

▶ **Which is easier to create, a macro or a module, and why?**

Macros are generally easier to create because you don't have to know any programming syntax. The hardest part of creating a macro is choosing the correct action (Access presents a limited list of about 50 actions from which you must choose). But once the action is chosen, the arguments associated with that action are displayed automatically in the Action Arguments pane, eliminating the need to learn any special programming syntax. To create a module, however, you must know a robust programming language, VBA, as well as the correct **syntax** (rules) for each VBA statement. The additional flexibility and power of VBA means that it is inherently more complex as well.

▶ **When must I use a macro?**

You must use macros to make global, shortcut key assignments. You can also use an automatic macro that executes when the database first opens.

▶ **When should I use a module?**

- Class modules, like the one shown in Figure O-2, are stored as part of the form or report object in which they are created. If you develop forms and reports in one database and copy them to another, class module VBA automatically travels with the object that stores it.

- You must use modules to create unique functions. Macros cannot create functions. For instance, you might want to create a function called COMMISSION that calculates the appropriate commission on a sale using your company's unique commission formula.

- Access error messages can be confusing to the user. But using VBA procedures, you can detect the error when it occurs and display your own message.

- You can't use a macro to accomplish many tasks outside of Access, but VBA code stored in modules works with other products in the Microsoft Office suite.

- VBA code can contain nested If statements, Case statements, and other programming logic which makes them much more powerful and flexible than macros. Some of the most common VBA keywords are shown in Table O-2. VBA keywords appear blue in the Code window.

CLUES TO USE

Converting macros to Visual Basic

You can convert existing macros to Visual Basic. Click the Macros button on the Objects bar, then click the name of the macro you want to convert. Click the File menu, click Save As, click the As list arrow, click Module, then click OK. If the macro is stored in a form or report, open the form or report in Design View, click the Tools menu, point to Macro, then click Convert Form's (or Report's) Macros to Visual Basic.

FIGURE O-2: Code window for a class module

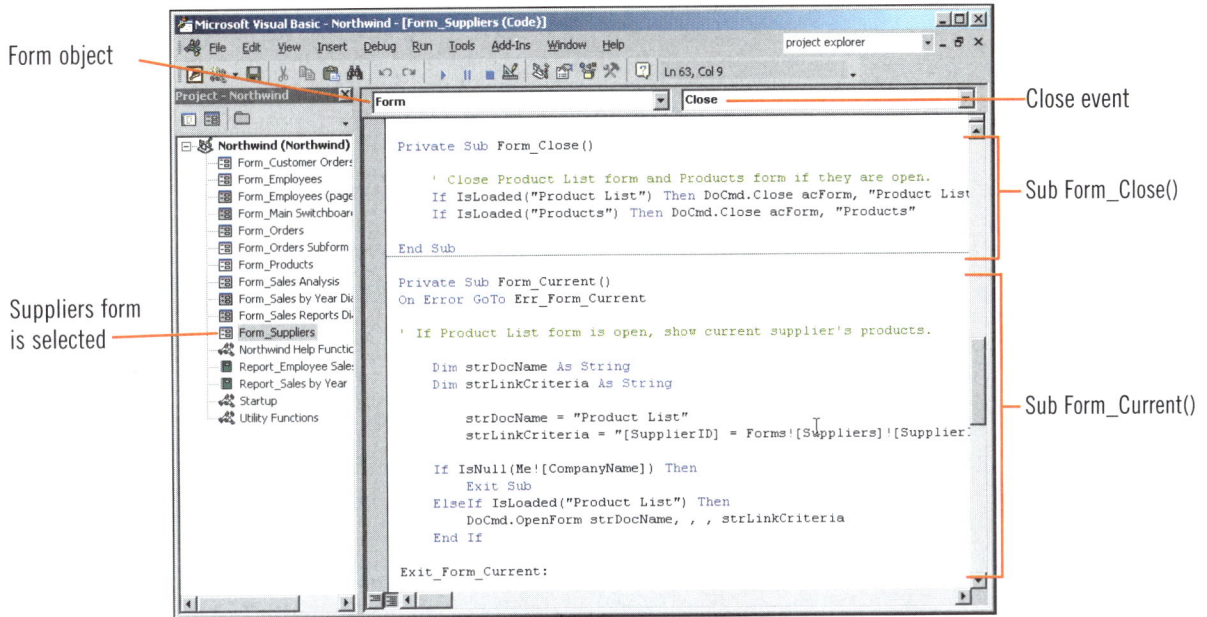

Form object →

Suppliers form is selected →

→ Close event

→ Sub Form_Close()

→ Sub Form_Current()

```
Private Sub Form_Close()

    ' Close Product List form and Products form if they are open.
    If IsLoaded("Product List") Then DoCmd.Close acForm, "Product List"
    If IsLoaded("Products") Then DoCmd.Close acForm, "Products"

End Sub

Private Sub Form_Current()
On Error GoTo Err_Form_Current

' If Product List form is open, show current supplier's products.

    Dim strDocName As String
    Dim strLinkCriteria As String

        strDocName = "Product List"
        strLinkCriteria = "[SupplierID] = Forms![Suppliers]![Supplier]"

    If IsNull(Me![CompanyName]) Then
        Exit Sub
    ElseIf IsLoaded("Product List") Then
        DoCmd.OpenForm strDocName, , , strLinkCriteria
    End If

Exit_Form_Current:
```

TABLE O-2: Common VBA keywords

statement	explanation
Function	Declares the name and arguments that create a new function procedure
End Function	When defining a new function, the End Function statement is required as the last statement to mark the end of the VBA code that defines the function
Sub	Declares the name for a new sub procedure; **Private Sub** indicates that the sub is accessible only to other procedures in the module where it is declared
End Sub	When defining a new sub, the End Sub statement is required as the last statement to mark the end of the VBA code that defines the sub
If...Then	Executes code (the code follows the Then statement) when the value of an expression is true (the expression follows the If statement)
End If	When creating an If...Then statement, the End If statement is required as the last statement
Const	Declares the name and value of a **constant**, an item that retains a constant value throughout the execution of the code
Option Compare Database	A declaration statement that determines the way string values (text) will be sorted
Option Explicit	A declaration statement that specifies that you must explicitly declare all variables used in all procedures; if you attempt to use an undeclared variable name, an error occurs at **compile time**, the period during which source code is translated to executable code
Dim	Declares a **variable**, a named storage location that contains data that can be modified during program execution
On Error GoTo	Upon error in the execution of a procedure, the On Error GoTo statement specifies the location (the statement) where the procedure should continue
Select Case	Executes one of several groups of statements called a **Case** depending on the value of an expression; use the Select Case statement as an alternative to using **ElseIf** in **If...Then...Else** statements when comparing one expression to several different values
End Select	When defining a new Select Case group of statements, the End Select statement is required as the last statement to mark the end of the VBA code

Creating Functions

While Access supplies hundreds of functions such as Sum and Count, you might need to create a new function to calculate a value based on the unique business rules used by your company. You would create a new function in a standard module so that it can be used in any query, form, or report in the database. MediaLoft has implemented a program that allows employees to purchase computer equipment when it is replaced. Equipment that is less than a year old will be sold to employees at 75% of its initial value, and equipment that is more than a year old will be sold at 50% of its initial value. Kristen defines a new function called EmployeePrice that will determine the employee purchase price of replaced computer equipment.

Steps 1234

1. Start Access, open the **Technology-O** database, click **Modules** on the Objects bar, click the **New button** on the Database window toolbar, then maximize the Code window and the Visual Basic window

   Access automatically inserts the Option Compare Database declaration statement, which determines the way string values (text) will be sorted.

2. Type **Function EmployeePrice(startingvalue)**, then press **[Enter]**

   The Function statement declares a new function name, EmployeePrice, which contains one argument, startingvalue. VBA automatically adds the End Function statement, a required statement to mark the end of the code that defines the new function. Because both Function and End Function are VBA keywords, they are blue. The insertion point is positioned between the statements so that you can further define how the new EmployeePrice function will calculate.

3. Press **[Tab]**, type **EmployeePrice = startingvalue * 0.5**, then press **[Enter]**

   Your screen should look like Figure O-3. The second statement explains how the EmployeePrice function will calculate. The function will return a value that is calculated by multiplying the startingvalue by 0.5. It is not necessary to indent statements, but indenting code between matching Function/End Function, Sub/End Sub, or If/End If statements enhances the program's readability. Also, it is not necessary to enter spaces around the equal sign and an asterisk used as a multiplication sign, but when you press [Enter], Access will add spaces as appropriate to enhance the readability of the statement.

4. Click the **Save button** on the Standard toolbar, type **Functions** in the Save As dialog box, then click **OK**

   Now that the function is created, it can be used in a query, form, or report.

5. Close the Visual Basic window, click **Queries** on the Objects bar, right-click the **Employee Pricing query**, then click **Design View** on the shortcut menu

   The Employee Pricing query opens in Query Design View. You can create calculated expressions in a query using either Access functions or the ones you define in standard modules.

6. Click the **blank Field cell** to the right of the InitialValue field, type **Price:EmployeePrice ([InitialValue])**, click the **Datasheet View button** on the Query Design toolbar, then maximize the datasheet

   Your screen should look like Figure O-4. In this query, you created a new field called Price that used the EmployeePrice function you created in a standard module. The value in the InitialValue field was used as the startingvalue argument. The InitialValue field was multiplied by 0.5 to create the new Price field.

7. Save the Employee Pricing query, then close the datasheet

FIGURE 0-3: Creating the EmployeePrice function

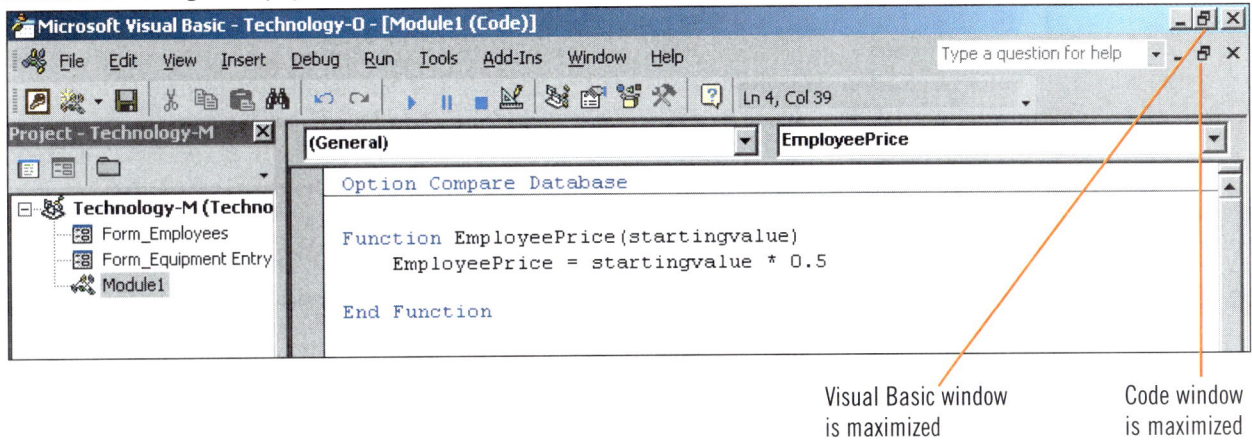

Visual Basic window is maximized

Code window is maximized

FIGURE 0-4: Creating the Price field using the EmployeePrice function

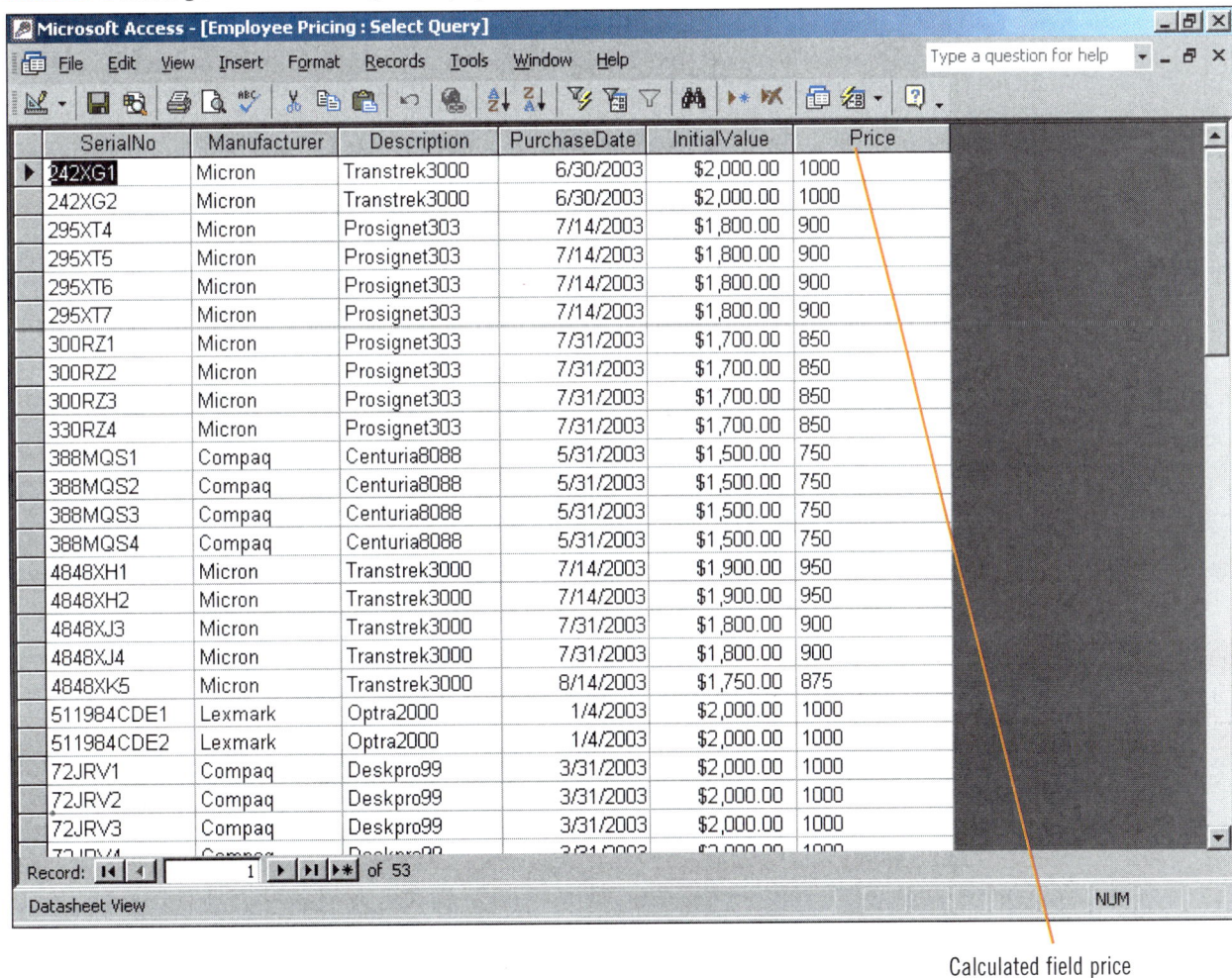

Calculated field price

Using If Statements

If...Then...Else logic allows you to test logical conditions and execute statements only if the conditions are true. If...Then...Else code can be composed of one or several statements, depending on how many conditions you want to test, how many possible answers you want to provide, and what you want the code to do based on the results of the tests. Kristen needs to add an If statement to the EmployeePrice function to test the age of the equipment, and then calculate the answer based on that age. As originally designed, the calculation *always* multiplies the startingvalue argument by 50%. But if the equipment is less than one year old, the function should return a value that multiplies the startingvalue argument by 75%.

Steps

1. Click **Modules** on the Objects bar, right-click the **Functions module**, then click **Design View**
   The Functions Code window with the EmployeePrice function opens. To determine the age of the equipment, the EmployeePrice function needs another argument, the purchase date of the equipment.

2. Click just before the **right parenthesis** in the Function statement, type **,** (a comma), press **[Spacebar]**, then type **purchasedate**
   The new function now contains two arguments. The statement is
   `Function EmployeePrice (startingvalue, purchasedate)`
   Now that another argument has been established, the argument can be used in the function.

3. Click to the right of the **right parenthesis** in the Function statement, press **[Enter]**, press **[Tab]**, type **If (Now() – purchasedate) >365 Then**, then press **[Enter]**
   This expression evaluates whether today's date, represented by the Access function Now(), minus the value represented by the purchasedate argument is greater than 365 days. If true, this would indicate that the equipment is older than one year.

QuickTip
Indentation doesn't affect the way the function works, but does make the code easier to read.

4. Indent, then enter the rest of the statements exactly as shown in Figure O-5
   The Else statement will be executed only if the expression is false (if the equipment is less than 365 days old). The End If statement is needed to mark the end of the If block of code.

5. Click the **Save button** 🖫 on the Standard toolbar, close the Visual Basic window, click **Queries** on the Objects bar, right-click the **Employee Pricing query**, then click **Design View** on the shortcut menu
   Now that the EmployeePrice function has two arguments, you need to modify the expression in the query to consider two arguments in order for it to calculate the correct answer.

6. Right-click the **Price field** in the query design grid, click **Zoom** on the shortcut menu, click between the **right square bracket** and **right parenthesis**, then type **,[PurchaseDate]**
   Your Zoom dialog box should look like Figure O-6. Both of the arguments used to calculate the EmployeePrice function are field names, so they must be typed exactly as shown, and surrounded by square brackets. Commas separate multiple arguments in the function.

Trouble?
If you get a compile or syntax error, open the Visual Basic window, check your function against Figure O-5, then correct any errors.

7. Click **OK** in the Zoom dialog box, then click the **Datasheet View button** 🔲 on the Query Design toolbar

8. Click any entry in the **PurchaseDate field**, then click the **Sort Ascending button** ⬆ on the Query Datasheet toolbar
   The EmployeePrice function now calculates two ways, depending on the age of the equipment determined by the date in the PurchaseDate field, as shown in Figure O-7. The new calculated Price field is based on the current date on your computer, so your results may vary.

9. Save, then close the Employee Pricing query

FIGURE N-1: Macro Design View of a macro group

Suppliers macro group

Macro Name column

Close action is selected

Condition column

Action column

Arguments for selected action (Close)

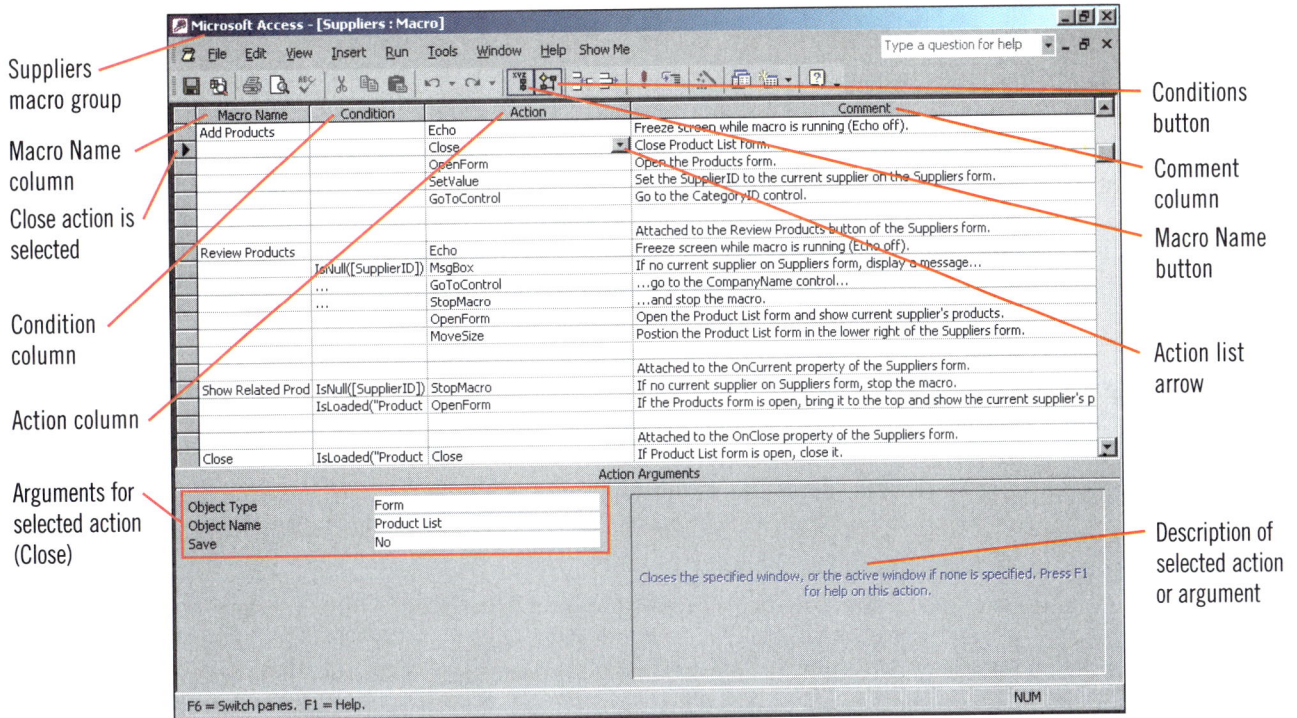

Conditions button

Comment column

Macro Name button

Action list arrow

Description of selected action or argument

TABLE N-1: Macro Design View components

Component	Description
Macro Name column	Contains the names of individual macros within a macro group. If the macro object contains only one macro, it isn't necessary to use this column because you can run the macro by referring to the macro by the macro object's name. View this column by clicking the Macro Names button ▦. The Macro Names button works as a toggle to open and close the Macro Name column.
Condition column	Contains conditional expressions that are evaluated either true or false. If true, the macro action on that row is executed. If false, the macro action on that row is skipped. View this column by clicking the Conditions button ▦. The Conditions button works as a toggle to open and close the Condition column.
Action column	Contains the actions, or the tasks, that the macro executes when it runs
Comment column	Contains optional explanatory text for each row
Action Arguments pane	Displays the arguments for the selected action
▶	Indicates which row is currently selected

Creating a Macro

In some software programs, you can create a macro by using a "macro recorder" to record, or save, the keystrokes and mouse clicks you use to perform a task. Access doesn't use that method. In Access, you create a macro by choosing a series of actions in Macro Design View that accomplish the job you want to automate. Therefore, if you are to become proficient with Access macros, you must be comfortable with macro actions. Access provides more than 50 macro actions. Some of the most common actions are listed in Table N-2. ✎ Kristen observes that time can be saved opening the All Equipment report from the Employees form, so she decides to create a macro to automate this task.

Steps

1. **Start Access, open the Technology-N database from where your Project Files are located, click Macros on the Objects bar, then click the New button on the Database window toolbar**
   Macro Design View opens, ready for your first action. The Macro Name and Condition columns are not visible by default, but can be toggled on by clicking their respective buttons on the Macro Design toolbar. They are only needed, of course, if you are creating multiple macros in the same macro object or using conditional expressions.

2. **Click the Action list arrow, press o to quickly scroll to the actions that start with the letter "o", then click OpenReport**
   The OpenReport action is added as the first line, and the arguments that further define the OpenReport action appear in the Action Arguments pane in the lower half of Macro Design View. The OpenReport action has two required arguments: Report Name and View. The Filter Name and Where Condition arguments are optional.

   > **QuickTip**
   > Press [F6] to jump between the actions and Action Arguments panes in Macro Design View.

3. **Click the Report Name argument text box in the Action Arguments pane, click the Report Name List arrow, then click All Equipment**
   All of the report objects in the Technology-N database display in the Report Name argument list.

4. **Click the View argument text box in the Action Arguments pane, click the View list arrow, then click Print Preview**
   Your screen should look like Figure N-2. Macros can be one or many actions long. In this case, the macro is only one action long and has no conditional expressions.

5. **Click the Save button on the Macro Design toolbar, type Preview All Equipment Report in the Macro Name text box, click OK, then close Macro Design View**
   The Technology-N database window shows the Print All Equipment Report object as a macro object.

6. **Click the Run button in the Database window toolbar**
   The All Equipment report opens in Print Preview.

7. **Close the All Equipment preview window**

Suppliers macro group

Macro Name column

Close action is selected

Condition column

Action column

Arguments for selected action (Close)

Conditions button

Comment column

Macro Name button

Action list arrow

Description of selected action or argument

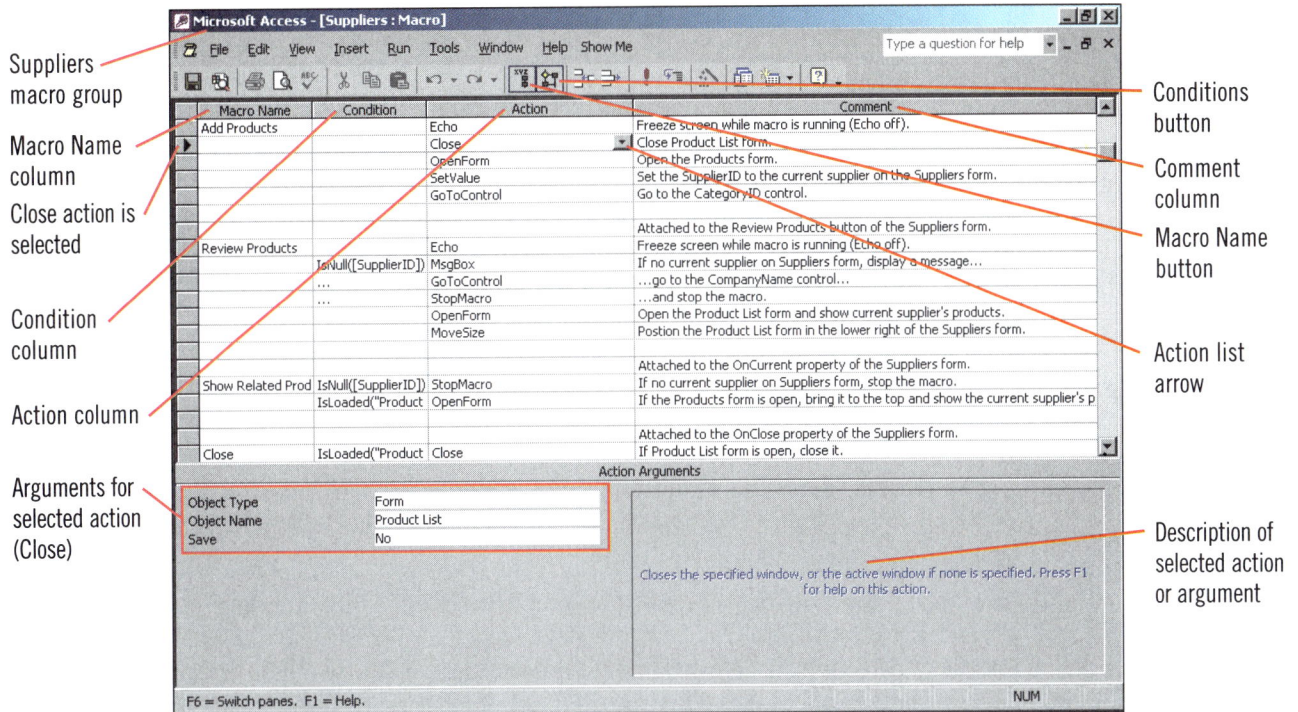

TABLE N-1: Macro Design View components

Component	Description
Macro Name column	Contains the names of individual macros within a macro group. If the macro object contains only one macro, it isn't necessary to use this column because you can run the macro by referring to the macro by the macro object's name. View this column by clicking the Macro Names button [icon]. The Macro Names button works as a toggle to open and close the Macro Name column.
Condition column	Contains conditional expressions that are evaluated either true or false. If true, the macro action on that row is executed. If false, the macro action on that row is skipped. View this column by clicking the Conditions button [icon]. The Conditions button works as a toggle to open and close the Condition column.
Action column	Contains the actions, or the tasks, that the macro executes when it runs
Comment column	Contains optional explanatory text for each row
Action Arguments pane	Displays the arguments for the selected action
[icon]	Indicates which row is currently selected

Access 2002

Creating a Macro

In some software programs, you can create a macro by using a "macro recorder" to record, or save, the keystrokes and mouse clicks you use to perform a task. Access doesn't use that method. In Access, you create a macro by choosing a series of actions in Macro Design View that accomplish the job you want to automate. Therefore, if you are to become proficient with Access macros, you must be comfortable with macro actions. Access provides more than 50 macro actions. Some of the most common actions are listed in Table N-2. Kristen observes that time can be saved opening the All Equipment report from the Employees form, so she decides to create a macro to automate this task.

Steps

1. Start Access, open the **Technology-N** database from where your Project Files are located, click **Macros** on the Objects bar, then click the **New button** on the Database window toolbar

Macro Design View opens, ready for your first action. The Macro Name and Condition columns are not visible by default, but can be toggled on by clicking their respective buttons on the Macro Design toolbar. They are only needed, of course, if you are creating multiple macros in the same macro object or using conditional expressions.

2. Click the **Action list arrow**, press **o** to quickly scroll to the actions that start with the letter "o", then click **OpenReport**

The OpenReport action is added as the first line, and the arguments that further define the OpenReport action appear in the Action Arguments pane in the lower half of Macro Design View. The OpenReport action has two required arguments: Report Name and View. The Filter Name and Where Condition arguments are optional.

QuickTip

Press [F6] to jump between the actions and Action Arguments panes in Macro Design View.

3. Click the **Report Name argument text box** in the Action Arguments pane, click the **Report Name List arrow**, then click **All Equipment**

All of the report objects in the Technology-N database display in the Report Name argument list.

4. Click the **View argument text box** in the Action Arguments pane, click the **View list arrow**, then click **Print Preview**

Your screen should look like Figure N-2. Macros can be one or many actions long. In this case, the macro is only one action long and has no conditional expressions.

5. Click the **Save button** on the Macro Design toolbar, type **Preview All Equipment Report** in the Macro Name text box, click **OK**, then close Macro Design View

The Technology-N database window shows the Print All Equipment Report object as a macro object.

6. Click the **Run button** in the Database window toolbar

The All Equipment report opens in Print Preview.

7. Close the All Equipment preview window

FIGURE N-2: Macro Design View with OpenReport action

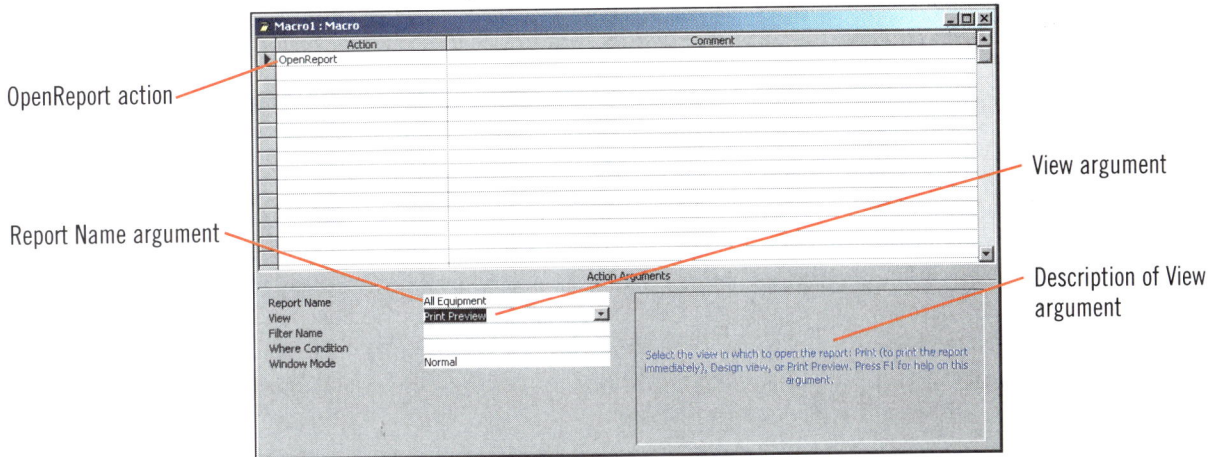

OpenReport action

Report Name argument

View argument

Description of View argument

TABLE N-2: Common macro actions

subject area	macro action	description
Handling data in forms	ApplyFilter	Restricts the number of records that appear in the resulting form or report by applying limiting criteria
	FindRecord	Finds the first record that meets the criteria
	GoToControl	Moves the focus (where you are currently typing or clicking) to a specific field or control
	GoToRecord	Makes a specified record the current record
Executing menu options	RunCode	Runs a Visual Basic function (a series of programming statements that do a calculation or comparison and return a value)
	RunCommand	Carries out a specified menu command
	RunMacro	Runs a macro or attaches a macro to a custom menu command
	StopMacro	Stops the currently running macro
Importing/Exporting data	TransferDatabase TransferSpreadsheet TransferText	Imports, links, or exports data between the current Microsoft Access database and another database, spreadsheet, or text file
Manipulating objects	Close	Closes a window
	Maximize	Enlarges the active window to fill the Access window
	OpenForm	Opens a form in Form View, Design View, Print Preview, or Datasheet View
	OpenQuery	Opens a select or crosstab query in Datasheet View, Design View, or Print Preview; runs an action query
	OpenReport	Opens a report in Design View or Print Preview, or prints the report
	OpenTable	Opens a table in Datasheet View, Design View, or Print Preview
	PrintOut	Prints the active object, such as a datasheet, report, form, or module
	SetValue	Sets the value of a field, control, or property
Miscellaneous	Beep	Sounds a beep tone through the computer's speaker
	MsgBox	Displays a message box containing a warning or an informational message
	SendKeys	Sends keystrokes directly to Microsoft Access or to an active Windows-based application

Modifying Actions and Arguments

Macros can contain as many actions as necessary to complete the process that you want to auto-mate. Each action is evaluated in the order in which it appears in Macro Design View, starting at the top. A macro stops executing actions when it encounters a blank row in Macro Design View. While some macro actions manipulate data or objects, others are used only to make the database easier to use. **MsgBox** is a useful macro action because it displays an informational message. ✎ Kristen decides to add an action to the Print All Equipment Report macro to clarify what is happening when the macro runs. She adds a MsgBox action to the macro to display a descriptive message for the user.

Steps 1 2 3 4

1. Click the **Design button** 📝 on the Database window toolbar
   The Print All Equipment Report macro opens in Macro Design View.

2. Click the **Action cell** for the second row, click the **Action list arrow**, press **m** to quickly scroll to the actions that start with the letter "m", then click **MsgBox**
   Each action has its own arguments that further clarify what the action will do.

3. Click the **Message argument text box** in the Action Arguments pane, then type **Click the Print button to print the All Equipment report**
   The Message argument determines what text appears in the message box. By default, the Beep argument is set to "Yes" and the Type argument is set to "None."

4. Click the **Type argument text box** in the Action Arguments pane, read the description in the lower-right corner of Macro Design View, click the **Type list arrow**, then click **Information**
   The Type argument determines which icon will appear in the dialog box that is created by the MsgBox action.

5. Click the **Title argument text box** in the Action Arguments pane, then type **To print this report...**
   Your screen should look like Figure N-3. The Title argument specifies what text will display in the title bar of the resulting dialog box. If you leave the Title argument empty, the title bar of the resulting dialog box will display "Microsoft Access."

6. Click the **Save button** 💾 on the Macro Design toolbar, then click the **Run button** ❗ on the Macro Design toolbar
   If your speakers are turned on, you should hear a beep, then the message box should appear, as shown in Figure N-4.

7. Click **OK** in the dialog box, close the All Equipment report, then close Macro Design View

FIGURE O-5: If...Then...Else statements

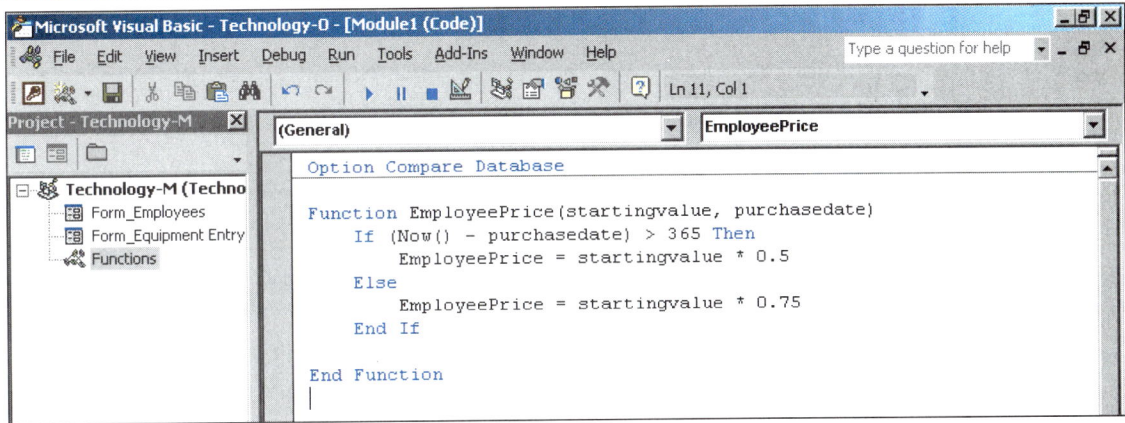

```
Option Compare Database

Function EmployeePrice(startingvalue, purchasedate)
    If (Now() - purchasedate) > 365 Then
        EmployeePrice = startingvalue * 0.5
    Else
        EmployeePrice = startingvalue * 0.75
    End If

End Function
```

FIGURE O-6: Modifying the expression

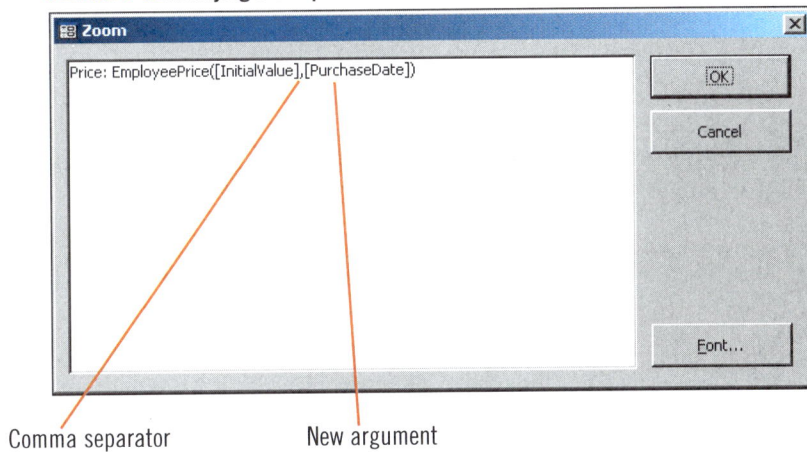

Price: EmployeePrice([InitialValue],[PurchaseDate])

Comma separator   New argument

FIGURE O-7: Price field is calculated two ways

SerialNo	Manufacturer	Description	PurchaseDate	InitialValue	Price
XPX5QRST2	HP	Deskjet 900XJ2	1/10/2000	$500.00	250
XPX5QRST1	HP	Deskjet 900XJ2	1/10/2000	$500.00	250
HKPF9	Dell	XPS480	1/4/2002	$2,000.00	1500
HKPF7	Dell	XPS480	1/4/2002	$2,000.00	1500
HKPF6	Dell	XPS480	1/4/2002	$2,000.00	1500
HKPF1	Dell	XPS480	1/4/2002	$2,000.00	1500
HKPF8	Dell	XPS480	1/4/2002	$2,000.00	1500
XPX5QRST3	HP	Deskjet 900XJ2	1/4/2002	$500.00	375

InitialValue *0.75   InitialValue *0.5

Documenting Procedures

Comment lines are statements in the code that document the code, and do not affect how the code runs. At any future time, if you want to read or modify existing code, you can write the modifications much more quickly if the code is properly documented. Comment lines start with an apostrophe, and appear in green in the Code window. ✎━━━ Kristen documents the EmployeePrice function in the Functions module with descriptive comments. This will make it easier for her to follow the purpose and logic of the function later.

Steps 1 2 3 4

1. Click **Modules** on the Objects bar, right-click the **Functions** module, then click **Design View**
   The Code window for the Functions module opens.

QuickTip

You also can create comments by starting the statement with Rem (for remark).

2. Click to the left of the **Function statement**, press [Enter], press [Up arrow], type **'This function is called EmployeePrice and has two arguments**, then press [Enter]
   As soon as you move to another statement, the comment statement will become green in the Code window.

Trouble?

Be sure to use an ' (apostrophe) and not a " (quotation mark) to begin the comment line.

3. Type **'Created by Your Name on Today's Date**, then press [Enter]
   Your screen should look like Figure O-8. You also can place comments at the end of a line by entering an apostrophe to mark that the next part of the statement is a comment. The utility project contains VBA code that helps Access with certain activities such as presenting the Zoom dialog box. It automatically appears in the Project Explorer window when you use the Access features that utilize this code.

4. Click to the right of **Then** at the end of the If statement, press [Spacebar], then type **'Now() is today's date**
   This comment explains that the Now() function is today's date. All comments are green, regardless of whether they are on their own line or at the end of an existing line.

5. Click to the right of **0.5**, press [Spacebar], then type **'If > 1 yr, value is 50%**

6. Click to the right of **0.75**, press [Spacebar], then type **'If < 1 yr, value is 75%**, then press [↓]
   Your screen should look like Figure O-9. Table O-3 provides more information about the Standard toolbar buttons in the Visual Basic window.

7. Click the **Save button** 🖫 on the Standard toolbar, click **File** on the menu bar, click **Print**, then click **OK**

8. Click **File** on the menu bar, then click **Close and Return to Microsoft Access**

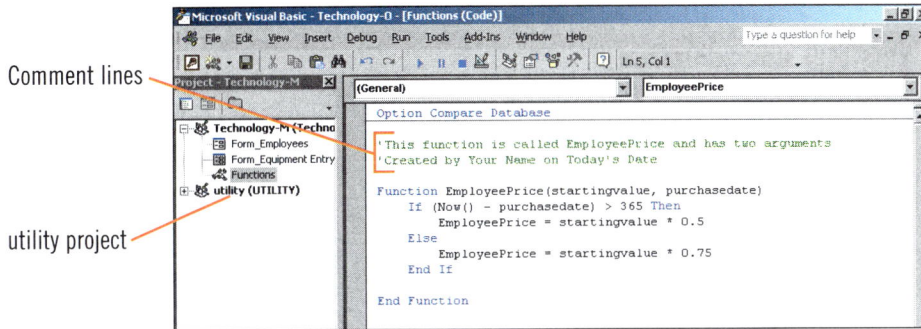

FIGURE O-8: Adding comments to the Code window

Comment lines

utility project

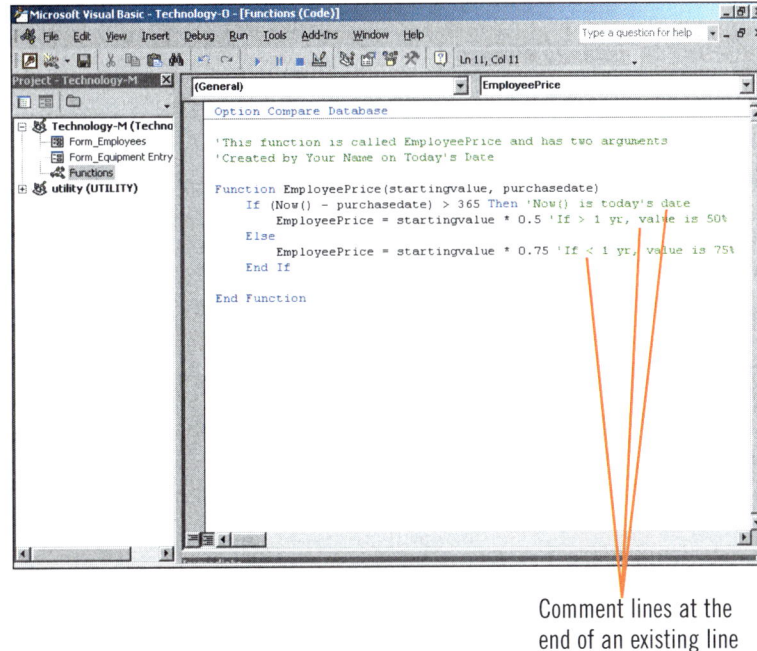

FIGURE O-9: Adding comments at the end of a statement

Comment lines at the
end of an existing line

TABLE O-3: Standard toolbar buttons in the Visual Basic window

button name	button	description
View Microsoft Access		Toggles between the Access and the active Visual Basic window
Insert Module		Opens a new module or class module Code window, or inserts a new procedure in the current Code window
Run Sub/UserForm		Runs the current procedure if the insertion point is in a procedure, or runs the UserForm if it is active
Break		Stops execution of a program while it's running, and switches to **break mode**, the temporary suspension of program execution in which you can examine, debug, reset, step through, or continue program execution
Reset		Resets the procedure
Project Explorer		Displays the Project Explorer, which displays a hierarchical list of the currently open projects (set of modules) and their contents
Object Browser		Displays the **Object Browser**, which lists the defined modules and procedures as well as available methods, properties, events, constants, and other items that you can use in the code

Examining Class Modules

Class modules are contained and executed within specific forms and reports. Class modules most commonly contain sub procedures and execute in response to an event such as the click of a command button. You do not always have to know VBA code to create class modules. The Command Button Wizard, for example, creates sub procedures. You can examine them to see how sub procedures work and how they are executed through specific events. ✎ Kristen used the Command Button Wizard to create four command buttons on the Equipment Entry Form. She examines the sub procedures in this form in order to understand class modules.

Steps 1 2 3 4

1. Click **Forms** on the Objects bar, right-click the **Equipment Entry Form**, click **Design View** on the shortcut menu, then maximize the form

   The form has four command buttons.

2. Click each command button while viewing the Object list on the Formatting (Form/Report) toolbar

   Your screen should look like Figure O-10. The Object list identifies the name of the selected control as determined by the control's Name property. In this case, the word "object" is used as a VBA programmer would use it. Within VBA, an object is any item that can be identified or manipulated, including the traditional Access objects (table, query, form, report, page, macro, module), and smaller pieces of the traditional objects including controls, sections, and existing procedures.

3. Click the **Code button** 🔲 on the Form Design toolbar

   The Code window for the VBA code stored in the Equipment Entry Form class module appears, as shown in Figure O-11. All of the code for each of the four command buttons was created by using the Command Button Wizard. The names of the subs, AddNewRecordButton and DeleteThisRecordButton, correspond with the names of the command buttons on the form. The _Click() suffix identifies the event that will cause the sub to execute.

4. Close the Visual Basic window, double-click the **Print This Record command button** to open its property sheet, click the **Event tab**, click **[Event Procedure]** in the On Click property, then click the **Build button** 🔲

   The class module is opened in the specific location where the PrintThisRecordButton_Click() sub is stored. To create a sub that executes based on a specific event associated with that command button (for example, to display a message box when the command button is double-clicked) you could use the property sheet to help you correctly name the new sub.

5. Close the Visual Basic window, click the **On Got Focus** property, click 🔲, click **Code Builder** in the Choose Builder dialog box, then click **OK**

   The class module Code window opens, as shown in Figure O-12. Because you entered the Code window through a specific event (On Got Focus) of a specific control (PrintThisRecordButton), VBA knew what to name the sub, PrintThisRecordButton_GotFocus(). It also automatically supplied the last line of the procedure, the End Sub statement. The rest of the sub's statements, however, would require individual programming, because you are not using a wizard to create the code.

6. Select the **Private Sub PrintThisRecordButton_GotFocus()** statement and the **End Sub** statement, press **[Delete]**, close the Visual Basic window, then save and close the Equipment Entry Form

FIGURE O-10: Four command buttons in Form Design View

Object list

Code button

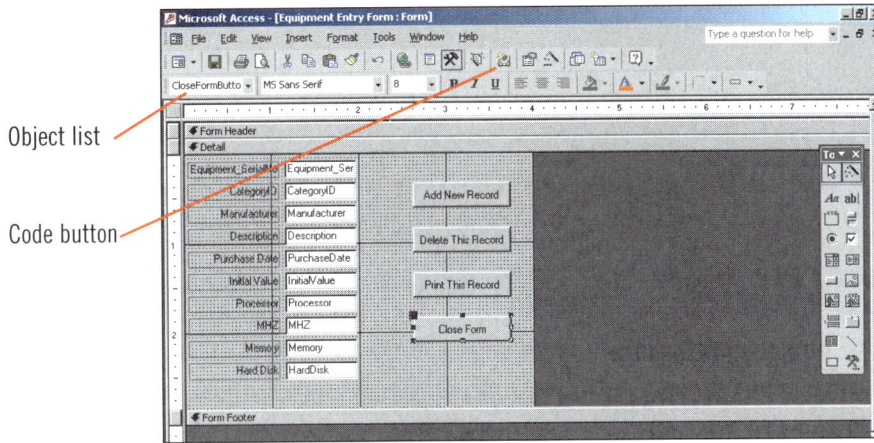

FIGURE O-11: Class module containing four sub procedures

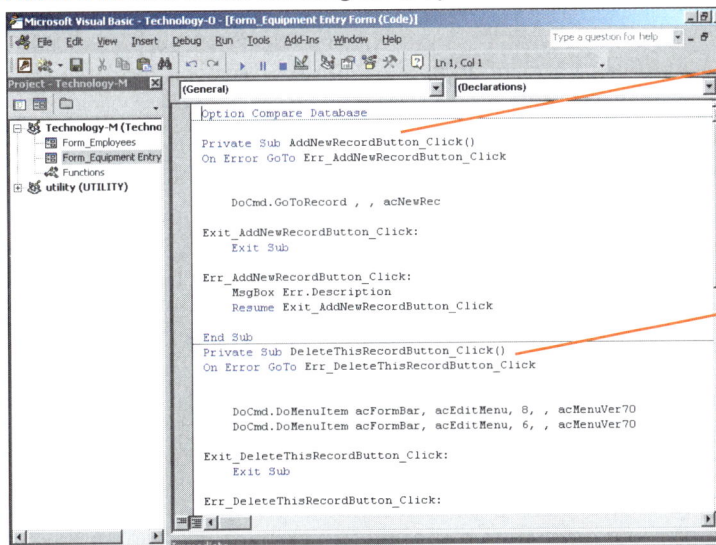

AddNewRecordButton_Click() sub

DeleteThisRecordButton_Click() sub

FIGURE O-12: Examining a new sub name

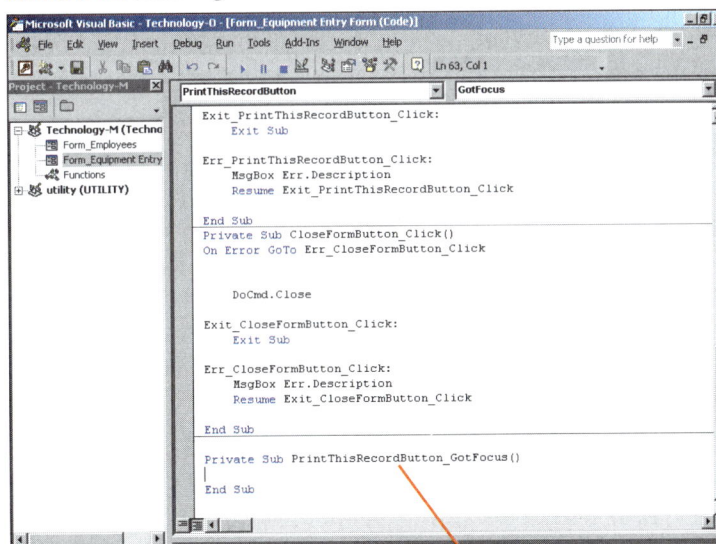

New sub attached to the On Got Focus
event of the PrintThisRecordButton

Creating Sub Procedures

While it is easiest to create class module sub procedures using wizards, not all subs can be created this way. The Command Button Wizard, for example, always attaches its code to the **On Click** event of a command button. You might want to create a sub that executes based on another action, such as double-click, or one that is assigned to a control other than a command button. 🥕 Kristen would like to add built-in documentation to a form that the user can access by clicking the form. To accomplish this, she writes a sub procedure in a form class module.

Steps 1234

1. Right-click the **Equipment Entry Form**, click **Design View** on the shortcut menu, then click the **Properties button** 🗔 on the Form Design toolbar to open the property sheet (if it's not already visible)

2. Click the **Event tab**, click the **On Click text box**, click the **Build button** […], click **Code Builder**, then click **OK**
   The class module opens with two new statements to identify the first and last lines of the new sub. The name of the new sub is Form_Click(). The name of the new sub references both the specific object and the specific event you chose in the property sheet. You can use the Object and Procedure lists within the Code window to change these choices, however.

3. Click the **Object list arrow** below the Standard toolbar, then click **FormFooter**
   A new sub, named FormFooter_Click(), is created.

4. Click the **Procedure list arrow** below the Standard toolbar, click **DblClick**, then scroll up to view the three new subs you just created, as shown in Figure O-13
   The Form_Click(), FormFooter_Click(), and FormFooter_DblClick(Cancel As Integer) were all created, but none of them contain anything more than the first and last statements. Now that you know how to use the Object and Procedure lists to create new subs, you can return to the original task of creating documentation for the form that appears when the user clicks the form.

5. Click the **Undo button** 🔙 on the Standard toolbar twice to remove both FormFooter subs, type **MsgBox ("Created by Your Name on Today's Date")** as the single statement for the Form_Click() sub, then click the **Save button** 💾 on the Standard toolbar
   Your screen should look like Figure O-14.

6. Close the Visual Basic window, click 🗔, click the **Form View button** 📧 on the Form Design toolbar, then click the **record selector** to the left of the record
   The MsgBox statement in the Form_Click() sub creates the dialog box, as shown in Figure O-15.

7. Click **OK** in the message box, then click the **Close Form** command button
   VBA is as robust and powerful as Access itself. It takes years of experience to appreciate the vast number of objects, events, methods, and properties that are available. With only modest programming skills, however, you can create basic sub procedures.

FIGURE O-13: Using the Object and Procedure lists

Undo button

Project - Technology-M

Technology-M (Techno
  Form_Employees
  Form_Equipment Entry
  Functions
utility (UTILITY)

Procedure list arrow

Object list arrow

Form_Click() sub

FormFooter_Click() sub

FormFooter_DblClick() sub

```
Err_DeleteThisRecordButton_Click:
    MsgBox Err.Description
    Resume Exit_DeleteThisRecordButton_Click

End Sub

Private Sub Form_Click()

End Sub

Private Sub FormFooter_Click()

End Sub

Private Sub FormFooter_DblClick(Cancel As Integer)

End Sub

Private Sub PrintThisRecordButton_Click()
On Error GoTo Err_PrintThisRecordButton_Click


    DoCmd.DoMenuItem acFormBar, acEditMenu, 8, , acMenuVer70
    DoCmd.PrintOut acSelection

Exit_PrintThisRecordButton_Click:
    Exit Sub
```

FIGURE O-14: Creating a sub procedure

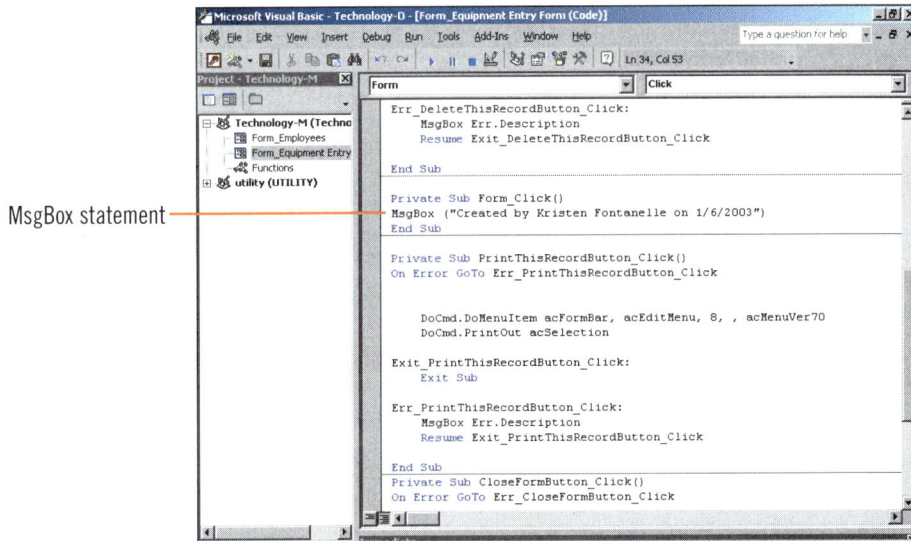

Project - Technology-M

Technology-M (Techno
  Form_Employees
  Form_Equipment Entry
  Functions
utility (UTILITY)

MsgBox statement

```
Err_DeleteThisRecordButton_Click:
    MsgBox Err.Description
    Resume Exit_DeleteThisRecordButton_Click

End Sub

Private Sub Form_Click()
MsgBox ("Created by Kristen Fontanelle on 1/6/2003")
End Sub

Private Sub PrintThisRecordButton_Click()
On Error GoTo Err_PrintThisRecordButton_Click


    DoCmd.DoMenuItem acFormBar, acEditMenu, 8, , acMenuVer70
    DoCmd.PrintOut acSelection

Exit_PrintThisRecordButton_Click:
    Exit Sub

Err_PrintThisRecordButton_Click:
    MsgBox Err.Description
    Resume Exit_PrintThisRecordButton_Click

End Sub
Private Sub CloseFormButton_Click()
On Error GoTo Err_CloseFormButton_Click
```

FIGURE O-15: Form_Click() sub executes the MsgBox statement

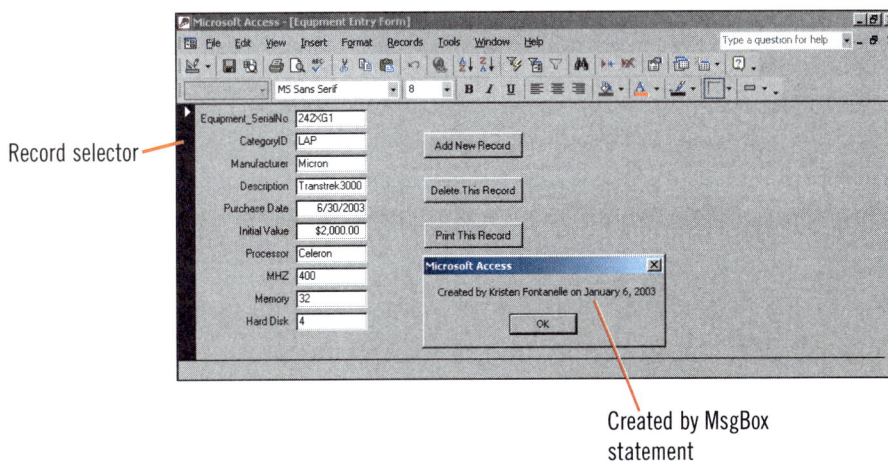

Record selector

Equipment_SerialNo 242XG1
CategoryID LAP
Manufacturer Micron
Description Transtrek 3000
Purchase Date 6/30/2003
Initial Value $2,000.00
Processor Celeron
MHZ 400
Memory 32
Hard Disk 4

Add New Record

Delete This Record

Print This Record

Microsoft Access
Created by Kristen Fontanelle on January 6, 2003
OK

Created by MsgBox
statement

Troubleshooting Modules

You might encounter three types of errors as your code runs, and Access provides several techniques to help you **debug** (find and resolve) these errors. **Compile-time errors** occur as a result of incorrectly constructed code. For example, you may have forgotten to write an End If statement following an If clause, or you may have a **syntax error**, such as a missing parenthesis. This type of error is easiest to find because your code will turn red as soon as it detects a syntax error. **Run-time errors** occur after the code starts to run, and include attempting an illegal operation such as dividing by zero or moving focus to a control that doesn't exist. When you encounter a run-time error, VBA will stop executing your procedure at the line in which the error occurred so you can examine it. **Logic errors** are the most difficult to troubleshoot because they occur when the code runs without problems, but the procedure still doesn't produce the desired result. ✎ Kristen studies debugging techniques using the Functions module.

1. Click **Modules** on the Objects bar, right-click **Functions**, click **Design View**, click to the right of the End If statement, type **your name**, then press [↓]
   Because entering your name is not a valid way to start a VBA statement, when you move out of that statement, VBA displays it in bright red.

2. Click **OK** in the Compile error message box, delete **your name**, then click anywhere in another statement
   The Option Compare Database statement changes to blue (reserved VBA keywords are blue) as soon as you successfully delete your name and click elsewhere in the Code window. Another VBA debugging tool is to set a **breakpoint**, a bookmark that suspends execution of the procedure at that statement to allow the user to examine what is happening.

QuickTip

Click the gray bar to the left of the VBA statement to toggle breakpoints on and off.

3. Click anywhere in the **If** statement, click **Debug** on the menu bar, then click **Toggle Breakpoint**
   Your screen should look like Figure O-16.

QuickTip

If you suspend the execution of a procedure by using a breakpoint, pointing to an argument in the Code window will display a ScreenTip with the argument's current value.

4. Click the **View Microsoft Access button** 📄 on the Standard toolbar, click **Queries** on the Objects bar, then double-click **Employee Pricing**
   When the Employee Pricing query opens, it immediately runs the EmployeePrice function. Because you set a breakpoint at the If statement, that statement is highlighted, as shown in Figure O-17, indicating that the code has been suspended at that point.

5. Click View on the menu bar, click **Immediate Window**, type **? purchasedate**, then press **[Enter]**
   Your screen should look like Figure O-18. The Immediate window is an area where you can determine the value of any argument at the breakpoint. If the date appears as a two-digit year and you would like it to appear as a four-digit year, you can specify that change for the existing database or for all databases using the Options dialog box. Click Tools on the menu bar, click Options, and the click then General tab to find the four-digit year formatting options.

6. Click **Debug** on the menu bar, click **Clear All Breakpoints**, click the **Continue button** ▶ on the Standard toolbar to execute the remainder of the function, then save, print, and close the Functions module
   The Employee Pricing query's datasheet should be visible.

7. Close the Employee Pricing datasheet, close the Technology-O database, then exit Access

FIGURE O-16: Setting a breakpoint

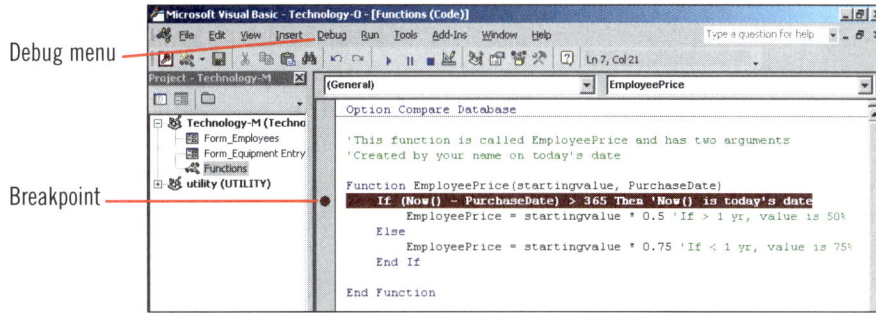

Debug menu

Breakpoint

FIGURE O-17: Stopping execution at a breakpoint

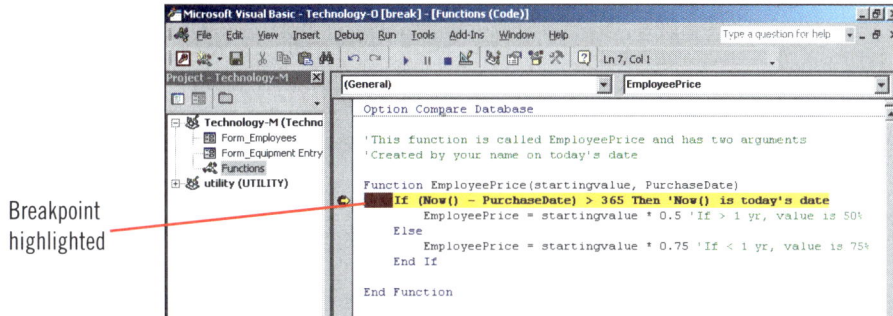

Breakpoint
highlighted

FIGURE O-18: Using the Immediate window

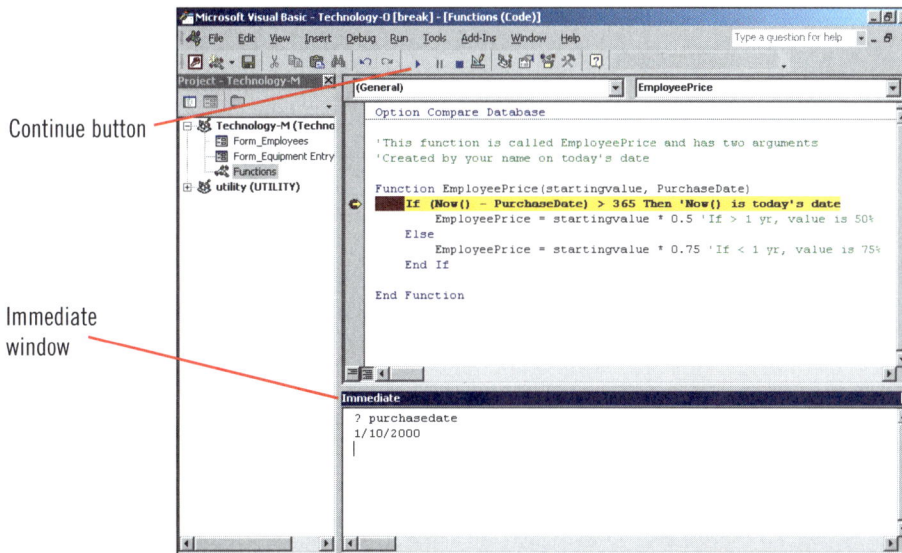

Continue button

Immediate
window

![CLUES TO USE]

Interpreting Visual Basic syntax

When you enter a Visual Basic keyword such as
MsgBox, shown in Figure O-19, Visual Basic prompts
appear to help you complete the statement. In the
MsgBox function syntax, the bold italic words are the
named arguments of the function. Arguments
enclosed in brackets are optional. (Do not type the
brackets in your Visual Basic code.) For the MsgBox
function, the only argument you must provide is the
text for the prompt.

FIGURE O-19: MsgBox function

```
MsgBox |
MsgBox(Prompt, [Buttons As VbMsgBoxStyle = vbOKOnly], [Title], [HelpFile], [Context])
As VbMsgBoxResult
```

Practice

► Concepts Review

Identify each element of the Visual Basic window shown in Figure O-20.

FIGURE O-20

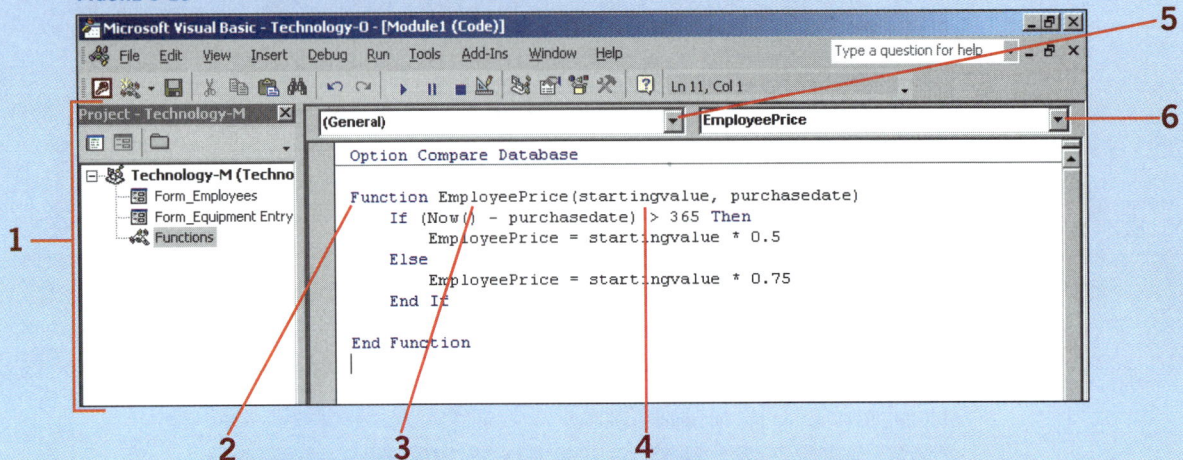

Match each term with the statement that describes its function.

7. Procedure
8. If…Then…Else statement
9. Debugging
10. Class modules
11. Visual Basic for Applications
12. Function
13. Arguments
14. Breakpoint
15. Module

a. Allows you to test a logical condition and execute commands only if the condition is true
b. The programming language used in Access modules
c. A line of code that automatically suspends execution of the procedure
d. A procedure that returns a value
e. Constants, variables, or expressions passed to a procedure to further define how it should execute
f. Stored as part of the form or report object in which they are created
g. The Access object where VBA code is stored
h. A series of VBA statements that perform an operation or calculate a value
i. A process to find and resolve programming errors

Select the best answer from the list of choices.

16. **A module contains VBA programming code organized in units called:**
a. Macros.
b. Arguments.
c. Breakpoints.
d. Procedures.

17. **Which type of procedure returns a value?**
a. Sub
b. Function
c. Sub procedure
d. Class module

18. **Which of the following is NOT a reason to use modules rather than macros?**
a. Modules are used to create unique functions.
b. Modules contain code that can work with other Microsoft Office software programs.
c. Modules can contain procedures that mask error messages.
d. Modules are usually easier to write than macros.

19. **Which of the following is NOT a type of VBA error?**
a. Compile time
b. Run time
c. Logic
d. Class action

20. **Which of the following is a specific action that occurs on or to an object, and is usually the result of a user action?**
a. Argument
b. Sub
c. Function
d. Event

▶ Skills Review

1. Understand modules.
a. Start Access, then open the **Basketball-O** database from the drive and folder where your Project Files are located.
b. Open the Code window for the Shot Statistics module.
c. Record your answers to the following questions on a sheet of paper.
   - What is the name of the function defined in this module?
   - What are the names of the arguments defined in this module?
   - In your own words, what is the purpose of the If statement?
   - What is the purpose of the End Function statement?
   - Why is the End Function statement in blue?
   - Why are some of the lines indented?

2. Compare macros and modules.
a. If not already opened, open the Code window for the Shot Statistics module.
b. Record your answers to the following questions on a sheet of paper.
   - Why was a module rather than a macro used to create this function?
   - Why is code written in the Shot Statistics Code window generally more difficult to create than a macro?
   - Identify each of the keywords or keyword phrases, and explain the purpose for each.

3. Create functions.
a. If not already opened, open the Code window for the Shot Statistics module.
b. Create a function called Contribution below the End Function statement of the TotalShotPercentage function by typing the following VBA statements: (*Hint:* Type the function exactly as written below.)
```
Function Contribution(fg, threept, ft, offreb, defreb, assists)
      Contribution = (fg * 2 + threept * 3 + ft + offreb * 2 + defreb + assists * 2)
End Function
```
c. Save the Shot Statistics module, then close the Visual Basic window.

d. Use Query Design View to create a new query using the First and Last fields from the Players table and all of the fields from the Stats table.

e. Create a calculated field named **Rank** in the first available column by carefully typing the Contribution function as follows:

Rank: Int(Contribution([FG], [3P], [FT], [Reb-O], [Reb-D], [Assists]))

(*Note:* The Int function converted the result to an integer rather than text for later sorting purposes.)

f. Sort the query in ascending order on the GameNo field, then in descending order on the Rank field. This will put the records in order from most valuable player to least for each game.

g. View the datasheet, as shown in Figure O-21, change PlayerNo 21 to your first and last name, then print the first page of the datasheet in landscape orientation.

h. Save the query with the name **Rankings**, then close the Rankings datasheet.

4. Use If statements.

a. Click Modules on the Objects bar, open the Shot Statistics Code window, click to the right of the Function Contribution statement, press [Enter], then modify the function with the statements shown below:

(*Hint:* You can use copy and paste to copy repeating statements, then edit for the differences.)

FIGURE O-21

First	Last	PlayerNo	GameNo	FG	FGA	3P	3PA	FT	FTA	Reb-O	Reb-D	Assists	Rank
Sydney	Freesen	4	1	3	4	2	2	1	1	1	2	2	21
Morgan	Tyler	51	1	1	5	0	0	2	4	4	6	1	20
Denise	Franco	42	1	2	5	1	2	4	4	2	3	1	20
Lisa	Friedrichsen	21	1	0	3	0	1	0	1	5	3	1	15
Ellyse	Howard	12	1	2	3	1	1	1	1	1	2	1	14
Megan	Hile	45	1	1	4	0	2	1	1	1	2	1	9
Denise	Franco	42	2	2	4	1	2	5	5	5	3	2	29
Sydney	Freesen	4	2	4	6	1	3	3	3	2	2	4	28
Morgan	Tyler	51	2	2	4	0	0	3	5	3	6	1	21
Ellyse	Howard	12	2	3	2	0	0	3	4	3	3	1	20
Megan	Hile	45	2	2	3	0	3	1	1	1	5	1	14
Lisa	Friedrichsen	21	2	1	2	0	0	1	4	0	0	1	5
Denise	Franco	42	3	5	3	2	4	4	5	5	3	1	35
Sydney	Freesen	4	3	5	6	2	3	2	4	2	1	2	27
Ellyse	Howard	12	3	5	6	0	0	2	4	4	3	1	25

```
Function Contribution(fg, threept, ft, offreb, defreb, assists)
   If fg+threept+ft = 0 Then
      Contribution = (fg * 2 + threept * 3 + ft + offreb * 2 + defreb + assists * 2)/2
   ElseIf offreb+defreb = 0 Then
      Contribution = (fg * 2 + threept * 3 + ft + offreb * 2 + defreb + assists * 2)/3
   Else
      Contribution = (fg * 2 + threept * 3 + ft + offreb * 2 + defreb + assists * 2)
   End If
End Function
```

b. Save the Shot Statistics module, then close the Visual Basic window.

c. Rename the Rankings query to **Rankings-your initials**, then open and print the first pages of the datasheet in landscape orientation. You should see the calculated Ranking field change for PlayerNo 21 for Games 1, 2, and 3 in which the player had either zero offense or zero rebounds.

d. Close the datasheet.

5. Document procedures.

a. Click Modules on the Objects bar, open the Shot Statistics Code window, and edit the Contribution function to include the following five comment statements:

```
Function Contribution(fg, threept, ft, offreb, defreb, assists)
'If no field goals, 3 pointers, or free throws were made
   If fg + threept + ft = 0 Then
'Then the Contribution statistic should be divided by 2
      Contribution = (fg * 2 + threept * 3 + ft + offreb * 2 + defreb + assists * 2) / 2
'If no offensive or defensive rebounds were grabbed
   ElseIf offreb + defreb = 0 Then
```

```
'Then the Contribution statistic should be divided by 3
      Contribution = (fg * 2 + threept * 3 + ft + offreb * 2 + defreb + assists * 2) / 3
   Else
      Contribution = (fg * 2 + threept * 3 + ft + offreb * 2 + defreb + assists * 2)
   End If
End Function
'This function was created by Your Name on today's date
```

   b. Save the changes to the Shot Statistics module, print the module, then close the Visual Basic window.

6. Examine class modules.

   a. Open the Player Entry Form in Form Design View.

   b. On the right side of the form, select the Command Button that is named PrintCurrentRecord and displays a printer icon.

   c. Open the property sheet for the button, click the Event tab, click the On Click property, then click the Build button to open the class module.

   d. Edit the comment on the last line to show your name and the current date; save and print the module, then close the Visual Basic window.

7. Create sub procedures.

   a. Open the Player Entry Form in Form Design View, if it's not already opened.

   b. Open the property sheet for the form, click the Event tab, click the On Mouse Move property text box, click the Build button, click Code Builder, then click OK.

   c. Enter the following statement between the Private Sub and End Sub statements:

```
[First].ForeColor = 255
```

   d. Enter a comment below this statement as follows:

```
'When the mouse moves, the First control will become red.
```

   e. Save, then close the Visual Basic window.

   f. Close the property sheet, save, then open the Player Entry Form in Form View.

   g. Move the mouse beyond the edge of the Detail section of the form. The color of the First text box should turn red.

   h. Save, then close the Player Entry Form.

8. Troubleshoot modules.

   a. Open the Code window for the Shot Statistics module.

   b. Click anywhere in the If fg + threept + ft = 0 statement.

   c. Click Debug on the menu bar, then click the Toggle Breakpoint option to set a breakpoint at this statement.

   d. Save and close the Visual Basic window, then return to Microsoft Access.

   e. Click Queries on the Objects bar, then double-click the Rankings-your initials query. This action will use the Contribution function, which will stop and highlight the statement where you set a breakpoint.

   f. Click View on the menu bar, click Immediate Window (if not already visible), type **?fg**, then press [Enter]. On a piece of paper, write down the current value of the fg variable.

   g. Type **?offreb**, then press [Enter]. On a piece of paper, write down the current value of the offreb variable.

   h. Click Debug on the menu bar, click Clear All Breakpoints, click the Continue button on the Standard toolbar.

   i. Return to the Rankings-your initials query in Datasheet View. Using both Query Design View and Query Datasheet View, answer the following questions:

     • When calculating the Rank field, what field was used for the fg argument?

     • When calculating the Rank field, what field is used for the offreb argument?

     • What is the value of the fg argument for the first record?

     • What is the value of the offreb argument?

   j. Close the Rankings-your initials query, close the Basketball-O database, then exit Access.

▶ Independent Challenge 1

As the manager of a doctor's clinic, you have created an Access database called Patients-O to track insurance claim reimbursements and general patient health. You want to modify an existing function within this database.

a. Start Access, then open the **Patients-O** database from the drive and folder where your Project Files are located.

b. Open the Body Mass Index module in Design View, then record your answers to the following questions on another sheet of paper:

- What is the name of the function in the module?
- What are the function arguments?
- How many comments are in the function?

c. Edit the BMI function by adding a comment at the end of the code with your name and today's date.

d. Edit the BMI function by adding a comment above the Function statement with the following information:
```
'A healthy BMI is in the range of 21-24.
```

e. Edit the BMI function by adding the following If statement between the Function and BMI statements:
```
If height = 0 Then BMI = 0 Else
```

f. Edit the BMI function by adding an End If statement between the BMI and End Function statements, then indent the code to clarify the If clause. The final BMI function code should look as follows:

```
'This function calculates BMI, body mass index.
'A high BMI indicates an unhealthy weight to height ratio.
'A healthy BMI is in the range of 21-24.
    Function BMI(weight, height)
        If height = 0 Then
            BMI = 0
        Else
            BMI = (weight * 0.4536) / (height * 0.0254) ^ 2
        End If
    End Function
'Your Name and today's date.
```

g. Save and print the module, then close the Visual Basic window.

h. Double-click the BMI Query to open its datasheet, then test the If statement by entering **0** in the Height field for the first record for Sara Johnson. When you press [Tab] to move to the Weight field, the bmicalc field should recalculate to 0.

i. Edit the first record to contain your first and last name, print, save, then close the BMI Query datasheet.

j. Close the Patients-O database, then exit Access.

▶ Independent Challenge 2

As the manager of a doctor's clinic, you have created an Access database called Patients-O to track insurance claim reimbursements. You want to study the existing sub procedures stored as class modules in the Claim Entry Form.

a. Start Access, then open the **Patients-O** database from the drive and folder where your Project Files are located.

b. Open the Claim Entry Form in Form Design View.

c. Click the Code button on the Form Design toolbar, then record your answers to the following questions on another sheet of paper:

- What are the names of the sub procedures in this class module?
- What Access functions are used in the PtFirstName_AfterUpdate() sub?
- How many arguments do the functions in the PtFirstName_AfterUpdate() sub have?
- What do the functions in the PtFirstName_AfterUpdate() sub do? (*Hint:* You may have to use the Visual Basic Help system if you are not familiar with the functions.)
- What is the purpose of the On Error command? (*Hint:* Use the Visual Basic Help system if you are not familiar with this command.)

d. Close the Visual Basic window, close the Claim Entry Form, then close the Patients-O database.

e. Exit Access.

▶ Independent Challenge 3

As the manager of a doctor's clinic, you have created an Access database called Patients-O to track insurance claim reimbursements that are fixed (paid at a predetermined fixed rate) or denied (not paid by the insurance company). You want to enhance the database with a class module.

a. Start Access, then open the **Patients-O** database from the drive and folder where your Project Files are located.

b. Open the CPT Form in Form Design View.

c. Expand the width of the CPT Form to about the 5" mark on the horizontal ruler.

d. Use the Command Button Wizard to add a command button in the Form Header section. Choose the Add New Record action from the Record Operations category.

e. Enter **Add Record** as the text on the button, then name the button **AddRecordButton.**

f. Use the Command Button Wizard to add a command button in the Form Header section to the right of the existing Add Record button. (*Hint:* Move and resize controls as necessary to put two command buttons in the Form Header section.)

g. Choose the Delete Record action from the Record Operations category.

h. Enter **Delete Record** as the text on the button, and name the button **DeleteRecordButton**.

i. Save and view the CPT Form in Form View, then click the Add Record command button.

j. Add a new record (it will be record number 65) with a CPTCode value of **999** and an RBRVS value of **1.5**.

k. To make sure that the Delete Record button works, click the new record you just entered, click the Delete Record command button, then click Yes to confirm the deletion.

l. In Form Design View, click the Delete Record command button, then press the [Delete] key.

m. Click the Code button on the Standard toolbar to examine the class module associated with this form, then record your answers to the following questions on another sheet of paper:
- How many subs exist in this class module and what are their names?
- What was the effect of deleting the command button in Form Design view on the associated Visual Basic code?

n. Add a comment as the last line of code in the Code window with your name and the current date, save, print, then close the Visual Basic window.

o. Save and close the CPT Form, close the Patients-O database, then exit Access.

e Independent Challenge 4

Learning a programming language is sometimes compared to learning a foreign language. But have you ever wondered how it would feel to learn a new software program or programming language if English wasn't your primary language, or if you had some other type of accessibility challenge? Advances in technology are helping to break down many barriers to those with vision, hearing, mobility, cognitive, and language impairments. In this exercise, you explore the Microsoft Web site for resources to address these issues.

a. Go to www.microsoft.com/enable, then print that page. Explore the Web site.

b. Go back to www.microsoft.com/enable, click the Guides by Disability link, then click the Cognitive and Language Impairments link.

c. After exploring the Web site (you may want to print some pages as well, but be careful as some articles are quite long), write a one-page, double-spaced paper describing some of the things that you learned about how Microsoft products accommodate people with Cognitive and Language impairments.

d. Go back to www.microsoft.com/enable, scroll to the bottom, click the International Sites list arrow, click Spanish, then click Go. Print that page, then exit Access.

▶ Visual Workshop

As the manager of a college basketball team, you are helping the coach build meaningful statistics to compare the relative value of the players in each game. The coach has stated that one offensive rebound is worth as much to the team as two defensive rebounds, and would like you to use this rule to develop a "rebounding impact statistic" for each game. Open the **Basketball-0** database and use Figure O-22 to develop a function called **ReboundImpact** in a new module called **Rebound Statistic** to calculate this statistic. Include your name and the current date as a comment in the last row of the function. Print the function.

FIGURE O-22

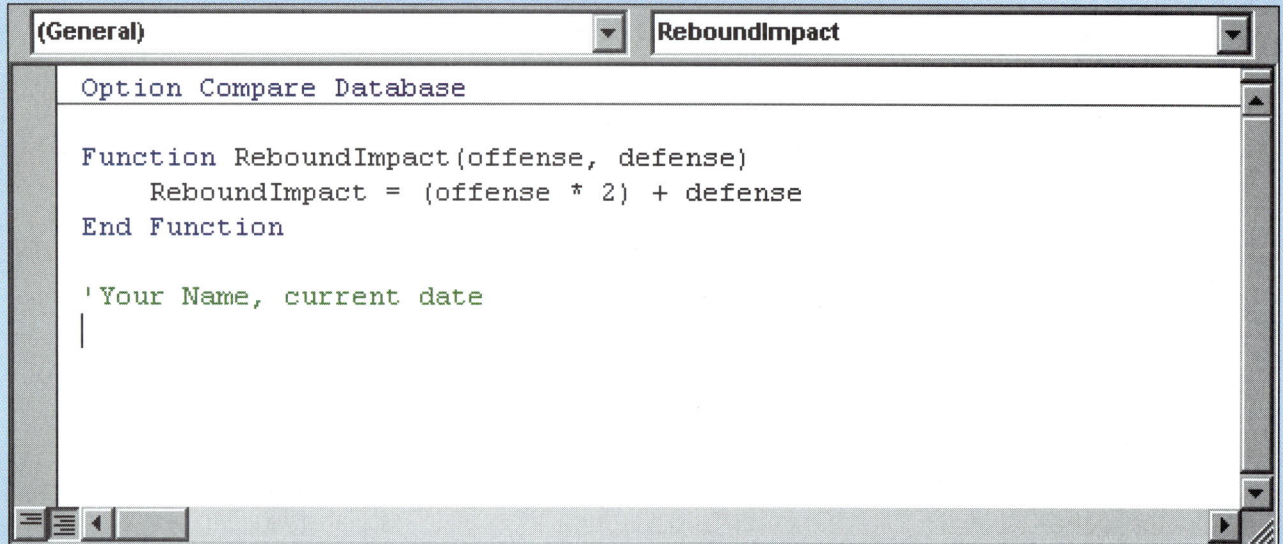

```
(General)                              ▼   ReboundImpact                              ▼

   Option Compare Database

   Function ReboundImpact(offense, defense)
       ReboundImpact = (offense * 2) + defense
   End Function

   'Your Name, current date
   |
```

Unit
P

Managing
the Database

Objectives

▶ **Convert databases**
MOUS ▶ **Set passwords**
MOUS ▶ **Change startup options**
MOUS ▶ **Encrypt a database**
▶ **Analyze performance**
MOUS ▶ **Split a database**
MOUS ▶ **Replicate using the Briefcase**
MOUS ▶ **Synchronize using the Briefcase**

Access databases are unlike the other Microsoft Office files in that they are typically used by more people and for much longer than Word documents or Excel spreadsheets. Therefore, spending a few hours to secure a database and improve its performance is a practical and wise investment. As more and more users become dependent on the database, any effort you take to make the database faster, easier, and more reliable will provide tremendous benefits. Database administration is an important responsibility. ✐ Kristen Fontanelle, network administrator at MediaLoft, will examine several administrative issues such as setting passwords, changing startup options, and analyzing database performance to protect, improve, and enhance her database.

Converting Databases

When you **convert** a database you change the file into one that can be opened in another version of Access. In Access 2002, however, the default file format for new databases is Access 2000, as evidenced by the information in the Database window title bar. This means that you can open an Access 2000 database in Access 2002 or Access 2000 without converting the database. While Microsoft Word and Microsoft Excel have enjoyed this type of backward and forward compatibility in previous versions, Access 2002 is the first version of Access that can share files with an older version of Access without first going through a conversion tool. If you want to open an Access 2000 database in Access 97, however, you need to convert it to an Access 97 database first. Kristen has been asked by the Training department to convert the Technology-P database to a version that they can open and use in Access 97 for a training class.

Steps 123 4

1. **Start Access, then open the Technology-P database from the drive and folder where your Project Files are located**
   To convert a database, you must make sure that no other users have it open. Because you are the sole user of this database, you can start the conversion process.

2. **Click Tools on the menu bar, point to Database Utilities, point to Convert Database, then click To Access 97 File Format**
   The Convert Database Into dialog box opens, prompting you for the name of the database.

3. **Make sure the Save In list references the drive and folder where your Project Files are located, then type Technology97 in the File name text box**
   Your screen should look like Figure P-1. Because both Access 2000 and Access 97 databases have the same **.mdb** file extension, it is helpful to identify the version of Access in the filename if you are going to be working with both file types on the same computer.

4. **Click Save in the Convert Database Into dialog box, then click OK when prompted about the Access 97 File Format**
   Access starts the conversion process; you can follow the progress on the status bar. Access creates a database file Technology97 in an Access 97 format. When the conversion is finished, you are returned to your original Access 2000 file, Technology-P.

5. **Right-click the Start button on the taskbar, click Explore on the shortcut menu, then scroll and locate your Project Files in the Folder list**
   You may need to click expand buttons ⊞ or collapse buttons ⊟ in the Folders list.

Trouble?

If you do not see the extensions on the file names, click Tools on the menu bar, click Folder Options, click the View tab, then uncheck the Hide file extensions for known file types check box.

6. **Click View on the menu bar, then click Details**
   Your screen should look similar to Figure P-2. By viewing file details, the Name, Size, Type, and Modified columns display the name, size in KB, file type, and date the file was last modified. Notice that the list includes Technology97, the database that was just created by converting the Technology-P Access 2000 database to an Access 97 version database. The filename Technology-P appears twice, though, both with an .mdb and an .ldb extension. The **.ldb** file is a temporary file that keeps track of record-locking information when the database is open. It helps coordinate the multiuser capabilities of an Access database so that several people can read and update the same database at the same time. The .ldb file may already be closed if your Project Files are stored on the hard drive.

7. **Close Windows Explorer**

FIGURE P-1: Convert Database Into dialog box

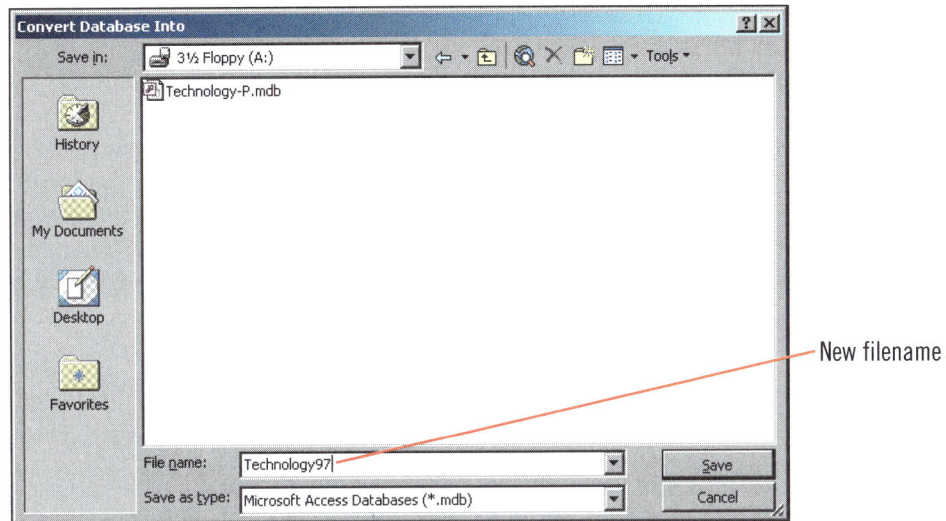

New filename

FIGURE P-2: Using Windows Explorer to view files

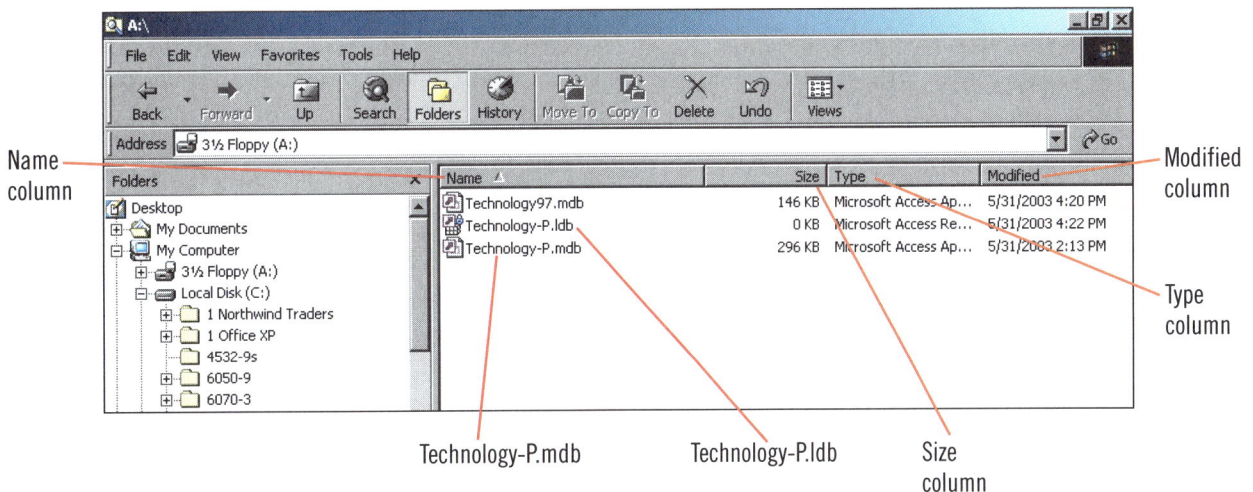

Name column

Technology-P.mdb

Technology-P.ldb

Size column

Modified column

Type column

Converting from Access 2000 to Access 2002

The *Access 2002 software application* provides some powerful new features not available in Access 2000 such as PivotTable View, PivotChart View, speech recognition, improved dynamic Web page connectivity, XML support, improved SQL Server connectivity, and more. *Access database files* themselves, however, have not dramatically changed between the Access 2000 and Access 2002 versions. Therefore, use the default Access 2000 version for new databases created in Access 2002 as shown in the Database window title bar unless your database is extremely large (a 2002 database will perform better if the database is very large), or are planning extensive future programming projects (a 2002 database will incorporate new properties and events for future releases of Access). By using the 2000 file format default option for new databases, you preserve seamless forward and backward compatibility with Access 2000 software users.

Setting Passwords

Setting passwords is a common strategy to secure information. You can set three types of passwords on an Access database: database, security account (also called user-level), and Visual Basic for Applications (VBA) passwords. If you set a **database password**, all users must enter that password before they are allowed to open the database, but once they open the database, they have full access to it. **Security account passwords** are applied to **workgroups**, files that determine the user(s), objects, and permissions to which the user(s) of that workgroup are granted (such as read, delete, or edit) for specific objects in the database. **VBA passwords** prevent unauthorized users from modifying VBA code. Other ways to secure an Access database are listed in Table P-1. Kristen uses a database password to further secure the information.

Steps

QuickTip

It's always a good idea to back up a database before creating a database password.

1. Click **File** on the menu bar, then click **Close**

   The Technology-P database closes, but the Access application window remains open.

2. Click the **Open button** 📂 on the Database toolbar, navigate to the drive and folder where your Project Files are stored, click **Technology-P**, click the **Open list arrow** in the Open dialog box, then click **Open Exclusive**

   To set a database password, you must open it in exclusive mode. **Exclusive mode** means that you are the only person who has the database open, and others will not be able to open the file during this time.

3. Click **Tools** on the menu bar, point to **Security**, then click **Set Database Password**

   The Set Database Password dialog box opens, as shown in Figure P-3. Passwords are case sensitive, and if you lose or forget your password, it can't be recovered. For security reasons, your password will not appear as you type; for each keystroke, an asterisk will appear. Therefore, you must enter the exact same password in both the Password and Verify text boxes to make sure you haven't made a typing error.

QuickTip

Check to make sure the Caps Lock light is not on before entering a password.

4. Type **cyclones** in the Password text box, press **[Tab]**, type **cyclones** in the Verify text box, then click **OK**

   Passwords should be easy to remember, but not as obvious as your name, the word "password," the name of the database, or the name of the company.

5. Click **File** on the menu bar, then click **Close**

   Of course, it's important to test the new password.

6. Click 📂 on the Database toolbar, navigate to the drive and folder where your Project Files are located, then double-click **Technology-P**

   The Password Required dialog box opens, as shown in Figure P-4.

7. Type **cyclones**, then click **OK**

   The Technology-P database opens, giving you full access to all of the objects. To remove a password, you must exclusively open a database, just as you did when you set a database password.

8. Click **File** on the menu bar, click **Close**, click 📂 on the Database toolbar, click **Technology-P**, click the **Open list arrow** in the Open dialog box, click **Open Exclusive**, type **cyclones** in the Password Required dialog box, then click **OK**

9. Click **Tools** on the menu bar, point to **Security**, click **Unset Database Password**, type **cyclones**, then click **OK**

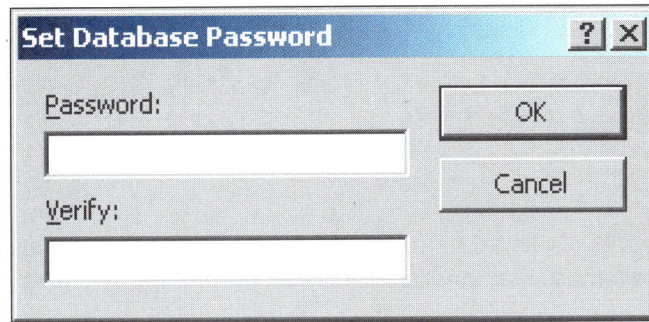

FIGURE P-3: Set Database Password dialog box

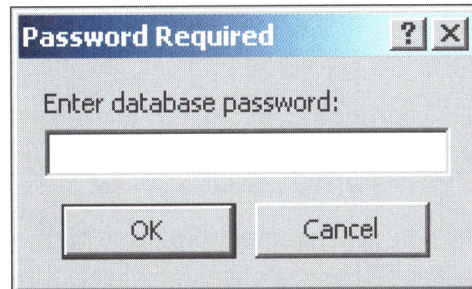

FIGURE P-4: Password Required dialog box

TABLE P-1: Methods to secure an Access database

method	description
passwords	Passwords can be set at the database, workgroup, or VBA level
encryption	Compacts the database and makes the data indecipherable to other programs
startup options	Hides or disables certain functions when the database is opened
show/hide objects	Shows or hides objects in the Database window; a simple way to prevent users from unintentionally deleting objects is to hide them in the Database window by checking the Hidden property in the object's property sheet
split a database	Separates the back-end data from the front-end objects (such as forms and reports) into two databases that work together; splitting a database allows you to give each user access to only those front-end objects they need as well as add additional security measures to the back-end database that contains the data

CLUES TO USE

Creating workgroups

The most extensive way to secure an Access database is to use the Workgroup Administrator to create workgroups that define the specific users and object permissions to which the users have access. To start the Workgroup Administrator, click Tools on the menu bar, point to Security, then click Workgroup Administrator. Using Workgroup Administrator, you can grant or deny permissions to any object in the database to any group or individual that is defined within the workgroup information file. Microsoft refers to a database that is protected with workgroup-level security as a secure database.

Access 2002

Changing Startup Options

Startup options are a series of commands that execute when the database is opened. Many common startup options can be defined through the Startup dialog box, such as what form and menu bar to display when the database opens. Other startup options require that a **command-line option**, a special series of characters added to the end of the path to the file (for example, C:\My Documents\MediaLoft.mdb /excl), execute a command when the file is opened. See Table P-2 for information on several startup command-line options. ✎ Because she knows that most users immediately open the Employees form as soon as they open the Technology-P database, Kristen uses the Startup dialog box to specify that the Employees form opens as soon as the Technology-P database opens.

Steps 1 2 3 4

1. Click **Tools** on the menu bar, then click **Startup**
The Startup dialog box opens, as shown in Figure P-5.

2. Click the **Display Form/Page list arrow**, then click **Employees**
In addition to specifying which form will open when the Technology-P database opens, the Startup dialog box provides several other options to customize and secure the database.

3. Click in the **Application Title text box**, type **MediaLoft Computer Assets**, click the **Allow Toolbar/Menu Changes check box** to clear the check box, then click **OK**
Clearing the Allow Toolbar/Menu Changes check box will not allow users to customize or change the view of toolbars or menus in any way. Provided the correct toolbars appear on each screen, not allowing the users to change them can simplify, secure, and improve the usability of the database. The text entered in the Application Title text box appears in the Access title bar.

QuickTip
Press and hold [Shift] while opening a database to bypass the startup options.

4. Close the Technology-P database, click the **Open button** 📂 on the Database toolbar, navigate to the drive and folder where your Project Files are located, then double-click **Technology-P**
The Technology-P database opens, followed by the Employees form, as shown in Figure P-6. If the database were password protected, you would have to remove the password before you could bypass the startup options.

5. Close the Employees form, then click **View** on the menu bar
The Toolbars option is no longer available because you disabled toolbar changes in the Startup dialog box.

6. Right-click the **Database toolbar**
No shortcut menus are available from any toolbars because you disabled toolbar changes in the Startup dialog box.

FIGURE P-5: Startup dialog box

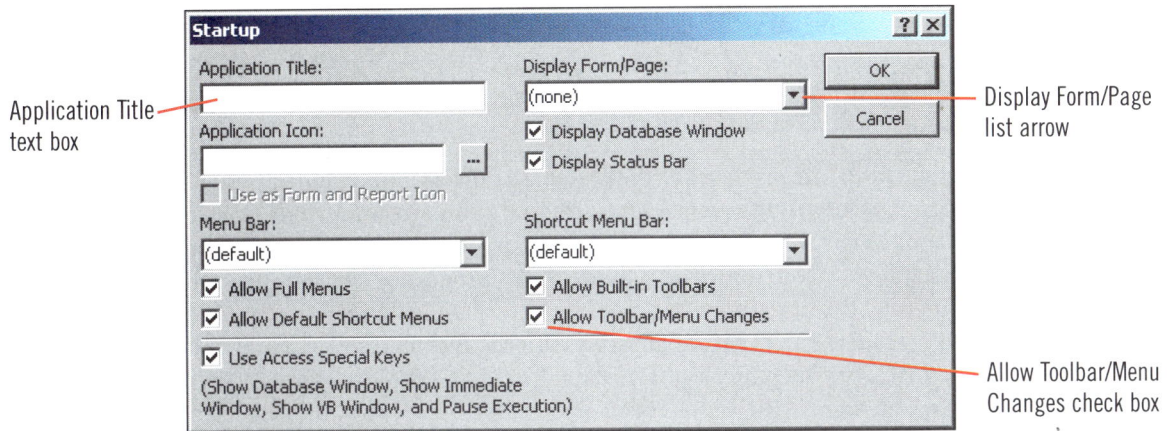

Application Title
text box →

Display Form/Page
list arrow →

Allow Toolbar/Menu
Changes check box

Startup

Application Title:

Display Form/Page:
(none)

☑ Display Database Window
☑ Display Status Bar

OK
Cancel

Application Icon:

☐ Use as Form and Report Icon

Menu Bar:
(default)

Shortcut Menu Bar:
(default)

☑ Allow Full Menus
☑ Allow Default Shortcut Menus

☑ Allow Built-in Toolbars
☑ Allow Toolbar/Menu Changes

☑ Use Access Special Keys

(Show Database Window, Show Immediate
Window, Show VB Window, and Pause Execution)

FIGURE P-6: Employees form automatically opens

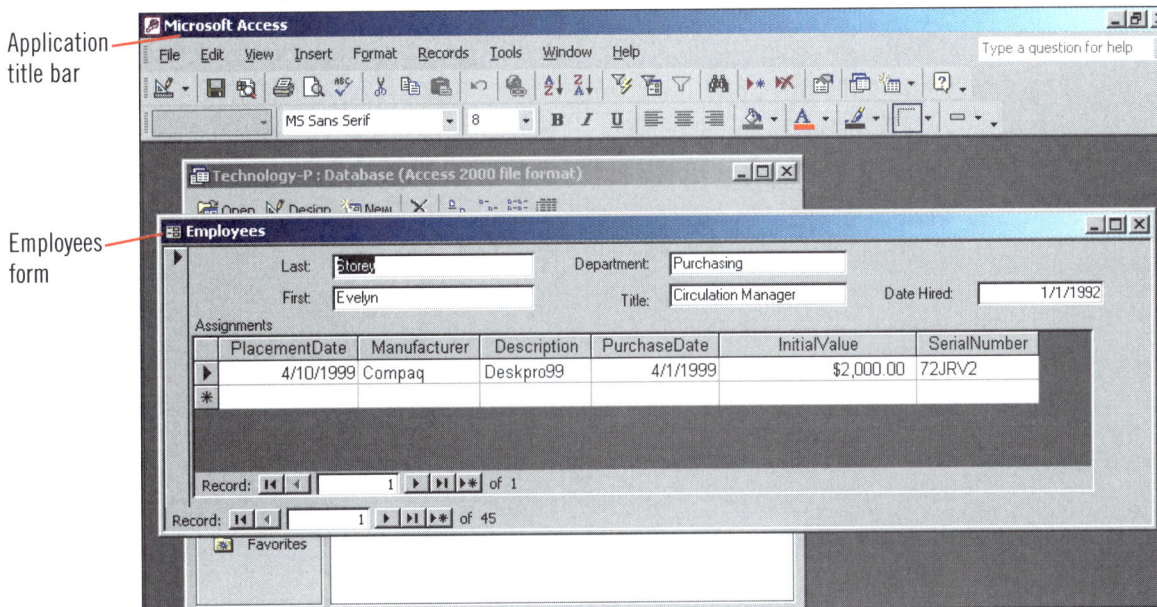

Application
title bar →

Microsoft Access

File Edit View Insert Format Records Tools Window Help

Type a question for help

MS Sans Serif   8   **B** *I* U

Technology-P : Database (Access 2000 file format)

Open Design New X

Employees
form →

Employees

Last: Storey   Department: Purchasing
First: Evelyn   Title: Circulation Manager   Date Hired: 1/1/1992

Assignments

	PlacementDate	Manufacturer	Description	PurchaseDate	InitialValue	SerialNumber
▶	4/10/1999	Compaq	Deskpro99	4/1/1999	$2,000.00	72JRV2
*						

Record: ◄◄ ◄ 1 ► ►► ►* of 1

Record: ◄◄ ◄ 1 ► ►► ►* of 45

Favorites

TABLE P-2: Startup command-line options

option	effect
/excl	Opens the database for exclusive access
/ro	Opens the database for read-only access
/pwd *password*	Opens the database using the specified *password*
/repair	Repairs the database (In Access 2000 and 2002, compacting the database also repairs it. If you choose the Compact on Close command, you don't need the /repair option.)
/convert *target database*	Converts a previous version of a database to an Access 2000 database with the *target database* name
/x *macro*	Starts Access and runs specified *macro*
/nostartup	Starts Access without displaying the task pane
/wrkgrp *workgroup information file*	Starts Access using the specified *workgroup information file*

Encrypting a Database

Encrypting means to make the Database objects and data itself indecipherable to other programs. **Decrypting** reverses encryption. If you are concerned that your Access database file might be stolen and the data stripped from it by another program (such as another database program, a word processor, or a utility program), encryption may be warranted. Other potential threats to your database are described in Table P-3. ✎ MediaLoft has recently connected their corporate file servers to the Internet, so Kristen is more concerned than ever before about keeping corporate data secure. She explores the encryption and decryption features of Access.

Steps 1234

QuickTip
It's always a good idea to back up a database before encrypting it.

1. Click **File** on the menu bar, then click **Close**

The Technology-P Database window closes, but the Access application is still running. You cannot encrypt an open database.

2. Click **Tools** on the menu bar, point to **Security**, click **Encrypt/Decrypt Database**, then navigate to the drive and folder where your Project Files are located

The Encrypt/Decrypt Database dialog box opens, as shown in Figure P-7.

3. Double-click **Technology-P** to choose it as the database to encrypt, double-click **Technology-P** again to choose it as the name for the encrypted database, then click **Yes** when prompted to replace the existing file

You can encrypt a database file to the same filename or to a new filename. In either case, a back-up copy of the database on a separate disk protects your file should the encryption be unsuccessful (unlikely but possible) or the equipment malfunctions during the encryption process. To users authorized to open the file, an encrypted database works in exactly the same way as the original file; it is not restricted until you create workgroup security accounts. Whether or not you are using workgroup accounts, though, encryption still helps protect data when it is sent over network connections. You decrypt a database using the same steps.

4. Click **Tools** on the menu bar, point to **Security**, then click **Encrypt/Decrypt Database**

5. Double-click **Technology-P** to choose it as the database to decrypt, double-click **Technology-P** again as the name for the decrypted database, then click **Yes** when prompted to replace the existing file

The status bar presents information about the progress of the encryption or decryption process.

CLUES TO USE

Creating an MDE File

An Access MDE file is a special copy of the database that prevents others from opening or editing form, report, or module objects in Design View. You can still enter data and use the MDE file just like the original database, but an MDE file gives you a way to distribute the database without revealing the development work you put into the forms, reports, and modules. An MDE file is also much smaller and runs faster than a regular database MDB file. To create an MDE file, close all open databases, but leave Access running. Click Tools on the menu bar, point to Database Utilities, and then click the Make MDE File option. Then enter the

names of the original database and the MDE file.

Also, if you are using an Access 2000 version database, you must first convert the database to an Access 2002 version database before you can convert it to an MDE file. To convert an Access 2000 version database to an Access 2002 version, click Tools on the menu bar, point to Database Utilities, point to Convert Database, and then click To Access 2002 File Format. You will be prompted for both the original database (if it is not currently open), as well as the name for the Access 2002 version database.

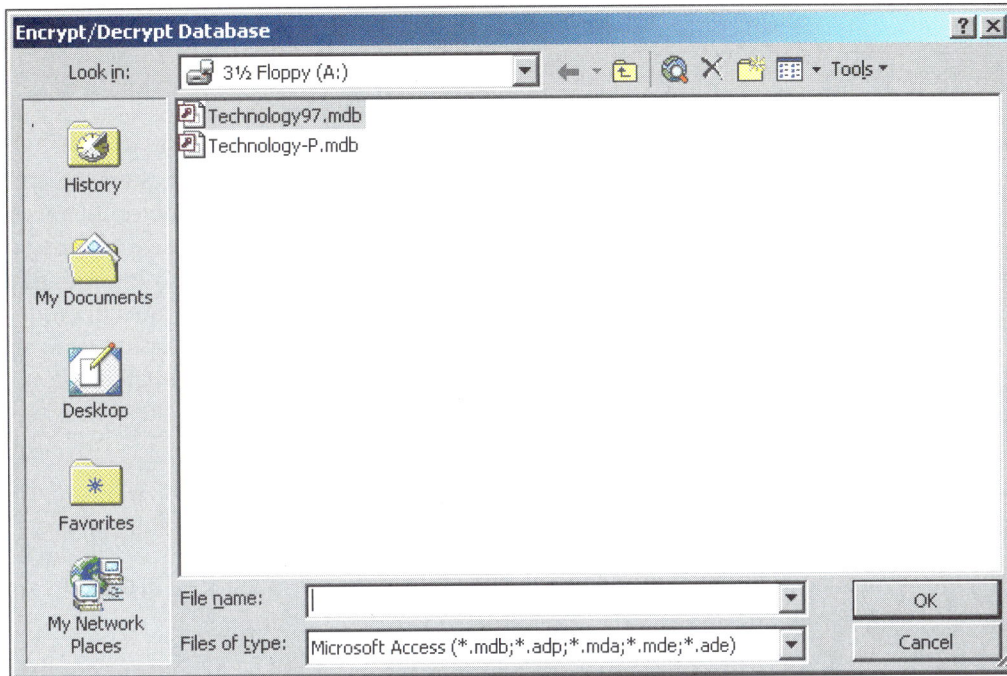

Encrypt/Decrypt Database

Look in: 3½ Floppy (A:)

History
My Documents
Desktop
Favorites
My Network Places

Technology97.mdb
Technology-P.mdb

File name:

Files of type: Microsoft Access (*.mdb;*.adp;*.mda;*.mde;*.ade)

OK
Cancel

TABLE P-3: Database threats

incident	what can happen	appropriate actions
Virus	Viruses can cause a vast number of damaging actions, ranging from profane messages to destruction of files.	Purchase the leading virus-checking software for each machine, and keep it updated.
Power outage	Power problems such as **brown-outs** (dips in power often causing lights to dim) and **spikes** (surges in power) can cause damage to the hardware, which may render the computer useless.	Purchase a **UPS** (Uninterruptible Power Supply) to maintain constant power to the file server (if networked). Purchase a **surge protector** (power strip with surge protection) for each end user.
Theft or intentional damage	Computer thieves or other scoundrels steal or vandalize computer equipment.	Place the file server in a room that can be locked after hours. Use network drives for end user data files, and back them up on a daily basis. Use off-site storage for backups. Set database passwords and encryption so that files that are stolen cannot be used. Use computer locks for equipment that is at risk, especially laptops.

Analyzing Performance

Access 2002

Access provides a tool called the **Performance Analyzer** that studies the structure and size of your database and makes a variety of recommendations on how you could improve its performance. With adequate time and Access skills, you can alleviate many performance bottlenecks by using software tools and additional programming techniques to improve database performance. With extra money, however, you can often purchase faster processors and more memory to accomplish the same thing. See Table P-4 for tips on optimizing the performance of your computer. Kristen uses the Performance Analyzer to see whether Access provides any recommendations on how to easily maintain peak performance of the Technology-P database.

Steps

1. Open the **Technology-P database** from the drive and folder where your Project Files are located, then close the **Employees form** that automatically opens

2. Click **Tools** on the menu bar, point to **Analyze**, click **Performance**, then click the **Forms tab**
   The Performance Analyzer dialog box opens, as shown in Figure P-8. You can choose to analyze selected tables, forms, other objects, or the entire database.

3. Click the **All Object Types tab**, click **Select All**, then click **OK**
   The Performance Analyzer examines each object and presents the results in a dialog box, as shown in Figure P-9. The key shows that the analyzer gives four levels of advice regarding performance: recommendations, suggestions, ideas, and items that were fixed.

4. Click **Table 'Assignments': Change data type of field 'SSN' from 'Text' to 'Long Integer'** in the Analysis Results list
   The icon tells you that this is an idea. The Analysis Notes section of the Performance Analyzer dialog box gives you additional information regarding that specific item. In this case, the idea is to change the data type of the field SSN from Text to Number (with a Long Integer field size). While this might not be an appropriate action for an SSN field, the three fields in the PCSpecs table—Memory, HardDisk, and MHz—all represent numeric values that could be changed from Text to Number with the suggested field size. All of the Performance Analyzer's ideas should be considered, but they are not as important as recommendations and suggestions.

5. Click **Close** to close the Performance Analyzer dialog box

FIGURE P-8: Performance Analyzer dialog box

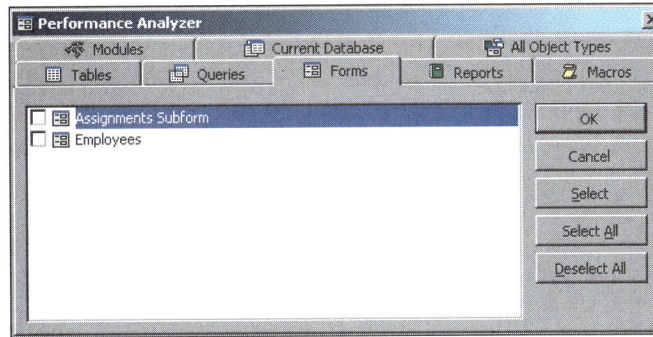

FIGURE P-9: Performance Analyzer results

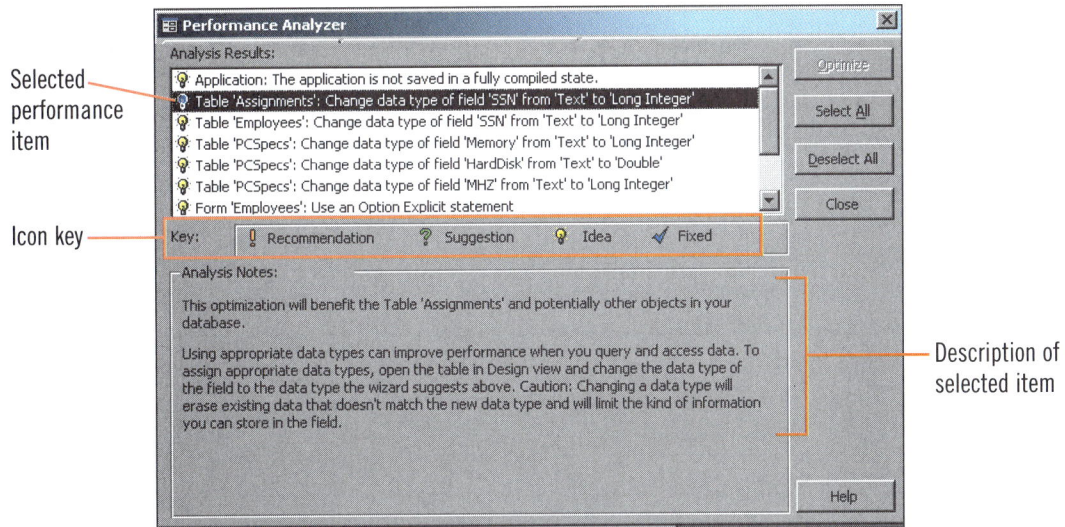

TABLE P-4: Tips for optimizing performance

degree of difficulty	tip
Easy	To free up memory and other computer resources, close all applications that you don't currently need
Easy	If they can be run safely on an "as-needed" basis, eliminate memory-resident programs such as complex screen savers, e-mail alert programs, and virus checkers
Easy	If you are the only person using a database, open it in exclusive mode
Easy	Use the Compact on Close feature to regularly compact and repair your database
Easy	Convert the database to an Access 2002 database
Moderate	Add more memory to your computer; once the database is open, memory is the single most important determinant of overall performance
Moderate	If others don't need to share the database, load it on your local hard drive instead of the network's file server (but be sure to back up local drives regularly, too)
Moderate	**Split** the database so that the data is stored on the file server, but other database objects are stored on your local, faster hard drive
Moderate to difficult	If using disk compression software, stop doing so or move the database to an uncompressed drive
Moderate to difficult	Run Performance Analyzer on a regular basis, examining and appropriately acting on each recommendation, suggestion, and idea
Moderate to difficult	Make sure that all PCs are running the latest versions of Windows and Access; this may involve purchasing more software or upgrading hardware to properly support these robust software products

Splitting a Database

A successful database grows and creates the need for higher levels of database connectivity. **Local area networks (LANs)** are installed to link multiple PCs together so they can share hardware and software resources. Once a LAN is installed, a shared database will often be moved to a **file server**, a centrally located computer from which every user can access the database by using the network. The more users share the same database, however, the slower it will respond. The **Database Splitter** feature improves the performance of a database shared among several users by allowing you to split the database into two files: the **back-end database**, which contains the actual table objects and is stored on the file server, and the **front-end database**, which contains the other database objects (forms, reports, so forth), and links to the back-end database tables. You copy the front-end database for as many users as needed because the front-end database must be located on each user's PC. You can also customize the objects and links each front-end database contains. Front-end databases not only improve performance, but also add a level of customization and security. ✎ Kristen uses the Database Splitter to split the Technology-P database into two databases in preparation for the new LAN being installed in the Information Systems Department.

Steps 1 2 3 4

QuickTip

It's always a good idea to back up a database before splitting it.

1. Click **Tools** on the menu bar, point to **Database Utilities**, then click **Database Splitter**
   The Database Splitter dialog box opens, and provides additional information on the process and benefits of splitting a database, as shown in Figure P-10.

2. Click **Split Database**, then navigate to the drive and folder where your Project Files are located
   The Create Back-end Database dialog box suggests the name Technology-P_be.mdb ("be" stands for "back-end") for your back-end database.

3. Click **Split**
   The status bar provides information about the split process.

4. Click **OK** when prompted that the split was successful
   The Technology-P database has become the front-end database, with all database objects intact except for the table objects. Technology-P no longer contains any table objects, but rather, contains links to the Technology-P_be database that stores the actual data, as shown in Figure P-11.

5. Click **Forms** on the Objects bar, then double-click the **Employees form**
   Even though the data is physically stored in the Technology-P_be.mdb database, the other objects in the Technology-P database can access this data through the linked tables.

6. Close the Employees form, click **Tables** on the Objects bar, right-click **Equipment**, click **Design View**, then click **Yes** when warned that some properties cannot be modified

7. Press **[F6]** to move the focus to the Field Size property for the SerialNo field, then press **[↓]** to move through the properties while viewing the right side of the Field Properties pane
   Most field properties cannot be modified in a linked table, including those that affect the actual size or structure of the data being stored. Properties that do not affect the physical data, but only how it appears to the user, such as Format and Input Mask, may be modified in a linked table.

8. Close the Equipment table, close the Technology-P database, then exit Access

FIGURE P-10: Database Splitter dialog box

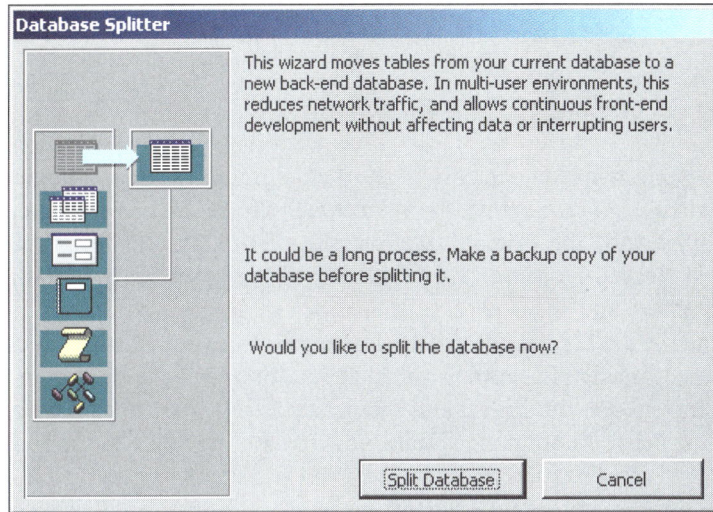

FIGURE P-11: Tables are linked in the front-end database

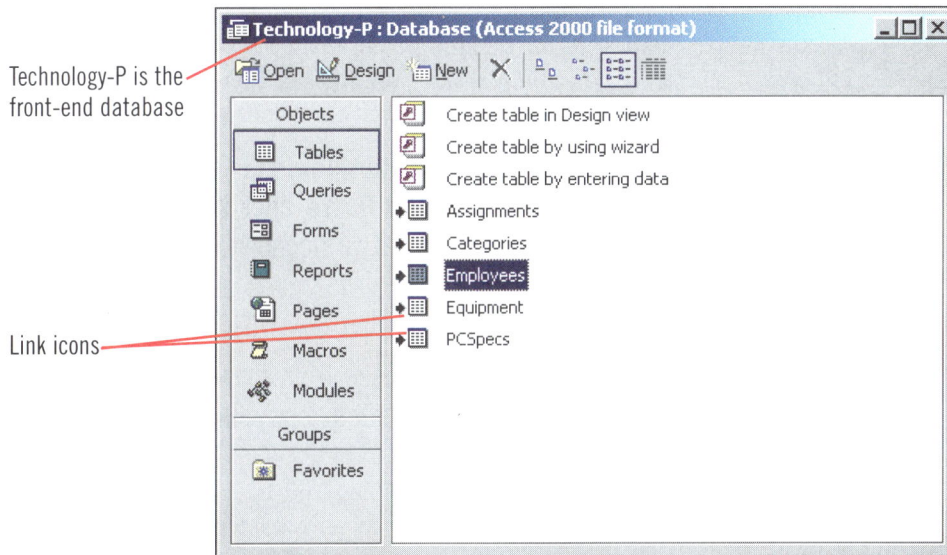

Technology-P is the front-end database

Link icons

Access 2002

Client/Server computing

Splitting a database into a front-end and back-end database that work together is an excellent example of client/server computing. **Client/Server computing** can be defined as two or more information systems cooperatively processing to solve a problem. In most implementations, the **client** is defined as the user's PC and the server is defined as the shared file server, mini-, or mainframe computer. The **server** usually handles corporate-wide computing activities such as data storage and management, security, and connectivity to other networks. Within Access, client computers generally handle those tasks specific to each user, such as storing all of the objects (other than table objects) used by that particular user. Effectively managing a vast client/server network in which many front-end databases link to a single back-end database is a tremendous task, but the performance and security benefits are worth the effort.

MANAGING THE DATABASE ACCESS P-13

Replicating Using the Briefcase

If you want to copy a database to another computer, such as a home PC or a laptop computer that you use when traveling, the Windows Briefcase can help you keep the copied database synchronized with the original database. The **Briefcase** makes a special copy of the original database (called a **replica**) and keeps track of changes made in both the original database (called the **master**) and the replica so that they can be resynchronized at a later date. The master database and all replica database files created from the master are called the **replica set**. The process of making the copy is called **replication**, and the process of reconciling and updating changes between the replica and the master is called **synchronization**. Kristen works with the Briefcase program to learn how to replicate and synchronize a database.

Steps

QuickTip

It's always a good idea to back up a database before replicating it.

1. Right-click the **Start button** on the taskbar, click **Explore** on the shortcut menu, locate your Project Files in the Folder list, right-click **Technology-P_be**, click **Copy** on the shortcut menu, then close Explorer

   You placed the Technology-P_be.mdb file on the Windows Clipboard.

2. Minimize all open windows, right-click the **desktop**, then click **Paste**

   You copied the master database to the desktop because you can't create a replica set with a master and replica both stored on floppy disks. Continue the exercise using the copy of the database on the desktop as the master database, and creating the replica on a new floppy disk.

Trouble?

If the My Briefcase window contains other files, move or delete them.

3. Right-click the **Technology-P_be** file on the desktop, click **Copy**, double-click **My Briefcase** 📂, click **Edit** on the menu bar, click **Paste**, click **Yes** to continue, click **No** when prompted about a backup, then click **OK** to accept the Original copy as the database that will allow design changes

   Your screen should look like Figure P-12.

4. Close the My Briefcase window, remove any disks from **drive A**, insert a blank formatted disk into **drive A**, right-click 📂 on the desktop, point to **Send To**, then click **3½ Floppy (A)**

   The floppy disk with the replica database can now be removed and used on another computer. Any changes made to the replica can be synchronized later with the master because you used the Briefcase to create the replica.

5. Double-click the **My Computer icon** 💻, double-click **3½ Floppy (A)**, double-click **My Briefcase**, double-click **Technology-P_be**, click **OK** if prompted about synchronization, then double-click the **Employees table**

   The Replicated Employees table opens. You can enter, delete, or edit data in this table just as you could in the master database.

6. Press **[Tab]**, type **Mike** in the First field for the first record, then close the Employees table

   Your screen should look like Figure P-13. Both the title bar of the database and the table icons indicate that you are working with a replica. The replica contains the record you just added, but the master does not.

7. Click **File** on the menu bar, then click **Exit**

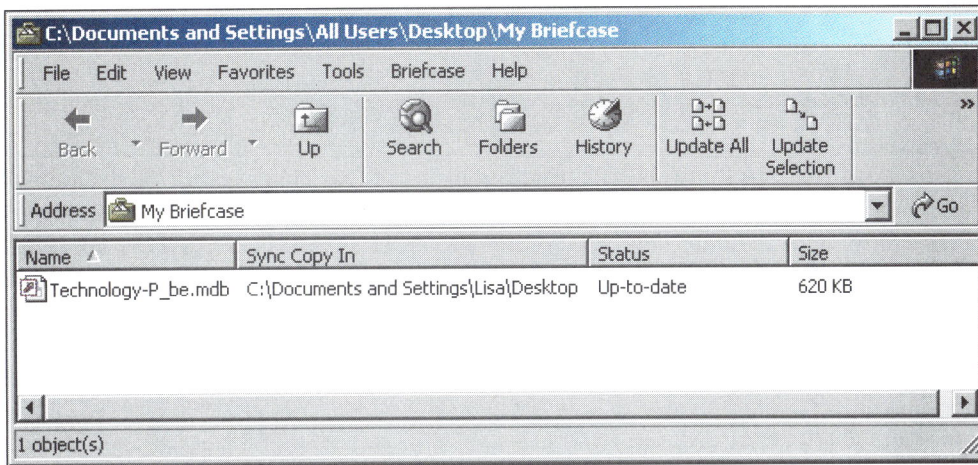

FIGURE P-12: My Briefcase

C:\Documents and Settings\All Users\Desktop\My Briefcase

File   Edit   View   Favorites   Tools   Briefcase   Help

Back   Forward   Up   Search   Folders   History   Update All   Update Selection

Address My Briefcase   Go

Name △	Sync Copy In	Status	Size
Technology-P_be.mdb	C:\Documents and Settings\Lisa\Desktop	Up-to-date	620 KB

1 object(s)

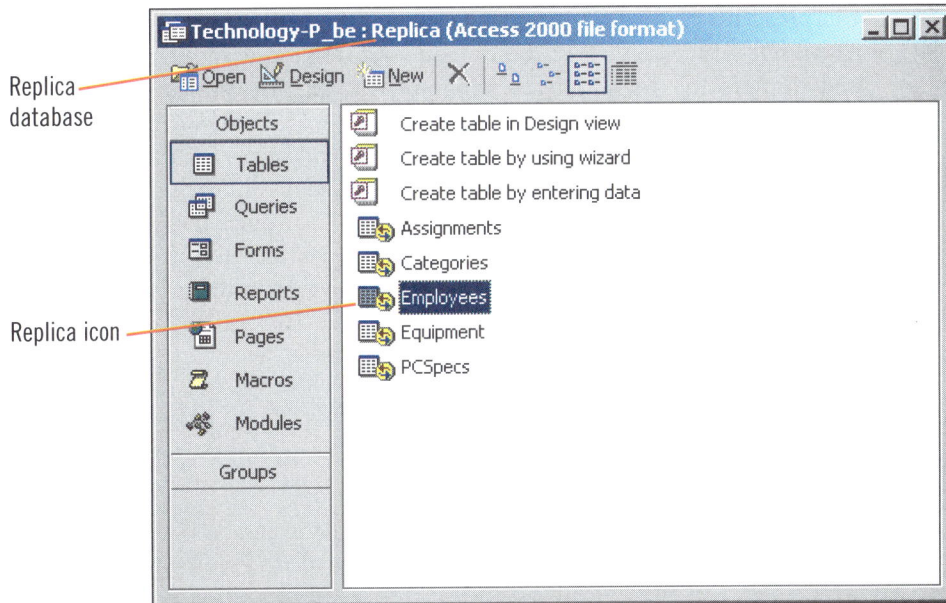

FIGURE P-13: Replica database

Replica database

Technology-P_be : Replica (Access 2000 file format)

Open   Design   New   X

Objects

Tables
Queries
Forms
Reports
Pages
Macros
Modules

Groups

Create table in Design view
Create table by using wizard
Create table by entering data
Assignments
Categories
Employees
Equipment
PCSpecs

Replica icon

Access 2002

Creating a Briefcase folder

By default, the desktop displays a single Briefcase icon called "My Briefcase." A **Briefcase** is actually a special type of folder designed to help users with two computers to keep the files that are used on both computers updated. If there is no Briefcase folder on the desktop, you can easily create as many new Briefcase folders as you need. You create, delete, copy, move, and rename a Briefcase folder in exactly the same manner as with a regular folder. For example, if you want to create a new Briefcase folder on the desktop, you can right-click the desktop, point to New, then click Briefcase.

Synchronizing Using the Briefcase

The Briefcase controls synchronization of the master and replica databases. If the Briefcase folder that contains the replica were stored on a floppy disk, the disk would have to be inserted into the computer on which the master is stored before synchronization could occur. Synchronization updates all records and objects in each member of the replica set. The Briefcase also reports on any synchronization discrepancies that it cannot resolve. ✐ Kristen has created a replica of the Technology-P_be database and has edited a record. She will synchronize it with the master to see how the Briefcase keeps the replica set up-to-date.

Steps 1 2 3 4

1. **Click the My Briefcase button** on the taskbar (if not already selected), then click the **Update All button** ⊞ on the My Briefcase Standard Buttons toolbar
   Your screen should look like Figure P-14. The Briefcase program reads both the master and the replica and determines that the replica has been updated but the master has not. Therefore, it recommends the replace action. If the Briefcase contained many files, each one would be listed with a suggested action (replace, skip, merge).

2. Click **Update**
   The Briefcase replaces the master file on your desktop with the replica file on your floppy and displays the My Briefcase window with an "Up-to-date" Status message for the Technology-P_be.mdb file, as shown in Figure P-15. Had you made changes to both the master and the replica, the Briefcase window would have recommended a more complex action: merge. The **merge** action evaluates the changes in each object and applies them to the other. For example, the merge action will resynchronize the two databases if you edit or add records in both the master and replica. You also can add new objects to both. You can make design changes only to existing objects, however, in the master database.

3. Close the My Briefcase window

4. Close the 3½ Floppy (A:) window, then close the My Computer window

5. Double-click the **Technology-P_be Design Master** database on the desktop, then double-click the **Employees** table
   Your screen should look like Figure P-16. Because the databases were synchronized, the first record of the master database contains the edit made to the first record in the replica.

6. Close the Employees table, close the Technology-P_be Design Master database, then exit Access

7. Right-click the **Technology-P_be Design Master** on the desktop, then click **Delete** on the shortcut menu

FIGURE P-14: Update My Briefcase window—Replace action

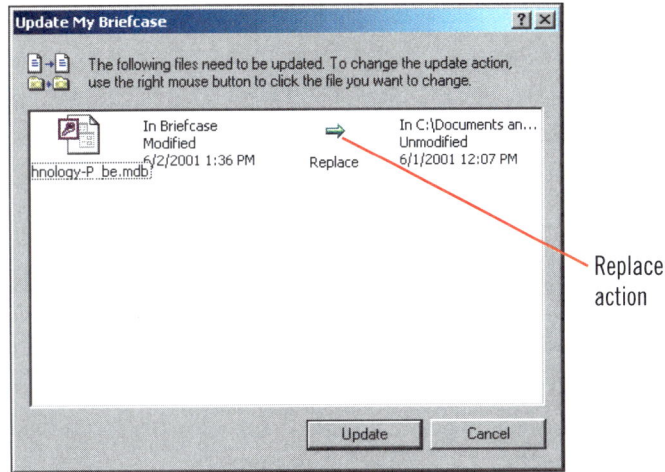

Replace action

FIGURE P-15: My Briefcase window showing an up-to-date file

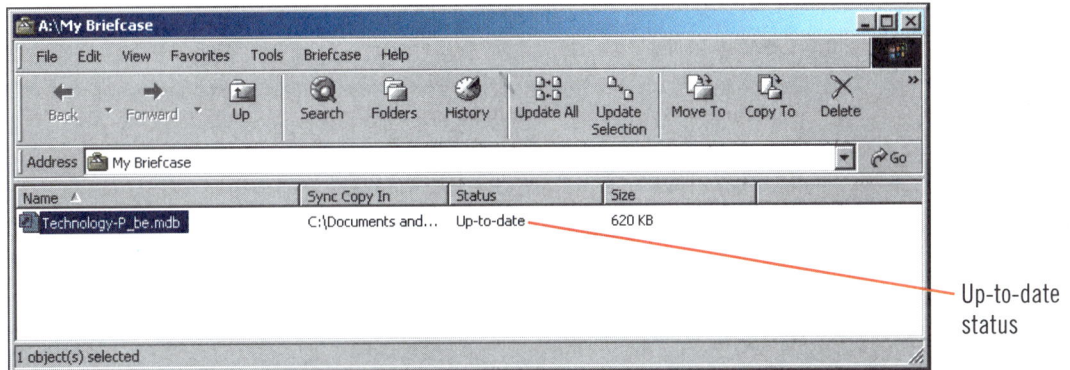

Up-to-date status

FIGURE P-16: Master database is synchronized

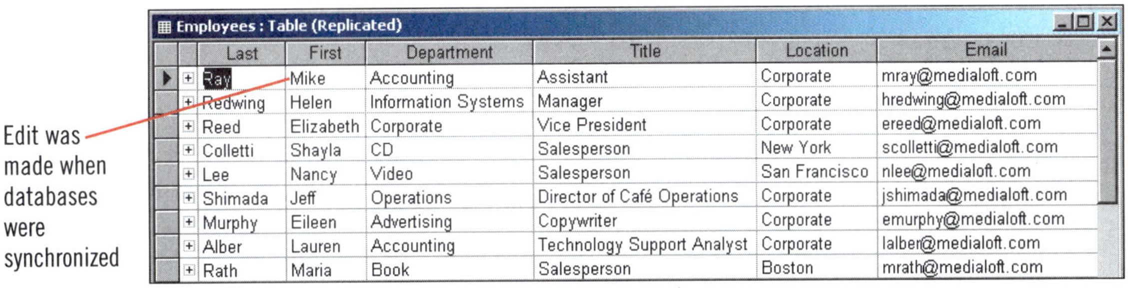

Edit was made when databases were synchronized

CLUES TO USE

Using the Briefcase with a laptop computer

You might use the Briefcase when a master database is stored on a file server and the replica is stored on the hard drive of a laptop computer. When you are in the office, your laptop computer is connected to the network through a docking station, so you would use the master database just like all of the other users.

When you are in the field, however, you would work on the replica stored in a Briefcase folder on the laptop's hard drive. When you return to the office, you would use the Briefcase update features to resynchronize the master on the hard drive and replica database on your laptop.

Practice

► Concepts Review

Identify each element of the Startup dialog box in Figure P-17.

FIGURE P-17

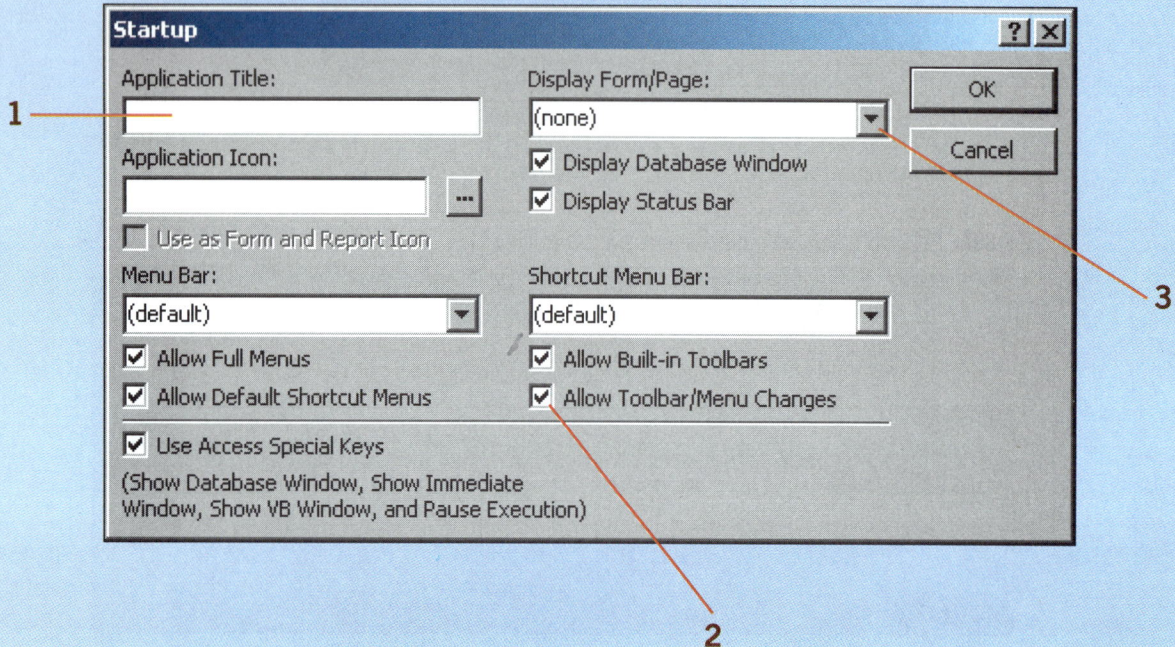

Match each term with the statement that describes its function.

4. **Exclusive Mode**
5. **Database Splitter**
6. **Encrypting**
7. **Performance Analyzer**
8. **Synchronization**

a. Studies the structure and size of your database, and makes a variety of recommendations on how you can improve its speed.

b. Breaks the database into two files to improve performance. One database contains the tables and the other contains the rest of the objects with links to the tables.

c. Updates the files in a replica set so that they all have the same information.

d. Scrambles data so that it is indecipherable when opened by another program.

e. Means that no other users will have access to the database file while it's open.

Select the best answer from the list of choices.

9. **Changing a database file into one that can be opened in Access 97 is called:**
   a. Splitting.
   b. Analyzing.
   c. Converting.
   d. Encrypting.

10. **Which is NOT a type of password that can be set on an Access database?**
   a. Database
   b. Security account
   c. Object
   d. Visual Basic for Applications

11. **Which of the following determines the users, objects, and permissions to which the users are granted?**
   a. Passwords
   b. Workgroups
   c. Permission logs
   d. Briefcase names

12. **Which character precedes a command-line option?**
   a. !
   b. @
   c. /
   d. ^

13. **Which of the following is NOT an advantage of splitting the database using the Database Splitter?**
   a. It keeps the data centralized in the back-end database for all users to access.
   b. It gives the users local control over form and report objects.
   c. It helps increase the overall performance of a database used on a LAN.
   d. It creates replica sets that can be used to synchronize files on laptops.

14. **Startup command-line options are:**
   a. A special series of characters added to the end of the file path that start with a forward slash.
   b. Entered in the Startup dialog box.
   c. Used to automate the synchronization of a replica set.
   d. Special objects that execute first when the database is opened.

15. **Client/server computing can be defined as:**
   a. Two or more information systems cooperatively processing to solve a problem.
   b. A process to resynchronize a replica set.
   c. A LAN, WAN, or the Internet.
   d. A way to study the structure and size of your database to make a variety of recommendations on how you could improve its performance.

16. **If you want to copy a database to another computer, such as a home or laptop computer, which of the following features would keep the databases up-to-date?**
   a. Database Splitter
   b. Performance Analyzer
   c. Startup options
   d. Briefcase

17. **After you split a database, the original is referred to as the:**
   a. Replica set.
   b. Replica.
   c. Synchronization set.
   d. Master.

18. **The Briefcase is a special type of:**
   a. Folder.
   b. File.
   c. Drive.
   d. Object.

19. **Which of the following is NOT a way to improve performance?**
   a. Convert the database to an Access 2002 database.
   b. Encrypt the database.
   c. Compact and repair the database.
   d. Open the database in exclusive mode.

20. **Which of the following is NOT a startup command-line option?**
   a. /ro
   b. /compact
   c. /excl
   d. /nostartup

▶ Skills Review

1. **Convert a database.**
   a. Start Access, then open the **Basketball-P** database from the drive and folder where your Project Files are stored.
   b. Click Tools on the menu bar, point to Database Utilities, point to Convert Database, then click To Access 97 File Format.
   c. Navigate to the drive and folder where your Project Files are stored, enter **Basketball97** as the File Name, click Save in the Convert Database Into dialog box, then click OK when prompted.
   d. Start Windows Explorer, navigate to the drive and folder where your Project Files are stored, then check to make sure that both the Basketball-P and Basketball97 databases are present. You also will see a Basketball-P.ldb file, because Basketball-P.mdb is currently open.
   e. Close Explorer.

2. **Set passwords.**
   a. Close the Basketball-P database, but leave Access open.
   b. Click the Open button on the Database toolbar, navigate to the drive and folder where your Project Files are located, then click **Basketball-P**.
   c. Click the Open list arrow, then click Open Exclusive.
   d. Click Tools on the menu bar, point to Security, then click Set Database Password.
   e. Check to make sure the Caps Lock light is not on, type **big12** in the Password text box, press [Tab], type **big12** in the Verify text box, then click OK. (Remember that passwords are case sensitive.)
   f. Close the Basketball-P database, but leave Access open.
   g. Reopen the **Basketball-P** database in exclusive mode. Type **big12** as the password.
   h. Click Tools on the menu bar, point to Security, click Unset Database Password, type **big12**, then click OK.
   i. On a piece of paper, explain why it was necessary for you to open the database in Exclusive Mode in steps c. and g.

3. **Change startup options.**
   a. Click Tools on the menu bar, then click Startup to open the Startup dialog box.
   b. Type **Iowa State Cyclones** in the Application Title text box, click the Display Form/Page list arrow, click the Player Entry Form, clear the Allow Toolbar/Menu Changes check box, then click OK. Notice the change in the Access title bar.
   c. Close the Basketball-P database, but leave Access open.
   d. Open the **Basketball-P** database.
   e. Close the Player Entry Form that automatically opened when the database was opened.
   f. Right-click the Database toolbar to make sure that you are unable to change or modify any of the toolbars.
   g. On a piece of paper, identify one reason for changing each of the three startup options modified in step b.
   h. Close the Basketball-P database, but leave Access open.

4. **Encrypt a database.**
   a. To encrypt the database, click Tools on the menu bar, point to Security, then click Encrypt/Decrypt Database.
   b. Navigate to the drive and folder where your Project Files are stored, click Basketball-P, then click OK.
   c. In the Encrypt Database As dialog box, click **Basketball-P**, then click Save.
   d. Click Yes when asked to replace the existing Basketball-P file.
   e. To decrypt the database, click Tools on the menu bar, point to Security, then click Encrypt/Decrypt Database.
   f. In the Encrypt/Decrypt Database dialog box, click **Basketball-P**, then click OK.
   g. In the Decrypt Database As dialog box, click **Basketball-P**, click Save, then click Yes.
   h. On a piece of paper, identify two database threats for which encryption could be used to protect the database.

5. **Analyze performance.**
   a. Open **Basketball-P**, then close the Player Entry Form.
   b. Click Tools on the menu bar, point to Analyze, then click Performance.
   c. Click the All Object Types tab, click Select All, then click OK.
   d. Click each of the Analysis Results, and read the Analysis notes.
   e. On a piece of paper, record the analysis results (there should be three entries), and identify whether they are recommendations, suggestions, ideas, or items that were fixed.
   f. Close the Performance Analyzer dialog box.

6. **Split a database.**
   a. Click Tools on the menu bar, point to Database Utilities, then click Database Splitter.
   b. Click Split Database, make sure that the Save in list shows the drive and folder where your Project Files are stored, then click Split to accept the default name of **Basketball-P_be** as the file name.
   c. Click OK when prompted that the database was successfully split.
   d. On a sheet of paper, identify two reasons for splitting a database.
   e. On the paper, identify the back-end and front-end database filenames, then explain what these databases contain.
   f. On the paper, explain what the table icons in the front-end database look like and what they represent.
   g. Close the Basketball-P database.

7. **Replicate using the Briefcase.**
   a. Copy the **Team-P** database from the drive and folder where your project files are stored, then paste it to the desktop of your computer.
   b. Copy the **Team-P** database from your desktop, then paste it to an empty Briefcase folder. Click Yes when asked to continue, click No when asked to make a back-up copy, then click OK to choose the Original Copy as the one that allows changes to the design of the database. (*Hint*: If you need to create a new Briefcase folder, right-click the desktop, point to New, then click Briefcase.)
   c. Double-click the Team-P database in the Briefcase window, double-click the Players table, then modify the record for PlayerNo 21 with your own first and last name.
   d. Close the Players table, close the Team-P Replica database, then exit Access. Close the Briefcase window.
   e. Open the **Team-P Design Master** database from your desktop, then open the Players table. PlayerNo 21 is not modified.
   f. Change PlayerNo 22 to that of a friend's first and last name.
   g. Close the Players table, then close the Team-P Design Master database and Access window.

8. **Synchronize using the Briefcase.**
   a. Open the Briefcase on the desktop where the replicated Team-P database is stored, click the Update All button, then click the Update button to merge the databases.
   b. Double-click the **Team-P** entry in the Briefcase window to open the replica database, double-click the Players table, then print the Players datasheet. Both PlayerNo 21 and 22 should show the changes you made. Print the datasheet.
   c. Close the Players datasheet, close the Team-P Replica, and close the Briefcase window.
   d. Open the **Team-P Design Master** database, then open the Players table. Both PlayerNo 21 and 22 should show the changes you made.
   e. Close the Players table, then close the Team P-Design Master.
   f. Delete any files you created in the desktop.

► Independent Challenge 1

As the manager of a doctor's clinic, you have created an Access database called Patients-P to track insurance claims. You want to set a database password on this file, and also encrypt the database.

a. Start Access.

b. Click the Open button on the Standard toolbar, navigate to the drive and folder where your Project Files are stored, click **Patients-P**, click the Open list arrow, then click Open Exclusive.

c. Click Tools, point to Security, then click Set Database Password.

d. Enter **health** in the Password text box as well as the Verify text box, then click OK.

e. Close the Patients-P database, but leave Access running.

f. To encrypt the database, click Tools, point to Security, then click Encrypt/Decrypt Database.

g. In the Encrypt/Decrypt Database dialog box, click Patients-P, then click OK.

h. Enter **health** as the password, then click OK.

i. In the Encrypt Database As dialog box, click Patients-P, click Save, click Yes to replace the existing file, enter **health** when prompted, then click OK.

j. Exit Access.

► Independent Challenge 2

As the manager of a doctor's clinic, you have created an Access database called Patients-P to track insurance claims. You want to change the startup options.

a. Start Access, then open the database **Patients-P** from the drive and folder where your Project Files are located.

b. If prompted for a password (if you completed Independent Challenge 1, the file will be password protected), enter **health**, then click OK.

c. To set startup options, click Tools on the menu, then click Startup.

d. In the Startup dialog box, enter **Drs. Aaron and Kelsey** in the Application Title text box, choose the Claim Entry Form as the choice for the Display Form/Page option, clear the Allow Toolbar/Menu Changes check box, then click OK.

e. Close the Patients-P database.

f. Open the **Patients-P** database to test the Startup options. Enter **health** as the password if prompted, then click OK.

g. Close the Claim Entry Form, then right-click the toolbar to make sure that toolbars cannot be modified. Check to make sure that Drs. Aaron and Kelsey appears in the title bar of the Access window.

h. Close the Patients-P database, then exit Access.

► Independent Challenge 3

As the manager of a doctor's clinic, you have created an Access database called Patients-P to track insurance claims. You want to use the Briefcase to synchronize a replica set.

a. Open Windows Explorer, locate the **Patients-P** database from the drive and folder where your Project Files are located then copy the database to the desktop. Close Explorer.

b. Start Access, then open the **Patients-P** database stored on your desktop using the Open Exclusive option. If a password is set on the Patients-P database, you must remove it before you can use the database to create a replica set. If you were not prompted for a password, close the database, close Access, and skip the next step.

c. Enter **health** as the password, close the Claim Entry Form if it automatically opened, click Tools, point to Security, click Unset Database Password, enter **health**, click OK, then close the Patients-P database and close Access.

d. Copy the **Patients-P** database on your desktop, then paste it into an empty Briefcase. (*Hint*: If you need to create a new Briefcase folder, right-click the desktop, point to New, then click Briefcase.)

e. Click Yes to continue, click No when asked about making a back-up copy, then click OK to choose the Original Copy as the one that allows changes to the design of the database.

f. Double-click the **Patients-P** database in the Briefcase window, close the Claims Entry Form if it is opened, double-click the Doctors table, then enter your own information as a new record in the PodFirstName (your first name initial), PodLastName (your last name), and PodCode (your first and last name initials, which must be unique from the other records because it is the key field) fields.

g. Close the Doctors datasheet, then close the Patients-P Replica database.

h. Open the **Patients-P Design Master** stored on the desktop.

i. Close the Claim Entry Form if it is opened, then double-click the Doctors table to open its datasheet.

j. Add a friend's name as a new record in the table, making sure that you enter unique initials in the PodCode field.

k. Close the Doctors datasheet, then close the Patients-P Design Master.

l. Open the Briefcase folder that contains the Patients-P replica, click the Update All button, then click Update to merge the changes in the Replica and Design Master.

m. Double-click either the **Patients-P Replica** or **Patients-P Design Master** file to open it, close the Claim Entry Form if it opens, double-click the Doctors table, then print the datasheet. You should see both your name and your friend's name entered as records in the datasheet.

n. Close the Doctors datasheet, close the Patients-P database, then close Access.

o. Delete any files you created on the desktop.

e Independent Challenge 4

Microsoft provides extra information, templates, files, and ideas at a Web site called Tools on the Web. In this exercise, you'll explore the Tools on the Web services.

a. Start Access, but do not open any databases.

b. Click Tools on the menu bar, then click Tools on the Web.

c. If prompted to identify the area of the world where you live, click the appropriate area.

d. Print the Tools on the Web home page.

e. Explore the site at your own pace. You may want to print some articles, but be careful as some articles are quite long.

f. Go back to the Tools on the Web home page, then click the Office Worldwide link.

g. Click the Canada (French) link. Notice that your browser is capable of displaying the characters in French words. Print the first page of the Canada (French) Web page, then click the Back button on your browser toolbar.

h. Click the China link. You may be prompted to install a language pack in order to display the Chinese language characters. Unless you are working on your own computer and have access to the Office XP CD, click Cancel. If you did not install the Chinese language pack, notice what characters your browser uses to represent the Chinese language.

i. Print the first page of the Chinese Web page (in whatever form it is in), then click the Back button on your browser toolbar.

j. Explore as many country sites as you like. Explore the More International Downloads link below the list of countries on the Welcome to Office Worldwide Web page.

k. Write a one-page, double-spaced paper describing some of the things you learned.

► Visual Workshop

As the manager of a doctor's clinic, you have created an Access database called **Patients-P** to track insurance claims. Use the Performance Analyzer to generate the results shown in Figure P-18 by analyzing all object types.

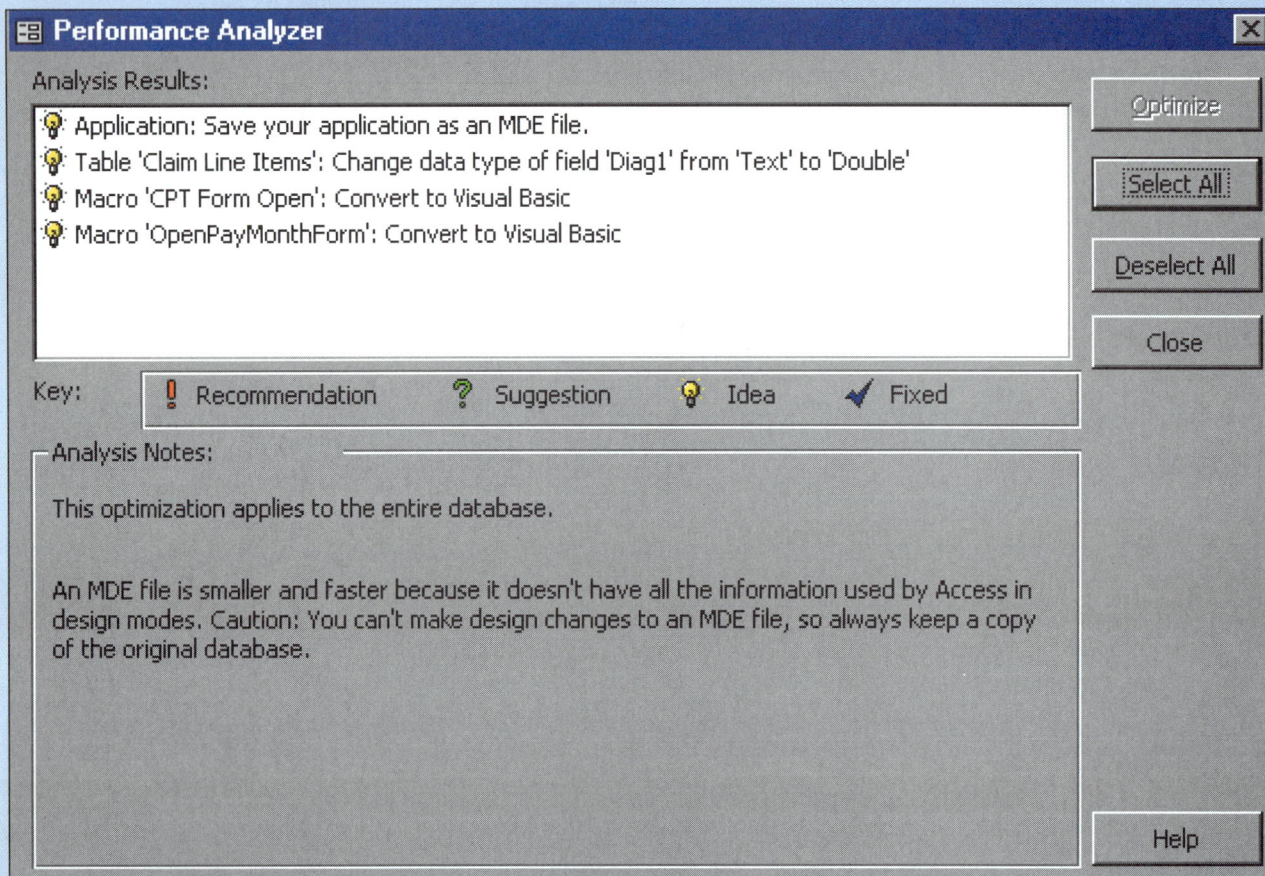

Performance Analyzer

Analysis Results:

- Application: Save your application as an MDE file.
- Table 'Claim Line Items': Change data type of field 'Diag1' from 'Text' to 'Double'
- Macro 'CPT Form Open': Convert to Visual Basic
- Macro 'OpenPayMonthForm': Convert to Visual Basic

Optimize
Select All
Deselect All
Close

Key: ! Recommendation   ? Suggestion   💡 Idea   ✔ Fixed

Analysis Notes:

This optimization applies to the entire database.

An MDE file is smaller and faster because it doesn't have all the information used by Access in design modes. Caution: You can't make design changes to an MDE file, so always keep a copy of the original database.

Help

Project Files List

Read the following information carefully!

Find out from your instructor the location of the Project Files you need and the location where you will store your files.

- To complete many of the units in this book, you need to use Project Files. Your instructor will either provide you with a copy of the Project Files or ask you to make your own copy.

- If you need to make a copy of the Project Files, you will need to copy a set of files from a file server, stand-alone computer, or the Web to the drive and folder where you will be storing your Project Files.

- Your instructor will tell you which computer, drive letter, and folders contain the files you need, and where you will store your files.

- You can also download the files by going to www.course.com. See the inside back cover of the book for instructions on how to download your files.

Copy and organize your Project Files.

Floppy disk users

- If you are using floppy disks to store your Project Files, the list on the following pages shows which files you'll need to copy onto your disk(s).

- Unless noted in the Project Files List, you will need one formatted, high-density disk for each unit. For each unit you are assigned, copy the files listed in the **Project File Supplied column** onto one disk.

- Make sure you label each disk clearly with the unit name (e.g., Access Unit I).

- When working through the unit, save all your files to this disk.

Users storing files in other locations

- If you are using a zip drive, network folder, hard drive, or other storage device, use the Project Files List to organize your files.

- Create a subfolder for each unit in the location where you are storing your files, and name it according to the unit title (e.g., Access Unit I).

- For each unit you are assigned, copy the files listed in the **Project File Supplied column** into that unit's folder.

- Store the files you modify or create for each unit in the unit folder.

Find and keep track of your Project Files and completed files.

- Use the **Project File Supplied column** to make sure you have the files you need before starting the unit or exercise indicated in the **Unit and Location column**.

- Use the **Student Creates File column** to find out the filename you use when saving a file you create new for the exercise.

Unit and Location	Project File Supplied	Student Creates File

Note: In Access, you do not save the database files with a different name. It is a good practice to make a backup copy of the files before you use them, in case you need to go back and repeat any of the exercises.

Access Unit I

Lessons	Training-I.mdb CourseMaterials.xls study.xml study.xsd	Access Courses Report.rtf Access Courses Report.xls acct.xml acct.xsd
Skills Review	Machinery-I.mdb Vendors.xls employ.xml employ.xsd	Every Product We Lease.rtf Products.xls prod.xml prod.xsd
Independent Challenge 1	Basketball-I.mdb	
Independent Challenge 2	Basketball-I.mdb	Player Statistics.rtf
Independent Challenge 3	Basketball-I.mdb	Games.xls
Independent Challenge 4	Languages-I.mdb	
Visual Workshop	Basketball-I.mdb	

Access Unit J

Lessons	Training-J.mdb	dept.htm instruct.htm pivot.htm chart.htm
Skills Review	Machinery-J.mdb	garden.htm products.htm units.htm uchart.htm
Independent Challenge 1	Basketball-J.mdb	pstats.htm
Independent Challenge 2	Basketball-J.mdb	games.htm
Independent Challenge 3	Basketball-J.mdb	gstats.htm
Independent Challenge 4	Languages-J.mdb	trans.htm
Visual Workshop	Basketball-J.mdb	scoring.htm

Access Unit K

Lessons	Training-K.mdb	
Skills Review	Seminar-K.mdb	
Independent Challenge 1	Basketball-K.mdb	
Independent Challenge 2	Basketball-K.mdb	
Independent Challenge 3	Basketball-K.mdb	
Independent Challenge 4	Chocolate-K.mdb	
Visual Workshop	Basketball-K.mdb	

Access Unit L

Lessons	Training-L.mdb	
Skills Review	Seminar-L.mdb	
Independent Challenge 1	Basketball-L.mdb	
Independent Challenge 2	Basketball-L.mdb	

Unit and Location	Project File Supplied	Student Creates File
Independent Challenge 3	Basketball-L.mdb	
Independent Challenge 4	(no files provided or created)	
Visual Workshop	Basketball-L.mdb	
Access Unit M		
Lessons	Technology-M.mdb	
Skills Review	Basketball-M.mdb	
Independent Challenge 1	Patients-M.mdb	
Independent Challenge 2	Patients-M.mdb	
Independent Challenge 3	Patients-M.mdb	
Independent Challenge 4	(no files provided or created)	
Visual Workshop	Patients-M.mdb	
Access Unit N		
Lessons	Technology-N.mdb	
Skills Review	Basketball-N.mdb	
Independent Challenge	1Patients-N.mdb	
Independent Challenge 2	Patients-N.mdb	
Independent Challenge 3	Patients-N.mdb	
Independent Challenge 4	Chocolate-N.mdb	
Visual Workshop	Patients-N.mdb	
Access Unit O		
Lessons	Technology-O.mdb	
Skills Review	Basketball-O.mdb	
Independent Challenge 1	Patients-O.mdb	
Independent Challenge 2	Patients-O.mdb	
Independent Challenge 3	Patients-O.mdb	
Independent Challenge 4	(no files provided or created)	
Visual Workshop	Basketball-O.mdb	
Access Unit P		
Lessons	Technology-P.mdb	Techonolgy-P_be.mdb Technology97.mdb
Skills Review	Basketball-P.mdb Team-P.mdb	Basketball-P_be.mdb Basketball97.mdb
Independent Challenge 1	Patients-P.mdb	
Independent Challenge 2	Patients-P.mdb	
Independent Challenge 3	Patients-P.mdb	
Independent Challenge 4	(no files provided or created)	
Visual Workshop	Patients-P.mdb	

Access 2002 Core MOUS Certification Objectives

Below is a list of the Microsoft Office User Specialist program objectives for Core Access 2002 skills, showing where each MOUS objective is covered in the Lessons and Practice. The skills with references to units A-H are covered in *Microsoft Access 2002—Illustrated Introductory*, and the skills with references to units I-P are covered in *Microsoft Access 2002—Illustrated Second Course. Microsoft Access 2002—Illustrated Introductory* is approved courseware for preparation for the Access 2002 Core MOUS exam.

MOUS standardized coding number	Activity	Lesson page where skill is covered	Location in lesson where skill is covered	Practice
AC2002-1	**Creating and Using Databases**			
AC2002-1-1	Create Access databases	ACCESS B-4	Steps 1–2	Skills Review Independent Challenges 1, 3
		ACCESS H-2	Steps 1–6	Skills Review
AC2002-1-2	Open database objects in multiple views	ACCESS A-4	Table A-2	Skills Review
		ACCESS A-10	Step 1	Independent Challenges 2, 3
		ACCESS A-16	Step 1	Visual Workshop
		ACCESS B-6	Step 7	(Units B, C, D, F)
		ACCESS B-16	Steps 5, 7	Skills Review
		ACCESS C-6	Steps 1, 7	Independent Challenges 1, 2, 3
		ACCESS D-6	Steps 1, 7	Visual Workshop
		ACCESS F-4	Step 6	
		ACCESS F-16	Steps 2, 7	
		ACCESS H-12	Step 4	Skills Review Independent Challenges 1, 2, 3, 4 Visual Workshop
AC2002-1-3	Move among records	ACCESS A-10	Steps 1–6	Skills Review
		ACCESS A-11	Table A-4	Independent Challenge 2, 3 Visual Workshop
		ACCESS C-4	Steps 5–6	Skills Review
		ACCESS C-12	Steps 5–7	Independent Challenges 1, 2, 3, 4
AC2002-1-4	Format datasheets	ACCESS B-8	Steps 3–5	Skills Review Independent Challenges 2, 3
AC2002-2	**Creating and Modifying Tables**			
AC2002-2-1	Create and modify tables	ACCESS B-2	Clues to Use	Skills Review
		ACCESS B-3	Table B-1	Independent Challenges 1, 3
		ACCESS B-4	Steps 3–7	
		ACCESS B-6	Steps 1–6	
		ACCESS B-7	Clues to Use	
		ACCESS E-6	Steps 2–7	Skills Review Independent Challenge 1 Visual Workshop
AC2002-2-2	Add a pre-defined input mask to a field	ACCESS E-8	Step 5	Skills Review
		ACCESS E-12	Step 5	
AC2002-2-3	Create Lookup fields	ACCESS E-4	Detail 5	Skills Review
		ACCESS E-5	Table E-2	
		ACCESS E-18	Steps 1–8	
AC2002-2-4	Modify field properties	ACCESS B-6	Steps 2–6	Skills Review
		ACCESS B-7	Clues to Use	Independent Challenges 1, 4
		ACCESS E-6	Steps 2–7	Skills Review
		ACCESS E-8	Steps 1–6	Independent Challenges 1, 4
		ACCESS E-9	Table E-3	Visual Workshop
		ACCESS E-10	Steps 1–4	
		ACCESS E-11	Table E-4	
		ACCESS E-12	Steps 1–5	
		ACCESS E-13	Steps 1–3	

MOUS standardized coding number	Activity	Lesson page where skill is covered	Location in lesson where skill is covered	Practice
AC2002-3	**Creating and Modifying Queries**			
AC2002-3-1	Create and modify Select queries	ACCESS B-16 ACCESS B-18	Steps 1–7 Steps 1–8	Skills Review Independent Challenges 2, 3 Visual Workshop
		ACCESS F-2 ACCESS F-4 ACCESS F-6 ACCESS F-7 ACCESS F-8 ACCESS F-9	Steps 2–6 Steps 1–3 Steps 1–5 Table F-1 Steps 1–4 Clues to Use	Skills Review Independent Challenges 1, 2, 3, 4 Visual Workshop
AC2002-3-2	Add calculated fields to Select queries	ACCESS F-10	Steps 2–6	Skills Review
AC2002-4	**Creating and Modifying Forms**			
AC2002-4-1	Create and display forms	ACCESS C-4 ACCESS C-5 ACCESS C-5	Steps 2–4 Table C-2 Clues to Use	Skills Review Independent Challenges 1, 2, 3, 4 Visual Workshop
		ACCESS G-4 ACCESS G-5	Steps 2–6 Table G-1	
AC2002-4-2	Modify form properties	ACCESS C-2 ACCESS C-6 ACCESS C-7 ACCESS C-8 ACCESS C-9 ACCESS C-10 ACCESS C-12 ACCESS C-13 ACCESS C-16	Table C-1 Steps 1–6 Table C-3 Steps 1–6 Table C-4 Steps 1–7 Steps 2–4 Table C-5 Steps 1–5	Skills Review Independent Challenges 1, 2, 3 Visual Workshop
		ACCESS G-8 ACCESS G-10 ACCESS G-12 ACCESS G-14 ACCESS G-15 ACCESS G-16	Steps 1–7 Steps 1–7 Steps 1–8 Steps 1–7 Table G-3 Steps 1–8	Skills Review Independent Challenges 1, 2, 3, 4 Visual Workshop
AC2002-5	**Viewing and Organizing Information**			
AC2002-5-1	Enter, edit, and delete records	ACCESS A-12 ACCESS A-14 ACCESS A-15	Steps 2–5 Steps 1–9 Table A-5	Skills Review Independent Challenge 3 Visual Workshop
		ACCESS B-16	Step 4	Skills Review Independent Challenges 1, 2, 3, 4 Visual Workshop
		ACCESS C-12 ACCESS C-14 ACCESS C-16	Steps 1, 5–7 Steps 1–5 Step 6	Skills Review Independent Challenges 1, 2, 3, 4 Visual Workshop
AC2002-5-2	Create queries	ACCESS B-16 ACCESS B-18 ACCESS B-19	Steps 1–8 Steps 1–7 Clues to Use	Skills Review Independent Challenges 2, 3 Visual Workshop
		ACCESS F-2 ACCESS F-4 ACCESS F-6 ACCESS F-7 ACCESS F-8 ACCESS F-9 ACCESS F-12 ACCESS F-13 ACCESS F-14	Steps 2–6 Steps 1–3 Steps 1–5 Table F-1 Steps 1–4 Clues to Use Steps 1–6 Table F-4 Steps 1–7	Skills Review Independent Challenges 1, 2, 3, 4 Visual Workshop

MOUS standardized coding number	Activity	Lesson page where skill is covered	Location in lesson where skill is covered	Practice
AC2002-5-3	Sort records	ACCESS B-11 ACCESS B-12 ACCESS B-13 ACCESS B-18	Table B-2 Steps 1–3 Clues to Use Step 4	Skills Review Independent Challenges 2, 3 Visual Workshop
		ACCESS C-4	Step 5	Skills Review Independent Challenge 2
		ACCESS F-4	Steps 1–3	Skills Review Independent Challenges 1, 2, 3
AC2002-5-4	Filter records	ACCESS B-11 ACCESS B-14 ACCESS B-17	Table B-2 Steps 1–5 Table B-4	Skills Review Independent Challenge 2
		ACCESS C-4 ACCESS C-14	Step 7 Steps 6–8	Skills Review Independent Challenge 3
AC2002-6	**Defining Relationships**			
AC2002-6-1	Create one-to-many relationships	ACCESS E-2 ACCESS E-4 ACCESS E-16	Details 1–3 Details 1–4 Steps 1–5	Skills Review Independent Challenge 1
AC2002-6-2	Enforce referential integrity	ACCESS E-16 ACCESS E-17	Steps 3–4 Clues to Use	Skills Review Independent Challenge 1
AC2002-7	**Producing Reports**			
AC2002-7-1	Create and format reports	ACCESS D-3 ACCESS D-4 ACCESS D-14 ACCESS D-15 ACCESS D-16	Table D-1 Steps 2–6 Steps 1–6 Table D-3 Steps 1–7	Skills Review Independent Challenges 1, 2, 3, 4 Visual Workshop
		ACCESS H-6 ACCESS H-8 ACCESS H-10	Steps 1–8 Steps 1–7 Steps 1–8	Skills Review Independent Challenges 1, 2 Visual Workshop
AC2002-7-2	Add calculated controls to reports	ACCESS D-6 ACCESS D-10	Steps 4–6 Steps 1–3	Skills Review Independent Challenge 2 Visual Workshop
AC2002-7-3	Preview and print reports	ACCESS D-8 ACCESS D-14	Steps 3–5 Steps 6–7	Skills Review Independent Challenges 1, 2, 3, 4 Visual Workshop
AC2002-8	**Integrating with Other Applications**			
AC2002-8-1	Import data to Access	ACCESS H-4 ACCESS H-5	Steps 1–6 Table H-1	Skills Review
		ACCESS I-6	Steps 1–3	Skills Review
AC2002-8-2	Export data from Access	ACCESS H-14 ACCESS H-15	Steps 1, 5 Table H-2	Skills Review
		ACCESS I-10 ACCESS I-11 ACCESS I-12 ACCESS I-14 ACCESS I-16	Step 1 Table I-3 Step 1 Steps 1–6 Steps 1–3	Skills Review Independent Challenges 2, 3 Visual Workshop
AC2002-8-3	Create a simple data access page	ACCESS H-12	Steps 1–6	Skills Review Independent Challenge 3
		ACCESS J-6 ACCESS J-8	Steps 1–6 Steps 1–4	Skills Review Independent Challenges 1, 2, 4

Access 2002 Expert MOUS Certification Objectives

Below is a list of the Microsoft Office User Specialist program objectives for the Expert Access 2002 skills, showing where each MOUS objective is covered in the Lessons and Practice. The skills with references to units A-H are covered in *Microsoft Access 2002—Illustrated Introductory*, and the skills with references to units I-P are covered in *Microsoft Access 2002—Illustrated Second Course*. When used in a sequence, these two titles cover all the Expert objectives and are approved courseware for preparation for the Access 2002 Expert MOUS exam.

MOUS standardized coding number	Activity	Lesson page where skill is covered	Location in lesson where skill is covered	Practice
AC2002e-1	**Creating And Modifying Tables**			
AC2002e-1-1	Use data validation	ACCESS E-14	Steps 1–2	Skills Review
		ACCESS E-15	Table E-5	Independent Challenge 1
AC2002e-1-2	Link tables	ACCESS I-8	Steps 1–3	Skills Review
AC2002e-1-3	Create lookup fields and modify Lookup field properties	ACCESS E-4	Details	Skills Review
		ACCESS E-5	Table E-2	Independent Challenge 4
		ACCESS E-18	Steps 1–7	Skills Review
AC2002e-1-4	Create and modify input masks	ACCESS E-9	Table E-3	Skills Review
		ACCESS E-12	Step 5	
AC2002e-2	**Creating And Modifying Forms**			
AC2002e-2-1	Create a form in Design View	ACCESS L-2	Steps 1–8	Skills Review
		ACCESS L-4	Steps 1–4	Skills Review
		ACCESS L-8	Steps 1–5	Skills Review
		ACCESS M-10	Steps 1–7	Skills Review
		ACCESS M-12	Steps 3–6	Skills Review
				Independent Challenge 3
AC2002e-2-2	Create a Switchboard and set startup options	ACCESS M-14	Steps 1–8	Skills Review
				Visual Workshop
		ACCESS M-16	Steps 1–5	Skills Review
				Visual Workshop
		ACCESS P-6	Steps 1–5	Skills Review
				Independent Challenge 2
AC2002e-2-3	Add Subform controls to Access forms	ACCESS G-4	Steps 1–6	Skills Review
		ACCESS G-6	Steps 1–8	Independent Challenges 1, 2, 3
		ACCESS G-7	Clues to Use	Visual Workshop
AC2002e-3	**Refining Queries**			
AC2002e-3-1	Specify multiple query criteria	ACCESS B-18	Step 7	Skills Review
		ACCESS B-19	Clues to Use	
		ACCESS F-6	Steps 1–4	Skills Review
		ACCESS F-8	Steps 1–4	Independent Challenge 2
AC2002e-3-2	Create and apply advanced filters	ACCESS B-14	Steps 1–5	Skills Review
AC2002e-3-3	Create and run parameter queries	ACCESS K-4	Steps 3–6	Skills Review
				Independent Challenge 1
				Visual Workshop
AC2002e-3-4	Create and run action queries	ACCESS K-8	Steps 1–6	Skills Review
		ACCESS K-9	Table K-2	Independent Challenge 2
		ACCESS K-10	Steps 1–6	
		ACCESS K-12	Steps 1–6	
		ACCESS K-14	Steps 1–5	
AC2002e-3-5	Use aggregate functions in queries	ACCESS F-12	Steps 1–5	Skills Review
		ACCESS F-13	Table F-4	Independent Challenges 1, 3

MOUS standardized coding number	Activity	Lesson page where skill is covered	Location in lesson where skill is covered	Practice
AC2002e-4	**Producing Reports**			
AC2002e-4-1	Create and modify reports	ACCESS D-3	Table D-1	Skills Review
		ACCESS D-6	Steps 1–6	Independent Challenges 1, 2, 4
		ACCESS D-8	Steps 1–3	Visual Workshop
		ACCESS D-10	Steps 1–3	
		ACCESS D-12	Steps 1–6	
		ACCESS D-14	Steps 1–6	
		ACCESS L-16	Steps 1–6	Skills Review
AC2002e-4-2	Add Subreport controls to Access reports	ACCESS L-14	Steps 1–4	Skills Review
				Independent Challenge 2
AC2002e-4-3	Sort and group data in reports	ACCESS D-6	Steps 1–3	Skills Review
		ACCESS D-8	Steps 1–3	Independent Challenges 2, 3
				Visual Workshop
AC2002e-5	**Defining Relationships**			
AC2002e-5-1	Establish one-to-many relationships	ACCESS E-2	Table E-1	Skills Review
				Independent Challenge 1
		ACCESS I-4	Steps 4–8	Skills Review
		ACCESS I-5	Table I-2	Independent Challenges 1, 4
AC2002e-5-2	Establish many-to-many relationships	ACCESS E-3	Clues to Use	Skills Review
		ACCESS I-4	Steps 6–7	Skills Review
		ACCESS I-5	Table I-2	Independent Challenges 1, 4
		ACCESS K-15	Clues to Use	
AC2002e-6	**Operating Access on the Web**			
AC2002e-6-1	Create and Modify a Data Access Page	ACCESS J-10	Steps 1–4	Skills Review
		ACCESS J-11	Table J-4	Independent Challenges 1, 2, 3, 4
		ACCESS J-12	Steps 1–7	Visual Workshop
AC2002e-6-2	Save PivotTables and PivotCharts views to Data Access Pages	ACCESS J-10	Steps 1–6	Skills Review
		ACCESS J-12	Steps 1–7	Independent Challenge 3
				Visual Workshop
AC2002e-7	**Using Access tools**			
AC2002e-7-1	Import XML documents into Access	ACCESS I-6	Steps 1–3	Skills Review
AC2002e-7-2	Export Access data to XML documents	ACCESS I-16	Steps 1–2	Skills Review
AC2002e-7-3	Encrypt and decrypt databases	ACCESS P-8	Steps 1–3	Skills Review
				Independent Challenge 1
AC2002e-7-4	Compact and repair databases	ACCESS H-16	Steps 1–2	Skills Review
AC2002e-7-5	Assign database security	ACCESS P-4	Steps 1–9	Skills Review
				Independent Challenge 1
AC2002e-7-6	Replicate a database	ACCESS P-14	Steps 1–5	Skills Review
		ACCESS P-16	Steps 1–2	Independent Challenge 3
AC2002e-8	**Creating Database Applications**			
AC2002e-8-1	Create Access Modules	ACCESS O-6	Steps 1–7	Skills Review
				Independent Challenge 1
				Visual Workshop
		ACCESS O-8	Steps 1–9	
		ACCESS O-10	Steps 1–8	
		ACCESS O-12	Steps 1–6	
		ACCESS O-14	Steps 1–6	
AC2002e-8-2	Use the Database Splitter	ACCESS P-12	Steps 1–8	Skills Review
AC2002e-8-3	Create an MDE file	ACCESS P-8	Clues to Use	

.ldb The file extension for a temporary file that exists when an Access database is open that keeps track of record locking information when the database is opened.

.mdb The file extension for Access databases.

Action query A query that makes changes to underlying data. There are four types of action queries: delete, update, append, and make-table.

ActiveX control A control that follows ActiveX standards.

ActiveX standards Programming standards developed by Microsoft to allow developers to more easily share software components and functionality across multiple applications.

Aggregate function A special function used in a summary query that calculates information about a group of records rather than a new field of information about each record such as Sum, Avg, and Count.

Alignment Commands used in Form or Report Design View to either left-, center-, or right-align a value within its control, or to align the top, bottom, right, or left edge of the control with respect to other controls.

Analyze it with Microsoft Excel An OfficeLink feature that allows you to quickly copy Access data to Excel.

AND criteria Criteria placed in the same row of the query design grid. All criteria on the same row must be true for a record to appear on the resulting datasheet.

AND query A query that contains AND criteria (two or more criteria present on the same row of the query design grid. Both criteria must be true for the record to appear on the resulting datasheet).

Append query An action query that appends records to another table.

Argument Information that a function uses to create the final answer. In an expression, multiple arguments are separated by commas. All of the arguments are surrounded by a single set of parentheses.

Arguments The pieces of information a function needs to create the final answer.

Argument (macros) For a macro, arguments are additional information for each action of a macro that further clarifies how the action is to execute. For a module, arguments are constants, variables, or expressions that are passed to a procedure and are required for it to execute.

Argument (modules) The pieces of information a function needs to create the final answer. In an expression, multiple arguments are separated by commas. All of the arguments are surrounded by a single set of parentheses.

Arithmetic operator Plus (+), minus (−), multiply (*), divide (/), or exponentiation (^) character used in a mathematical calculation.

Ascending order A sequence in which information is placed in alphabetical order or arranged from smallest to largest.

Auto Center A form property that determines whether a form will be centered in the database window.

AutoFormat Predefined format that you can apply to a form or report to set the background picture, font, color, and alignment formatting choices.

AutoKeys A special name reserved for the macro group object that contains key combinations (such as Ctrl+L) that are used to run associated macros.

AutoNumber A field data type in which Access enters a sequential integer for each record added into the datasheet. Numbers cannot be reused even if the record is deleted.

AutoReport A tool used to quickly create a new report based on the selected table or query.

Back-end database When a database has been split using the Database Splitter, a back-end database is created which contains all of the data and is stored on a computer that is accessible by all users (which is usually the file server in a LAN).

Backup An up-to-date copy of data files.

Bang notation Syntax used to separate parts of an object (the parts are separated by an exclamation point, hence "bang") in the Visual Basic programming language.

Border Style A form property that determines the appearance of the borders around a form.

Bound control A control used in either a form or report to display data from the underlying record source; also used to edit and enter new data in a form.

Bound image control A bound control used to show OLE data such as a picture on a form or report.

Browser Software such as Microsoft Internet Explorer used to find, download, view, and use Web pages.

Breakpoint A bookmark set in VBA code that temporarily suspends execution of the procedure at that point in time so that the user can examine what is happening.

Briefcase A Windows program used to help synchronize two computers that regularly use the same files.

Calculated control A control that uses information from existing controls to calculate new data such as subtotals, dates, or page numbers; used in either a form or report.

Calculated field A field created in Query Design View that results from an expression of existing fields, Access functions, and arithmetic operators. For example the entry Profit: [RetailPrice]-[WholesalePrice] in the field cell of the query design grid creates a calculated field called Profit that is the difference between the values in the RetailPrice and WholesalePrice fields.

Calculation A new value that is created by entering an expression in a text box on a form or report.

Calendar control An ActiveX control that shows the current date selected on a small calendar. You can use this control to find or display a date in the past or future.

Caption A field property used to override the technical field name with an easy-to-read caption entry when the field name appears on datasheets, forms, and reports.

Caption property A field property used to override the technical field name with an easy-to-read caption when the field name appears on datasheets, forms, and reports.

Cascade Delete Related Records An option that can be applied to referential integrity that automatically deletes all records in the "many" table if the record with the matching key field in the "one" table is deleted.

Cascade Update Related Fields An option that can be applied to referential integrity that means that data in the foreign key field of the "many" table will automatically change when primary key fields values in the "one" table are changed.

Case In VBA, a group of statements.

Category axis On a PivotChart, the horizontal axis. Also called the x-axis.

Chart Graph. Visual representation of numeric data that helps a user see comparisons, patterns, and trends in data.

Chart Field List A list of the fields in the underlying record source for a PivotChart.

Chart Wizard Access Wizard that steps you through the process of creating charts within forms and reports.

Check box Bound control used to display "yes" or "no" answers for a field. If the box is "checked" it indicates "yes" information in a form or report.

Child record In a pair of tables that have a one-to-many relationship, the "many" table contains the child records.

Class module A module used only within a particular form or report object and therefore stored within the form or report object.

Client In Internet terminology, this would be your computer.

Client/server applications An application which uses both a server (typically used to manage data and communications process) and clients (typically used to manage the user interface such as forms) for one application.

Client/server computing Two or more information systems cooperatively processing to solve a problem.

Collapse button A button that looks like a "minus sign" to the left of a record displayed in a datasheet that when clicked, collapses the subdatasheet that is displayed.

Combo box A bound control used to display a list of possible entries for a field in which you can also type an entry from the keyboard. It is a "combination" of the list box and text box controls.

Command button An unbound control used to provide an easy way to initiate an action or run a macro.

Command Button Wizard A Wizard that steps you through the process of creating a command button.

Command-line option A special series of characters added to the end of the path to the database file that start with a forward slash and modify the way that the database is opened.

Comment line A VBA statement that does not execute any actions but is used to clarify or document other statements. Comment lines appear in green in the Code window and start with a single apostrophe.

Compacting Rearranging the data and objects on the storage medium so space formerly occupied by deleted objects is eliminated. Compacting a database doesn't change the data, but reduces the overall size of the database.

Comparison operators Characters such as > and < that allow you to find or filter data based on specific criteria.

Compile time The period during which source code is translated to executable code.

Compile time error A VBA error that occurs because of incorrectly constructed VBA code.

Conditional expression An expression that results in either a "true" or "false" answer that determines whether a macro action will execute or not.

Conditional formatting Formatting that is based on specified criteria. For example, a text box may be conditionally formatted to display its value in red if the value is a negative number.

Constant In VBA, a constant is an item that retains a constant value throughout the execution of the code.

Control Any element on a form or report such as a label, text box, line, or combo box. Controls can be bound, unbound, or calculated.

Control Source The most important property of a bound control on a form or report because it determines which field the bound control will display.

ControlTip Text property Property of a control that determines what text displays in tip that pops up when you point to that control with the mouse.

Convert To change a database file into one that can be opened by an earlier version of Access.

Criteria The entry that determines which records are displayed when finding or filtering records in a datasheet or form, or when building a query.

Crosstab query A query that presents data in a cross-tabular layout (fields are used for both column and row headings), similar to PivotTables in other database and spreadsheet products.

Crosstab Query Wizard A wizard used to create crosstab queries that helps identify which fields will be used for row and column headings, and which fields will be summarized within the datasheet.

Crosstab row A row in the query design grid used to specify the column and row headings and values for the crosstab query.

Currency A field data type used for monetary values.

Current record box See specific record box.

Current record symbol A black triangle symbol that appears in the record selector box to the left of the record that has the focus in either a datasheet or a form.

DAP See Data access page.

Data The unique information you enter into the fields of the records.

Data access page See page.

Database A collection of related information, such as a list of employees.

Database password A Password that is required to open a database.

Database software Software used to manage data that can be organized into lists of things such as customers, products, vendors, employees, projects, or sales.

Database Splitter An Access feature that improves the performance of a shared database by allowing you to split it into multiple files.

Database window The window that includes common elements such as the Access title bar, menu bar, and toolbar.

Database Wizard An Access wizard that creates a sample database file for a general purpose such as inventory control, event tracking, or expenses. The objects created by the Database Wizard can be used and modified.

Datasheet View A view that lists the records of the object in a datasheet. Table, query, and most form objects have a Datasheet View.

Data type A required property for each field that defines the type of data that can be entered in each field. Valid data types include AutoNumber, Text, Number, Currency, Date/Time, OLE Object, and Memo.

Date/Time A field data type used for date and time data.

Date function Access function that returns today's date.

Debug To determine why a macro doesn't run properly.

Decimal Places A field property that determines the number of digits that should be displayed to the right of the decimal point (for Number or Currency fields).

Declaration statement A VBA statement that precedes procedure statements and helps set rules for how the statements in the module are processed.

Decrypt To reverse the encryption process.

Default Switchboard When working with switchboards, the default switchboard is the first switchboard in the database, and the one used to link to additional switch board pages.

Default Value A field property that provides a default value, automatically entered for a given field when a new record is created.

Default View A form property that determines whether a subform automatically opens in Datasheet or Continuous Forms View.

Delete query An action query that deletes records based on an expression.

Delimited text file A file with only text (no formatting) that typically stores one record on each line with field values separated by a common character such as a comma, tab, or dash.

Design grid See query design grid.

Design View A view in which the structure of the object can be manipulated. Every Access object has a Design View.

Detail A section of the form or report that contains the controls that are printed for each record in the underlying query or table.

Detail section The section of a form or report that contains the controls that are printed for each record in the underlying query or table.

Dialer Software that helps you dial and connect to your Internet Service Provider.

Dialog box A special form that displays information or prompts a user for a choice.

Dialog property option An option for the Border Style form property that adds a thick border to the form, and prevents the form from being maximized, minimized, or resized.

Display Control A field property that determines how a Yes/No field appears in Datasheet View and Form View.

Display When A control property that determines whether the control will appear only on the screen, only when printed, or at all times.

Documenter An Access feature that creates reports on the properties and relationships between the objects in your database.

Domain name The middle part of a URL, such as www.course.com.

Drop area A position on a PivotChart or PivotTable where you can drag and place a field. Drop areas on a PivotTable include the Filter Field, Row Field, Column Field, and Totals or Detail Field. Drop areas on a PivotChart include the Filter Field, Category Field, Series Field, and Data Field.

Dynamic Web page A Web page automatically updated with the latest changes to the database each time it is opened. Web pages created by the page object are dynamic.

Dynaset A type of recordset displayed within a query's datasheet that allows you to update all fields except for those on the "one" side of a one-to-many relationship.

Edit mode The mode in which Access assumes you are trying to edit a particular field, so keystrokes such as [Ctrl][End], [Ctrl][Home], [←], and [→] move the insertion point within the field.

Edit record symbol A pencil-like symbol that appears in the record selector box to the left of the record that is currently being edited in either a datasheet or a form.

E-mail Electronic mail.

Enabled Control property that determines whether the control can have the focus in Form View.

Encrypt To make the database objects and data within the database indecipherable to other programs.

End tag In markup languages such as HTML and XML, an end tag is used to mark the end of data.

Enforce Referential Integrity An option that can be applied to a one-to-many relationship. When applied, it ensures that no orphan records are entered or created in the database by making sure that the "one" side of a linking relationship (CustomerNumber in a Customer table) is entered before that same value can be entered into the "many" side of the relationship (CustomerNumber in a Sales table).

Event Something that happens within a database (such as the click of a command button or the entry of a field) that can be used to initiate the execution of a macro. Events are associated with toolbars, objects, and controls, and can be viewed by examining that item's property sheet.

Expand button A button that looks like a "plus sign" to the left of a record displayed in datasheet view that when clicked, will show related records in a sub-datasheet.

Exporting A process to quickly convert data from access to another file format such as an Excel workbook, a Word document, or a static Web page.

Expression A combination of values, functions, and operators that calculates to a single value. Access expressions start with an equal sign and are placed in a text box in either Form Design View or Report Design View.

Extensible Markup Language A set of tags and codes that allow one application to deliver data to another application using Web pages.

Extensible Schema Document A file format that stores structural information about a database. It accompanies and helps describe the data in an XML file.

Extensible Stylesheet Language A file format that stores presentation (formatting characteristics) about data. It accompanies and helps describe the data in an XML file.

Favorites group A group on the Groups bar that organizes frequently used objects.

Field The smallest piece of information in a database such as the customer's name, city, or phone number.

Field list A list of the available fields in the table or query that it represents.

Field names The names given to each field in Table Design or Table Datasheet View.

Field property See properties.

Field selector button The button to the left of a field in Table Design View that indicates which field is currently selected.

Field Size A field property that determines the largest number that can be entered in a field (for Number or Currency fields) or the number of characters that can be entered in a field (for Text fields).

Field Size property A field property that determines the number of characters or digits allowed for a field.

File transfer Uploading and downloading files containing anything from text to pictures to music to software programs.

Filter A temporary view of a subset of records. A filter can be saved as a query object if you wish to apply the same filter later without recreating it.

Filter window A window that appears when you click the Filter By Form button when viewing data in a datasheet or in a form window. The Filter window allows you to define the filter criteria.

Find A command used to locate specific data within a field or entire datasheet that the user specifies.

Find Duplicates Query Wizard A wizard used to create a query that determines whether a table contains duplicate values in one or more fields.

Find Unmatched Query Wizard A wizard used to create a query that finds records in one table that doesn't have related records in another table.

Fit (print option) An option that automatically adjusts a preview to display all pages in a report.

Foreign key field In a one-to-many relationship between two tables, the foreign key field is the field in the "many" table that links the table to the primary key field in the "one" table.

Focus The property that indicates which field would be edited if you were to start typing.

Form An Access object that provides an easy-to-use data entry screen that generally shows only one record at a time.

Form Design toolbar The toolbar that appears when working in Form Design View with buttons that help you modify a form's controls.

Form Design View The view of a form in which you add, delete, and modify the form's properties, sections, and controls.

Form Header A section that appears at the top of the screen in Form View for each record, but prints only once at the top of all records when the form is printed.

Form Footer A section that appears at the bottom of screen in Form View for each record, but prints only once at the end of all records when the form is printed.

Form Wizard An Access wizard that helps you create a form.

Format Painter A tool that you can use within Form Design View and Report Design View to copy formatting characteristic from one control, and paint them on another.

Format Field property that controls how information will be displayed and printed.

Front-end database When a database has been split using the Database Splitter, a front-end database is created which contains links back to the data stored in the back-end database as well as any objects needed by the user. The front-end database is stored on the user's computer, which is also called the client computer.

Function A special, predefined formula that provides a shortcut for a commonly used calculation, for example, SUM or COUNT.

Graphic *See* image.

Graphical user interface An interface that is comprised of buttons, lists, graphical elements, and other controls that can be controlled using the mouse rather than just the keyboard.

Group A collection of objects.

Groups bar Located just below the Objects bar in the database window, the Groups bar displays the Favorites and any user-created groups, which in turn contain shortcuts to objects. Groups are used to organize the database objects into logical sets.

Group Footer A section of the report that contains controls that print once at the end of each group of records.

Group Header A section of the report that contains controls that print once at the beginning of each group of records.

Grouping To sort records in a particular order plus provide a section before and after each group of records.

Grouping records In a report, to sort records based on the contents of a field, plus provide a group header section that precedes the group of records as well as a group footer section that follows the group of records.

Grouping controls Allows you to identify several controls as a group to quickly and easily apply the same formatting properties to them.

GUI *See* Graphical user interface

Handles *See* sizing handles.

Hide Duplicates Control property that when set to "Yes," hides duplicate values for the same field from record to record in the Detail section.

Home page The first page displayed when you enter a new URL in your browser.

HTML HyperText Markup Language, a set of codes inserted into a text file that browser software such as Internet Explorer can use to determine the way text, hyperlinks, images, and other elements appear on a Web page.

Hyperlink Address Property of an image on a Web page that stores address information so that if you click the image, it functions like a hyperlink.

HyperText Markup Language *See* HTML.

Hyperlink A field data type that stores World Wide Web addresses. A hyperlink can also be a control on a form that when clicked, opens another database object, external file, or external Web page.

If...Then...Else A series of VBA statements that allow you to test for a logical condition and execute one set of commands if the condition is true and another if the condition is false.

Image A nontextual piece of information such as a picture, piece of clip art, drawn object, or graph. Because images are graphical (not numbers or letters), they are sometimes referred to as graphical images.

Immediate window In the VBA Code window, the area where you can determine the value of any argument at the breakpoint.

Importing A process to quickly convert data from an external source, such as Excel or another database application, into an Access database.

Input Mask A field property that controls the type of data that can be entered into a field and also provides a visual guide as the data is entered.

Insert Merge Field A dialog box within Word that lists all of the fields you can use to merge into the main document to create a customized mass mailing.

Internet A worldwide network of computer networks that sends and receives information such as Web pages and e-mail through a common protocol called TCP/IP.

Internet Service Provider A company that connects your computer to the Internet.

Intranet A wide area network uses the same technologies as the Internet (TCP/IP protocol, e-mail, Web pages), but is built for the internal purposes of a company.

Is Not Null Criterion that finds all records in which any entry has been made in the field.

Is Null Criterion that finds all records in which no entry has been made in the field.

ISP *See* Internet Service Provider.

Junction table A table created for the purpose of establishing separate one-to-many relationships to two tables that have a many-to-many relationship.

Key field *See* primary key field.

Key field combination Two or more fields that as a group contains unique information for each record.

Key field symbol In Table Design View, the symbol that appears as a miniature key in the field indicator box to the left of the field name. It identifies the field that contains unique information for each record.

Key symbol In Table Design View, the symbol that appears as a miniature key in the field indicator box to the left of the field name. It identifies the field that contains unique information for each record.

Label An unbound control that displays static text on forms and reports.

Label Wizard A report-generation tool that helps you create mailing labels.

LAN *See* Local area network.

Layout The general arrangement in which a form will display the fields in the underlying recordset. Layout types include Columnar, Tabular, Datasheet, Chart, and PivotTable. Columnar is most popular for a form, and Datasheet is most popular for a subform.

Left function Access function that returns a specified number of characters starting with the left side of a value in a Text field.

Len function Access function that returns the count of the number of characters in a given field.

Like operator An Access comparison operator that allows queries to find records that match criteria that include a wildcard character.

Line control An unbound control used to draw lines on a form or report that divide it into logical groupings.

Linked table A table created in another database product or application such as Excel, that is stored outside an Access database, but which can still be used within an Access database.

Link Child Fields A subform property that determines which field will serve as the "many" link between the subform and main form.

Link Master Fields A subform property that determines which field will serve as the "one" link between the main form and the subform.

Linking Connects an Access database to an external file such as another Access, dBase, or Paradox database; an Excel spreadsheet, or a text file.

List box A bound control that displays a list of possible choices for the user. Used mainly on forms.

Local area network Connects local resources such as files servers, user computers, and printers by a direct cable.

Locked A control property that specifies whether you can edit data in a control in Form View.

Lookup A reference table or list of values used to populate the values of a field.

Lookup field A field that has lookup properties. Lookup properties are used to create a drop-down list of values to populate the field.

Lookup Wizard A wizard used in Table Design View that allows one field to "lookup" values from another table or entered list. For example, you might use the Lookup Wizard to specify that the CustomerNumber field in the Sales table display the CustomerName field entry from the Customers table.

Macro An Access object that stores a collection of keystrokes or commands such as those for printing several reports in a row or providing a toolbar when a form opens.

Macro Design View An Access view you use to create macros and list macro actions in the order you want them to run.

Macro Group An Access macro object that contains more than one macro.

Mail Merge toolbar Word toolbar that assists in the process of a mail merge.

Main document A Word document that contains the standard text that will be used for each letter in a mass mailing.

Main form A form that contains a subform control.

Main report A report that contains a subreport control is called the main report.

Make-table query An action query that creates a new table.

Many-to-many relationship The relationship between two tables in an Access database in which one record of one table relates to many records in the other table and vice versa. You cannot directly create a many-to-many relationship between two tables in Access. To relate two tables with such a relationship, you must establish a third table called a junction table that creates separate one-to-many relationships with the two original tables.

Master The original Access database file that is copied to the Briefcase.

Memo A field data type used for lengthy text such as comments or notes. It can hold up to 64,000 characters of information.

Merge fields The variable pieces of data that are merged from an Access database into a Word main document during a mail merge process.

Merge It with Microsoft Word An OfficeLink feature that allows you to quickly merge Access database records with a Word document for mass mailing purposes.

Method An action that an object can perform.

Modem Short for modulate-demodulate. Hardward that converts digital computer signals to analog telephone signals

Module An Access object that stores Visual Basic programming code that extends the functions an automated processes of Access.

MsgBox A macro action that displays an informational message.

Multi-user Access databases are inherently multi-user, so that many people can enter and update information at the same time.

Name property Property of a text box that gives the text box a meaningful name.

Named argument In VBA, a value that provides information to an action, event, method, procedure, property, or function.

Navigation buttons Buttons in the lower-left corner of a datasheet or form that allow you to quickly navigate between the records in the underlying object as well as add a new record.

Navigation mode A mode in which Access assumes that you are trying to move between the fields and records of the datasheet (rather than edit a specific field's contents), so keystrokes such as [Ctrl][Home] and [Ctrl][End] move you to the first and last field of the datasheet.

Navigation toolbar Toolbar at the bottom left corner of Datasheet View, Form View, or a Web page that helps you navigate between records.

Network administrator Person who builds and maintains a network.

Newsgroups SImilar to e-mail, but messages are posted in a "public mailbox" that is available to any subscriber, rather than sent to one individual.

Normalization The process of creating a relational database that involves determining the appropriate fields, tables, and table relationships.

NorthwindCS A sample Access database that illustrates how an Access database can connect to an SQL Server database.

Notepad A free Windows accessory text editing program.

Null The state of "nothingness" in a field. Any entry such as 0 in a numeric field or a space in a text field is not null. It is common to search for empty fields by using the Null criteria in a filter or query. Is Not Null criteria finds all records where there is an entry of any kind.

Number A field data type used for numeric information used in calculations, such as quantities.

Object A table, query, form, report, page, macro, or module in Access.

Object (VBA) An item that can be identified or manipulated, including the traditional Access objects, such as a table, query, or form, and smaller parts of these objects, such as controls, sections, and procedures.

Object list box In Form Design view and Report Design view, this box is located on the Formatting (Form/Report) toolbar and displays the name or caption for the currently selected control.

Objects bar In the opening database window, the toolbar that presents the seven Access objects and groups.

ODBC *See* Open Database Connectivity.

OfficeLinks Three tools within Access (Publish It with Microsoft Word, Publish It with Microsoft Excel, and Merge It with Microsoft Word) that allow you to quickly send data from an Access database to another Microsoft Office software product.

OLE Object A field data type that stores pointers that tie files created in other programs to a record such as pictures, sound clips, or spreadsheets.

On Click An event property that causes a macro to run when a command button is clicked.

One-to-many line The line that appears in the Relationships window that shows which field is duplicated between two tables to serve as the linking field. The one-to-many line displays a "1" next to the field that serves as the "one" side of the relationship and an infinity symbol next to the field that serves as the "many" side of the relationship when referential integrity is specified for the relationship. Also called one-to-many join line.

One-to-many relationship The relationship between two tables in an Access database in which a common field links the tables together. The linking field is called the primary key field in the "one" table of the relationship and the foreign key field in the "many" table of the relationship.

Open Database Connectivity Standards that allow data sources to share data with one another

Operators Symbols such as add (+), subtract (−), multiply (*), and divide (/) used in an expression.

Option button A bound control used to display a limited list of mutually exclusive choices for a field such as "female" or "male" for a gender field in a form or report.

Option group A bound control placed on a form that is used to group together several option buttons that provide a limited number of values for a field.

Option Group Wizard An Access wizard that guides the process of developing an option group with option buttons.

Option Value Property for each option button within an option group that identifies what value will be placed in the field when that option button is clicked.

OR criteria Criteria placed on different rows of the query design grid. A record will appear in the resulting datasheet if it is true for any single row.

OR query A query that contains OR criteria (two or more criteria present on different rows in the query design grid. A record will appear on the resulting datasheet if it is true for either criteria.)

Orphan record A record in a "many" table that doesn't have a linking field entry in the "one" table. Orphan records can be avoided by using referential integrity.

Page An Access object that creates Web pages from Access objects as well as provides Web page connectivity features to an Access database. Also called Data Access Page.

Page Design View A view that allows you to modify the structure of a data access page.

Page Footer A section of a form or report that contains controls that print once at the bottom of each page.

Page Header A section of a form or report that contains controls that print once at the top of each page. On the first page of the report, the Page Header section prints below the Report Header section.

Page View A view that allows you to see how your dynamic Web page will appear when opened in Internet Explorer.

Parameter query A query that displays a dialog box prompting you for criteria each time you run it.

Parent record In a pair of tables that have a one-to-many relationship, the "one" table contains the parent records.

Parent/Child relationship The relationship between the main form and subform. The main form acts as the parent, displaying the information about the "one" side of a one-to-many relationship between the forms. The subform acts as the "child" displaying as many records as exist in the "many" side of the one-to-many relationship.

Performance Analyzer An Access feature that studies the size and structure of your database and makes a variety of recommendations on how you could improve its performance.

PivotChart A graphical presentation of the data in a PivotTable.

PivotChart View The view in which you build a PivotChart.

PivotTable An arrangement of data that uses one field as a column heading, another as a row heading, and summarizes a third field, typically a Number field, in the body.

PivotTable An organization of data that groups and summarizes records according to a field that serves as a row heading, and another field that serves as a column heading.

PivotTable List A control on a Web page that summarizes data by columns and rows to make it easy to analyze.

PivotTable View The view in which you build a PivotTable.

Pixel One pixel is the measurement of one picture element on the screen.

PMT function Access function that returns the monthly payment for a loan.

Pop-up form A special type of form that stays on top of other open forms, even when another form is active.

Primary key field A field that contains unique information for each record. A primary key field cannot contain a null entry.

Primary sort field In a query grid, the left-most field that includes sort criteria. It determines the order in which the records will appear and can be specified "ascending" or "descending."

Procedure A series of VBA programming statements that perform an operation or calculate an answer. There are two types of procedures: functions and subs.

Project A special Access file that contains no data, but rather, form and report objects. The data for the database is typically located on a file/server to which the project file is linked to.

Properties Characteristics that further define the field (if field properties), control (if control properties), section (if section properties), or object (if object properties).

Property sheet A window that displays an exhaustive list of properties for the chosen control, section, or object within the Form Design View or Report Design View.

Publish It with Microsoft Excel An OfficeLink feature that allows you to quickly copy a query, form, or report object object to Excel.

Publish It with Microsoft Word An OfficeLink feature that allows you to quickly copy a query, form, or report object object to Word.

Publishing Saving Web files to Web folders on a server.

Query An Access object which provides a spreadsheet-like view of the data similar to tables. It may provide the user with a subset of fields and/or records from one or more tables. Queries are created when the user has a "question" about the data in the database.

Query design grid The bottom pane of the Query Design View window in which you specify the fields, sort order, and limiting criteria for the query.

Query Design View The window in which you develop queries by specifying the fields, sort order, and limiting criteria that determine which fields and records are displayed in the resulting datasheet.

Record A group of related fields, such as all demographic information for one customer.

Record locking A feature of Access databases that prevents two users from updating the same record at the same time.

Record selector box The small square to the left of a record in a datasheet that marks the current record or the edit record symbol when the record has the focus or is being edited.

Recordset Type A query property that determines if an how records displayed by a query are locked.

Record Source In a form or report, the property that determines which table or query object contains the fields and records that the form or report will display. It is the most important property of the form or report object. A bound control on a form or report also has a Record Source property. In this case, the Record Source property identifies the field to which the control is bound.

Recordset The value of the Record Source property.

Rectangle control An unbound control used to draw rectangles on the form that divide the other form controls into logical groupings.

Referential integrity Ensures that no orphan records are entered or created in the database by making sure that the "one" side of a linking relationship (CustomerNumber in a Customer table) is entered before that same value can be entered in the "many" side of the relationship (CustomerNumber in a Sales table).

Relational database A database in which more than one table, such as the customer, sales, and inventory tables, can share information. The term "relational database" comes from the fact that the tables are linked or "related" with a common field of information. An Access database is relational.

Replica The copy of the Access database file that is stored in the Briefcase.

Replica set Both the original (master) and replicated (replica) database file. There may be more than one replica in a replica set, but there is only one master.

Replication The process of making replicas of a master database file using the Briefcase.

Report An Access object that creates a professional printout of data that may contain such enhancements as headers, footers, and calculations on groups of records.

Report Design View View of a report in which you add, delete, and edit the report's properties, sections, and controls.

Report Footer On a report, a section that contains controls that print once at the end of the last page of the report.

Report Header On a report, a section that contains controls that print once at the top of the first page of the report.

Report section properties Properties that determine what information appears in different report sections, and how it is formatted.

Report Wizard An Access wizard that helps you create a report.

Required A field property that determines if an entry is required for a field.

Resize bar The bar that separates the upper and lower panes in Query Design View. You drag the resize bar up or down to provide more room for one of the panes.

Rich text format A file format that does not support all advanced Word features, but does support basic formatting embellishments such as font types and colors.

Right function Access function that returns a specified number of characters starting with the right side of a value in a Text field.

Row selector The small square to the left of a field in Table Design View.

Row Source A field Lookup property that provides values for the drop-down lookup list for that field.

RTF *See* Rich text format.

Schema A pictoral representation of how the tables of the database are related. Access presents the database schema in the Relationships window.

Section A location of a form or report that contains controls. The section in which a control is placed determines where and how often the control prints.

Secondary sort field In a query grid, the second field from the left that includes sort criteria. It determines the order in which the records will appear if there is a "tie" on the primary sort field. (For example, the primary sort field might be the State field. If two records both contained the data "IA" in that field, the secondary sort field, which might be the City field, would determine the order of the IA records in the resulting datasheet.)

Security account password A password applied to workgroups used to determine which objects each workgroup has access to and at what level.

Select query The most common type of query that retrieves data from one or more linked tables and displays the results in a datasheet.

Server In Internet terminology, this would be the computer that serves the information to you from the Internet such as a Web page or an e-mail message.

Simple Query Wizard A wizard used to create a select query.

Single step To run a macro one line at a time, and observing the effect of each line as it is executed.

Sizing handles Small squares at each corner of a selected control in Access. Dragging a handle resizes the control. Also known as handles.

Snapshot A type of recordset displayed within Query Datasheet View that does not allow you to update any field.

Sorting Reordering records in either ascending or descending order based on the values of a particular field.

Specific record box Part of a box in the lower-left corner in Datasheet view and Form view of the Navigation buttons that indicates the current record number. You can click in the specific record box, then type a record number to quickly move to that record. Also called the current record box or record number box.

Speech recognition A feature that allows you to speak directly to your computer and have it respond to your commands.

Spreadsheet control An ActiveX control that provides similar functionality.

SQL Server A database program provided by Microsoft for databases that are larger and more complex than those managed by Access.

Standard module A module stored as objects within the database window. Standard modules can be executed from anywhere within the database.

Start tag In markup languages such as HTML and XML, a start tag is used to mark the beginning of data.

Startup option A series of commands that execute when a database is opened.

Statement A line of VBA code.

Status bar The bar at the bottom of the Access window that provides informational messages and other status information (such as whether the Num Lock is active or not).

Status Bar Text property Property of a control that determines what text displays in the status bar when that control has the focus.

Structured Query Language (SQL) A standard programming language for selecting and manipulating data stored in a relational database.

Static Web page Web pages created by exporting a query or report to HTML from an Access database are static because they never change after they are created.

Structured query language See SQL.

Subdatasheet A datasheet that shows related records in the "many" table. It appears when the user clicks a record's expand button.

Sub A procedure that performs a series of VBA statements but does not return a value nor can it be used in an expression. You create subs to manipulate controls and objects.

Subform A form placed within a form that shows related records from another table or query. A subform generally displays many records at a time in a datasheet arrangement.

Sub procedure See Sub.

Subreport A report placed as a control within another report.

Summary query A query used to calculate and display information about records grouped together.

Switchboard A special type of form that uses command buttons to simplify and secure access to database objects.

Switchboard Manager An Access feature that simplifies the creation and maintenance of switchboard forms.

Synchronization The process of reconciling and updating changes between the master and replicas of a replica set.

Syntax The technical rules that govern a language or program.

Syntax error A VBA error which occurs because of a typing error or misspelling. Syntax errors are highlighted in the Code window in red.

Tab control An unbound control used to create a three-dimensional aspect to a form so that other controls can be organized and shown in Form View by clicking the "tabs."

Tab order The sequence in which the controls on the form receive the focus when the user presses [Tab] or [Enter] in Form view.

Table Datasheet toolbar The toolbar that appears when you are viewing a table's datasheet.

Table Design View The view in which you can add, delete, or modify fields and their associated properties.

Table Wizard An interactive tool used to create a new table from a list of sample tables and sample fields.

Target table A table to which an append query adds a record set.

Templates Sample databases that you can use and modify for your own purposes.

Text A field data type that allows text information or combinations of text and numbers such as a street address. By default, it is 50 characters but can be changed to 50 characters. The maximum length of a text field is 255 characters.

Text box A common control used on forms and reports to display data bound to an underlying field. A text box can also show calculated controls such as subtotals and dates.

Toggle button A bound control used to indicate "yes" or "no" answers for a field. If the button is "pressed" it displays "yes" information.

Toolbox toolbar The toolbar that has common controls that you can add to a report or form when working in Report Design View or Form Design View.

Top values A feature within Query Design View that allows you to limit the number of records in the resulting datasheet to a value or percentage of the total.

Unbound control A control that does not change from record to record and exist only to clarify or enhance the appearance of the form, such as labels, lines, and clip art.

Unbound image control An unbound control that is used to display clip art and that doesn't change as you navigate from record to record on a form or report.

UNC See Universal Naming Convention.

Uniform Resource Locator A Web page address that allows other computers to find that Web page.

Universal Naming Convention The address you give a file on a local area network.

Unmatched record See orphan record.

Update query An action query that updates data based on an expression.

Upsize Convert an Access database to an SQL Server database.

URL See Uniform Resource Locator.

Validation Rule A field property that helps eliminate unreasonable entries by establishing criteria for an entry before it is accepted into the database.

Validation Text A field property that determines what message will appear if a user attempts to make a field entry that does not pass the validation rule for that field.

Value axis On a PivotChart, the vertical axis. Also called the y-axis.

Variable A named storage location that can contain data that can be modified during program execution.

VBA (Visual Basic for Applications) The Access programming language that is very similar to Visual Basic and which is stored within module objects.

VBA password A password that prevents unauthorized users from modifying VBA code.

View buttons Four buttons in the database window that determines how the object icons are displayed (as Large Icons, Small Icons, List, and Details).

Visual Basic Editor Code window (Code window) The window you use to write Visual Basic programming code.

WAN See Wide area network.

Web folder Special folders dedicates to organizing Web pages.

Web page A file that is viewed using browser software such as Microsoft Internet Explorer.

Web server A computer that stores and serves Web pages to clients.

Webmaster Person who builds and maintains a Web server.

What-if analysis A reiterative analysis, usually performed in Excel, where you change values in a workbook and watch related calculated formulas update instantly.

Wide area network Created when a LAN is connected to an existing telecommunications network.

Wildcard characters Special characters used in criteria to find, filter, and query data. The asterisk (*) stands for any group of characters. For example, the criteria I* in a State field criteria cell would find all records where the state entry was IA, ID, IL, IN, or Iowa. The question mark (?) wildcard stands for only one character.

Word wrap A feature within Microsoft Word that determines when a line of text extends into the right margin of the page, and automatically forces text to the next line without you needing to press Enter.

Workgroup A description of users, objects, and permissions to which those users have access to the objects stored as a file.

World Wide Web A global network of networks that use Web servers, Web pages, browser software, and other common technologies to share documents across the world.

XML See Extensible Markup Language.

XML file A text file that contains Extensible Markup Language (XML) tags that identify fields and contain data.

XSD See Extensible Schema Document.

XSL See Extensible Stylesheet Language.

Yes/No A field data type that stores only one of two values, "Yes" or "No."

Zoom pointers Mouse pointers displayed in Print Preview that allow you to change the zoom magnification of a printout.

Index

olution in wri   g

·sh literary respons   to
French Revolution

N
ïϵ

Ideas and Production

Over recent years the study of the humanities has changed beyond all recognition for many of us. The increasing attention given to theories of interpretation and writing has altered the intellectual circumstances and perspectives of the various disciplines which compose the group. The studies of literature, history, society, politics, gender and philsophy are increasingly finding common ground in shared assumptions about intellectual procedure and method. **Ideas and Production** addresses this common ground.

We are interested in the investigation of the particular historical circumstances which produce the culture of a period or group, and the exploration of conventionally unregarded or understudied work. We are also interested in the relationship of intellectual movements to institutions, and the technological and economic means of their production. It is through the study of the circumstances and conditions in which ideas are realised that the humanities can develop fresh approaches in a period of rapid and exciting social and intellectual change.

As thought and learning become increasingly international and older political and intellectual structures give way, **Ideas and Production** is concerned to investigate new intellectual horizons from the perspective of competing theories and methods, and through the rethinking of old or settled definitions.

Ideas and Production welcomes the potential of debate and intervention, as well as the careful study of materials. The series is aimed at the student, teacher and general reader and encourages clarity and directness in argument, language and method.

Edward J. Esche, Penelope Kenrick,
Rick Rylance, Nigel Wheale